ZAGAT SURVEY

Back in 1979, we never imagined that an idea born during a wine-fueled dinner with friends would take us on an adventure that's lasted three decades – and counting.

The idea – that the collective opinions of avid consumers can be more accurate than the judgments of an individual critic – led to a hobby involving friends rating NYC restaurants. And that hobby grew into Zagat Survey, which today has over 350,000 participants worldwide weighing in on everything from airlines, bars, dining and golf to hotels, movies, shopping, tourist attractions and more.

By giving consumers a voice, we – and our surveyors – had unwittingly joined a revolution whose concepts (user-generated content, social networking) were largely unknown 30 years ago. However, those concepts caught fire with the rise of the Internet and have since transformed not only restaurant criticism but also virtually every aspect of the media, and we feel lucky to have been at the start of it all.

And that wasn't the only revolution we happily stumbled into. Our first survey was published as a revolution began to reshape the culinary landscape. Thanks to a host of converging trends – the declining supremacy of old-school formal restaurants; the growing sophistication of diners; the availability of ever-more diverse cuisines and techniques; the improved range and quality of ingredients; the rise of chefs as rock stars – dining out has never been better or more exciting, and we've been privileged to witness its progress through the eyes of our surveyors. And it's still going strong.

As we celebrate Zagat's 30th year, we'd like to thank everyone who has participated in our surveys. We've enjoyed hearing and sharing your frank opinions and look forward to doing so for many years to come. As we always say, our guides and online content are really "yours."

We'd also like to express our gratitude by supporting **Action Against Hunger,** an organization that works to meet the needs of the hungry in over 40 countries. To find out more, visit www.zagat.com/action.

Nina and Tim Zagat

ZAGAT®
CELEBRATING 30 YEARS

Long Island Restaurants 2009/10

LOCAL EDITORS
John Capone and Laura Weiss

SENIOR LOCAL EDITOR
Suzi Forbes Chase

STAFF EDITOR
Karen Hudes

Published and distributed by
Zagat Survey, LLC
4 Columbus Circle
New York, NY 10019
T: 212.977.6000
E: longisland@zagat.com
www.zagat.com

ACKNOWLEDGMENTS

We thank Courtney Humiston and Steven Shukow, as well as the following members of our staff: Stacey Slate (editorial assistant), Brian Albert, Sean Beachell, Maryanne Bertollo, Jane Chang, Sandy Cheng, Reni Chin, Larry Cohn, Alison Flick, Jeff Freier, Andrew Gelardi, Roy Jacob, Ashunta Joseph, Cynthia Kilian, Natalie Lebert, Mike Liao, Christina Livadiotis, Dave Makulec, Andre Pilette, Kimberly Rosado, Becky Ruthenburg, Donna Marino Wilkins, Sharon Yates, Anna Zappia and Kyle Zolner.

The reviews in this guide are based on public opinion surveys. The ratings reflect the average scores given by the survey participants who voted on each establishment. The text is based on quotes from, or paraphrasings of, the surveyors' comments. Phone numbers, addresses and other factual data were correct to the best of our knowledge when published in this guide.

© 2009 Zagat Survey, LLC
ISBN-13: 978-1-60478-148-9
ISBN-10: 1-60478-148-3
Printed in the
United States of America

Contents

Ratings & Symbols

Zagat Top Spot	Name	Symbols		Cuisine	Zagat Ratings			
					FOOD	DECOR	SERVICE	COST

Area, Address & Contact

▼ Ƶ **Tim & Nina's** ◑ *American*   ▽ 23 | 9 | 13 | $15

East Hampton | 1 Main St. (Maidendive Ln.) |
631-555-1212 | www.zagat.com

Review, surveyor comments in quotes

Locals, "major celebrities" and "congenial drifters" alike "storm the hedgerows" for a taste of the "haute campground grub" at this East Hampton American, where cognoscenti crow over the "classy" yet "comforting", "cheap" cuisine; aesthetes object to "eating in a trailer" "without air-conditioning or even a fan", and say the "surly" staff "should be used as fish bait."

Ratings

Food, Decor and **Service** are rated on the Zagat 0 to 30 scale.

0	– 9	poor to fair
10	– 15	fair to good
16	– 19	good to very good
20	– 25	very good to excellent
26	– 30	extraordinary to perfection
	▽	low response	less reliable

Cost

Our surveyors' estimated price of a dinner with one drink and tip. Lunch is usually 25 to 30% less. At prix fixe–only places we show the charge for the lowest-priced menu plus 30%. For unrated **newcomers** or **write-ins,** the price range is shown as follows:

I	$25 and below	E	$41 to $65
M	$26 to $40	VE	$66 or more

Symbols

Ƶ	highest ratings, popularity and importance
◑	serves after 11 PM
Ƨ	closed on Sunday
Ṁ	closed on Monday
⊄	no credit cards accepted

About This Survey

Here are the results of our **2009/10 Long Island Restaurants Survey,** covering 852 eateries in the Long Island area. Like all our guides, this one is based on the collective opinions of avid consumers – 5,854 all told. We've also included a list and map of 40 wineries and vineyards on Long Island's East End.

WHO PARTICIPATED: Input from these enthusiasts forms the basis for the ratings and reviews in this guide (their comments are shown in quotation marks within the reviews). These surveyors are a diverse group: 51% are women, 49% men; 5% are in their 20s; 16%, 30s; 22%, 40s; 29%, 50s; and 28%, 60s or above. Collectively they bring roughly 867,000 annual meals' worth of experience to this Survey. We sincerely thank these participants – this book is really "theirs."

HELPFUL LISTS: See Key Newcomers (page 7), Most Popular (page 9), Top Ratings (pages 10–14), Best Buys (pages 15–16) and the 44 handy indexes starting on page 162.

OUR EDITORS: Special thanks go to our editors, John Capone, a dining, nightlife and lifestyle writer for *Black Book, New York* and NBC New York online; Suzi Forbes Chase, author of *The Hamptons Book: A Complete Guide* as well as other travel guides and cookbooks; and Laura Weiss, a food and travel journalist who has written for the *New York Times,* the *New York Daily News* and the Food Network.

ABOUT ZAGAT: This marks our 30th year reporting on the shared experiences of consumers like you. Today we have over 350,000 surveyors and now cover airlines, bars, dining, entertaining, fast food, golf, hotels, movies, music, resorts, shopping, spas, theater and tourist attractions in over 100 countries.

INTERACTIVE: Up-to-the-minute news about restaurant openings plus menus, photos and more are free on **ZAGAT.com** and the award-winning **ZAGAT.mobi** (for web-enabled mobile devices). They also enable reserving at thousands of places with just one click.

VOTE AND COMMENT: We invite you to join any of our surveys at **ZAGAT.com.** There you can rate and review establishments year-round. In exchange for doing so, you'll receive a free copy of the resulting guide when published.

AVAILABILITY: Zagat guides are available in all major bookstores as well as on **ZAGAT.com.** You can also access our content when on the go via **ZAGAT.mobi** and **ZAGAT TO GO** (for smartphones).

FEEDBACK: To improve this guide, we invite your comments about any aspect of our performance. Have we missed anything? Just contact us at **longisland@zagat.com.**

New York, NY
April 29, 2009

Nina and Tim

Nina and Tim Zagat

What's New

Has the state of the economy affected the Long Island dining scene? You bet: 41% of our surveyors say they're eating out less, 40% are paying more attention to prices and 32% are choosing less expensive places – and it's no wonder. The average cost of a meal on LI is now $41.41, topping NYC ($40.78) and well above the U.S. average ($34.49). These facts aren't lost on restaurateurs, many of whom are crafting more affordable menus and launching prix fixe deals.

WINNING COMBINATIONS: Showing that you don't need flashy digs or mad wine markups to take home the gold, the recently relocated **Kitchen A Bistro** in St. James was voted No. 1 for Food by admirers of its artful French fare paired with BYO bottles. Meanwhile, sophisticated yet comforting country inns on the North Fork took top honors for both Decor (**Jedediah's** in Jamesport) and Service (**North Fork Table & Inn**), while Great Neck's **Peter Luger** claimed the Most Popular title for the 16th year running, proving that a plunging portfolio can't curb cravings for an aged porterhouse.

STIMULUS PACKAGES: A number of restaurants have been transformed in response to the financial downturn. Chef Kent Monkan reopened his former Heirloom space in Locust Valley as the budget-friendly **Brass Rail.** In Huntington, Aix en-Provence is now the more sporty **Crew Kitchen & Cocktails,** and Mazzi is now **Rocco's Italian Kitchen.** Big-name chefs are downscaling too – see Bobby Flay's new **Bobby's Burger Palace** in Lake Grove.

PIT PERFORMERS: Smoke is on fire, with Islip's new **Island BBQ & Grill** and **Ruby's Famous BBQ Joint** in East Meadow taking a 'cue from recent arrivals like Port Washington's **Harbor-Q** and Sagaponack's **Townline BBQ.** With Bay Shore's **Smokin' Al's Famous BBQ** having just branched out to Massapequa Park, the trend shows no sign of burning out.

LI LUXURY: Despite the current climate, several spectacularly lavish restaurants opened, among them Roslyn's marble-accented **Limani,** showcasing a huge select-your-own seafood display, and Woodbury's **Speranza Fine Italian Food Studio,** with cooking by chef Michael Meehan (ex **Mill River Inn**).

EAST END ACTION: Montauk arrivals include **Surf Lodge,** with a large waterside deck; **Backyard,** in the Solé East resort, boasting cushy beds for poolside dining; and the Southern-geared **Gulf Coast,** about to open in the revamped Montauk Yacht Club. The market-driven, minuscule **Dish** has customers coveting tables in Water Mill, while Sagaponack's **Old Stove Pub** has been revived by Colin Ambrose (**Estia's Little Kitchen**). On the North Fork, Tom Schaudel, who opened Mattituck's **A Mano** last year, has left Jedediah's, where new chef Matt Murphy (**Antares Cafe**) is crafting a more casual menu.

Key Newcomers

Our editors' take on the year's top arrivals. See page 202 for a full list.

Alexandros | *Mediterranean*

A Mano | *Italian*

Black & Blue Seafood | *Seafood/Steak*

Bobby's Burger | *Burgers*

Brasserie Persil | *French*

Brass Rail | *American*

Brooks & Porter | *Steak*

Circa Ristorante | *Italian*

Dish | *American*

Grappa | *Italian*

Grey Horse Tavern | *American*

Haiku Bistro | *Asian/Japanese*

Jin East | *Japanese*

Kiraku | *Japanese*

Kitchen A Trattoria | *Italian*

La Strada | *Italian*

La Tavola | *Italian*

Limani | *Med./Seafood*

Lola's | *American*

Mill Creek Tavern | *Seafood/Steak*

Mirabelle Tavern | *American*

Mumon | *Japanese*

Oevo | *Italian*

Osteria Toscana | *Italian*

Palio Ristorante | *Italian*

Pasta Vino | *Italian*

Porters on the Lane | *Seafood/Steak*

Ruby's Famous BBQ | *BBQ*

Simply Fondue | *Fondue*

Speranza | *Italian*

Surf Lodge | *American*

Table 9 | *Italian*

Tel Aviv | *Israeli/Kosher*

Tequila Jacks | *Caribbean*

Coming up in spring 2009, **Sripraphai,** a branch of the highly acclaimed Thai in Woodside, Queens, is slated to open in Williston Park, leading a slew of offshoots in the works, including a new outpost of **Bliss** in a pretty roadside house in Blue Point. The owners of **Four Food Studio** have plans for a New Hyde Park newcomer, while the Bohlson Group (**Tellers, Prime**) is expanding from surf 'n' turf to Italian cooking with a new Islip addition in May, plus NYC vet Eric Miller will be helming the upcoming **Catch Seafood Tavern** in Port Jefferson. Among the most anticipated comebacks this year, Guy Reuge will relaunch **Mirabelle Restaurant** in Stony Brook's Three Village Inn (where **Mirabelle Tavern** opened in March), and East Buffet, the elaborate all-you-can-eat Chinese-Eclectic that had a serious fire in 2008, is returning to Huntington Station as **Best Buffet.**

Out on the East End, word has it that a consortium of owners including Jon Bon Jovi and Ron Perelman plan to resurrect the **Blue Parrot** (or a reasonable facsimile) in East Hampton. Meanwhile, NYC's **Mezzaluna** is set to open a branch in the space formerly known as Gordon's in Amagansett in mid-May. Tom Schaudel plans summertime launches for an Italian wine bar and a sushi spot, both in Greenport, while in Sag Harbor, Sen Spice & Lounge is transforming into **Phao Thai Kitchen** (which had a prior incarnation across the street) and Ed 'Jean-Luc' Kleefield plans to open a patisserie adjacent to **JLX Bistro.**

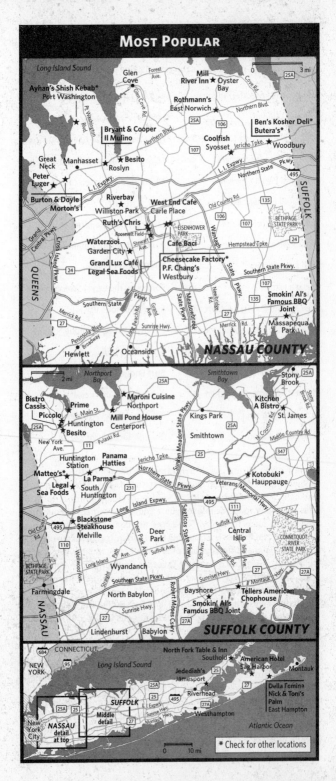

MOST POPULAR

Long Island Sound

Glen Cove · Forest Ave.

Mill River Inn ★ Oyster Bay

Ayhan's Shish Kebab* Port Washington

Rothmann's East Norwich · Northern Blvd.

Bryant & Cooper **Il Mulino** · Northern Blvd.

Ben's Kosher Deli* **Butera's***

Coolfish Syosset

Jericho Tpke. · Woodbury

Great Neck · Manhasset · **Besito** Roslyn

Peter Luger

L. I. Expwy. · Northern State Pkwy. · 495 · **SUFFOLK**

Burton & Doyle **Morton's**

Riverbay Williston Park

West End Cafe Carle Place · Old Country Rd.

BETHPAGE STATE PARK

Ruth's Chris Roosevelt Field · EISENHOWER PARK

Waterzooi Garden City

Cafe Baci · Hempstead Tpke.

Grand Lux Café **Legal Sea Foods**

Cheesecake Factory* **P.F. Chang's** Westbury

Southern State Pkwy.

QUEENS

Southern State · Pkwy.

Smokin' Al's Famous BBQ Joint Massapequa Park

Hewlett · Oceanside

Merrick Rd. · Sunrise Hwy.

NASSAU COUNTY

Northport Bay · *Smithtown Bay* · Stony Brook

Bistro Cassis · **Prime** Huntington

Maroni Cuisine Northport

Kitchen A Bistro St. James

Piccolo · **Besito**

Mill Pond House Centerport

Kings Park

Matteo's* · **Panama Hatties**

Huntington Station

La Parma* South Huntington

Kotobuki* Hauppauge

Legal Sea Foods

Blackstone Steakhouse Melville

Deer Park

Central Islip

CONNETQUOT RIVER STATE PARK

Wyandanch

NASSAU

Farmingdale

North Babylon

Bayshore

Smokin' Al's Famous BBQ Joint

Tellers American Chophouse

Lindenhurst · Babylon

SUFFOLK COUNTY

CONNECTICUT

North Fork Table & Inn Southold

American Hotel Sag Harbor · Montauk

NEW YORK

Long Island Sound

Jedediah's Jamesport

SUFFOLK

Riverhead

Della Femina **Nick & Toni's** **Palm** East Hampton

NASSAU detail at top

Middle detail

Westhampton

Atlantic Ocean

NEW YORK CITY

* Check for other locations

Most Popular

1. Peter Luger | *Steak*
2. Cheesecake Factory | *American*
3. Bryant & Cooper | *Steak*
4. Kotobuki | *Japanese*
5. Besito | *Mexican*
6. West End | *American*
7. Il Mulino NY | *Italian*
8. American Hotel | *Amer./French*
9. North Fork Table | *American*
10. Ruth's Chris | *Steak*
11. Morton's | *Steak*
12. Jedediah's | *American*
13. Legal Sea Foods | *Seafood*
14. Kitchen A Bistro | *French*
15. Coolfish | *Seafood*
16. Blackstone Steak | *Steak*
17. Della Femina | *American*
18. Bistro Cassis | *French*
19. Maroni Cuisine | *Eclectic/Italian*
20. Nick & Toni's | *Italian/Med.*
21. Smokin' Al's BBQ | *BBQ*
22. Mill Pond | *Seafood/Steak*
23. Prime | *American*
24. Waterzooi | *Belgian*
25. Mill River Inn | *American/Eclectic*
26. Palm | *Seafood/Steak*
27. Riverbay | *Seafood*
28. Grand Lux | *Eclectic*
29. Matteo's | *Italian*
30. Tellers | *Steak*
31. Piccolo | *American/Italian*
32. Cafe Baci | *Italian*
33. Rothmann's Steak | *Steak*
34. Ben's Deli | *Deli*
35. Burton & Doyle | *Steak*
36. La Parma | *Italian*
37. Panama Hatties* | *American*
38. Ayhan's Shish Kebab | *Med.*
39. Butera's | *Italian*
40. P.F. Chang's | *Chinese*

It's obvious that many of the above restaurants are among the Long Island area's most expensive, but if popularity were calibrated to price, we suspect that a number of other restaurants would join their ranks. Thus, we have added two lists comprising 90 Best Buys on page 15 as well as Prix Fixe Dinner Deals on page 16.

---

* Indicates a tie with restaurant above

Top Food Ratings

Excludes places with low votes, unless indicated by a ▽.

28 Kitchen A Bistro | *French*
North Fork Table | *American*
Maroni Cuisine | *Eclectic/Italian*
Chachama Grill | *American*

27 Lake House | *American*
Aji 53 | *Japanese*
Mill River Inn | *Amer./Eclectic*
Dario's | *Italian*
Kotobuki | *Japanese*
Peter Luger | *Steak*
Vine Street | *American*
Le Soir | *French*

26 Stone Creek | *French/Med.*
In Season | *American*
Mosaic | *American*
Mirko's | *Eclectic*
Piccolo | *American/Italian*
Vintage Prime | *Steak*
Panama Hatties | *American*
Barney's | *American/French*

Plaza Cafe | *American*
Nagahama | *Japanese*
Bryant & Cooper | *Steak*
Dave's Grill | *Continental/Sea.*
Siam Lotus | *Thai*
Da Ugo | *Italian*
Tellers | *Steak*
Nisen Sushi | *Japanese*
Orient | *Chinese*
Jedediah's | *American*
La Plage | *Eclectic*
Il Mulino NY | *Italian*
La Piccola Liguria | *Italian*
Rialto | *Italian*
Thai Gourmet | *Thai*
Solé | *Italian*
Bravo Nader! | *Italian*

25 Polo | *American*
Branzino | *Italian*
Maureen/Daughters' | *Amer.*

BY CUISINE

AMERICAN (NEW)
28 North Fork Table
Chachama Grill
27 Lake House
Mill River Inn
26 In Season Amer.

AMERICAN (TRAD.)
27 Vine Street
25 Maureen/Daughters'
24 American Hotel
PeraBell
Ivy Cottage

ASIAN FUSION
24 West East Bistro
Taiko
Toku
23 Yokohama
Blue Fin

BBQ/SOUTHWESTERN
24 Smokin' Al's BBQ
23 Big Daddy's
21 Swingbelly's Beachside
Turtle Crossing
RS Jones

CAJUN/SOUTHERN
23 Bayou
Cooke's In
Big Daddy's
21 LL Dent
20 Wild Harvest

CHINESE
26 Orient
24 Orchid
23 Hunan Taste
Fortune Wheel
Pearl East

CONTINENTAL
26 Dave's Grill
25 Soigné
Barolo
1770 House
24 Palm Court

ECLECTIC
28 Maroni Cuisine
27 Mill River Inn
26 Mirko's
La Plage
24 PeraBell

FRENCH

27	Le Soir
26	Stone Creek
	Barney's
25	Soigné
	La Marmite
	Oliver Bon Dinant
	Brasserie Persil
24	La Coquille
	Chez Noëlle
	American Hotel

FRENCH (BISTRO)

28	Kitchen A Bistro
25	Sage Bistro
24	Bistro Cassis
	Bistro du Village
23	Emerson's

GREEK

23	Med. Snack Bar
22	Trata East
21	Ethos
20	Hellenic Snack
	Chicken Kebab

INDIAN

23	Kiran Palace
	House of Dosas
	Rangmahal
22	House of India
	Hampton Chutney

ITALIAN

28	Maroni Cuisine
26	Piccolo
	Solé
25	Sempre Vivolo
	Casa Rustica

ITALIAN (NORTHERN)

27	Dario's
26	Da Ugo
	Il Mulino NY
	La Piccola Liguria
	Rialto

ITALIAN (SOUTHERN)

26	Bravo Nader!
24	La Ginestra
23	La Parma
	Mamma Lombardi's
	Matteo's

JAPANESE

27	Aji 53
	Kotobuki
26	Nagahama
	Nisen Sushi
25	Nisen

MEDITERRANEAN

26	Stone Creek
25	Harvest/Ft. Pond
23	Pier 95
	Med. Snack Bar
	Pita House

MEXICAN

23	Oaxaca Mexican
	Besito
	Salsa Salsa
21	Green Cactus
	La Panchita

MIDDLE EASTERN

23	Pita House
22	Kabul Afghani
21	Azerbaijan Grill
	Ariana
	Colbeh

PIZZA

25	Massa's
24	Salvatore's
23	Nick's
	Grimaldi's
	King Umberto

SEAFOOD

26	Dave's Grill
25	Starr Boggs
	Palm
	Mill Pond
24	Black & Blue

STEAKHOUSES

27	Peter Luger
26	Vintage Prime
	Bryant & Cooper
	Tellers
25	Palm

THAI

26	Siam Lotus
	Thai Gourmet
24	Onzon Thai
22	Thai Table
	Sarin Thai

BY SPECIAL FEATURE

BREAKFAST
25 Maureen/Daughters'
24 Robinson's
23 Toast
   JT's Corner Cafe
   Thomas's Ham

BRUNCH
25 Polo
   Rothmann's Steak
24 Bistro Cassis
   Stonewalls
   Palm Court

BYO
28 Kitchen A Bistro
26 Thai Gourmet
24 Onzon Thai
   Bistro du Village
19 Paradise Island∇

DINING ALONE
24 Frisky Oyster
   Coolfish
   Sen
22 Hampton Chutney
   Sushi Ya

HOTEL DINING
28 North Fork Table
   (North Fork Inn)
26 Jedediah's
   (Jedediah Hawkins Inn)

25 Polo
   (Garden City Hotel)
   Palm
   (Huntting Inn)
   1770 House

NEWCOMERS (RATED)
25 Brasserie Persil
24 Black & Blue Seafood
22 Brooks & Porter
   A Mano
19 Cherrystones

PEOPLE-WATCHING
27 Mill River Inn
   Peter Luger
26 Stone Creek
   Panama Hatties
   Barney's

SINGLES SCENES
26 Bryant & Cooper
   Tellers
   Nisen Sushi
25 Rothmann's Steak
24 Burton & Doyle

VIEWS
27 Lake House
26 Dave's Grill
   La Plage
25 Harvest/Ft. Pond
   Mill Pond

BY LOCATION

EAST HAMPTON TOWNSHIP
26 Dave's Grill
25 Palm
   Harvest/Ft. Pond
   1770 House
24 Della Femina

NASSAU COUNTY
27 Mill River Inn
   Dario's
   Kotobuki
   Peter Luger
26 Barney's

NORTH FORK & SHELTER ISLAND
28 North Fork Table
27 Vine Street

26 Jedediah's
   La Plage
24 Jamesport Manor

SOUTHAMPTON TOWNSHIP
26 Stone Creek
   Mirko's
   Plaza Cafe
25 Starr Boggs
24 American Hotel

SUFFOLK COUNTY
28 Kitchen A Bistro
   Maroni Cuisine
   Chachama Grill
27 Lake House
   Aji 53

Top Decor Ratings

28 Jedediah's	Q East
27 Nisen Sushi	Aji 53
Prime	Lombardi's
Toku	Brooks & Porter
Palm Court	Blackstone Steak
Jamesport Manor	Garden Grill
26 Tellers	American Hotel
Pine Island	Mill Pond
East Hampton Point	Lake House
Country House	
Polo	**23** Mac's Steak
25 Oak Room	Rist. Gemelli
North Fork Table	Ram's Head
Honu	East by Northeast
Annona	Four Food Studio
Trumpets	Burton & Doyle
Tierra Mar	Robinson's
Nonnina	Besito
1770 House	City Cellar
24 Stone Creek	Soigné
	Barney's

OUTDOORS

Annona	Madame Tong's
Backyard	On 3
Cipollini	Ram's Head
Della Femina	Savanna's
East Hampton Point	Starr Boggs

ROMANCE

American Hotel	Lake House
Barney's	Ram's Head
Country House	Robert's
Jamesport Manor	1770 House
Jedediah's	Stone Creek

ROOMS

Four Food Studio	1770 House
Jedediah's	Speranza
Limani	Tellers
Nisen Sushi	Toku
Palm Court	Tula Kitchen

VIEWS

B. Smith's	Pine Island Grill
Dockers Waterside	Riverview
East Hampton Point	Sunset Beach
Harvest/Ft. Pond	Trumpets
Oakland's	Wall's Wharf

Top Service Ratings

27 | North Fork Table

26 | Polo
Mill River Inn
Dario's
Chachama Grill
Jedediah's

25 | Lake House
La Piccola Liguria
Maroni Cuisine
Soigné
Plaza Cafe
Rialto
Camille's
Mosaic
Barney's
Panama Hatties
San Marco

24 | Galleria Dominick
Voila!
Piccolo

La Marmite
Sempre Vivolo
Stone Creek
Caracalla
Siam Lotus
Mirko's
Tellers
Aji 53
Benny's
Casa Rustica
Mario
Vintage Prime
Oak Room
Il Mulino NY
Da Ugo
Vittorio's
Palm Court
Page One
Branzino
Le Soir

Best Buys

In order of Bang for the Buck rating.

1. American Burger	21. Massa's
2. Maureen/Daughters'	22. Oaxaca Mexican
3. House of Dosas	23. Bridgehampton Candy
4. Robinson's	24. Hildebrandt's
5. Thomas's Ham	25. Greenport Tea
6. Green Cactus	26. Kiran Palace
7. Salsa Salsa	27. JT's Corner Cafe
8. Salvatore's	28. Thai Gourmet
9. Hampton Coffee	29. International Delight
10. Toast	30. La Panchita
11. Hampton Chutney	31. Thai Table
12. Fresco Crêperie	32. Thai Green Leaf
13. Pie	33. Eddie's Pizza
14. Ancient Ginger	34. Nick's
15. Baja Grill	35. Orient
16. Sweet Mama's	36. Pita House
17. La Bottega	37. Lemonleaf Grill
18. Grimaldi's	38. Spicy's BBQ
19. Bay Burger	39. Emilio's
20. Bigelow's	40. Mama's

OTHER GOOD VALUES

Aji 53	Lucy's Café
Albert's Mandarin	Med. Snack Bar
Asian Moon	Milk & Sugar Café
Azerbaijan Grill	Mitchell's
BayKery Café	Once Upon a Moose
Ben's Deli	Onzon Thai
Benten	Orchid
Big Daddy's	Pancho's
Blue Moon	Pasta-eria
BobbiQue	Pastrami King
Bobby's Burger	Seeda Thai
Bozena	Shang Hai Pavilion
Chefs of New York	Siam Lotus Thai
Cooke's Inn	Simply Thai
Curry Club	Smokin' Al's BBQ
Famous Dave's	Sri Thai
Fortune Wheel	Star Confectionery
George Martin's Grill	Steven's Pasta
Gonzalo's	Sundried Tomato
Hotoke	Swingbelly's Beachside
House of India	Tandoor Grill
Kabul Afghani	Toast & Co.
La Piazza	Umberto's
LL Dent	Wild Fig
Los Compadres	Zorba the Greek

PRIX FIXE DINNER DEALS

Since hours may be limited and prices can change, please call ahead to confirm.

$26-$30

Barney's	26	Nick & Toni's	30
Casa Rustica	30	Oliver Bon Dinant	29
Chez Noëlle	28	On 3	28
Coolfish	28	red bar	29
Fifth Season	28	Rist. Gemelli	30
Fresno	28	Romantico of Capri	26
Gabrielle's	30	Ruvo	26
H2O	30	Snaps	30
Jamesport Manor	29	Soigné	29
Jolly Fisherman	28	Stone Creek	30
Jonathan's Rist.	29	Stonewalls	28
La Primavera	26	Tratt. Diane	30
Le Chef	30	Voila!	30
Maxxels	28	Wild Honey	26

$25 AND UNDER

Almond	25	Honu Kitchen	25
Argyle Grill	25	Horace & Sylvia's	22
Azerbaijan Grill	13	Hudson's Mill	25
Babylon Carriage	22	JT's Corner Cafe	23
Bellport	19	JT's Place	20
Big Daddy's	16	La Bella Vita	24
Bistro 44	25	La Tavola	20
Bistro Toulouse	19	Lodge B&G	25
Bobby Van's	25	Lola's	20
Bob's Place	22	Mama's	12
Brick & Rail	25	Matsulin	25
Broadway Beanery	22	Michaels'/Maidstone	25
Butterfields	22	New Hyde Park Inn	25
Cafe Max	23	Nicholas James	24
Cho-Sen	23	Ozumo	10
Cielo	19	Page One	24
Cimino's	24	Peppercorns	22
City Café	25	Pierre's	25
Collins & Main	25	Roots	18
Crossroads Cafe	22	RS Jones	19
Declan Quinn's	21	Runyon's	25
Delano Mansion	25	Schooner	23
Desmond's	23	75 Main St.	23
Duke Falcon's	22	Shagwong	22
Elaine's Asian	24	34 New St.	20
Fiddleheads	25	Thyme	24
Fisherman's Catch	24	Trumpets	25
Garden Grill	25	Uncle Bacala's	25
George Martin	20	Villa D'Este	22
George Martin's Grill	15	Westhampton Steak	22
George Martin's Coastal	22	Wild Harvest	25
Hemingway's	25	Wildthyme	25

RESTAURANT DIRECTORY

	FOOD	DECOR	SERVICE	COST

Abel Conklin's *Eclectic/Steak*
22 | 17 | 21 | $53

Huntington | 54 New St. (W. Carver St.) | 631-385-1919 | www.abelconklins.com

At this "old-fashioned but well-done" chophouse, "hearty" prime cuts and "steady" Eclectic dishes are served by a "courteous" staff to a "senior"-leaning crowd of Huntington "regulars"; "dark" and "cozy", its 19th-century surroundings seem "stuck in a time warp" to some, but many find it a "tried-and-true", "good-value" alternative to modern "mega-steakhouses."

Absolutely Mario Ⓜ *Italian*
21 | 17 | 22 | $40

Farmingdale | 10 Allen Blvd. (Broad Hollow Rd.) | 631-694-7416 | www.absolutelymario.com

"Hands-on" owner Mario Garcia "makes sure everyone is happy" at this Farmingdale "neighborhood" place providing "above-average" Italian fare; while both the decor and the wine list "could use a little work", most appreciate the "accommodating" service and "moderate cost."

Ⓩ Aji 53 *Japanese*
27 | 24 | 24 | $39

Bay Shore | 53 E. Main St. (3rd Ave.) | 631-591-3107 | www.aji53.com

Admirers say *"arigato"* for the "spectacular presentations" of "outstanding" sushi ("Manhattan rolls without the train trip") and "beyond delicious" cooked Japanese dishes at this "Bay Shore jewel" whose owner's "Nobu pedigree" also shows in the "hip" surroundings and "steep" but "tasty" cocktails; with "convivial" service to boot, the "secret is out" – so "definitely call ahead for reservations."

Akari *Japanese*
21 | 14 | 17 | $32

Merrick | 2063 Merrick Rd. (Orr St.) | 516-378-9888

"Fine" "fresh" fish is the draw at this Merrick "favorite" for sushi and a "mean miso soup"; it "could use a sprucing up" – and is a bit heavy on "Long Island rich kids" for some – but its "consistent" quality ensures a "big take-out business."

Akbar *Indian*
21 | 18 | 19 | $35

Garden City | 2 South St. (Stewart Ave.) | 516-357-8300

Loyalists "love the buffet lunch" for a "bargain" at this otherwise "upscale" Garden City Indian offering "fabulous", "flavorful" feasts that are "on the spicy side"; "plush surroundings" and an "eager, helpful" staff enhance the experience for "family" get-togethers and "private parties."

Albert's Mandarin Gourmet *Chinese*
21 | 15 | 19 | $29

Huntington | 269 New York Ave. (bet. Gerard St. & Union Pl.) | 631-673-8188

"Everyone is treated like a regular" by owner Albert Leung at this Huntington "go-to" offering a "top-notch" Mandarin menu and the "old-time" ambiance of a "'70s-style Chinese restaurant" (just "like the kind our parents took us to as kids"); with "friendly" service and affordable tabs, it's a "reliable" "local standby" that brings back fond "memories."

	FOOD	DECOR	SERVICE	COST

NEW Alexandros *Mediterranean* — | — | — | M

Mount Sinai | 1060 Rte. 25A (Pipe Stave Hollow Rd.) | Mt. Sinai | 631-928-8600

Chef-owner Sam Constantis has reopened his classic Greek-Mediterranean (formerly in Miller Place) after an absence of several years, renovating the former Eddie G's Steak House on Route 25A in Mount Sinai; the new interior, with a small front bar, wood floors and a mural of Alexander the Great, provides a warm backdrop for favorites such as gyros, lamb chops and whole grilled fish; N.B. no alcohol is served, but a liquor license is pending.

Allison's Amalfi Risorante *Italian/Mediterranean* 22 | 20 | 22 | $52

Sea Cliff | 400 Glen Cove Ave. (Glenola Ave.) | 516-656-4774 | www.allisonsamalfi.com

The "gracious" married team of owner Allison Izzo and chef O'Michael Zara "makes the experience special" at this Sea Cliff "star" offering "wonderful" Med-Italian dishes in a frescoed strip-mall space with a "nice grotto feel"; though a few find the menu "limited" and service "inconsistent", most call it "reasonable" overall; N.B. closed Tuesdays.

Almarco *Italian* 18 | 17 | 20 | $39

Huntington | 13 Wall St. (bet. Gerard & Main Sts.) | 631-935-1690

"Dining outside is pleasant during the warmer months" at this "little" Huntington Italian, though the fairly "standard" food gets mixed reviews, and many agree the "dated" Tuscan decor "needs upgrading"; on the plus side, service is "friendly", and the bill "won't leave you running for the nearest ATM."

Almoncello *Italian* 20 | 18 | 19 | $47

Wainscott | 290 Montauk Hwy. (bet. Daniels Hole & Wainscott Rds.) | 631-329-6700 | www.almoncello.com

"Charming" co-owner and host Eric Lemonides (Almond) "makes everyone feel at home" at this "welcome" Wainscott addition – a more "refined" redo of the former Almondito – delivering "satisfying", "rustic" Northern Italian eats in a "lively" atmosphere; though a few critics "miss" its former Mex incarnation, and cite "forgettable" food and "spotty" service, the Saturday night karaoke is still "a total hoot"; N.B. closed Tuesday–Wednesday in the off-season.

Almond *French* 21 | 18 | 21 | $48

Bridgehampton | 1970 Montauk Hwy. (bet. Hayground & Snake Hollow Rds.) | 631-537-8885 | www.almondrestaurant.com

A "flat-out favorite" for "frites with the fellas on Fridays", this "casual" but "high-quality" "roadside" Bridgehampton bistro (which recently spun off a Manhattan branch) "hums loudly with the chatter of summer Hamptonites" in season; though it can get "jammed", the "gracious" service, "European feel" and "easy-on-the-pocketbook" prices "more than make up for any waiting at the bar"; N.B. closed Tuesday–Wednesday in the winter.

NEW A Mano *Italian* | 22 | 18 | 21 | $46 |

Mattituck | 13550 Main Rd. (bet. Love Ln. & Wickam Ave.) | 631-298-4800 | www.amanorestaurant.com

Chef/co-owner Tom Schaudel's new "laid-back" osteria in Mattituck offers Italian dishes made "by hand" with "ingenious" combinations of "fresh ingredients", including "unique" pizzas from the "wood-burning oven"; the "superb selection of Long Island and Italian wines" and "local cheeses" "showcases the North Fork bounty", and while service varies from "attentive" to "amateurish", its "later" hours are appreciated by those "who like to eat after 8 PM."

Z American Hotel, The *American/French* | 24 | 24 | 23 | $68 |

Sag Harbor | The American Hotel | 49 Main St. (bet. Bay Ave. & Washington Sts.) | 631-725-3535 | www.theamericanhotel.com

Both "locals and city-dwellers warm to the charms" of this "grande dame" in an "iconic" Sag Harbor hotel where the American-French cuisine is "terrific" (despite frequently "changing chefs"), the "legendary" wine list is "longer than *War and Peace*" and the "celebrity sightings are just a bonus"; though its "rich, dark decor" might be "stuffy" for some and the staff "a little haughty", most find the "costly" meal "well worth it."

American Roadside Burgers *Burgers* | 17 | 12 | 14 | $12 |

Huntington | 337 New York Ave. (bet. Main & W. Carver Sts.) | 631-935-0300

Smithtown | 80 E. Main St. (bet. Hauppauge Rd. & Maple Ave.) | 631-382-9500

www.americanburgercompany.com

Patty pundits find an appealing "alternative to Mc-meals" at these "neat industrial" Huntington and Smithtown joints, voted Best Bang for the Buck on Long Island, whose "juicy" burgers are accompanied by an "abundance" of free toppings, "must-try" sweet potato fries and "thick" milkshakes; though a few are disappointed by "smaller than expected" eats, most judge there's just the "right amount of greasy crunchy goodness" to cure a "craving"; P.S. finish a four-decker RoadStar and "get your name on the wall."

Amici *Italian* | 21 | 18 | 19 | $36 |

Massapequa | 4348 Merrick Rd. (Roxbury Ln.) | 516-799-4100 | www.amici-ristorante-italiano.com

"Huge portions that will bust your belt" are a hallmark of this "old-fashioned" Massapequa Italian serving "family-style" "Neapolitan feasts" to lots of "large groups"; the room gets "loud" and critics call the cooking only "adequate", but many are fond of the "homey" feel and "excellent value."

Ancient Ginger *Chinese* | 21 | 17 | 19 | $24 |

St. James | 556 N. Country Rd. (Lake Ave.) | 631-584-8883 | www.ancientginger.com

"Definitely a step above most Chinese restaurants in the area", this "creative" St. James option offers "gourmet", "healthful eating" in a "quiet", earth-toned setting – "no goldfish tanks here"; bolstered by an "eager-to-please" staff and "reasonable prices", fans affirm it's a "real find."

Angelina's *Italian*
22 | 18 | 21 | $45

East Norwich | Christina's Shopping Ctr. | 1017 Oyster Bay Rd. (bet. Johnson Ct. & Northern Blvd.) | 516-922-0033

Angelina's II *Italian*
Syosset | 30 Berry Hill Rd. (East St.) | 516-364-8234 | www.angelinas2.com

"Big" plates of "hearty", "high-end Italian basics" served by a "warm", "accommodating" staff draw a "loyal clientele" to this pair of separately owned trattorias; while the strip-mall location in East Norwich is a "favorite" of many, the Syosset branch in a "cozy house" has an extra touch of "old-world elegance", along with prix fixe lunches and dinners for a "good deal."

ⓩ Annona *Italian*
23 | 25 | 22 | $59

Westhampton Beach | Manhattan Motorcars | 112 Riverhead Rd., 2nd fl. (bet. Montauk Hwy. & Rogers Ave. Ext.) | 631-288-7766 | www.annona.com

"Where else will you find a Lamborghini as the most expensive item on the menu?" ask enthusiasts about this Westhampton Beach "hot spot" "perched above" an "ultraluxury" car showroom with plenty to "ogle"; the "sophisticated" Italian food and "dynamic decor" (enhanced by a "neat bar" and terrace dining in the summer) get pulses racing too, so despite a touch of "attitude", it's a "pleasure" to hop in.

Antares Cafe *American/Caribbean*
24 | 16 | 18 | $50

Greenport | Brewer Yacht Yard | 2530 Manhanset Ave. (bet. Beach Rd. & Champlain Pl.) | 631-477-8839

Chef-owner Matt Murphy "really has a touch" with "wonderfully inventive" cuisine at this "offbeat" Greenport "gem", formerly a New American spot that he's reopening in 2009 with a Caribbean emphasis – including frozen drinks and tiki decor – and lower prices; while the "bulk of the dining is alfresco", the room can be "cozy as a ship's cabin" ("especially in the winter"), and though the "service varies", most find it a "worthwhile trip to the end of the North Fork"; N.B. closed Tuesday–Wednesday in the off-season.

Aqua East *Italian*
20 | 21 | 19 | $49

Montauk | 17 S. Edison St. (S. Etna Ave.) | 631-668-4147

Reviewers report "lots of flavor" at this slightly "upscale" Italian that's "found a home in Montauk" with Tuscan-style digs and largely "attentive" service; though the cooking strikes some as "average at best", the "active bar" is part of the draw; N.B. closed mid-November to April.

Argyle Grill & Tavern *American*
21 | 20 | 19 | $38

Babylon | 90 Deer Park Ave. (bet. Grove Pl. & Main St.) | 631-321-4900 | www.theargylegrill.com

"Perfect for meeting and eating with friends", this "bustling" Babylon pub with a "Manhattan" vibe is "jammed on the weekends" with "lots of singles" sipping "martinis" and sampling a "solid menu" of "interesting", "not too expensive" New American fare; though some complain about "long waits" (no reservations are taken) and a deafening "din", the "friendly" service and crowd keep it a "favorite" local stomping ground.

Ariana *Afghan/Vegetarian*   21 | 18 | 19 | $37

Huntington | 255 Main St. (bet. New St. & New York Ave.) | 631-421-2933 | www.arianacafe.com

"Relax and relish the meal" of "distinctive", "carefully prepared" dishes that please "vegetarians and non-vegetarians" alike at this "cluttered but comfy" Huntington Afghan furnished with lots of patterned "pillow seating"; while a few fault "iffy" service, most appreciate the moderate price and the opportunity to try "something a little different."

Armand's *Italian*   17 | 15 | 18 | $38

Southampton | 1271 Noyac Rd. (Roses Grove Rd.) | 631-283-9742

Drive along the Peconic to reach this Southampton "hole-in-the-wall" dishing up "solid" Italian and brick-oven pizza from the open kitchen; a "little neighborhood spot for the locals", it's "casual and not expensive", though some complain it's "priced too high" for the "shabby" interior.

Arturo's *Italian*   23 | 18 | 23 | $46

Floral Park | 246-04 Jericho Tpke. (Colonial Rd.) | 516-352-7418 | www.arturorestaurant.com

"Wonderful old-world Italian dishes" gratify guests at this family-owned Floral Park "standby" where "overflowing" antipasto and dessert carts complement the "pleasant", "traditional" space; an "owner who circulates the room" and "attentive" service are part of the charm, so while it feels "old hat" and "expensive" to some, others say it's "been around forever and it's easy to see why."

Asian Moon *Pan-Asian*   23 | 22 | 21 | $33

Garden City | 825 Franklin Ave. (bet. 9th St. & Stewart Ave.) | 516-248-6161

"Modern" and "unique", this "affordable" Garden City eatery is applauded for "fresh", "eclectic" Pan-Asian cuisine that's prepared with "top-quality ingredients" and "beautifully presented" by a "professional" staff; as it's "lovely in the evening" with "upscale", "tranquil" surroundings (including a waterfall), admirers agree the "decor sets the mood and the food heightens it."

A Taberna *Portuguese*   23 | 17 | 18 | $36

Island Park | 4135 Austin Blvd. (bet. Saratoga & Trafalgar Blvds.) | 516-432-0455

"Sangria and sausage are a great way to start" at this "authentic" new Island Park Portuguese that "takes its heritage seriously" while maintaining a "lighthearted" feel with sunny colors, fresh flowers and nautical details; though a frequently "packed" house and "slow" service leave many "waiting for a table even with reservations", "reasonable" tabs help compensate.

	FOOD	DECOR	SERVICE	COST

Ayhan's Fish Kebab *Seafood/Turkish*

	19	16	19	$33

Port Washington | 286 Main St. (bet. Carlton Ave. & Shore Rd.) | 516-883-1515 | www.ayhans.com

"Crispy whole grilled fish" is the daily catch at this Turkish seafooder in Port Washington where the early-bird specials and Monday–Tuesday lobster deals "have the place jumping" with both "kids" and "seniors"; true, the "open" room in a former bank can get a bit "noisy", but the "consistent" quality and "family-friendly" service keep it a "favorite."

Ayhan's Mediterranean Cafe & Marketplace *Mediterranean/Turkish*

	18	15	18	$28

Port Washington | 293 Main St. (bet. Bank St. & Carlton Ave.) | 516-767-1400

Ayhan's Shish Kebab *Mediterranean/Turkish*

Baldwin | 550 Sunrise Hwy. (bet. Lancaster & Rockwood Aves.) | 516-223-1414

Plainview | Plainview Ctr. | 379 S. Oyster Bay Rd. (Woodbury Rd.) | 516-827-5300

Port Washington | 283 Main St. (bet. Bank St. & Carlton Ave.) | 516-883-9309

Rockville Centre | 201 Sunrise Hwy. (N. Village Ave.) | 516-255-0005

Westbury | Mall at the Source | 1504 Old Country Rd. (Evelyn Ave.) | 516-222-8000

www.ayhans.com

Customers "count on" the "killer salads", skewers and other Turkish-Med plates at this "powerhouse" local chain founded by Ayhan Hassan some 30 years ago; even if the decor is on the "cheesy" side (reminiscent of *yaya*'s house"), it offers "good value for the money", particularly during the "outrageous Sunday brunch buffet"; P.S. the Mediterranean Cafe in Port Washington is "picturesque" with "views of Manhasset Bay."

Azerbaijan Grill *Mideastern*

	21	14	20	$29

Westbury | 1610 Old Country Rd. (Post Ave.) | 516-228-0001 | www.azerbaijangrill.com

"You can't find a better kebab in Tehran" insist advocates of this Westbury "strip-mall surprise" grilling up "marvelous", "aromatic" Med, Persian and Turkish specialties; the service is "warm" and "prompt", so even if the "sparse decor ranks just above an office cafeteria", it's still an "inexpensive" "delight."

Azuma Sushi
Asian Fusion *Asian Fusion/Japanese*

	-	-	-	M

Greenlawn | 252 Broadway (Little Plains Rd.) | 631-262-7200 | www.azumasushiasianfusion.com

Succeeding in a site that's seen a lot of turnover through the years, this Greenlawn go-to offers a wide selection of sushi and cooked Japanese dishes, as well as Asian fusion eats that encompass Chinese and Thai flavors; while the setting is humble, reasonable prices help keep it crowded on weekend nights.

	FOOD	DECOR	SERVICE	COST

Babette's *Eclectic*

	20	13	17	$39

East Hampton | 66 Newtown Ln. (bet. Main St. & Osborne Ln.) | 631-329-5377 | www.babetteseasthampton.com

"Vegetarians" and others "feel virtuous" even as they sip a "blow-your-head-off Bloody Mary" at this "Newtown Lane landmark" where the "imaginative" Eclectic menu is big on "tofu, sprouts and fruit drinks" (with a few fish and poultry choices too); though critics cite "long waits", lackluster looks and "break-your-wallet" breakfasts, many feel it's the "only real choice if you want organic, healthy cuisine" and an "Alec Baldwin" sighting at the same time; N.B. closed Wednesday nights.

Babylon Carriage House *Continental*

	19	22	19	$42

Babylon | 21 Fire Island Ave. (Main St.) | 631-422-5161 | www.babyloncarriagehouse.com

Admirers "love the look" of this Babylon Continental set in a converted carriage house, where the bar is "happening" (especially during "Friday happy hour") and the rooms are "homey"; most report "finely prepared", "inventive" food (*Top Chef* contestant Danny Gagnon is chef de cuisine), and if some feel it's too "inconsistent and expensive for what you get", bargain-hunters call the Wednesday lobster bake the "best deal around."

Baby Moon *Italian*

	19	13	17	$33

Westhampton Beach | 238 Montauk Hwy. (bet. Rogers Ave. & S. Country Rd.) | 631-288-6350 | www.babymoonrestaurant.com

"A favorite for pizza" since 1970, this "family destination" in Westhampton Beach packs a "crowd" for "reliable" Southern Italian cooking and wood-fired pies; the decor is "early pizzeria", so even if some find it a bit "overpriced", it "still feels like an old-time neighborhood" place.

Backyard *Mediterranean*

	-	-	-	E

Montauk | Solé East | 90 Second House Rd. (S. Eldert Ln.) | 631-668-2105 | www.soleeast.com

Sleek and chic, this seasonal hideaway inside Solé East, a hotel in a historic Tudor building in Montauk, features a Mediterranean menu bolstered by local seafood and organic produce; with a large bar and fireplace, as well as outdoor poolside dining on oversized beds to the tune of DJ sets, it's a hot summertime scene.

Baja Grill *Mexican*

	17	13	16	$19

East Northport | Elwood Shopping Ctr. | 1920 Jericho Tpke. (Elwood Rd.) | 631-462-2252
Smithtown | 20 E. Main St. (bet. Hauppauge Rd. & Maple Ave.) | 631-979-2252
www.bajagrillny.com

"Big, honking burritos" and "sizzling fajitas" satisfy at these "festive" Mexicans that work "for a quick bite" on a "budget"; they're "steady, predictable" places where "the kids are happy" and the adults enjoy the "sizable margaritas."

	FOOD	DECOR	SERVICE	COST

Bamboo Restaurant & Sushi Lounge *Pan-Asian*

| 20 | 17 | 17 | $48 |

East Hampton | 47 Montauk Hwy. (bet. Baiting Hollow & Cove Hollow Rds.) | 631-329-9821

The "bustling" scene "swings well into the night" (especially "Thursdays and weekends") at this "chic" East Hampton sushi bar and lounge where a "young crowd" mingles over "respectable" rolls and Pan-Asian dishes; some feel it "costs more than it delivers", but the summer evening prix fixe is "attractive", and all in all it "can be fun as long as you're not taking things too seriously."

☑ Barney's Ⓜ *American/French*

| 26 | 23 | 25 | $63 |

Locust Valley | 315 Buckram Rd. (Bayville Rd.) | 516-671-6300 | www.barneyslv.com

"There's no better place on a chilly autumn night" "when the fireplace is aglow" than this "snug" Locust Valley "charmer" where the New American–French cooking is as "delectable as the atmosphere"; a "fine wine list" (with "affordable" options) and "superb" service make it "outstanding in every way", so no wonder it's still "hot with the chichi set."

Barolo *Continental/Italian*

| 25 | 20 | 23 | $52 |

Melville | 1197 Walt Whitman Rd. (Sweet Hollow Rd.) | 631-421-3750

"An oasis" in Melville, this "little" "romantic" "find" impresses guests with its "excellent" Continental-Italian cuisine provided by a "terrific" staff; while tabs are a touch "high" and the "dated" "interior could use a refresh", many prize it as an "adult restaurant" that's on their "short list for special occasions."

Barrister's *American*

| 16 | 13 | 17 | $34 |

Southampton | 36 Main St. (Wall St.) | 631-283-6206 | www.barristersouthampton.com

"Good for late lunches" or "comfort dinners", this "sociable" Southampton pub serves "typical", "consistent" burgers, sandwiches and other American grub in a prime location "right on Main Street"; true, it's a bit "ordinary" all around, but offers "a break from pricier alternatives" in the area.

Basil Leaf Cafe *Italian*

| 19 | 18 | 19 | $40 |

Locust Valley | Plaza Shops | 7B Birch Hill Rd. (bet. Elm St. & Underhill Rd.) | 516-676-6252 | basilleaf.kpsearch.com

"Ladies love it for lunch" and other "Loc-Is" are fond of the "refined", "fairly priced" Italian food served by a "pleasant" staff at this "cute" cafe "tucked away in a mall"; with both a "quiet patio" and "fireside" dining, it has year-round appeal, leading to "lots of repeat customers."

Bay Burger ⌀ *Burgers*

| 19 | 9 | 12 | $17 |

Sag Harbor | 1742 Bridgehampton-Sag Harbor Tpke. (Carroll St.) | 631-899-3915 | www.bayburger.com

"They grind their own beef and bake their own buns" to create a "fabulous" burger at this "updated" "counter-service" "joint" just south of Sag Harbor where "the only thing that can go wrong is eating too much"; it's "quick" and the "kids love it", and though some peeved patrons "wish" the "nondescript" surroundings "held up to the food", most are content to chow down "alfresco" at umbrella-topped tables; P.S. "they serve local wines" and beers too, as well as homemade ice cream.

BayKery Café *Bakery*
▽ 19 | 20 | 16 | $20

Oyster Bay | 124 South St. (bet. Orchard & W. Main Sts.) | 516-922-7002

"Fine panini", "homemade soups" and "great breakfast and baked goods" provide a "nice change" at this daytime Oyster Bay eatery decorated with bookcases and artwork for sale; though the service can be "lackluster", regulars say the "sociable owner loves to schmooze" and honor "requests."

Bayou, The 🅼 *Cajun/Creole*
23 | 17 | 20 | $35

North Bellmore | Omni Plaza | 2823 Jerusalem Ave. (Pea Pond Rd.) | 516-785-9263 | www.bayou4bigfun.com

"When you're cravin' Cajun" and have a "hankerin' for some gumbo, andouille and étouffée" ("hot or not"), this New Orleans-style roadhouse in North Bellmore is just "the ticket", complete with an "adult atmosphere" and "Mardi Gras" trappings; while there's often a "wait", potent libations are a perk – though "two Hurricanes are the limit if you want to walk out"; N.B. only AmEx and cash accepted.

Bayview Inn & Restaurant 🅼 *American/Continental*
21 | 18 | 20 | $45

South Jamesport | Bayview Inn | 10 Front St. (S. Jamesport Ave.) | 631-722-2659 | www.northforkmotels.com

While it's "not the flashiest" on the North Fork, this "restored inn" brings "urban-quality" New American–Continental cuisine to South Jamesport in a "simple" setting staffed by "servers who care"; many consider it the "best bet" around for the price, and while there's barely a bay view, most agree "summertime eating on the porch is delightful."

BBQ Bill's *BBQ*
18 | 15 | 16 | $29

Greenport | 47 Front St. (2nd St.) | 631-477-2300

"Greenport has a hit" in this joint combining "tender" BBQ with "killer views from the upstairs deck"; though some 'cue critics call it "only ok", it works as an easy "family place", especially "considering the dearth of decent, inexpensive food in the area."

Beacon *American*
24 | 22 | 21 | $58

Sag Harbor | 8 W. Water St. (Bridge St.) | 631-725-7088

"The rare waterfront restaurant where the food is as good as the view", this "hip" second-story seasonal favorite in Sag Harbor wins praise for both its "fabulous" (if "expensive") New American dishes and "fantastic" sunsets over the marina; service is "welcoming", but they "don't take rezzies – so don't be in a rush, and relax with a cocktail" at the zinc bar.

	FOOD	DECOR	SERVICE	COST

Bella Vita City Grill *American/Italian*

| 21 | 16 | 20 | $43 |

St. James | Colonial Shopping Ctr. | 430-16 N. Country Rd. (Clinton Ave.) | 631-862-8060 | www.bellavitacitygrill.com

"Lots of locals" go for a "well-rounded" menu of Italian–New American fare "done with creativity and style" at this St. James "gem", complete with "martinis" and a "Manhattan" feel; it's a bit "costly" and often so "cramped" and "noisy" that you might want to "bring your PDA so you can communicate" with your dining companions, but the "friendly" service helps compensate.

Bellport, The *American/Continental*

| 23 | 19 | 20 | $47 |

Bellport | 159 S. Country Rd. (bet. Station Rd. & Woodruff St.) | 631-286-7550 | www.bellport.com

"An 'in' funky restaurant in an old-money town", this Bellport "charmer" helmed by "original" chef-owner Taylor Alonso offers a "different", "unpretentious" setting to dine on "excellent" New American–Continental meals with a "personal touch"; though some feel the "snug" space could use some "primping up", most simply "go with the mood" and appreciate that it's "upscale but not over-priced"; N.B. a $19 prix fixe is offered Monday nights.

Benihana *Japanese*

| 18 | 17 | 19 | $37 |

Manhasset | Bed, Bath & Beyond Shopping Plaza | 2105 Northern Blvd. (Port Washington Blvd.) | 516-627-3400
Westbury | 920 Merchants Concourse (opp. Mall at the Source) | 516-222-6091
www.benihana.com

"Dinner and a show" take on new meaning at these "entertaining" Manhasset and Westbury branches of the Japanese steakhouse chain, the "original teppanyaki experience" complete with "acrobatic", "knife-flipping" chefs who "slice and dice" your meal tableside; party-poopers protest "bland" grub, "hokey" theatrics and "chop-chop" service, noting that "if you go without kids", it helps to "drink a lot."

Benkei Japanese *Japanese*

| ▽ 20 | 17 | 16 | $37 |

Northport | 16 Woodbine Ave. (bet. Main St. & Scudder Ave.) | 631-262-7100

"Plentiful", "nicely presented" sushi and "well-done" Japanese dishes appeal at this family-owned Northport newcomer, "but, and there is a big but", the "rushed" service "could use a bit of work"; even with a fairly "cramped" sushi bar too, a few find the atmosphere "pleasant" nonetheless.

NEW Bennett's *Eclectic*

| - | - | - | M |

Locust Valley | 23 Birch Hill Rd. (bet. Elm St. & Forest Ave.) | 516-676-2620 | www.bennettswineandcheese.com

Owner Bennett Schwartz has created a destination for Eclectic small plates at this loungey newcomer in the former home of Bin 23 in Locust Valley; a selection of cheeses, fondue, crostini and panini are some of the light bites available for weary workers returning from Manhattan on the nearby train, whether for a full meal or to accompany a glass of vino.

	FOOD	DECOR	SERVICE	COST

Benny's Ristorante ⸱ ⊠ *Italian* | 25 | 18 | 24 | $53 |

Westbury | 199 Post Ave. (Maple Ave.) | 516-997-8111 |
www.bennysristorante.com

"A haven for old-world bliss", this "upscale" Westbury "mainstay" provides "classic" Northern Italian dishes in a "relaxing" (if somewhat "dated") atmosphere; service is "warm yet professional", and though a few feel the staff "caters to their crowd", most applaud the "caring" owner for "making sure everything runs smoothly."

Ben's Kosher Deli *Deli* | 19 | 12 | 15 | $24 |

Baldwin | 933 Atlantic Ave. (bet. Bayview Ave. & Grand Blvd.) |
516-868-2072
Carle Place | 59 Old Country Rd. (Glen Cove Rd.) | 516-742-3354
Greenvale | 140 Wheatley Plaza (bet. Glen Cove Rd. & Northern Blvd.) |
516-621-3340
Woodbury | 7971 Jericho Tpke. (Southwoods Rd.) | 516-496-4236

Ben's Express Deli *Deli*

Garden City | Roosevelt Field Mall | 630 Old Country Rd. (bet. Clinton Rd. &
Meadowbrook Pkwy.) | 516-294-3354
www.bensdeli.net

"Fressers" "forget the calories and chow down" on "jaw-aching" pastrami sandwiches, "wonderful" homemade soups and other "solid" kosher fare at this "authentic Jewish deli" mini-chain; though some cite "slapdash" service, "nondescript" settings and a "commercial" trend, most savor the chance to hark back to their "childhood in Brooklyn" with eats "like grandma used to make."

Benten *Japanese* | 25 | 16 | 21 | $32 |

Miller Place | 331 Rte. 25A (Miller Place Rd.) | 631-473-7878
Chef Ken Lee crafts "unique rolls" at this "amazing", "family-run" Japanese standout in Miller Place that does a "booming take-out business" ("call early"); the staff is "wonderful" and the "complete box dinners are an excellent deal", though the "small", "uninspiring" digs leave diners "yearning" for more space; N.B. closed Tuesdays.

⊠ Besito *Mexican* | 23 | 23 | 21 | $46 |

Roslyn | Harborview Shoppes | 1516 Old Northern Blvd.
(bet. Northern Blvd./Rte. 25A & Remsen Ave.) | 516-484-3001
Huntington | 402 New York Ave. (bet. Carver & Fairview Sts.) |
631-549-0100
www.besitomex.com

"Vibrant" Mexican food with a "modern flair" (including "must-have" guac made tableside) "kisses the palate" at this "hip" Huntington and Roslyn duo that also boasts "boutique margaritas", "beautiful people" and "dark", "gorgeous" ambiance ("candles lit against the back wall make it look phenomenal"); despite some complaints of "upselling", most maintain the "terrific" service suits the "sophisticated" meal.

Bevanda *Italian* | 21 | 17 | 23 | $46 |

Great Neck | 570 Middle Neck Rd. (bet. Breuer Ave. & Brokaw Ln.) |
516-482-1510
The "ever-present owners" "could not be more attentive to their guests" at this Great Neck veteran known for "super service" and "sub-

stantial" Northern Italian fare; so even if the cooking is fairly "predict-able", and the decor a bit "long in the tooth", complimentary "nice touches" and "reasonable" tabs keep "longtime" customers loyal.

Big Daddy's *BBQ/Cajun*

| 23 | 17 | 20 | $33 |

Massapequa | 1 Park Ln. (Front St.) | 516-799-8877 | www.bigdaddysny.com

Big-flavored, "big Cajun dishes" pack a "powerful kick" ("beware when they say 'hot'") and the drinks "knock your socks off" at this "noisy", "down-home" slice of "Bourbon Street" in Massapequa that also dishes up "delicious" BBQ; "waits on the weekends" can hold up some partyers, but most just relax and "let the good times roll."

Bigelow's ⊟ *New England*

| 24 | 8 | 19 | $22 |

Rockville Centre | 79 N. Long Beach Rd. (Sunrise Hwy.) | 516-678-3878

"Deep yearnings" for the "freshest" fried Ipswich clams and "excellent" chowder ("the best south of New England") draw "third-generation" diners to this 60-year-old Rockville Centre "seafood shack"; though some claim it's "getting a little too pricey" considering the "counter-only" "luncheonette" digs, defenders insist "in their case less is better – I wouldn't change a thing."

Birchwood on the Park *American/Polish*

| ▽ 18 | 14 | 19 | $28 |

Southampton | 76C Jobs Ln. (Pond Ln. & S. Main St.) | 631-283-4316 | www.birchwoodonthepark.com

Birchwood Tap Room *American/Polish*

Riverhead | 512 Pulaski St. (Hamilton Ave.) | 631-727-4449

"Hearty grub and drink" can be had at this old-and-new duo offering Polish and American pub fare ("spackle up those arteries") at "reasonable prices"; the "rustic" Riverhead location in Polishtown has an atmosphere out of the "1950s" with "original decor" from when it opened 80 years ago, while the new Southampton branch just off Main Street is a world away, featuring DJ and karaoke nights.

🅉 Bistro Cassis *French*

| 24 | 20 | 22 | $44 |

Huntington | 55B Wall St. (bet. Central & Gerard Sts.) | 631-421-4122 | www.bistrocassis.com

A "rare down-to-earth French eatery", this Huntington *soeur* to Bistro Citron "wows" with "aromatic" mussels and other "classic" dishes delivered by a "charming" staff; true, the tables are so "close together" you could "eat off the plate next to you", but for many the "bustle and noise" are part of the "exhilarating" experience; N.B. reservations accepted only for six or more.

Bistro Citron *French*

| 21 | 20 | 19 | $43 |

Roslyn | 1362 Old Northern Blvd. (bet. E. Broadway & Main St.) | 516-403-4400 | www.bistrocitron.com

Sporting a "sophisticated vibe", this Roslyn spin-off of Bistro Cassis offers "must-try" mussels with "crusty bread" among other "tasteful" French bistro bites, complemented by "simple", "cozy" surroundings and a "pastoral" view of the duck pond in back; with "professional", "pleasant" service and a "fabulous" Sunday

	FOOD	DECOR	SERVICE	COST

brunch to boot, no wonder it's usually "full to the brim" (and "noisy") on the weekends.

Bistro du Village ⓜ *French*   24 | 19 | 20 | $44

Port Washington | 172 Main St. (bet. Madison & Monroe Sts.) | 516-883-1010

"*Mon dieu!*", it's "a shock to find a splendid French place here" exclaim Gallic gourmets about this Port Washington "neighborhood bistro" where chef Eric Le Dily prepares "amazing" dishes set down by a "knowledgeable" staff; its "petite" space is "intimate as they come", but a few find it "cramped" with "close-together" tables; N.B. the BYO-only policy makes it a "bargain."

Bistro 44 *American*   21 | 19 | 19 | $46

Northport | 44 Main St. (bet. School St. & Woodbine Ave.) | 631-262-9744 | www.bistro44restaurant.com

"Nestled in the town of Northport", this "welcome addition to the reawakening scene" offers "fresh", "well-prepared" New American fare in a "warm" setting with a "delightful" patio; the location makes it "perfect for pre-theater dinners" or paired with a "Main Street stroll", though some patrons find it "pricey" given the "close quarters" and somewhat "uneven" service.

Bistro M Ⓢ *American*   25 | 17 | 23 | $58

Glen Head | 70 Glen Head Rd. (Railroad Ave.) | 516-671-2498 | www.bistromrestaurant.com

Reviewers recommend the "exquisite dining experience" at this Glen Head "rarity" where "unique", "delicious" seasonal New American dishes are prepared by "creative" chef/co-owner Mitch SuDock, who often "comes out to greet" guests; though its location by the train tracks can detract, many are pleased by the "intimate", "well-appointed" space and "attentive" staff, and call the prix fixe an "excellent deal."

Bistro Toulouse ⓜ *French*   21 | 19 | 22 | $41

Port Washington | 43 Main St. (bet. Bayles & Maryland Aves.) | 516-708-1852

Iva and Pablo Cecere "run a charming little bistro" in the heart of Port Washington, where the "inventive" French menu "changes seasonally", the "help is earnest" and the room is "relaxed yet elegant", if a bit "tight"; all in all it's a satisfying "sleeper", plus the prix fixe dinner is a "real bargain."

B.K. Sweeney's Parkside Tavern *American*   18 | 16 | 18 | $30

Bethpage | 356 Broadway (Powell Ave.) | 516-935-9597

B.K. Sweeney's Uptown Grille *American*

Garden City | 636 Franklin Ave. (bet. 6th & 7th Sts.) | 516-746-3075 | www.bksweeneys.com

These "local hangouts" in Garden City and Bethpage ("the 19th hole" for golfers) complement the suds with "tasty burgers" and other "steady" American "pub grub" for a "value"; "cheerful" service, a "hopping" bar scene and lots of big-screen TVs make them just right for "unwinding or catching a game."

	FOOD	DECOR	SERVICE	COST

NEW Black & Blue
Seafood Chophouse Ⓜ *Seafood/Steak* — **24** | **21** | **22** | **$53**

Huntington | 65 Wall St. (bet. Central & Gerard Sts.) | 631-385-9255
"New on the Huntington scene", this "ambitious" surf 'n' turfer "impresses" with "creative", "beautifully presented" dishes and largely "polished" service; even if the "dark", "plush" supper-club decor strikes some as "mediocre", most warm up to the "enjoyable" bar.

Blackbirds' Grille *Cajun/Southern* — ▽ **18** | **14** | **18** | **$30**

Sayville | 553 Old Montauk Hwy. (Broadway Ave.) | 631-563-4144 |
www.blackbirdsgrille.com
Folks find "affordable" Cajun-Southern eats that are "surprisingly good" if a little "lacking in NOLA flair" at this "homey" Sayville bar and grill; a "nice meeting place", it tends to get "crowded" and "noisy" on the weekends with customers who "really come" to have a drink and see the live bands.

Ⓩ Blackstone Steakhouse ● *Steak* — **23** | **24** | **22** | **$67**

Melville | 10 Pinelawn Rd. (Broad Hollow Rd.) | 631-271-7780 |
www.blackstonesteakhouse.com
"First-rate" steak and "fabulous", "top-dollar" sushi keep this Melville "power" place on the 110 corridor "full of suits" who are "closing deals" and being "treated like royalty" by the "A+" staff; the "gorgeous" main room is "sleek" and "spacious", though some balk at the "high decibels" and "über-expensive" bill.

Blackwells Ⓜ *Steak* — **21** | **23** | **22** | **$49**

Wading River | Great Rock Resort & Golf Club | 141 Fairway Dr.
(Sound Ave.) | 631-929-1800 | www.blackwellsrestaurant.com
"After visiting the wineries" or hitting the links, this Wading River steakhouse provides a "truly wonderful vista" of the Great Rock golf course from a "spacious", "mahogany-accented" dining room that "looks like an old-fashioned men's club"; duffers and others affirm the "flavorful" cuts are a "decent value", and the staff is "responsive without being overbearing"; N.B. the Food score does not reflect a post-Survey chef change.

Bliss Ⓜ *American* — **22** | **19** | **21** | **$48**

East Setauket | 766 Rte. 25A (Nicolls Rd.) | 631-941-0430 |
www.blissli.com
"Each plate comes out like a piece of art" at this "bright spot" in East Setauket featuring "novel" New American cuisine by chef Danny Avalos; "excellent martinis", "courteous service" and a "lovely" room decorated with local artwork make it a "popular" "date spot", though the "tiny" space is too "tight" for some, and the meal a bit "pricey."

Blond *American* — **22** | **19** | **21** | **$52**

Miller Place | Aliano Shopping Ctr. | 691 Rte. 25A (Oakland Ave.) |
631-821-5969 | www.blondrestaurant.com
You may feel like you're in a "trendy Brooklyn neighborhood" rather than a Miller Place strip mall at this "chic", "crisp" and "ambitious" New American where the upscale, "innovative" dishes are "plated

with style"; given its "cheerful" service and "romantic" ambiance, many deem it a "discovery in the middle of nowhere"; N.B. the Food score may not reflect a recent chef-owner change.

Blue *American*   ▽ 19 | 21 | 18 | $47

Blue Point | 7 Montauk Hwy. (Nicolls Rd.) | 631-363-6666 | www.restaurantblue.com

"Tasty" New American cuisine is upstaged by the "singles scene" at this Blue Point restaurant and club where the "over-35 crowd" can dance to DJ sets "into the late evening" on the weekends; it's "spacious, comfortable" and a little "decadent", though some find the service "remiss" and the menu "overpriced."

Blue Fin 🅼 *Asian Fusion/Japanese*   23 | 21 | 21 | $42

Great Neck | 148 Middle Neck Rd. (Cedar Dr.) | 516-487-9000

"I'm glad it's still a secret" admit admirers of this Great Neck "find" delivering "fresh fish" and "excellent" cooked Japanese and Asian fusion dishes for "moderate" tabs; "beautiful" decor and an "accommodating" staff add to its "chic" appeal.

Blue Moon *Pizza*   21 | 17 | 18 | $28

Rockville Centre | 26 N. Park Ave. (bet. Merrick Rd. & Sunrise Hwy.) | 516-763-4900 | www.bluemoonpizzeria.com

"More than a pizza place", this "affordable", "old-time" Rockville Centre Italian turns out "pleasing" red-sauce dishes and "delicious" panini along with "home-run" coal-oven pies; fans say both the staff and the "Little Italy"-style surroundings make you feel "comfortable", plus the "clutch" location next to a multiplex makes it a cinch for "pre- or post-movie" meals.

Blue Ocean Asian   ▽ 24 | 17 | 19 | $36
Bistro & Sushi Bar *Pan-Asian*

Bethpage | 300 Central Ave. (Stewart Ave.) | 516-822-2888

"Unique combinations" of sushi and "delicious", "unusual" Pan-Asian specials make enthusiasts "happy" to have this "hidden find" in Bethpage; though the aqua-accented space gets mixed reviews, it's "cute", "convenient" and a "value" to boot.

Blue Room 🅼 *American*   24 | 19 | 21 | $48

East Northport | 93 Larkfield Rd. (9th Ave.) | 631-261-5761

The "original menu" of New American cuisine with a touch of "Southern inspiration" "soars" at this "terrific" East Northport "find" housed in a "tiny", "unlikely spot" with "quirky but attractive" decor; "good" service, "reasonable" prices and live blues on Wednesdays all add to the "down-home" appeal.

Blue Sky Bistro 🖻🅼 *American*   ▽ 23 | 18 | 21 | $46

Malverne | 366 Hempstead Ave. (Arlington Ave.) | 516-599-9002

Its strip-mall location is a bit "strange", but this "small", "attractive" arrival in Malverne defies expectations with its "innovative interpretations" of market-driven American fare, a "well-versed" staff and "homey" atmosphere; while it's on the "expensive" side, patrons say perks like "30-plus wines by the glass" make it "worth a trip."

	FOOD	DECOR	SERVICE	COST

BobbiQue *BBQ* — 19 | 16 | 16 | $26

Patchogue | 70 W. Main St. (bet. Havens & N. Ocean Aves.) |
631-447-7744 | www.bobbique.com

"Authentic BBQ in Patchogue! woo-hoo!" exclaim smoke hounds about
this "go-to" slice of Memphis serving up "sumptuous", "slow-cooked"
meats and more than 100 "special brews" for a "great value"; though
its "industrial" setting and "awkward" ordering system aren't for
everyone, fans agree the live blues on the weekends "adds some zest."

NEW Bobby's Burger Palace *Burgers* — - | - | - | I

Lake Grove | Smith Haven Mall | 355 Smith Haven Mall
(bet. Middle Country Rd. & Nesconset Hwy.) | 631-382-9590 |
www.bobbysburgerpalace.com

"Renowned" TV personality, restaurateur and cookbook author Bobby
Flay hits Long Island with a burger bang, opening this sleek, casual
chain link in the Smith Haven Mall in Lake Grove; faithful fans who
flank the lime- and orange-accented curvy counter say the "creative
selections" provide "another grillicious meal from the grillmaster",
which accounts for those lines that snake out the door.

Bobby Van's Steakhouse *Steak* — 22 | 19 | 20 | $60

Bridgehampton | 2393 Main St. (bet. Ocean Rd. & School St.) |
631-537-0590 | www.bobbyvans.com

An "oldie but a goodie", this "see-and-be-seen" steakhouse in the
"hub" of Bridgehampton is "hopping" with guests who savor the
"steady" if "expensive" food and "generous" drinks set down by a
"knowledgeable" staff; indeed, the bar scene can become a "meat
market in every respect on summer evenings", but some guests go
purely for the early prix fixe "deal."

Bob's Place Ⓜ *American* — 21 | 21 | 20 | $43

Floral Park | 230 Jericho Tpke. (bet. Flower Ave. & Park Pl.) |
516-354-8185 | www.bobsplacerestaurant.com

"Publike and elegant at the same time", this revamped Floral Parker
(formerly Gebhardt's) is "taking off" with an "attractive" New
American menu that's especially economical during the "awesome"
Tuesday–Thursday prix fixe dinner; to some, the ambiance is just
"so-so", but "timely" service is a plus.

Boccaccio Ⓜ *Italian* — 23 | 17 | 23 | $48

Hicksville | 275 W. Old Country Rd. (Newbridge Rd.) | 516-433-6262 |
www.boccacciony.com

"Big" plates of "old-school" Northern Italian fare make for "top-shelf"
meals at this 1977 Hicksville mainstay that gets a boost in business
from its popular "birthday special"; the "pleasant" owner and "wonderful" staff provide "personal attention", so while some detractors
deem it "dated" and "overpriced", regulars feel "right at home."

Bonbori Tiki *Japanese/Thai* — 19 | 17 | 18 | $34

Huntington | 14 Elm St. (bet. Nassau Rd. & New York Ave.) | 631-673-0400
Huntington diners find a "decent mix" of "enjoyable" Thai and
Japanese food at this "quiet" two-floor space with modest prices;

while critics feel they "fall short" on both cuisines and cite a "tired" interior, at least the "charming" outdoor garden is "pretty in the summer" and service has "improved" of late.

Bonsai *Japanese* | 22 | 16 | 19 | $33 |

Port Washington | 92 Main St. (bet. Evergreen & Haven Aves.) | 516-883-0103

"Beautifully presented" sushi, "satisfying entrees" and bento boxes with a "nice variety" keep this Port Washington Japanese "one step ahead" of the rest; "fair prices" and an atmosphere "without the stuffy pretense" make it a popular "place to take children" – so some grown-ups recommend "going late to avoid all the kids at early seatings."

Bostwick's on the Harbor *Seafood* | 20 | 17 | 19 | $46 |

East Hampton | Harbor Marina | 39 Gann Rd. (off Three Mile Harbor Rd.) | 631-324-1111

"Sail in for the sunsets, steamers and beer" at this seasonal East Hampton seafooder with a "picture-perfect" locale right on Three Mile Harbor; the "simply prepared" fish, "informal atmosphere" and "moderate" prices all appeal, though for some customers "sitting on the steps with a glass of wine, waiting for a table, is the best part."

Bozena Polish-European Restaurant Ⓜ *Polish* | ▽ 22 | 13 | 21 | $26 |

Lindenhurst | 485 W. Montauk Hwy. (bet. 7th & 8th Sts.) | 631-226-3001 | www.polishdinner.com

Those in search of a "pierogi fix" need not "suffer on the BQE anymore", since this Lindenhurst locale provides "deliciously fattening", "authentic Polish cuisine" for an "excellent value"; servers are "friendly and helpful", but since it's essentially a "big catering hall", watch out for "loud DJs" playing Eastern European music during your meal; N.B. reservations accepted for six or more.

Branzino *Italian* | 25 | 21 | 24 | $54 |

Lynbrook | 152 Union Ave. (Scranton Ave.) | 516-599-6161 | www.branzinoristorante.com

Lovers of "leisurely" Northern Italian meals adore this "out-of-the-way" Lynbrook "oasis" for its "superb" (if somewhat "steep") menu and "high-quality" service; since the "cozy" skylit space only seats 50, it can become "impossibly crowded on the weekends", so cognoscenti opt for "delightful" weeknight dinners.

Brasserie Cassis *French* | 23 | 21 | 21 | $45 |

Plainview | Plainview Ctr. | 387 S. Oyster Bay Rd. (Woodbury Rd.) | 516-653-0090 | www.reststarinc.com

"So authentic, I want to pay in Euros" affirm *amis* of this "stylish" "new favorite" that "teleports you" from a Plainview strip mall "straight into a small French brasserie"; the "classic bistro fare" is plated with "superb sauces" and served by a "well-informed" staff, so while some sniff that it's "crowded" and a bit "pretentious", others dub it "busy, noisy and everything it needs to be."

	FOOD	DECOR	SERVICE	COST

NEW Brasserie Persil *French*   25 | 19 | 22 | $39

Oceanside | 2825 Long Beach Rd. (bet. Merle Ave. & Poole St.) |
516-992-1742 | www.persilrestaurant.com

"Oceanside has hit the big time!" trumpet fans of this new brasserie (sister to Sage Bistro) turning out "fresh", "top-notch"
French fare that's a "real bargain"; despite complaints about the
noise level ("conversation is impossible"), most find the room "attractive" and the staff "attentive", providing a "much-needed" addition to "this neck of the woods"; N.B. reservations accepted for
parties of six or more.

NEW Brass Rail M *American*   - | - | - | M

Locust Valley | 107 Forest Ave. (bet. Birch Hill Rd. & Weir Ln.) |
516-723-9103

After a short stint as chef at Nisen Sushi in Woodbury, chef-owner
Kent Monkan is back at his old digs (previously called Heirloom) in
Locust Valley; the handsome marble-topped mahogany bar with its
brass rail is still there, but the layout is more open and there's a new
slant to the cuisine – an American menu ranging from sandwiches to
small plates to entrees such as stuffed boneless short ribs, offering
some options when it comes to cost.

Bravo Nader! *Italian*   26 | 14 | 23 | $55

Huntington | 9 Union Pl. (bet. New York Ave. & Wall St.) | 631-351-1200 |
www.bravonader.com

Though the name may resemble a chant for an all-star soccer forward, this "shoebox" Huntington haunt is "beloved" for the "marvelous", "worth-every-penny" Southern Italian food ("specials are the
sweet spot") crafted by "amazing" chef-owner Nader Gebrin, who
"works magic in the kitchen" and "makes you feel at home"; even if
the space often gets so "crammed" "you could eat off your neighbor's plate by mistake", fans love that the "wine is flowing and
loud conversations abound."

Breakwater Cafe *American*   - | - | - | E

Montauk | Montauk Manor | 236 Edgemere St. (bet. Elwell St. &
S. Erie Ave.) | 631-668-3949 | www.montaukmanor.com

Tucked away in the "stately" Montauk Manor near the center of the
village, this "quiet dining room" serves a "casual" New American
menu that's outshined by its hilltop views; while the cuisine is more
upscale than at many of its neighbors, some surveyors find the
menu "a little pricey" for the area; N.B. closed Monday–Tuesday
from October–April.

NEW Brick & Rail *Eclectic*   - | - | - | E

Wantagh | 3274 Railroad Ave. (bet. Beech St. & Wantagh Ave.) |
516-308-3476 | www.brickandrail.com

All aboard the Wantagh express, an Eclectic newcomer near the
train station whose upscale yet relaxed digs feature railroad posters
and other retro accents; prix fixe deals Sunday–Thursday and bar
specials on Wednesdays keep it budget-friendly for both early birds
and happy-hour lovers; N.B. closed Tuesdays.

	FOOD	DECOR	SERVICE	COST

Bridgehampton Candy Kitchen ⏚ *Diner*

15 | 12 | 18 | $20

Bridgehampton | Main St. (School St.) | 631-537-9885

"Time-warp back to a '50s diner" and "indulge your sweet tooth" with housemade ice cream and milkshakes at this "classic" Bridgehampton "throwback" steeped in "soda fountain appeal"; while the other "homestyle" American grub tends to be "greasy" and just a "touch above ok", its unchanging, "unpretentious" "luncheonette" style keeps it "filled with families" (including some "celebs") and "swamped in the summer."

Broadway Beanery Ⓜ *American*

22 | 22 | 21 | $37

Lynbrook | 23 Atlantic Ave. (bet. Merrick Rd. & Sunrise Hwy.) | 516-596-0028 | www.broadwaybeanery.com

"Not a beanery at all", this "ambitious" Lynbrook New American delivers "creative" dishes and "sinful" sweets that make it worth going "for a meal, a drink or dessert"; the "relaxed" candlelit setting with Victorian details and "live music on the weekends" makes it "great for a date"; N.B. a recent chef change may not be fully reflected by the Food score.

Brook House *American*

- | - | - | ı

Stony Brook | Stony Brook Village Ctr. | 123 Main St. (bet. Christian Ave. & Rte. 25A) | 631-751-4617

This homey little place in the midst of the Stony Brook Village Center is high on nostalgia, decorated with huge Norman Rockwell prints, bentwood chairs and a big old stove at the entrance holding flyers about upcoming local events; hearty fare like meatloaf, steaks and Reubens dominate the American menu, followed up by treats from the in-house ice cream parlor.

🆕 Brooks & Porter *Steak*

22 | 24 | 21 | $61

Merrick | 16 Merrick Ave. (Sunrise Hwy.) | 516-379-9400 | www.brooksandporter.com

"Welcome to Merrick!" salute meat eaters who savor the "excellent", "enormous cuts" of beef at this "hot" new steakhouse with a busy bar, oversized booths and a side of "Manhattan chic"; it's an appealing option "when you want to stay away from the more crowded chains", though a few feel "service is lacking" for the "New York City price."

🅉 Bryant & Cooper Steakhouse *Steak*

26 | 20 | 23 | $67

Roslyn | 2 Middle Neck Rd. (Northern Blvd.) | 516-627-7270 | www.bryantandcooper.com

The prime cuts are "consistently tops" and the "seafood and sides are terrific too" at this "steakhouse extraordinaire" on the "corridor of carnivores" in Roslyn; while the "old-time" dining room can be a "tight squeeze", it's tended to by "professional, witty waiters", and loyalists love that it's "loud, full of testosterone" and a "fun scene" with a crowd "six-deep" at the bar – just be sure to "check your 401(k)" before footing the bill; N.B. don't miss the butcher and retail shop next door.

	FOOD	DECOR	SERVICE	COST

B. Smith's *Cajun/Southern* | 16 | 23 | 17 | $53 |

Sag Harbor | Long Wharf Promenade (Bay St.) | 631-725-5858 |
www.bsmith.com

"Location, location, location" rules the day at this "captivating space on the wharf" offering a "stunning" view of "Sag Harbor yachts" from its "chic" dining room and bar; despite the entertaining expertise of celeb co-owner Barbara Smith, however, the service is of the "summer-student" variety and the "mediocre", "expensive" Cajun-Southern fare "doesn't quite live up to the magnificent setting – but then again the setting is so good it doesn't have to."

Buckram Stables Cafe *American* | 18 | 17 | 18 | $33 |

Locust Valley | 31 Forest Ave. (bet. Birch Hill Rd. & Weir Ln.) |
516-671-3080

"Blue-blooded" Locust Valley pals make a "home base" of this "neighborhood steady" known for "great burgers" and other "tasty" American "pub grub that's proven itself over time"; though critics call it "a bit expensive for the type of food", that hardly daunts fans who often "jam" the "inviting" digs (that "really feel like a converted stable"), so reservations are recommended.

Buoy One *Seafood* | 22 | 7 | 17 | $31 |

Riverhead | 1175 W. Main St. (Mill Rd.) | 631-208-9737

"Unbelievable" "fresh seafood at fair prices is a formula that works well" at this "rustic fish monger" and restaurant that's a "hidden gem" in Riverhead; so "ignore the setting" – "basically a take-out counter with tables" – or "go when the weather's nice and sit outdoors" for a "perfect" summertime repast.

Burton & Doyle Steakhouse *Steak* | 24 | 23 | 23 | $67 |

Great Neck | 661 Northern Blvd. (Summer St.) | 516-487-9200 |
www.burtonanddoyle.com

"Quality steaks", a "phenomenal wine list" and a "lively atmosphere" lead canny carnivores to this "top-shelf" Great Neck meatery on "Steakhouse Row", where there's also a sushi bar for those who wish "to go a little lighter"; fond of the "superb" staff "without a side of snobbiness", the "clubby, pubby" crowd keeps it so packed "you wouldn't know there's a recession when you're here on a Friday or Saturday night."

Butera's *Italian* | 21 | 17 | 19 | $35 |

NEW **Seaford** | 3930 Sunrise Hwy. (bet. Jackson & Washington Aves.) |
516-795-6321

Woodbury | Woodbury Village Shopping Ctr. | 7903 Jericho Tpke.
(Southwoods Rd.) | 516-496-3633

Smithtown | 65 E. Main St. (Landing Ave.) | 631-979-9113
www.buteras.com

"Humongous" portions of "tasty, reliable" "red-sauce Italian" cooking is dished up at this trio of "family" favorites offering "quite a value" for the money; though the "crowded" Woodbury and Smithtown branches draw praise, "disappointed" diners wonder "what were they thinking?" by shuttering the two former Massapequa lo-

	FOOD	DECOR	SERVICE	COST

cations and opening a "glorified pizza joint" in Seaford that's "more like a cafeteria with not a lot of character"; P.S. to avoid a wait, "go before 6 PM."

Butterfields ⌧ American
20 | 19 | 19 | $40

Hauppauge | 661 Old Willets Path (Engineers Rd.) | 631-851-1507 | www.butterfieldsrestaurant.biz

This hopping Hauppauge "hideaway" "keeps the industrial park locale alive after dark", attracting the "after-work crowd" with "surprisingly good" New American fare and a "beautiful" mahogany bar; DJs on the weekends make it an "all-purpose" hit, though some complain of "spotty" service and feel it would have more dining potential "if they could lower the noise to that of a hockey game."

Cafe Baci Italian
22 | 16 | 20 | $33

Westbury | 1636 Old Country Rd. (bet. Post Ave. & S. Fulton St.) | 516-832-8888 | www.cafebacirestaurant.com

You'll "never leave hungry" from this Westbury "staple" where fans cheer the "heaping" plates of "well-made" pastas and other "satisfying" Italian eats that are "enough for a second meal"; an "eager-to-please" staff manages to keep the "mob scene" in check, though critics cite "long waits on the weekends" as well as "lackluster" digs and "difficult" parking that's "so bad you can't count on dining there."

Café Buenos Aires Argentinean
23 | 21 | 22 | $44

Huntington | 23 Wall St. (bet. Gerard & Main Sts.) | 631-603-3600 | www.cafebuenosaires.net

Customers say *que bueno!* to this Huntington "destination" for its "heavenly" empanadas and "superb" steaks among other "Argentinean delights", served in a "dressy" setting with "nice ambiance"; "charming" co-owner Hugo García and his staff provide "cordial" service, and the "boisterous" bar is an appealing "place to sit for hot or cold tapas" while checking out the Friday night tango dancers.

Café Formaggio Italian
20 | 19 | 20 | $35

Carle Place | 307 Old Country Rd. (E. Gate Blvd.) | 516-333-1718 | www.cafeformaggio.com

"Consistent", "generous" plates of "Italian basics at fair prices" (including "gluten-free options") attract customers to this Carle Place eatery, though some feel it's "too expensive" for "nothing-special" cuisine and "unspectacular" ambiance; since reservations are only taken for six or more, prepare to wait "during prime time."

NEW Cafe Havana Cuban
17 | 18 | 14 | $33

Smithtown | 944 W. Jericho Tpke. (bet. 9th & 10th Aves.) | 631-670-6277 | www.cafehavanali.com

"You can't go wrong with the Cuban sandwiches" say those who've sampled this "lively" Smithtown newcomer, but they still "need to work out a few kinks in the kitchen", so "avoid anything complicated"; the "erratic" service could use "some serious work" too, and the palm-tree decor with flowing white fabric is too *Miami Vice* for some, but at least the live Latin jazz on weekends is "enjoyable", and so are the "outstanding" mango mojitos.

	FOOD	DECOR	SERVICE	COST

Cafe Joelle on Main St. *American/Eclectic*

| 23 | 16 | 20 | $34 |

Sayville | 25 Main St. (Railroad Ave.) | 631-589-4600 |
www.cafejoelle.net

A "notch above" other "casual" options, this "solid Sayville institution" delivers "delicious" New American–Eclectic dishes, "amazing specials" and "wonderful desserts"; it's "pleasant" with a "warm community feel", though some find the space too "tight", especially since the no-reservations policy means there's "often a long wait" at the "small", "packed" bar.

Cafe La Strada *Italian*

| 24 | 16 | 22 | $45 |

Hauppauge | 352 Wheeler Rd. (Central Ave.) | 631-234-5550 |
www.cafelastradarestaurant.com

Champions cheer the "kitchen hits a home run" with "real-deal" traditional dishes at this "shopping-center gem" in Hauppauge that's "like coming home to your favorite Italian Sunday dinner"; the muralled decor "could use an upgrade", but the "white-glove" service is "very accommodating" (especially if you're a "regular") and the "legendary" wine list is "well priced."

Cafe Max *American/Eclectic*

| 21 | 15 | 21 | $48 |

East Hampton | 85 Montauk Hwy. (Cove Hollow Rd.) | 631-324-2004 |
www.unhampton.com

"Leave the airs at home and prepare to eat well" at this East Hamptoner where chef-owner Max Weintraub has a "steady cadre of regulars who like his traditional presentation" of American-Eclectic cuisine with a focus on "great seafood"; though some complain it's too much of "the same" ("give us a break, Max, do something different") and the former speakeasy space is otherwise "nothing special", the "civilized" service and "popular prix fixe" dinners are huge selling points; N.B. Sunday brunch is served in the off-season only.

Cafe Rustica *Italian/Mediterranean*

| 21 | 18 | 21 | $40 |

Great Neck | 200 Middle Neck Rd. (bet. Cedar Dr. & Linden Blvd.) |
516-829-6464 | www.caferusticarestaurant.com

"Feel-good" Italian-Mediterranean meals can be found at this Great Neck "standby" where the food is "skillfully prepared and plentiful", servers are "prompt and courteous" and the "brick wall adds warmth" to the "cozy" atmosphere; bargain-hunters also tout its "lunch specials" and "extensive early-bird menu" for offering "terrific value."

Cafe Symposio *Italian*

| 18 | 16 | 17 | $35 |

Bellmore | 2700 Sunrise Hwy. (bet. Bedford & Washington Aves.) |
516-785-6097 | www.cafesymposio.com

This "South Shore stalwart" dishes up "ample" portions of "dependable Italian" for Bellmore residents craving a place "quiet enough to have a conversation with your tablemate"; service is "hit-or-miss" and the "converted diner" setting "leaves a bit to be desired", but the "relaxing" live piano music Wednesday–Sunday is a "definite plus."

	FOOD	DECOR	SERVICE	COST

Cafe Testarossa ⓜ *Continental* | 20 | 18 | 20 | $45 |

Syosset | 499 Jericho Tpke. (bet. Jackson Ave. &
Seaford-Oyster Bay Expwy.) | 516-364-8877 |
www.cafetestarossa.com

Continental "comfort" fare is a "real crowd-pleaser" at this "spacious" "Syosset standby" that "keeps getting better with age"; the staff "treats you right" (especially if you're among the "local glitterati"), and it's "fine for the money" with "lots of food" and one of the "best sunset menus in the area."

Caffe Laguna ⓜ *Italian* | 19 | 18 | 18 | $40 |

Long Beach | 960 W. Beech St. (bet. New Hampshire St. & Tennessee Ave.) |
516-432-2717

"Spend time with friends over a casual meal" or have an "intimate dinner" at this Long Beach Italian whose brick-oven dishes satisfy "on a wintry night"; some cite "inconsistent" cooking and tricky summer parking, but the "decent" service and "date"-friendly ambiance generally hold up to the "not moderate, not expensive" tabs.

ⓩ Camille's ⓜ *Continental* | 24 | 22 | 25 | $46 |

Carle Place | 490 Westbury Ave. (bet. Cherry Ln. & Rushmore Ave.) |
516-338-0848 | www.camillesfinecuisine.com

Reviewers recommend this Carle Place "rarity" for "first-class" Continental fare that's strong on German cooking, served in a "wonderful" setting with a "restful" ambiance brightened by fresh flowers; the "warm", "welcoming" service and an "excellent" prix fixe some nights keep it a "special" destination; N.B. closed Monday–Tuesday.

Canterbury Ales
Oyster Bar & Grill *American/Eclectic* | 18 | 17 | 18 | $34 |

Oyster Bay | 46 Audrey Ave. (bet. South & Spring Sts.) | 516-922-3614 |
www.canterburyalesrestaurant.com

More than a "neighborhood tavern", this American-Eclectic "does fish and seafood well" along with providing hearty "high-end pub food" and an "excellent selection of craft beers"; even if the staff "needs to be jolted into action from time to time", few mind since the Old English–style rooms "covered head-to-toe in Teddy Roosevelt and Oyster Bay memorabilia" offer an "interesting" distraction.

Caracalla Ristorante ⓩ *Italian* | 23 | 20 | 24 | $56 |

Syosset | 102 Jericho Tpke. (bet. Michael & Oak Drs.) | 516-496-3838 |
www.caracallaristorante.com

"Authentic Italian" cuisine by an "A+" chef earns raves for this "real treat" in Syosset boasting "unbeatable" service too; though the Roman decor is a bit "old-world" and the menu can be "expensive", frugal guests go for the "great lunch specials."

Carnival ⓞ *Italian* | 20 | 15 | 18 | $32 |

Port Jefferson Station | 4900 Nesconset Hwy. (Terryville Rd.) |
631-473-9772 | www.carnivalrestaurant.net

Diners debate whether this "trustworthy" red-saucer in Port Jefferson Station is a "pizza parlor" with an Italian restaurant in back or a "restaurant that's also a very good pizzeria", but all agree it excels at "*abbondanza*" ("if you finish your main course, you're a *gavone*"); servers can "seem inexperienced at times" and you don't come for the ambiance, but it's a "family-friendly", "inexpensive night out."

Caruso's *Italian* ▽ 22 | 14 | 21 | $33

Rocky Point | 41 Broadway (Rte. 25A) | 631-744-1117 | www.carusosrestaurant.com

"Exceeding expectations from the modest appearance", the "able kitchen" turns out "super pizza" among other "special" Italian fare at this stuccoed "sleeper in Rocky Point"; it's "pleasant and quiet", and the "lovely patio with a fireplace" is a plus.

Casa Luis Ⓜ *Spanish* 23 | 13 | 21 | $37

Smithtown | 1033 Jericho Tpke. (Cornell Dr.) | 631-543-4656

"Sangria is a must" at this moderately priced, "tried-and-true" Spanish in Smithtown that "still maintains its luster" with "terrific" food, "attentive" service and a "hopping" bar; while the "cramped", "dark" dining room "lacks a little" in decor, the "crowds don't seem to mind, since getting a table on a Saturday night is nearly impossible" without reservations.

Casa Rustica *Italian* 25 | 22 | 24 | $53

Smithtown | 175 W. Main St. (bet. Edgewood Ave. & Elliot Pl.) | 631-265-9265 | www.casarustica.net

"Simple, fresh" and "exceptional" Italian dishes presented by an "impeccable" staff make this Smithtown "mainstay" the place to go for a "romantic dinner or special occasion"; admirers overwhelmingly approve of the dining room's "beautiful" recent renovation and appreciate that while "expensive", it "won't leave your wallet totally empty."

Catfish Max *American/Seafood* 23 | 14 | 21 | $42

Seaford | 3681 Naomi St. (Ocean Ave.) | 516-679-2020 | www.catfishmax.com

Habitués are "hooked" on this "hard-to-find" Seaford "secret that's no longer a secret", an "outstanding little joint on the water" whose "amazing" seafood and New American combinations "manage to be creative without being weird"; it's a bit "ramshackle", but with "gracious" service and a "vintage feel", it's "delightful" for "unwinding on a summer night."

🅩 Chachama Grill *American* 28 | 20 | 26 | $49

East Patchogue | Swan Nursery Commons | 655 Montauk Hwy. (S. Country Rd.) | 631-758-7640 | www.chachamagrill.com

"Dinner is nothing short of a magical experience" for ardent fans of the "artistic" New American fare by chef Elmer Rubio that's a "true treat for the palate" at this "surprising" "storefront extraordinaire" in East Patchogue (whose short-lived Commack spin-off has closed); featuring a "wonderful" staff, "reasonably priced wine list" and prix fixe deals, it's one of the "best bets" on the island.

FOOD | DECOR | SERVICE | COST

Chadwicks
at the Station *American/Continental*

- | - | - | E

Rockville Centre | 49 Front St. (bet. Clinton & N. Park Aves.) | 516-766-7800 | www.chadwicksli.com

A two-room interior warmed by chocolate brown wainscoting, peach-colored walls and a fireplace in the lounge offers a relaxing setting for the American-Continental cuisine of this Rockville Centre venue; rich, rarefied dishes such as rack of lamb finished with a Merlot demi glace and St. Peter's fish crusted with lobster are some of the menu highlights.

Chalet Bar & Lounge ◑ *American/Eclectic*

▽ 18 | 19 | 19 | $33

Roslyn | 1 Railroad Ave. (bet. Roslyn Rd. & Warner Ave.) | 516-621-7975 | www.roslynchalet.com

Renovated and reopened in October 2008, this formerly funky, bi-level Roslyn restaurant and lounge has been reborn with a Miami vibe, flaunting white leather chairs, low white tables and a white marble bar, along with a bluestone terrace for summer dining; the American-Eclectic menu (served till 2 AM on the weekends) still offers what some patty partisans call the "best burgers on LI", along with "light bites" for sharing with a group; N.B. the makeover may not be fully reflected by the Decor score.

Chaophaya Ⓜ *Thai*

▽ 21 | 14 | 18 | $30

Kings Park | 25 Main St. (Henry St.) | 631-269-2818

"Ignore the unwelcoming outside" since the "extremely friendly owners aim to please" at this "nice little Thai restaurant" where the food is "spiced just right" and sometimes "superb"; a few customers cite "spotty" service, but overall it "seems to have found a good home in Kings Park" after moving from Lindenhurst.

NEW Charlotte's Bistro *American*

▽ 20 | 19 | 18 | $43

Cold Spring Harbor | 55 Main St. (bet. Shore Rd. & Spring St.) | 631-692-8345

"Fresh and updated" since the space housed Bedlam Street, this Cold Spring Harbor arrival "deserves a try", offering "interesting" New American dishes in "portions that look small but are quite filling"; "friendly" service and details like "horse pictures" and sunflowers on the tables warm up the ambiance, making it the "perfect place on a summer night" when the French doors are open to the sidewalk and you can "follow the meal with a walk to the water."

☒ Cheesecake Factory *American*

20 | 19 | 17 | $30

Westbury | Mall at the Source | 1504 Old Country Rd. (Evelyn Ave.) | 516-222-5500 ◑
Huntington Station | Walt Whitman Mall | 160 Walt Whitman Rd. (Weston St.) | 631-271-8200
Lake Grove | Smith Haven Mall | 610 Smith Haven Mall (bet. Middle Country Rd. & Nesconset Hwy.) | 631-361-6600
www.cheesecakefactory.com

The menu's "mammoth" – and "so are the crowds" – at these "family-pleasing" chain links where the "endless" American options arrive in equally "colossal" portions (ironically, "they give you so much there's no room" for their "heavenly" namesake desserts); despite "ordinary" settings, "spotty" staffing and "lots of commotion", these "well-oiled machines" are so "busy, busy, busy" that they're best accessed "off-hours" to avoid a "long wait."

Chefs of New York *Italian*
▽ | 20 | 11 | 18 | $24

East Northport | 508 Larkfield Rd. (Clay Pitts Rd.) | 631-368-3156

Known for more than just its "delish" thin-crust pies, this neighborhood pizzeria in East Northport plates "affordable" Italian food in "portions so large, you'll have meals for days"; the servers "always have smiles on their faces", and parents appreciate that it's so "casual" you can "take the kids and let them run amok."

Chequit Inn *American/Eclectic*
19 | 20 | 17 | $46

Shelter Island Heights | Chequit Inn | 23 Grand Ave. (Waverly Pl.) | 631-749-0018 | www.shelterislandinns.com

A "lovely" location is the key to this "relaxing" American-Eclectic in Shelter Island Heights, an "old-fashioned place with an outstanding view" from the porch and terrace; many say the "service leaves a lot to be desired" ("if you get the right college student, your meal can be wonderful") and the "expensive chow", while "much improved", can be "uneven", so "basics" are the best bet; N.B. hours vary with the season, so call ahead.

ꞁ**NEW**ꞁ Cherrystones
Clam & Lobster Shack Ⓜ *Seafood*
19 | 12 | 14 | $31

East Hampton | 277 Pantigo Rd. (Cross Hwy.) | 631-324-9020

"When you don't want a fuss", this counter-service "seafood shack", a new East Hampton offshoot of Bostwick's on the Harbor, hits the spot with "great lobster rolls" and other "fresh shellfish" dished on "paper plates" in a "kid-friendly" environment; the "marginal" service and "white-tablecloth prices" put off some, but others call it a "nice casual addition to the Hamptons scene"; N.B. open May–September.

Chez Kama Ⓜ *Continental/Japanese*
- | - | - | E

Great Neck | 77 Middle Neck Rd. (bet. Cedar Dr. & Grace Ave.) | 516-482-8360

An unusual juxtaposition of Continental cuisine, sushi and other Japanese fare (served side by side on the menu, rather than as fusion dishes) defines this Great Neck eatery; while its scope is ambitious, the decor is simple, consisting primarily of a huge poster of Central Park's Great Lawn covering one wall.

Chez Noëlle Ⓜ *French*
24 | 17 | 22 | $54

Port Washington | 34 Willowdale Ave. (S. Bayles Ave.) | 516-883-3191 | www.cheznoellerestaurant.com

"Fine French food from the old school" makes for "marvelous" meals at this Port Washington "favorite that's aged well", assisted by "energetic, amusing" servers who know the "regular clientele"; though

FOOD DECOR SERVICE COST

some assess the "stale" decor "could use some sprucing up", the atmosphere is "conducive to conversation" and prices are "fair", especially if you go for the prix fixe.

Chi ⑤Ⓜ *Chinese/Eclectic* ▽ 25 | 24 | 24 | $53

Westbury | 103 Post Ave. (bet. Lexington & Madison Aves.) | 516-385-3795

"Chic" and "sleek", this Westbury Chinese with a "lounge" ambiance dishes up "delicious" Eclectic fare to go with its "great martinis"; some night owls "wish there were more of a scene", however, while others stay away due to "over-the-top" prices.

Chicken Kebab *Greek/Turkish* 20 | 9 | 17 | $26

Roslyn Heights | 92 Mineola Ave. (Elm St.) | 516-621-6828 | www.chickenkebab.com

"They charcoal-grill it and that makes all the difference" at this Roslyn Heights kebabery delivering "simple", "pleasing" Greek-Turkish specialties in "friendly" fashion; though the decor is decidedly "dowdy", that's "easily overlooked" considering the big "bang for the buck", so "don't look around, just eat."

Cho-Sen Island *Asian Fusion/Kosher* 18 | 15 | 17 | $33

Lawrence | 367 Central Ave. (Frost Ln.) | 516-374-1199 | www.chosengarden.com

Cho-Sen Village *Asian Fusion/Kosher*

Great Neck | 505 Middle Neck Rd. (Baker Hill Rd.) | 516-504-1199 | www.cho-senvillage.com

"Paradise" for kosher customers "craving chicken lo mein", this Asian fusion eatery in Great Neck (with a Lawrence sib) "rivals the rest" when it comes to "spiced-just-right" fare; even if the Chinese dishes and sushi are "not particularly imaginative", the shareable "big portions" and "family atmosphere" appeal; N.B. closed Fridays and opens after sundown Saturdays.

Churrascaria Riodizio *Brazilian* 21 | 17 | 20 | $44

Roslyn Heights | 388 Willis Ave. (Cambridge St.) | 516-621-4646 | www.churrascariariodizio.com

"Bring your inner caveman" to this Roslyn Heights Brazilian "carnivorgy", a Manhattan spin-off that satisfies with "succulent meats" and "sides galore" that "keep on coming", all presented by a "well-choreographed" staff and washed down with caipirinhas ("a couple of those and you'll be doing the samba"); "long waits for a table" are part of the package, but fans assure that once you sit down you'll "feel like you're in Rio."

Churrasqueira Bairrada Ⓜ *Portuguese* 24 | 14 | 21 | $34

Mineola | 144 Jericho Tpke. (Willis Ave.) | 516-739-3856 | www.churrasqueira.com

"Waiters with meat on spits" deliver an "endless", "terrific" "red meat fix" along with "fabulous chicken dinners" and "irresistible" sangria at this "addictive", relatively "inexpensive" Mineola Portuguese; since it draws "monumental crowds", vets advise "get there early to avoid a huge wait."

	FOOD	DECOR	SERVICE	COST

Ciao Baby *Italian*
18 | 17 | 17 | $37

Carle Place | 246 Voice Rd. (Glen Cove Rd.) | 516-248-7600
Massapequa Park | 50-74 Sunrise Hwy. (Block Blvd.) | 516-799-5200
Commack | Mayfair Shopping Ctr. | 204 Jericho Tpke. (Harned Rd.) | 631-543-1400
www.ciaobabyrestaurant.com

"The ersatz goomba style is as thick as Sunday gravy" at this "gimmicky" Italian trio where the "joking" waiters are "over-the-top" and so are the "almost comedic" portions that "give family-style a whole new meaning"; while all the "noise" has "chased away" some conversation lovers, others keep it "mobbed on the weekends", since it's "a fun place to go with a lot of people."

NEW Ciao Bella Ⓜ *Italian*
- | - | - | M

Valley Stream | 149 S. Franklin Ave. (Station Plaza) | 516-568-7411
Tucked away underneath the LIRR tracks and close enough to the station to entice commuters to stop, this Valley Stream Italian has a nondescript brick exterior and limited signage suggesting a speakeasy state-of-mind; indeed, open the door and a convivial atmosphere prevails, encouraged by both the retro decor (black-and-white hexagon-tile floor, tin ceiling and Italian promotional product posters on the wall) and a hearty, reasonably priced menu.

Cielo *Italian*
18 | 16 | 20 | $33

Hauppauge | 321 Nesconset-Port Jefferson Hwy. (bet. Brookside Dr. & Rte. 111) | 631-724-1918 | www.cielocuisine.com

"Generous" plates of "dependable" Italian food are set down by a "personable" staff that "really wants you to be happy" at this Hauppauge go-to for "great deals"; often "full to the brim", the quarters are too "cramped" for some, but fair-weather friends "love the outdoor eating during warmer months."

Cielo Ristorante Italiano Ⓜ *Italian*
19 | 18 | 20 | $46

Rockville Centre | 208 Sunrise Hwy. (bet. N. Park & N. Village Aves.) | 516-678-1996 | www.cieloristorante.com

This Rockville Centre "staple" succeeds with "solid" Northern Italian fare served by a "courteous" staff in a Tuscan-style interior adorned with marble and cherry wood; some feel it's "not fancy" and "overpriced", but others recommend it as a "good place for a date."

Cimino's Italian Seafood Ⓜ *Italian*
∇ 18 | 18 | 19 | $44

Southold | 62375 Main Rd. (Laurel Ave.) | 631-765-5700
Though few surveyors have sampled it, this Southern Italian in Southold, opposite the Port of Egypt marina and under the same ownership as BBQ Bill's, tends to please with "simple but delicious" dishes served in a "classy" roadside building with tile floors, brick walls and an abundance of plants; despite its "potential", however, "disappointed" detractors call it "unpolished" and "overpriced for what you get."

Cinelli's Pizzeria & Restaurant *Italian*
- | - | - | M

Franklin Square | 1195 Hempstead Tpke. (Doris Ave.) | 516-352-1745

(continued)

(continued)

Cinelli's Trattoria & Grill *Italian*

Oceanside | 156 Davison Ave. (Oceanside Rd.) | 516-678-9494
www.cinellis-ny.com

Founded in Franklin Square in 1986 by the Cinelli family, who migrated from a village in Southern Italy after WWII, this moderately priced eatery and its Oceanside offshoot provide traditional Italian entrees and pastas as well as panini and burgers; with an efficient, tech-savvy delivery system, they're especially popular among take-out lovers.

Cipollini *Italian*   20 | 20 | 19 | $49

Manhasset | The Americana | 2110C Northern Blvd. (Searingtown Rd.) | 516-627-7172 | www.cipollinirestaurant.com

"Who knew there was a scene like this on Long Island?" ask "glamour"-struck guests of this "sophisticated, lively" Italian in The Americana showcasing "people-watching at its best" among its parade of post-Prada "Gold Coast women" (i.e. "ladies gone wild"); fortunately, the food is "gorgeous" too ("especially the thin-crust pizzas"), and though the "service can be iffy" and the noise reaches "assault" levels, both the "entertaining" bar and "European-feeling" patio are still "the place to be", since "no one eating here has any clue there's a financial crisis."

NEW Circa Ristorante Enoteca *Italian*   - | - | - | M

Mineola | CVS Shopping Ctr. | 348 E. Jericho Tpke. (Jay Ct.) | 516-280-2234 | www.circali.com

A sharp newcomer with a Sbarro as an owner (sibling to Burton & Doyle, Rothmann's), this enoteca brings a new era of Italian dining to Mineola; embellished with a gold-toned granite bar, a glass-enclosed wine cellar and a two-sided fireplace, the room invites feasting on signatures such as tuna crudo and whole branzino with gremolata, as well as on wine- and wallet-friendly pizzas and pastas.

Cirella's *Continental/Italian*   21 | 16 | 20 | $39

Melville | 14 Broadhollow Rd. (Arlington St.) | 631-385-7380

Cirella's at Saks Fifth Avenue *American/Eclectic*

Huntington Station | Saks Fifth Avenue, Walt Whitman Mall | 230 Walt Whitman Rd. (Weston St.) | 631-350-1229
www.cirellarestaurant.com

"Catch up with all the locals" at this "popular" (if "packed-in") Melville mainstay where "they spoil you" with "homestyle" Continental and Northern Italian dishes served by a "pleasant, eager" crew; those looking for a "change of pace at the mall" stop at the "cute" Saks location for American-Eclectic offerings from panini to sushi.

cittanuova ● *Italian*   18 | 18 | 16 | $43

East Hampton | 29 Newtown Ln. (bet. Main St. & Park Pl.) | 631-324-6300 | www.cittanuova.com

It "feels like Milano" "in the heart of East Hampton" at this "spiffy" Italian serving "standout pizzas", "regional specialties" and gelato matched by "wine by the quartino"; the outdoor "summer scene is a big draw", though some decry the "dicey" service and say it's "too trendy" and "expensive for what is offered"; P.S. no reservations are taken, so "timing is everything" to avoid a wait.

City Café *Italian*

17	17	18	$41

Garden City | 987 Stewart Ave. (bet. Selfridge Ave. & South St.) | 516-222-1421 | www.citycafe.biz

"Go for the music and dancing" at this "enjoyable" Garden City Italian where the "older set" is "hot to trot" to live bands; considering the "mediocre" fare, many feel it's "better for cocktails" than for food, but at least prices are "fairly reasonable."

City Cellar Wine Bar & Grill *American*

20	23	20	$43

Westbury | 1080 Corporate Dr. (bet. Ellison Ave. & Zeckendorf Blvd.) | 516-693-5400 | www.bigtimerestaurants.com

A "stunning wine cellar wall" calls attention to this "impressive" vino selection at this "sleek", "Manhattan-like" Westbury chain link where the New American plates are generally "creative and flavorful" if at times "uneven" and "costly"; some say the "attentive" staff could still use some seasoning too, but overall it works for "dates" or a "girls' night out."

Clam Bar at Napeague ⊅ *Seafood*

19	12	15	$27

Amagansett | 2025 Montauk Hwy. (on Napeague Stretch) | 631-267-6348

"Nothing says vacation like wonderful seafood on a paper plate", so "belly up to the bar" at this "classic" "shack" on the Napeague Stretch to savor an "amazing" (if "pricey") lobster roll and other delicacies just "off the boats that day"; the outdoor setting, "basically a collection of plastic tables adjoining a parking lot on Route 27", combines a "roadside" vibe with the "roar of the ocean in the distance" – just watch out "at dusk" when "the mosquitoes are as hungry as the patrons."

Claudio's *American/Continental*

15	17	17	$40

Greenport | 111 Main St. (bet: Front St. & Greenport Harbor) | 631-477-0627 | www.claudios.com

"Million-dollar views" mean the "crowds are automatic" at this waterside "Greenport tradition" (dating back to 1870) that's a "trip back in time" with its "nautical theme" and "historical photos"; true, the "high-priced" "fried-to-a-frizzle" seafood and other American-Continental eats "don't match the quality of the harbor setting", but "stick to the uncomplicated" and "go for the scene, not the cuisine."

Cliff's Elbow Room *Steak*

21	10	18	$38

Jamesport | 1549 Main Rd. (S. Jamesport Ave.) | 631-722-3292 | www.elbowroomli.com

Cliff's Elbow Too Ⓜ *Steak*

Laurel | 1085 Franklinville Rd. (off Main Rd./Rte. 25) | 631-298-3262 | www.elbowroomli.com

Cliff's Rendezvous *Steak*

Riverhead | 313 E. Main St. (Maple Ave.) | 631-727-6880

The "famous marinated steaks" "cannot be matched" at these family-owned chophouses where regulars "hobnob at the bar" and the staff "makes you feel like a local"; though the decor is knocked as "caught in a time warp" and space is so "tight" you might find your neighbor's elbow in your rib, these "blasts from the past" are some of the last places on the North Fork "where you don't have to pay a crazy price for a small portion of fancy food."

Clubhouse, The *Steak*
22 | 17 | 22 | $54

Huntington | 320 W. Jericho Tpke. (W. Hills Rd.) | 631-423-1155 | www.clubhousesteaks.com

It "looks like a joint from the outside", but this "small" "hidden treasure of Huntington" "surprises" with its "solid steaks", "rustic", "romantic" atmosphere and "personal service"; while it's not cheap, beef eaters appreciate that it "doesn't require taking out a second mortgage" to dine here.

Coach Grill & Tavern *American*
22 | 12 | 21 | $43

Oyster Bay | 22 Pine Hollow Rd. (bet. High St. & Lexington Ave.) | 516-624-0900 | www.coachgrillandtavern.com

A "longtime local standby" in Oyster Bay, this "comfortable" pub "you can bring your family to" serves up "varied", "generous" plates of often "wowing" New American dishes; overseen by an owner who "knows everyone", the service is "terrific", so "ignore the dated decor" and settle in for a "casual evening at the right price"; N.B. reservations accepted for five or more.

Coast Grill *American/Seafood*
18 | 14 | 16 | $52

Southampton | 1109 Noyac Rd. (Turtle Pond Rd.) | 631-283-2277

Fans affirm it's "always a pleasure" to pop into this "reliable old-timer" on Peconic Bay in Southampton, delivering "simply prepared" New American seafood and an "occasionally stellar bar scene"; though the "uninteresting" decor could use "an uplift", the "nice view" at sunset keeps locals and vacationers coming "off the beaten path" for "summertime marina dining"; N.B. closed Monday-Thursday in the off-season.

Colbeh *Persian*
21 | 16 | 19 | $43

Great Neck | Andrew Hotel | 75 N. Station Plaza (Barstow Rd.) | 516-466-8181
Roslyn Estates | 1 The Intervale (Warner Ave.) | 516-621-2200
www.colbeh.com

"Authentic, tasty and kosher make a great triple play" pronounce partisans about these "Persian phenomenons" (with sibs in Manhattan and Queens), where the food is "plentiful" and the "caring staff" provides appetizing "amenities"; despite the somewhat "dull" decor, the Great Neck location is a "quiet oasis" at lunch, and the more "elegant" Roslyn Estates branch delivers as a "date place"; N.B. closes one hour before sundown Fridays and opens one hour after sundown Saturdays.

Collins & Main 🗷 Ⓜ *American/Eclectic*
24 | 23 | 23 | $51

Sayville | 100 S. Main St. (Collins Ave.) | 631-563-0805 | www.collinsandmain.com

It's "exceedingly relaxing" to dine at this "upscale" New American-Eclectic "gem" "tucked away in Sayville", where the "thoughtfully prepared" food, "exceptional" service and "attractive" setting (with "tables far enough apart so that you can have a conversation") add up to a "wonderful" experience; on Saturday nights, live piano makes it an extra "nice way to start the evening."

Cooke's In, The Ⓜ *Caribbean/Southern*   23 | 11 | 21 | $30

Huntington | 767 New York Ave. (Holdsworth Dr.) | 631-424-2181
"Best ever" fried chicken is the "standout dish" and "those sides can't be beat" at this Caribbean-Southern "find" in a converted Huntington diner, where "charming" owner Juanita Cooke makes it a "party", "personally greeting" guests and "sometimes singing" along with the live piano music on weekends; as it's a "special place" all around, even critics of the "1950s-style suburban kitchen" decor let it slide, since "you don't eat the walls."

Ⓩ Coolfish *Seafood*   24 | 21 | 22 | $51

Syosset | North Shore Atrium | 6800 Jericho Tpke. (Michael Dr.) | 516-921-3250 | www.tomschaudel.com
"Once you get past" its office building setting, a "sophisticated experience" awaits at this "high-end" Syosset seafooder by chef-owner Tom Schaudel, executing "absolutely superb" "original" preparations of the daily catch; with an "attractive", "comfortable" interior and "just right" service, it's a "cool place that remains remarkably hot"; N.B. an "excellent" prix fixe is served before 6:30 PM nightly (except Saturday).

Cooperage Inn *American/Continental*   20 | 21 | 20 | $42

Baiting Hollow | 2218 Sound Ave. (bet. Edwards & National Blvds.) | 631-727-8994 | www.cooperageinn.com
Vineyard travelers on the North Fork stop for "hearty" American-Continental "home cooking with a touch of class" at this "beautiful" Baiting Hollow "favorite" with a "farmhouse atmosphere"; service is "a little slow" at times and some find the food "overly complicated" (and the setting "too country clutter"), but few can quibble with the "amazing" all-you-can-eat Sunday brunch – one of the "best bargains on Long Island."

Ⓩ Country House, The *American*   22 | 26 | 23 | $58

Stony Brook | 1175 Rte. 25A (Main St.) | 631-751-3332 | www.countryhouserestaurant.com
"Right out of a storybook", this "tea-roomy" New American in a "historic" Stony Brook home ("George Washington probably slept here") is the "place to be pampered" with "exceptional", "expensive" meals; they "go all out" with seasonal decorating ("don't miss it at Christmastime"), so even if it's too "froufrou" for some, most rave it's a "real treat."

NEW Cove Star *Asian Fusion/Japanese*   - | - | - | M

Glen Cove | 18 Cottage Row (Brewster St.) | 516-676-8578 | www.covestarbistro.com
Renovated under new ownership, this distinctive Glen Cove house decked out with wooden floors, a stone wall and fireplace has an

earthy feel that suits its Japanese and Asian fusion menu; a variety of lunch specials packs extra value for daytime diners, while martinis and tiki drinks entice at night.

Cozymel's Mexican Grill *Mexican*

| 16 | 16 | 16 | $27 |

Westbury | 1177 Corporate Dr. (Merchants Concourse) | 516-222-7010 | www.cozymels.com

"Frozen margaritas abound" at this Westbury chain link where the "tableside guacamole" is a "highlight" on the menu of "basic Americanized Mexican fare"; despite complaints that it's a "commercialized" "cliché", it's "family-friendly" with "distractions for the children" and "not bad for a low-cost dinner."

Crabtree's *Continental/Mediterranean*

| 20 | 18 | 21 | $40 |

Floral Park | 226 Jericho Tpke. (bet. Emerson & Hinsdale Aves.) | 516-326-7769 | www.crabtreesrestaurant.com

"*Little Rascals* images" set an old-time tone at this "quirky" Floral Park Continental-Med with "lovely backyard dining" on a leafy patio; "reliable" food and "attentive" service keep it a "midweek" "favorite", though some feel it's only "fair" and the menu "never seems to change."

NEW Crew Kitchen & Bar Ⓜ *American*

| 25 | 21 | 23 | E |

(fka Aix en-Provence)

Huntington | 134 New York Ave. (Ketewomoke Dr.) | 631-549-3338 | www.crewli.com

Though renamed, reconceived and redecorated post-Survey, this former Huntington home of Aix en-Provence (and sister to Barney's) is still run by the same owners and chef, now focusing on the "New American flair" that has long distinguished the "fantastic" food, with the new option of a less expensive bar menu; while the "charming" interior has fresh new accents with a rowing-team motif, guests can expect the "seamless" service to remain the same.

Crossroads Cafe *American*

| 20 | 13 | 19 | $40 |

East Northport | 26 Laurel Rd. (bet. Bellerose Ave. & LIRR) | 631-754-2000 | www.thecrossroadscafe.com

"Restaurant week lives here all year" with "all kinds of special nights" that'll "make your wallet happy" proclaim patrons of this East Northport "sleeper" turning out "satisfying" New American fare with "enough variety to please everyone"; still, critics compare the dining room to a "banquet hall that hasn't been set up yet", urging "renovate please."

Cull House *Seafood*

| 19 | 11 | 17 | $32 |

Sayville | 75 Terry St. (River Rd.) | 631-563-1546 | www.cullhouse.com

"Fresh lobster" and other "seaside eats" are "served as they should be – on paper plates with plenty of butter and napkins" at this "extremely casual" fish house "by the ferries" in Sayville; it looks a bit "rough" and "run-down" and the cost is "a little high" considering the modest amenities, but "nightly drink and dinner specials" add to the "fun, friendly" vibe.

	FOOD	DECOR	SERVICE	COST

Curry Club *Indian*

| 22 | 17 | 20 | $30 |

East Setauket | 10 Woods Corner Rd. (Nicolls Rd.) | 631-751-4845
Lake Grove | 2811 Middle Country Rd. (Stony Brook Rd.) |
631-580-1777
www.curryclubli.com

Offering "some of the best Indian in Suffolk County", this eatery has expanded from East Setauket to a second branch in Lake Grove, with both dialing the heat up "from mild to as much as you can stand" when requested; both the "bargain" lunch buffet and "welcoming" service are assets, plus the "pleasant" deity-decorated dining room at the original gets a boost from the adjoining lounge hosting DJ and karaoke nights.

Cyril's Fish House ⊗ *Seafood*

| 18 | 12 | 15 | $35 |

Amagansett | 2167 Montauk Hwy. (on Napeague Stretch) |
631-267-7993 | www.cyrilsfishhouse.com

"It isn't summer without a trip" to this seasonal Amagansett "beach bar without the beach" say road-tripping reviewers, who tend to agree that the "better-than-expected" seafood is nevertheless out-shined by the "wild", rum-drenched scene where "bikers, bankers, young and old" "spread out over Montauk Highway"; "of course, there's Cyril" himself sitting at his perch at the bar, who many say "makes the place"; N.B. cash only.

Danú Ⓜ *Asian Fusion*

| ▽ 19 | 22 | 20 | $48 |

Huntington | 368 New York Ave. (bet. Carver & Elm Sts.) |
631-549-5757

"South Beach ambiance" infuses this upscale Huntington arrival that's decked out in "dramatic" white-toned decor and pulses on the weekends with live salsa music; though some applaud the "different" Asian fusion menu with "adventurous" Latin touches, others feel the "strange combos of food don't work" and prefer it for the "fun bar scene."

Ⓩ Dario's Ⓢ *Italian*

| 27 | 18 | 26 | $57 |

Rockville Centre | 13 N. Village Ave. (bet. Merrick Rd. & Sunrise Hwy.) |
516-255-0535

"You can eat simply or elaborately – just let them feed you" at this Rockville Centre "winner" known for Northern Italian cuisine "at its finest" ("the best veal chop on Long Island") and a "cordial" staff that "sets the standard for service"; even though the decor and am-biance are "not comparable" to the food, most agree it's "pricey but worth it" for a "fabulous" meal.

Daruma of Tokyo *Japanese*

| 21 | 13 | 16 | $36 |

Great Neck | 95 Middle Neck Rd. (Maple Dr.) | 516-466-4180

"Practically a Great Neck landmark", this "old mainstay" still satis-fies customers with "solid sushi" and "pleasing" Japanese cooked dishes that are on the "traditional" side; yes, "service can be slow during peak hours", but it's generally "attentive and friendly", and the staff's uniforms with Mets logos "add a quirky note" to the otherwise "drab" digs.

	FOOD	DECOR	SERVICE	COST

Z Da Ugo Z *Italian* — 26 | 18 | 24 | $54

Rockville Centre | 509 Merrick Rd. (Long Beach Rd.) | 516-764-1900
The "specials are always prepared to perfection" at this "rare find" in Rockville Centre serving "top-notch" Northern Italian fare to a crowd "full of regulars" that packs the "tight" room; though the "dedicated staff" tends to dote on familiar faces, most newcomers still say it lives up to the cost, so be sure to "make reservations early."

Z Dave's Grill *Continental/Seafood* — 26 | 17 | 21 | $59

Montauk | 468 W. Lake Dr. (bet. Flamingo Ave. & Soundview Dr.) | 631-668-9190 | www.davesgrill.com
Fans effuse "the fish practically flop onto your plate straight off the dock out back" at this Montauk mainstay that cooks up a "memorable", "high-end" Continental menu of "outstanding" seafood; the dining room may be "cramped" and "stuck in the '80s" and there's a chorus of complaints about the "frustrating" same-day reservation policy (it's "tough unless you get there or phone right at opening"), but most conclude it's "always worth it."

Declan Quinn's *American* — ∇ 19 | 14 | 18 | $26

Bay Shore | 227 Fourth Ave. (bet. Cherry & E. Garfield Sts.) | 631-206-2006 | www.declanquinns.net
"When you're in the mood for a pub menu", this "local hangout" in Bay Shore hits the spot with "comforting" and at times "adventurous" American eats that are "full of flavor"; it boasts a "lively atmosphere" and a beach volleyball court out back for warmer months, plus Thursday is 'steak and brew night' and "wow, is it good."

Dee Angelo's Pleasant Ave. Café *Italian* — ∇ 17 | 16 | 18 | $41

Westhampton Beach | 149 Main St. (Library Ave.) | 631-288-2009
"Pleasant outdoor seating for people-watching" attracts patrons to this "tiny", "friendly" Westhampton Beach Italian serving "steady, though predictable" fare; while even fans find the "portions do not match the prices" and lament a "limited" dinner menu, most agree it's "very nice for lunch."

**Delano Mansion
at the Woodlands** Z M *American* — - | - | - | E

Woodbury | 1 Southwoods Rd. (bet. Convent Rd. & Jericho Tpke.) | 516-921-5707 | www.thedelanomansion.com
A prominent fixture on the Town of Oyster Bay Golf Course in Woodbury, this grand 1918 mansion designed by Delano & Aldrich is now the destination for a New American menu that's high-end but highly accessible with a nightly prix fixe; decorated in beiges and browns, the second-floor dining room offers a subdued setting, while a large terrace expands the space in the summer.

Deli King *Deli* — 18 | 9 | 14 | $23

New Hyde Park | Lake Success Shopping Ctr. | 1570 Union Tpke. (New Hyde Park Rd.) | 516-437-8420
This "true staple" of the Lake Success Shopping Center could easily reside "on the Lower East Side", offering "reliable", "old-fashioned"

kosher deli eats that are "just right for a family meal"; despite the "plain setting" and "inconsistent" service, surveyors say it works when you need a "pastrami fix."

Z Della Femina *American* | 24 | 22 | 22 | $67 |

East Hampton | 99 N. Main St. (Cedar St.) | 631-329-6666 | www.dellafemina.com

Still the "place to be seen on a Saturday night" in East Hampton, this "hot ticket" rewards its "tony" clientele with "spectacular" New American fare "emphasizing fresh, local seasonal ingredients that never fail to please"; service is "smooth" (if a touch "smug"), and the "light, airy setting" designed with "well-spaced tables" and celebrity caricatures creates an "elegant" atmosphere that's especially inviting on "quieter" (and more affordable) winter nights.

Desmond's *American* | ∇ 22 | 22 | 21 | $42 |

Wading River | Inn at East Wind | 5720 Rte. 25A (¼ mi. south of Sound Ave.) | 631-846-2335 | www.eastwindlongisland.com

"If you're going east and don't want to break the bank in the Hamptons", this Wading River stop in the Inn at East Wind fits the bill with "excellent specials" on the New American menu served in "dark", mahogany-accented environs; though some feel it's "just ok", many recommend it for a "pleasant evening" or "lavish" Sunday brunch.

DiMaggio's Trattoria *Italian* | 18 | 14 | 18 | $30 |

Port Washington | 706 Port Washington Blvd. (Davis Ave.) | 516-944-6363 | www.dimaggios.net

"Classic" pasta dishes and "NY-style pizza" are "quick and consistent" at this veteran Italian in Port Washington that's "more comfortable" following a recent makeover; the staff is "helpful" and it's "inexpensive" too, making for a "child-friendly" meal.

NEW Dish ⊠ Ⓜ *American* | - | - | - | M |

Water Mill | Water Mill Shoppes | 760 Montauk Hwy., Ste. 5C (bet. Nowedonah Ave. & Station Rd.) | 631-726-0246

Adventurous and bold, this tiny discovery in the Water Mill Shoppes has a maximum capacity of about 16 people, but chef-owners Merrill Indoe and Peter Robertson, both CIA graduates, put together a different market-driven New American menu every weekend, making these seats highly coveted; copper pots on the walls and blue-and-white checked napkins lend a splash of color, while the BYO policy provides extra stimulus; N.B. open Friday–Saturday nights only (at press time), serving a $35 prix fixe.

Diwan *Indian* | - | - | - | M |

Hicksville | Patel Plaza | 415 S. Broadway (Ludy St.) | 516-513-1057

NEW Port Washington | 37 Shore Rd. (Mill Pond Rd.) | 516-439-4200

Recently reopened in its old Port Washington digs, with a new Hicksville location too, this brand-name Indian pair (with a branch in Jackson Heights) has a popular lunch buffet and an extensive menu of curries and tandoor oven specialties at night; the Shore

Road location features wraparound windows (but a minimal view of the nearby marina), while the simple Hicksville setting is bright and airy, adorned with paintings of Indian royalty.

Diya *Indian*

| - | - | - | M |

Valley Stream | 43 Rockaway Ave. (E. Lincoln Ave.) | 516-872-2223 | www.diyalounge.com

Serving a buffet lunch and an à la carte dinner, this Indian fusion newcomer to the Valley Stream dining scene offers a large, gold-accented space with a separate bar/lounge and dining room; the menu includes a variety of curries, vegetarian dishes and numerous tandoori specialties, with lunch going for under $10 and a happy hour from 4–7 PM.

Dockers Waterside Restaurant & Marina *Seafood/Steak*

| 19 | 22 | 17 | $49 |

East Quogue | 94 Dune Rd. (Dolphin Ln.) | 631-653-0653 | www.dockerswaterside.com

"What a treasure!" trumpet sunset-seekers who say the "unbelievable" view "dwarfs all other considerations" but the seafood and steak are "better than you'd expect" at this seasonal baysider in East Quogue; raucous happy hours on the deck with live bands score it "extra" points, but unimpressed eaters cite "Hamptonian" service and wonder "how much is a sunset worth?"

Dockside Bar & Grill *Seafood*

| 19 | 15 | 18 | $40 |

Sag Harbor | American Legion Hall | 26 Bay St. (Ryson St.) | 631-725-7100

It "doesn't look like much from the outside", as it's set in an American Legion Hall, but this "lucky find" in Sag Harbor "over-performs" when it comes to the "reasonably priced" seafood and opens up to a "magical" patio "facing the yachts"; though service is "friendly" if not always "crisp", some reviewers relish the "relaxed, unpretentious" vibe; N.B. off-season hours vary, so call ahead.

Dodici *Italian*

| 23 | 21 | 21 | $43 |

Rockville Centre | 12 N. Park Ave. (bet. Merrick Rd. & Sunrise Hwy.) | 516-764-3000 | www.dodicirestaurant.com

"Light, fresh" and "wonderful" Italian dishes (including "pizzas from the wood-burning oven") matched by a wine list "like a book" draw diners to this "upscale" destination "in the heart of Rockville Centre"; while the "pretty" Tuscan-style surroundings "need some sound absorption", most say the "friendly" yet "unobtrusive" staff helps make the meal "enjoyable."

Downtown *American*

| - | - | - | E |

Mineola | 197 Mineola Blvd. (Grant Ave.) | 516-741-4597 | www.downtownbarandgrill.com

In a smart setting complete with a granite bar, tile floor and oak wainscoting, this urbane Mineola magnet delivers upscale New American fare, from burgers to shrimp skewers to double-cut pork chops; an extensive martini list and small-plates bar menu add to its after-work appeal.

	FOOD	DECOR	SERVICE	COST

Driver's Seat *American* · 15 · 14 · 16 · $32

Southampton | 62 Jobs Ln. (S. Main St.) | 631-283-6606

"Don't expect gourmet food", but this Southampton "standby" (since the '60s) works for "basic" American fare, especially the "good burgers", and has "decent prices for the area"; most prefer the outdoor tables to the "quaint" pub interior with dark-wood booths and a fireplace, though the service "can be surly" either way.

Duke Falcon's Global Grill *American/Eclectic* · 23 · 17 · 21 · $39

Long Beach | 36 W. Park Ave. (bet. Edwards & National Blvds.) | 516-897-7000

"Exotic" Eclectic–New American cuisine and themed decor made up of "mementos of 'Duke's' worldwide travels" encourage "multiple visits" to this "steady", moderately priced performer in Long Beach; the "wide variety" makes it "great for picky eaters", and the staff is "informative", so most savor the sensation of "dining on safari", even if "some of the combinations are rather strange."

Duryea's Lobster Deck ⊄ *Seafood* · 21 · 13 · 10 · $36

Montauk | 65 Tuthill Rd. (bet. Flamingo Ave. & Fleming Rd.) | 631-668-2410 | www.duryealobsters.com

"Dine with the seagulls" at this "no-frills" seasonal seafooder in Montauk with a "spectacular waterside" locale, where you "order at a window" and find a spot in the sun to soak in the "essence of summer"; opinions are split on whether the prices are fair, but the "lobster is just out of the water" and that's the point for most; N.B. the popular BYO policy is likely to return this season.

Dynasty of Port Washington *Chinese* · 18 · 16 · 20 · $29

Port Washington | 405 Main St. (2nd Ave.) | 516-883-4100

"In a sea of Chinese restaurants", the "cut-above" Cantonese cuisine and personal service earn a following for this "fairly priced" Port Washington staple where "everyone is doted on like a family friend"; despite complaints that the cooking is "too American", most find it "pleasant" in a "pretty" (if not quite up-to-date) setting.

East by Northeast *American/Pan-Asian* · 21 · 23 · 19 · $55

Montauk | Stone Lion Inn | 51 S. Edgemere St. (bet. Elwell St. & S. Erie Ave.) | 631-668-2872 | www.harvest2000.com

Montaukers meet for "magnificent" dining at this Harvest spin-off complete with "glorious sunsets" over Fort Pond, "elegant" decor with couch seating and "inventive" New American–Pan Asian fare (the "rich" duck tacos are particularly "memorable"); critics cite "hefty" tabs and service that's "not top-rate", but allies attest it's "busy and rightfully so"; N.B. closed from January to mid-February.

Z East Hampton Point *American* · 20 · 26 · 18 · $58

East Hampton | 295 Three Mile Harbor Rd. (4 mi. north of Hook Windmill) | 631-329-2800 | www.easthamptonpoint.com

The "stunning sunsets" are a "knockout" at this "handsome", "romantic" seasonal East Hamptoner overlooking Three Mile Harbor,

FOOD | DECOR | SERVICE | COST

even if the "good" New American fare and "inconsistent" service don't quite measure up to the surroundings; it's a definite "splurge site", but tipsters point out the "limited menu on the outside deck is a better buy."

E. B. Elliot's *American*

`18` `18` `18` `$41`

Freeport | 23 Woodcleft Ave. (Front St.) | 516-378-8776 | www.ebelliots.com

Situated on Freeport's Nautical Mile, this "upbeat" New American eatery dishes up "creative seafood" as well as "beautiful" waterfront views and a "fun" bar downstairs, with live music on the weekends; critics complain that the kitchen is "overly ambitious" at times, the prices are "too expensive" and the scene too "young" if you're "over 35."

Eddie's Pizza ●✍ *Pizza*

`21` `7` `16` `$20`

New Hyde Park | 2048 Hillside Ave. (Denton Ave.) | 516-354-9780

Pizza lovers make a "pilgrimage" to this 1940s-era parlor in New Hyde Park for the "holy grail" – "super thin-crust bar pies!" that are hailed as some of the "best on the island" (even the "diet" pizzas "can't be beat"); sure, it's a "dump" with "gruff service from an array of interesting dames", but "what's not to like from this one-of-a-kind joint?"

Edgewater ✖Ⓜ *Italian*

`-` `-` `-` `E`

Hampton Bays | 295 E. Montauk Hwy. (bet. Ocean View & S. Valley Rds.) | 631-723-2323 | www.edgewaterrestaurant.com

Equipped with huge windows and a spacious deck, this seasonal Hampton Bays Italian presents a striking view of Shinnecock Bay, complemented by summery furnishings of blond and wicker furniture; its menu of pizzas and high-end entrees is matched by a wine list that includes a small selection of local vintages.

18 Bay Ⓜ *Italian*

`24` `18` `22` `$62`

Bayville | 18A Bayville Ave. (bet. Bayville Park Blvd. & Bayville Rd.) | 516-628-0124

"Vibrant", "inventive" Italian cuisine that incorporates "locally produced" ingredients distinguishes this "tiny gem by the sea" staffed by "personable", "informative" servers; still, despite its "cottagelike" setting, critics call it "small yet not so intimate", and feel its "big tabs" "push the high-end of pricing" for Bayville; N.B. closed Monday–Tuesday.

Elaine's Asian Bistro & Grill *Pan-Asian*

`23` `23` `21` `$39`

Great Neck | 8 Bond St. (bet. Grace Ave. & N. Station Plaza) | 516-829-8883 | www.elainesbistro.com

"Urban chic" remakes a "suburban basement" in Great Neck with the arrival of this "visually and gastronomically delicious" Pan-Asian providing "delicacies" from a "diverse", "affordable" menu of Chinese, Japanese and Thai dishes; "amazing" service is another plus, so all in all, "if you want an NYC feel" combined with "innovative" food, this is "your place."

	FOOD	DECOR	SERVICE	COST

Elbow East Steak

21 | 12 | 19 | $44

Southold | 50 N. Sea Dr. (Kenney's Rd.) | 631-765-1203

"Remarkable" marinated steaks are what this Southold chop-house is "all about" for the "local crowd" that craves its "consistently good", "priced-right" cuts of beef; formerly affiliated with the Cliff's chainlet, the locale has a "no-thrills atmosphere" courtesy of "ancient" decor, but the new outdoor deck for cocktails is certainly a plus.

El Parral Italian/Spanish

21 | 9 | 18 | $36

Syosset | 8 Berry Hill Rd. (Muttontown Eastwoods Rd.) | 516-921-2844 | www.elparral.com

"Where else can you get chicken *à la francese* while your dinner companion orders *arroz con pollo*?" ask admirers of this Spanish-Italian "neighborhood fixture" in Syosset that after more than 30 years still serves the "best paella this side of Madrid"; the "early ugly" decor is "stuck in 1981" ("they should update at least to 1994"), but with "family-style" service and "relatively cheap" tabs, it's always "packed on the weekends."

Emerson's Ⓜ American/French

23 | 16 | 20 | $42

Babylon | 69 Deer Park Ave. (bet. Grove Pl. & Main St.) | 631-669-2333 | www.emersonsrestaurant.com

Chef/co-owner Pierre Rougey (former exec chef at Raoul's in Manhattan) is a "godsend" gush guests who thrill to the "fantastic" New American–French fare prepared with "poise and verve" (and often with organic, "gluten-free" ingredients) at this "small", "quaint" Babylon bistro; some sniff the "pleasant" atmosphere is a bit "blah" and that the service can be "erratic", but most maintain it's a "must-try."

Emilio's Italian

23 | 15 | 18 | $27

Commack | Harrow's Shopping Ctr. | 2201 Jericho Tpke. (Ruth Blvd.) | 631-462-6267 | www.emiliosmenu.com

"Always jam-packed", this "reasonable" Commack Italian serves up "can't-be-beat" pizzas from the take-out counter along with "excellent" dishes that "go way beyond" what you'd expect in the back dining room; the "hit-or-miss" service gets lower marks, though, since some reviewers report "they know that the food is good and treat you like they don't care if you come back."

Epicurean Room Ⓜ Eclectic

– | – | – | M

Central Islip | Culinary Arts Ctr., NYIT | 300 Carleton Ave (bet. Manhattan Blvd. & Suffolk Ave.) | 631-348-3293 | www.nyit.edu/culinary

Inside the Culinary Arts Center at NY Institute of Technology in Central Islip, this Eclectic buffet restaurant is a teaching tool for aspiring chefs; the lunch (served Wednesday–Friday), dinner (Friday–Saturday) and Sunday brunch, all for less than $30, offer a potpourri of market-driven dishes, and wines are available by the glass and bottle; though the decor is rather institutional, an accommodating staff softens the edges.

	FOOD	DECOR	SERVICE	COST

Epiphany ☒ *Italian* — 22 | 19 | 23 | $42

Glen Cove | 284 Glen St. (bet. Elm & Hendrick Aves.) | 516-759-1913 | www.epiphanyrestaurant.com

Admirers affirm the "innovative" Italian dishes prepared with "quality" ingredients "will hook you", and so will the "short" but "wonderful" wine list, at this Glen Cove "favorite" where a "first-rate" staff paces a "pleasant evening"; "casual, comfortable" and "reasonable", it's decorated with shadow boxes and other artwork, and often plays host to "large parties."

Ernesto's East ☒ *Italian* — 20 | 12 | 23 | $45

Glen Head | 10 Railroad Ave. (bet. Glen Head Rd. & School St.) | 516-671-7828

"Gracious" greetings from the owners "make it worth coming back again and again" for guests at this "upscale" "mom-and-pop" Italian mainstay serving "fine food" by the railroad station in Glen Head; though many customers conclude the "service is better" than the cooking, the "small", "cozy" space still "fills up quickly", so reservations are recommended.

Estia's Little Kitchen *American* — 21 | 12 | 19 | $40

Sag Harbor | 1615 Bridgehampton-Sag Harbor Tpke. (bet. Carroll St. & Clay Pit Rd.) | 631-725-1045 | www.eatshampton.com

Loyalists "love" this "little roadside joint" on the Bridge-Sag Turnpike where chef-owner Colin Ambrose prepares "honest" American meals with "fixings from his own garden" in an "unassuming" (if sometimes "chaotic") atmosphere; it's a "value for lunch and breakfast", but if you come on the weekends, "be prepared to wait (and wait) if you're not an early-riser"; N.B. closes at 3 PM Monday-Thursday and all day Tuesday.

Ethos *Greek* — 21 | 20 | 18 | $45

Great Neck | 25 Middle Neck Rd. (bet. Grace Ave. & N. Station Plaza) | 516-305-4958 | www.ethosrestaurants.com

This "high-end" Greek addition to Great Neck (with two New York City siblings) boasts "fresh-from-the-dock grilled fish and classic sides" served in an "inviting", earth-toned dining room; though the service can be "immature", it's generally "friendly", so converts coo "let your taste buds go wild" and enjoy "Manhattan-level" cuisine in the 'burbs.

Fairway Restaurant *American* — 18 | 8 | 14 | $24

Sagaponack | Poxabogue Golf Course | 3556 Montauk Hwy. (Wainscott Harbor Rd.) | 631-537-7195

"A terrific breakfast and lunch dive" located off the front nine of the Poxabogue Golf Course in Sagaponack, this decidedly "un-trendy" daytime American dishes up "diner-quality", "tasty vittles" to an "interesting mix of locals and weekenders"; it's "family-friendly, which can get noisy at times", but most reviewers recommend it when you want a meal in the Hamptons "without having to make an ATM withdrawal."

	FOOD	DECOR	SERVICE	COST

Famous Dave's *BBQ*

	19	15	17	$27

Westbury | 1060 Corporate Dr. (bet. Ellison Ave. & Zeckendorf Blvd.) | 516-832-7300
Smithtown | 716 Smithtown Bypass (Terry Rd.) | 631-360-6490
www.famousdaves.com

"Don't get dressed up" for these "casual" BBQ chain links in Smithtown and Westbury where the "solid", "finger-lickin'" 'cue is dished out in "kitschy", "country-cabin" digs; the "mass-produced" meals may not "win any awards", but these "busy" joints are always a "welcome sight when on the road" – and a strong "value" to boot.

Fanatico *Italian*

	20	16	16	$27

Jericho | Waldbaum's Shopping Ctr. | 336 N. Broadway (bet. Burke & Scott Aves.) | 516-932-5080 | www.fanaticomenu.com

"Terrific" Italian fare does the trick for "quick family meals" "when you're not in the mood to be fancy" at this "crowded", fairly "modern" eatery tucked into a Jericho strip mall; "healthy choices" like whole-wheat pasta are a perk, and prices are "reasonable", though the "wait can be long on weekends" since reservations are only accepted for groups of seven or more.

fatfish Wine Bar & Bistro *Seafood*

	19	20	18	$43

Bay Shore | 28 Cottage Ave. (Clinton Ave.) | 631-666-2899 | www.fatfish.info

"You feel like you won the lottery if you're able to sit on the water" at this "casual", "summery" "hangout" overlooking (and partially floating on) the Great South Bay; most agree "they need to step it up a notch" with the Mediterranean-influenced seafood and "lacking" service, but even critics recommend checking out the "live music" and the "singles scene" on the weekend; N.B. closed Monday–Tuesday in the winter.

Fiddleheads Ⓜ *Seafood*

	23	16	21	$48

Oyster Bay | 62 South St. (bet. Audrey & Hamilton Aves.) | 516-922-2999 | www.fiddleheadsnewyork.com

The chef "whips up some amazing specials" that are "served beautifully" at this "inventive", "expensive" Oyster Bay seafooder that changed hands in 2007; "bland" decor is a downside, but the staff "makes you feel like you're a regular, whether you are or not", and "live music on weekends completes the package."

Fifth Season, The *American*

	24	21	21	$49

Port Jefferson | 34 E. Broadway (bet. Main St. & Mariners Way) | 631-477-8500 | www.thefifth-season.com

"Finally, a restaurant with a view worth visiting in Port Jefferson" proclaim patrons about this "don't-miss" New American that recently relocated from Greenport, bringing an "impressive" "eclectic" menu that "varies with the produce of the season"; set in a "simple, elegant" space with "attentive" (if at times "uneven") service, it's become "the place to be on weekend nights"; N.B. wine is served, but BYO is permitted, and there's no corkage fee for Long Island wines.

	FOOD	DECOR	SERVICE	COST

56th Fighter Group *American* — 15 | 20 | 16 | $34

Farmingdale | Republic Airport, gate 1 (Rte. 110) | 631-694-8280 | www.56thfgrestaurant.com

"Kids", "granddads" and "Grummanites" all "love to watch the planes" and check out the "Air Force memorabilia" at this "nostalgia" trip, located at Farmingdale's Republic Airport; still, while it's "fun for drinks or Sunday brunch" (reservations recommended), many say the "subpar", "slightly overpriced" American eats taste too much "like K-rations" to wing their way back.

NEW Fino Rosso *Italian* — ▽ 18 | 16 | 17 | $55

Glen Cove | 75 Cedar Swamp Rd. (bet. 3rd & 4th Sts.) | 516-759-7088 | www.finorosso.com

Following a "glitzy" redo of the former Veranda space, this Glen Cove restaurant has morphed again under new ownership into a dramatic Northern Italian venue with a "nightclub atmosphere"; customers can dine on pastas, pizzas and a wide array of entrees in the dining room, on the patio or at the bar with flat-screen TVs, though the "jury's still out" on whether it's "on the right track" or "just doesn't mesh."

NEW Fishbar *Seafood* — ▽ 16 | 15 | 15 | $46

Montauk | Gone Fishing Marina | 467 E. Lake Dr. (opp. Montauk Airport) | 631-668-6600 | www.freshlocalfish.com

It's basically a covered deck with tables, but the second-floor "view of the harbor can't be beat" at this new, seasonal Montauker that's a "work in progress" when it comes to the seafood and the service; still, beach bums find it "ideal" for drinks "on a warm summer day."

Fisherman's Catch *Seafood* — 19 | 17 | 19 | $40

Point Lookout | 111 Bayside Dr. (Hewlett Ave.) | 516-670-9717 | www.fishermanscatchrestaurant.com

"Simply prepared" seafood at this "old-fashioned" Point Lookout waterside spot generally fulfills expectations of "what a satisfying fish house on the South Shore of Long Island should be"; even if some cite "ordinary" offerings and a "catering-hall" feel, the locale comes through with a "view to die for" of "sunsets over the bay"; N.B. closed Monday–Tuesday in the winter.

Fishery, The *Seafood* — 19 | 14 | 18 | $35

East Rockaway | 1 Main St. (Atlantic Ave.) | 516-256-7117 | www.thefishery1.com

"It's all about sitting outside on the water" at this East Rockaway seafooder hosting nightly "live bands during the summer" and a "party atmosphere on the deck" that can get "extremely noisy"; though a bit "basic", the eats tend to be "above average", served by a "no-nonsense" staff for "fair" prices.

Foody's *BBQ/Pizza* — ▽ 19 | 11 | 17 | $30

Water Mill | Water Mill Shoppes | 760 Montauk Hwy. (Station Rd.) | 631-726-3663

Advocates advise "anything done in the wood-burning grill is delicious" – particularly the "excellent" BBQ chicken pizza – at this "reliable" eatery by chef/co-owner Bryan Futerman (formerly of Nick & Toni's) in the Water Mill Shoppes; it's "child-friendly", "low-cost" and colorful, so most don't mind the "casual" setting and service.

🆕 Fortune Asian Bistro Asian — | — | — | E

Westbury | 477 Old Country Rd. (bet. Evelyn & Rockaway Aves.) | 516-333-8686

Offering a full Japanese menu alongside numerous Chinese and Thai choices, this high-end Asian newcomer in Westbury, across from The Mall at the Source, is thoughtfully designed with mahogany floors and an entire wall of cubbyholes holding glass canisters filled with colorful fruits and veggies; booth seating and a sushi bar keep it comfortable for both dates and groups.

Fortune Wheel Chinese 23 | 10 | 16 | $26

Levittown | Nassau Mall | 3601 Hempstead Tpke. (Wantaugh Ave.) | 516-579-4700

Sinophiles say "it's worth the wait on weekends" for the "superior", "sparklingly fresh" seafood and "exceptional dim sum" plated up at this Levittown "jewel" in the Nassau Mall; the decor may be "the pits" and the service "brusque" ("it helps to speak Chinese"), but enthusiasts affirm it's just "like eating in Chinatown."

Four Food Studio 🗷 American 20 | 23 | 19 | $53

Melville | 515 Broadhollow Rd. (Baylis Rd.) | 631-577-4444 | www.fourfoodstudio.com

"Chic" and "wildly designed", this "ultramodern" Melvillean feels like being "in a *Jetsons* cartoon" to some, and its "cool" looks translate into a "huge singles scene" at the "screaming bar"; its equally "trendy" New American menu scores for being "innovative" and "seasonal" with "frequent changes" and "nice little touches", though disappointed diners deem it "pricey, pretty and pretentious", with a staff that's a little too "impressed with itself."

Franina Ristorante 🅼 Italian 23 | 21 | 22 | $56

Syosset | 58 W. Jericho Tpke. (bet. Haskett & Oak Drs.) | 516-496-9770 | www.franina.com

Grateful guests are "transported" by the "superb" "Italian with flair" proffered by a "gracious" staff at this "upscale" "surprise" in a Syosset strip mall; despite its "modest" facade, the "beautiful" interior, enhanced by rich fabrics and a "lovely fireplace", creates an atmosphere that's "pure Tuscany."

Frank's Steaks Steak 20 | 16 | 19 | $52

Jericho | Jericho Shopping Plaza | 4 Jericho Tpke. (Aintree Rd.) | 516-338-4595

Rockville Centre | 54 Lincoln Ave. (S. Village Ave.) | 516-536-1500 www.frankssteaks.com

"If steak is your thing, it's reliable" maintain meat hounds about this "middle-of-the-road" duo delivering "landmark dishes" like the Romanian skirt steak for "lower prices than the big names"; the Jericho location has been spiffed up with a mid-Survey renovation, while the Rockville Centre branch remains "quaint" and "family-friendly", with paper and crayons for both kids and adults who "enjoy the opportunity to doodle."

Fratelli Iavarone Cafe *Italian*

| 21 | 15 | 19 | $34 |

New Hyde Park | Lake Success Shopping Ctr. | 1534 Union Tpke. (bet. Lakeville & New Hyde Park Rds.) | 516-488-4500 | www.ibfoods.com/cafe

"The front-of-the-house pizza place and so-so decor mask the culinary treasures" in the dining room of this New Hyde Park Italian turning out "fresh", "well-prepared" grub for a "fair" price; "comforting" and "convenient" all around, it's located in a strip mall alongside a sister gourmet shop with its own "marvelous offerings" to take home.

Frederick's ⊠ *Continental*

| 22 | 15 | 22 | $50 |

Melville | 1117 Walt Whitman Rd. (bet. Arlington St. & Old Country Rd.) | 631-673-8550 | www.fredericksofli.com

"They do a little of everything" at this "consistent", family-owned Melville Continental where the slightly "expensive" "menu hasn't changed much" in 30 years ("why mess with old favorites?") and the room is still "geared for the older crowd" ("updating might be a good idea"); thankfully with all those years under its belt, the servers have "been there forever and know what they're doing."

Fresco Crêperie & Café ⊅ *French*

| 23 | 16 | 22 | $24 |

Long Beach | 150A E. Park Ave. (bet. Long Beach & Riverside Blvds.) | 516-897-8097

"You can't do better" for "cheap eats at the beach" declare diners of the "delightful" French crêpes that are suitable for "lunch, a light dinner or a delicious dessert" at this "casual" Long Beach cafe; though the decor is "very bare", most agree that the "nicest staff" and a "relaxed atmosphere" combine to ensure a leisurely "escape from the daily grind."

Fresno *American*

| 22 | 19 | 22 | $54 |

East Hampton | 8 Fresno Pl. (bet. Gingerbread Ln. & Railroad Ave.) | 631-324-8700 | www.fresnorestaurant.com

"Offbeat" New American dinners "satisfy" at this "winning" yearrounder (in the Beacon and red bar family) that's a little out of the way, near the train station in East Hampton, so it's "not part of the maddening crush"; a "courteous" staff and "cute" dining room with a "pretty" patio complete the "pleasant" ambiance, while the prix fixe helps take the edge off the "pricey" menu; N.B. closed Monday-Tuesday in the off-season.

Frisky Oyster *Eclectic*

| 24 | 19 | 20 | $58 |

Greenport | 27 Front St. (bet. 1st & Main Sts.) | 631-477-4265 | www.thefriskyoyster.com

The "clever" Eclectic cuisine is "fabulous", "fresh and local" at this "hip", "grown-up" "feast" that brings "a little bit of Manhattan to Greenport" (with "TriBeCa" prices to match); staffed by an "affable" crew, the "vibrant", "sophisticated room" is "packed even in midwinter", so reservations are highly recommended; N.B. closed Monday-Tuesday from Labor Day to Memorial Day.

	FOOD	DECOR	SERVICE	COST

Fulton & Prime
Fish and Steakhouse *Seafood/Steak*

22 | 20 | 22 | $55

Syosset | 352 Jericho Tpke. (bet. Bruce St. & Seaford-Oyster Bay Rd.) | 516-921-1690

Customers commend the "quality cuts of meat" and "nice", varied seafood options at this upmarket Syosset steakhouse that's suited to a "business meeting, family dinner" or low-key night out; though some say the "sides lack panache" and the decor is a bit "drab", many appreciate the refreshing "absence of pretense" from a staff that's "attentive without being over-the-top."

Gabrielle's Brasserie &
Wine Bar *American*

22 | 22 | 20 | $40

Rockville Centre | 22 N. Park Ave. (bet. Merrick Rd. & Sunrise Hwy.) | 516-536-6611 | www.gabriellesny.com

Right on Rockville Centre's "bustling Restaurant Row", this "chic" New American boasts a "lovely" design (with "mesmerizing" lights), a "lively" bar scene and "ambitious" kitchen that many feel "gets it right"; though it can be "pricey" apart from the "popular" prix fixe options, most agree it's the kind of place "every neighborhood should have."

Galleria Dominick *Italian*

25 | 20 | 24 | $54

Westbury | 238 Post Ave. (bet. Drexel & Winthrop Aves.) | 516-997-7373 | www.galleriadominick.com

"Dominick watches over everything" from the "delectable" Northern Italian "home cooking" to a "knowledgeable" staff that "takes pride" in its work at this "long-standing" "special-occasion" place in Westbury, where the "elegant", softly lit ambiance is elevated with live piano on the weekends; while some patrons report "waiting" even with reservations, savvy guests "always go with friends who are regulars" for the most "accommodating" treatment.

Garden Grill *American*

19 | 24 | 20 | $37

Smithtown | 64 N. Country Rd. (bet. Judges Ln. & Main St.) | 631-265-8771 | www.thegardengrill.com

"A charming old house converted into a charming restaurant", this Smithtown American is admired for its "beautifully decorated" Victorian interior that "affords the opportunity to have a quiet dinner in one of its many rooms"; though it's too "cutesy" for some, and the food is less "memorable" than the setting, many recommend the "early-bird specials" and "excellent" Sunday brunch buffet for "value."

Gasho of Japan *Japanese*

19 | 17 | 19 | $35

Hauppauge | 356 Vanderbilt Motor Pkwy. (bet. Kennedy Dr. & Marcus Blvd.) | 631-231-3400 | www.gasho.com

"Dinner is entertainment" at this Hauppauge hibachi haunt where the "chefs put on a show" (some are "funnier" than others) for lots of families taking in the "theatrics" and "decent" Japanese steakhouse fare at "communal-style" tables; true, it's "not for the serious diner" and the "tired" interior is "due for a renovation", but at least the "bang for the buck" beats out some competitors.

	FOOD	DECOR	SERVICE	COST

George Martin ● *American*　　　　| 22 | 19 | 21 | $44 |

Rockville Centre | 65 N. Park Ave. (bet. Front St. & Sunrise Hwy.) |
516-678-7272 | www.georgemartingroup.com

"Still going strong", this "Rockville Centre fixture" draws a "loyal following" of "friends and neighbors" for its "solid", "something-for-everyone" New American menu served by a "smart", "thoughtful" staff; it tends to get "crowded and noisy", especially at the bar, but a "comfortable" layout with lots of booths lends it a "great clubby feeling."

George Martin's Coastal Grill *Seafood*　| 20 | 22 | 21 | $43 |

Long Beach | 40 E. Park Ave. (bet. Edwards & Riverside Blvds.) |
516-432-2690 | www.georgemartingroup.com

This "seafood-oriented outpost" of the George Martin chain brings its sociable "flair" to Long Beach, turning out "simple" but "high-end" dishes in a polished setting that feels a little "like a cruise ship"; while the servers aim to "please", some diners are "disappointed", calling it "overpriced for basic surf 'n' turf choices."

George Martin's Grillfire *Burgers*　　| 21 | 18 | 20 | $32 |

NEW **Merrick** | 33 W. Sunrise Hwy. (Merrick Ave.) |
516-379-2222

Rockville Centre | 13 N. Park Ave. (bet. Merrick Rd. & Sunrise Hwy.) |
516-678-1290

www.georgemartingroup.com

"Nice for a quick bite", this "relaxed" Rockville Centre American (with a new Merrick branch that opened post-Survey) offers a seemingly "endless" selection of burgers as well as other "quality" "comfort food" for "reasonable" tabs; the furnishings are a little "boring", but the "buzzing, friendly bar" makes it an after-work "winner."

Giulio Cesare Ristorante ⑧ *Italian*　| 24 | 16 | 22 | $55 |

Westbury | 18 Ellison Ave. (Old Country Rd.) | 516-334-2982

"Can you say old-school?" ask supporters of this Westbury "standard with staying power" that offers "expensive" but "wonderful" Italian ("I dare you to find a better osso buco!"); though some grouse that "regulars come first" and the decor is the "same from the '80s", the majority shrugs that the usually "fine service" doled out by an "experienced" staff means "it doesn't matter."

Golden Pear Café, The *Coffeehouse*　| 17 | 10 | 14 | $20 |

Bridgehampton | 2426 Montauk Hwy. (bet. Bridgehampton-Sag Harbor Tpke. & Corwith Ave.) | 631-537-1100

East Hampton | 34 Newtown Ln. (bet. Main St. & Osborne Ln.) |
631-329-1600

Sag Harbor | 111 Main St. (Spring St.) | 631-725-2270

Southampton | 99 Main St. (Nugent St.) | 631-283-8900

Stony Brook | Stony Brook Village Ctr. | 97A Main St. (bet. Christian Ave. & Rte. 25A) | 631-751-7695

www.goldenpearcafe.com

"Fresh" "light fare", pastries and coveted coffee served in a "fast-food format" are "easy" enough for daytime eats "if you can fight your way through the crowds to get to the counter" at this "in" mini-chain dotting "many a Main Street in the Hamptons"; given the "outrageous" prices, however, peeved patrons pooh-pooh it as the "Platinum Pear."

Goldmine Mexican Grill *Mexican*   ▽ 18 | 8 | 17 | $16

Greenlawn | 99 Broadway (bet. Central St. & Pulaski Rd.) | 631-262-1775

Taco fanatics make like bandits for this "solid" counter-service Mexican in Greenlawn that serves "delicious" "cheap eats" for takeout or eat-in (though it's just a small "joint"); a few customers complain of "cranky" service, but most conclude that overall it's "good for its type."

Gonzalo's American Café *American*   ▽ 20 | 12 | 18 | $26

Glen Cove | 5 School St. (Highland Rd.) | 516-656-0003 | www.americancafeglencove.com

"Down-home" American favorites including "killer meatloaf", "great hamburgers" and "amazing" soups ("a little bit of heaven in a bowl") are the bread and butter of this little storefront in Glen Cove; while its looks are "unassuming", the "service is pleasant" and it's "kid-friendly", making it a "nice neighborhood place to eat before or after the movies."

Gosman's Dock *Seafood*   17 | 17 | 15 | $44

Montauk | 500 W. Lake Dr. (Soundview Dr.) | 631-668-5330 | www.gosmans.com

"Watch the lobster boats pull in while you eat the catch" (and the "seagulls watch you" back) at this harborside "icon" in Montauk whose "terrific views" make it a "tourist spot for sure"; despite complaints of "long waits", "listless" service and prices that have "outstripped the value", gung-ho types still say "ya gotta go" "at least once."

Graffiti *American*   20 | 16 | 19 | $32

Hewlett | Peninsula Shopping Ctr. | 1326 Peninsula Blvd. (Mill Rd.) | 516-791-2959

Woodbury | Woodbury Common | 8285 Jericho Tpke. (Woodbury Rd.) | 516-367-1340

www.graffitirestaurant.com

A "convenient" "go-to", this "moderately priced" Hewlett and Woodbury twosome plates up "super salads" and "serious specials" from an "extensive" New American roster that covers the bases for the "entire family" or "dining with the girls"; it's "cute" (with a "fun" "alfresco" scene at Woodbury Common), though some note that it's "noisy" and the service is "rather casual."

⧫ Grand Lux Cafe *Eclectic*   19 | 21 | 18 | $32

Garden City | Roosevelt Field Mall | 630 Old Country Rd. (bet. Clinton Rd. & Meadowbrook Pkwy.) | 516-741-0096 | www.grandluxcafe.com

"Spun-off from the Cheesecake Factory", this somewhat "fancier" version in the Roosevelt Field mall features an "everything-for-everybody" Eclectic menu that spans the globe and arrives in "huge", "tasty" portions; if "plush", vaguely Venetian decor and "speedy service" aren't enough, it's "not too expensive" either.

	FOOD	DECOR	SERVICE	COST

NEW Grappa ⓜ *Italian* ▽ 20 | 18 | 18 | $48

Sag Harbor | 62 Main St. (bet. Garden & Spring Sts.) | 631-725-7427 |
www.grappawinebar.com

"You can have a wonderful meal just ordering appetizers", and even
the half-portions of pasta are "more than enough" enthuse eaters
who have sampled this new, "not overly expensive" Sag Harbor
Italian, Ed 'Jean-Luc' Kleefield's latest Hamptons venture (and his
second concept at this frequently changing location); as it's largely
a wine bar, the wraparound zinc bar is a centerpiece, though some
deduct decor points for the "strange high-top seating."

Grasso's *American* 25 | 22 | 23 | $56

Cold Spring Harbor | 134 Main St. (bet. Elm & Poplar Pls.) | 631-367-6060 |
www.grassosrestaurant.com

"Phenomenal" New American fare keeps customers "celebrating" at
this "charming little restaurant" with a "romantic", upscale ambiance in the "quaint village" of Cold Spring Harbor; live jazz most
nights "adds spice", though some call it "better during the week unless you're into the bar scene."

Greek Village *Greek* 19 | 12 | 17 | $26

Commack | Macy's Plaza | 44 Veterans Memorial Hwy. (bet. Jericho Tpke. &
Sunken Meadows Pkwy. S.) | 631-499-6590 |
www.greekvillagecommack.com

"Can you say spanakopita?" ask advocates of the spinach pie
that's a favorite at this family-run "standby" serving "honest" Greek
fare in a Commack shopping center; sure, it's "dinerlike", but most
"don't mind the total lack of ambiance" because the "prices make
up for it."

Green Cactus Grill *Mexican* 21 | 8 | 14 | $14

Garden City Park | 2441 Jericho Tpke. (bet. Herricks Rd. & Marcus Ave.) |
516-248-0090
NEW Long Beach | 167 E. Park Ave. (bet. Long Beach & Riverside Blvds.) |
516-897-8226
Plainview | Plainview Shopping Ctr. | 397B S. Oyster Bay Rd.
(Woodbury Rd.) | 516-937-3444
Rockville Centre | 288 Sunrise Hwy. (Park Ave.) | 516-536-0700
Roslyn Heights | 215 Mineola Ave. (bet. MacGregor Ave. &
Old Powerhouse Rd.) | 516-626-3100
Wantagh | Cherrywood Shopping Ctr. | 1194 Wantagh Ave.
(Jerusalem Ave.) | 516-781-4900
North Babylon | 1209 Deer Park Ave. (bet. Mohawk Dr. & Woods Rd.) |
631-242-2008
Huntington | 1273 E. Jericho Tpke. (Manor Rd.) | 631-673-1010
NEW Huntington | 318 Main St. (bet. Green & Prospect Sts.) |
631-271-8900
Stony Brook | 1099 Rte. 25A (bet. Cedar St. & Hawkins Rd.) |
631-751-0700
www.greencactusgrill.com

"Consistently fresh and delicious" "not-so-fast fast Mexican food"
"hits the spot" (and the "salsa bar is a plus") at this growing chainlet
offering "total bang for your buck"; though some of the older locales

feel fairly "bleak", reviewers report a number of branches now look "way better" following a remodel with earthy tones.

Green Melody Kosher/Pan-Asian — | — | — | M

Jericho | Jericho Commons | 519 N. Broadway (bet. I-495 & Jericho Tpke.) | 516-681-5715

Offering the uncommon combo of kosher vegetarian Pan-Asian fare, this seitan specialist tucked away in a hard-to-find corner of Jericho Commons appeals to both restricted eaters and others with its moderately priced array of mock meat dishes; a setting with green carpeting and red walls and chairs keeps the tone simple and upbeat.

Greenport Tea Company Tearoom 20 | 20 | 20 | $26

Greenport | 119A Main St. (bet. E. Front St. & Greenport Harbor) | 631-477-8744 | www.greenportteacompany.com

"Owners Jan and Jenette cook up a storm", specializing in "high tea to die for" – complete with "light finger sandwiches", scones and mini-pastries – as well as "homemade soups" at this "tiny", "relaxing" and fragrant little teahouse in Greenport; "part-kitsch, part–*Alice in Wonderland*" and fine for "feeling Victorian", it's a "nice place to bring mom for lunch"; N.B. closed the first three weeks of January and Monday–Wednesday in the winter.

NEW Grey Horse Tavern American ▽ 22 | 24 | 22 | $43

Bayport | 291 Bayport Ave. (Montauk Hwy.) | 631-472-1868 | www.greyhorsetavern.com

"Long Island history whispers in the walls" at this "excellent" Bayport newcomer inside a "beautifully decorated" 140-year-old building (once a stagecoach stop) serving "superb" New American fare using "local and organic ingredients"; the staff is "warm" and "well-educated on food and wine", the bar's "terrific" and there's live jazz and bluegrass on the weekends, making it the kind of "welcoming upscale pub you wish were around the corner from your house."

Grill Room ☒ American 22 | 19 | 21 | $46

Hauppauge | 160 Adams Ave. (bet. Arkay & Commerce Drs.) | 631-436-7330 | www.thegrillroomrestaurant.com

A Hauppauge office park provides the unlikely setting for this "dark", "sexy" and "sophisticated" surprise that plates a "wonderful", somewhat "expensive" selection of New American dishes along with "generous pours" from the "beautiful" new granite bar; live music on the weekends "can make conversation impossible", but game guests like that it's "loud" "in an NYC kind of way."

Grimaldi's Pizza 23 | 15 | 19 | $24

Garden City | 980 Franklin Ave. (bet. 9th & 10th Sts.) | 516-294-6565 | www.grimaldisrestaurant.com

"If you love thin-crust pizza, this is the place!" approve pie-sani of this Garden City spin-off that's "just like the original" in Brooklyn but "without the bridge" and the "long lines" for its "crisp", coal-fired specialty; the "prompt service is nothing special" and neither is the "ordinary" room, but most agree that once you take a bite, it "blows away" the rest.

	FOOD	DECOR	SERVICE	COST

NEW Gulf Coast Kitchen *Caribbean/Southern*

| - | - | - | E |

Montauk | Montauk Yacht Club Resort & Marina | 32 Star Island Rd. (off W. Lake Dr.) | 631-668-3100 | www.montaukyachtclub.com

Scheduled to open just after press time, this newcomer at the Montauk Yacht Club (in the space last occupied by Lighthouse Grill) will offer local seafood and produce with a Southern-Caribbean twist; sporting a living-room feel, the relaxed dining room features bookshelves, Gulf Coast memorabilia and historic photos of the Yacht Club (which is celebrating its 80th anniversary), as well as views of Lake Montauk; other dining and drinking options set to open on-site by summer 2009 include Hurricane Alley, with a fish shack menu, and the loungey Barracuda Bar.

NEW Haiku Asian Bistro & Sushi Bar *Asian/Japanese*

| - | - | - | M |

Woodbury | Woodbury Town Plaza | 8025 Jericho Tpke. (bet. Southwoods & Woodbury Rds.) | 516-584-6782

New to Woodbury (with Westchester siblings), this far-reaching bistro features Chinese, Malaysian and Thai specialties along with sushi and other Japanese dishes, served in a contemporary interior with ivory walls, black trim and hanging lanterns with gold shantung-like fabric shades; a liquor license is pending, but BYO is permitted with no corkage fee.

Hampton Chutney Co. *Indian*

| 22 | 10 | 16 | $19 |

Amagansett | Amagansett Sq. | Main St. (Hedges Ln.) | 631-267-3131 | www.hamptonchutney.com

"Take the Jitney to nirvana" enthuse dosa-"addicted" day-trippers about this "sweet little" counter-service spot (that spawned two NYC outposts) hidden in the back of Amagansett Square; the "neat", "gourmet" Indian lunches can be eaten on outdoor picnic tables, as there's barely enough room inside for the "long lines during the prime season"; N.B. winter hours vary, so call ahead.

Hampton Coffee Company *Coffeehouse*

| 19 | 15 | 18 | $18 |

Water Mill | 869 Montauk Hwy. (Davids Ln.) | 631-726-2633
Westhampton Beach | 194 Mill Rd. (Oak St.) | 631-288-4480
www.hamptoncoffeecompany.com

Java junkies perk up at the "smells of freshly roasted coffee and warm scones baking" at this "chic" East End pair purveying "tasty" breakfast goods and "basic sandwich/salad fare" for "light lunches"; while the Westhampton Beach branch has limited seating, the Water Mill location is a full-service cafe that also has Mexican options.

Harbor Bistro *American*

| 22 | 19 | 22 | $51 |

East Hampton | Maidstone Marina | 313 Three Mile Harbor Rd. (4 mi. north of Hook Windmill) | 631-324-7300

"Beautiful views" are the star at this East Hamptoner at the Maidstone Marina, though many feel the New American food "equals the daily sunset", or at least comes close with "excellent", "creative" preparations; the "staff is a joy" too, the atmosphere

FOOD | DECOR | SERVICE | COST

"casual" and the bill "reasonable" for the Hamptons; N.B. closed November to mid-April.

Harbor Crab *Seafood*   18 | 16 | 18 | $36

Patchogue | 116 Division St. (bet. Clare Rose Blvd. & River Ave.) | 631-687-2722 | www.harborcrab.com

You can "dock your boat" at this "energetic eating and meeting place" on the Patchogue River and kick-start the night with a "vibrant bar scene" that keeps going year-round; the seafood is "decent" if "hit-or-miss depending on what you order", and some feel the tiki-accented space "needs upkeep", but many appreciate that it's "not overpriced or pretentious", and the floating outdoor deck is "a treat."

Harbor-Q *BBQ*   - | - | - | I

Port Washington | 84 Old Shore Rd. (Shore Rd.) | 516-883-4227 | www.harborq.com

"Just what the town needed", this budding BBQ joint in Port Washington serves "swoon"-worthy ribs, brisket and other staples with serious "smoke flavor", along with "customized salads" and "neat" sides; "unpretentious" and a little industrial (the space once housed a metal shipping company), it's staffed by "family-friendly" servers, and the Sunday–Thursday prix fixe deals make it extra easy on the wallet.

Harvest on Fort Pond *Italian/Mediterranean*   25 | 21 | 21 | $50

Montauk | 11 S. Emery St. (Euclid Ave.) | 631-668-5574 | www.harvest2000.com

"Bring some friends" as the "gigantic" Mediterranean-Tuscan plates are "meant to be shared" – and so "delicious" "it's tough to pick out just a few" – at this "best-for-the-money" Montauk "must" where revelers "sit outside in the garden", "catch a sunset" over Fort Pond and "love life"; "packed" and "happening", it's a "tough reservation", but even those who have "waited two hours" "would have to say it was worth it."

Havana Beach Club *Cuban*   - | - | - | M

Montauk | 448 W. Lake Dr. (bet. Flamingo Ave. & Soundview Dr.) | 631-668-6677 | www.havanabeachclubny.com

Down on the docks in Montauk, this Cuban cutie caters to summer customers with its large covered porch and 30-ft.-long bar topped by an awning, while also serving winter dinners (Thursday–Saturday) in a fireplace-warmed dining room; the menu includes a Cuban paella, grilled pork chops and a variety of sandwiches, complemented by mojitos and lively Latin music on the speakers.

Heart of Portugal *Portuguese*   20 | 17 | 20 | $43

Mineola | 241 Mineola Blvd. (bet. Jackson & Jefferson Aves.) | 516-742-9797 | www.heartofportugalrestaurant.com

"I may not go to Portugal anytime soon but at least I can savor the food" say fans of the "heartwarming" meals at this "slightly offbeat" and "retro" Mineola option; some sniff that it "looks like a dive bar", but most agree it's "more pleasant" on the verdant patio.

	FOOD	DECOR	SERVICE	COST

Hellenic Snack Bar & Restaurant *Greek*   20 | 11 | 17 | $30

East Marion | 5145 Main Rd. (bet. Maple & Shipyard Lns.) |
631-477-0138 | www.thehellenic.com

Satisfied surveyors "smile" about "scrumptious Greek cuisine in a
mom-and-pop setting" at this East Marion veteran that's been serving up "traditional", "reasonable" fare (and "famous lemonade") for
more than 30 years; yes, the service can be "slow" and the "dinerlike"
digs get "crowded with Orient Point ferry-goers", but many call the
patio the "perfect summer experience"; N.B. closed mid-November
to mid-January.

Hemingway's *American*   18 | 17 | 18 | $35

Wantagh | 1885 Wantagh Ave. (bet. Brooktree Ln. & Park Ave.) |
516-781-2700 | www.hemingwaysgrill.com

"A good place to gather", this "Wantagh favorite" has a "comfortable pub atmosphere" that would make "Papa proud", and a staff
that "lets you linger over martinis and apps"; while the "standard"
New American fare gets mixed marks, fans feel "for what this place
is, it does it right."

Hideaway, The *Eclectic*   ▽ 20 | 21 | 19 | $47

Fire Island | Housers Hotel | 785 Evergreen Walk (Bay Walk) |
631-583-8900

"Adorable" and "relaxing", this Ocean Beach eatery in a seaside
hotel is sought out for "fabulous sunsets on the deck" in the summer; while the Eclectic menu isn't always "consistent", most diners
deem it "decent" for Fire Island.

Higashi ⓜ *Japanese*   20 | 15 | 18 | $34

Syosset | 260 Jericho Tpke. (Burke Ln.) | 516-364-7571

"Flavorful", "nicely presented" sushi earns a satisfied "neighborhood" following at this affordable, "family-run" Japanese in Syosset;
the decor is "simple", but the atmosphere is abetted by owners who
"know how to treat regulars."

Hildebrandt's ⓜ *American*   19 | 12 | 19 | $22

Williston Park | 84 Hillside Ave. (bet. Roslyn Rd. & Willis Ave.) |
516-741-0608 | www.hildebrandts-wp.com

"Return to a simpler era" (namely the 1920s) at this "retro soda
fountain" in Williston Park whose enthusiasts say skip the "homestyle" American cooking, "throw caution to the wind" and make
one of their "hot fudge sundaes" "your main course at lunch";
with a "nice staff" too, it's a "prime example of why some things
should not change."

Hinata *Asian Fusion/Japanese*   22 | 17 | 20 | $39

Great Neck | 6 Bond St. (Grace Ave.) | 516-829-3811

"Beautiful" presentations of "terrific" Japanese and Asian fusion
dishes lend distinction to this Great Neck "contender" where the
food and service are generally "excellent"; though some say the
sushi tends to "stick to the routine", most maintain it's "always
worth a visit."

	FOOD	DECOR	SERVICE	COST

Hokkaido *Japanese*
| | 21 | 17 | 20 | $36 |

Albertson | 1162 Willis Ave. (Netz Pl.) | 516-621-1887 |
www.hokkaido-albertson.com

Albertson eaters appreciate the "talented" chefs who prepare "top-notch" rolls and "hibachi that never fails to entertain" at this "indie" Japanese (like "Benihana off steroids"); while the decor is fairly "functional", most assert that the "super-friendly" servers "who remember your previous orders and then guide you" make it a "local favorite."

Homura Sushi *Japanese*
▽ 24 | 15 | 20 | $35

Williston Park | 636 Willis Ave. (bet. Fordham & Franklin Sts.) |
516-877-8128

"Unique, fresh and satisfying" rolls along with "extras to keep you happy" make this sushi specialist a "small wonder in the small community" of Williston Park; the "simple" digs are comfortable enough for some, while others tend to opt for takeout.

⚡ Honu Kitchen & Cocktails Ⓜ *American*
22 | 25 | 21 | $51

Huntington | 363 New York Ave. (bet. Main & W. Carver Sts.) |
631-421-6900 | www.honukitchen.com

"This stunner really shines" applaud Huntington table-hoppers who say the former Blue Honu has "completely reinvented itself" with a "beautiful", "sexy" redesign, an "appealing" New American small-plates menu that "steps up the food quality" and "wonderful" martinis mixed by "fantastic bartenders"; while the bill can "add up like nobody's business" and the bar scene gets "overcrowded", many feel it's ideal for a "real night out"; N.B. a recent chef change may not be reflected by the Food score.

Horace & Sylvia's Publick House *American*
17 | 16 | 17 | $32

Babylon | 100 Deer Park Ave. (bet. Grove Pl. & Main St.) | 631-587-5081

"Decent", affordable New American "pub grub" and a "lively (but not crazy) bar scene" add up to a "down-to-earth fun place to meet" over eats and drinks at this Babylon bistro; still, as the service is often "mediocre" and the menu "could be a little more interesting", some maintain it's "middle-of-the-road in every way."

NEW Hotoke *Japanese*
▽ 26 | 28 | 22 | $37

Smithtown | 41 Rte. 111 (E. Main St.) | 631-979-9222 |
www.hotokejapanese.com

"Wow" say those who've sampled this "sophisticated" Smithtown newcomer offering both "imaginative" sushi and "traditional" hibachi tables where the "chefs put on a great show"; with its "chic" feel and "nice presentations", fans say it's "worth a visit – or five."

House of Dosas *Indian*
23 | 9 | 19 | $16

Hicksville | 416 S. Broadway (Boehme St.) | 516-938-7517 |
www.houseofdosas.com

"If you can't make it to Jackson Heights" or "Madras", "it's easy to get hooked on this Hicksville fixture" dishing out "spicy, delicious dosas" and other "excellent" Indian vegetarian specialties; it's little more than a "hole-in-the-wall", but the staff is "prompt and cordial", and it "fills you up without breaking the bank."

House of India *Indian* | 22 | 16 | 21 | $29 |

Huntington | 256 Main St. (New York Ave.) | 631-271-0059 | www.houseofindiarestaurant.com

"Huntington doesn't have too much to offer" when it comes to Indian food, but the cooking at this subcontinental – "always reliable" and "spiced to your liking" – succeeds "despite the lack of competition"; the service is generally "gracious", and while some assess the space "needs redecoration", it's "quiet" and the "price is right."

Houston's *American* | 21 | 19 | 19 | $35 |

Garden City | Roosevelt Field Mall | 630 Old Country Rd. (bet. Clinton Rd. & Meadowbrook Pkwy.) | 516-873-1454 | www.hillstone.com

A "chain that doesn't feel like one", this "reliable" Roosevelt Field option "clicks" thanks to a "pretty darn good" menu of "all-American comfort items" (including a notoriously "addicting spinach dip") and a "modern metropolitan" ambiance; despite debate on the cost – "inexpensive" vs. "overpriced" – most report "solid quality" here.

H.R. Singleton's *American* | 17 | 17 | 18 | $33 |

Bethpage | 150 Hicksville Rd. (Hempstead Tpke.) | 516-731-7065 | www.hrsingletonsrestaurant.com

This Bethpage American, a "souped-up bistro" with an "annexed bar for the older crowd", works for a "family night out" or grown-up get-togethers; the menu is "simple" and "steady", though even if it's "not pricey", some find it "overpriced for ok food."

H2O Seafood Grill *Seafood* | 23 | 21 | 21 | $53 |

Smithtown | 215 W. Main St. (Edgewood Ave.) | 631-361-6464 | www.h2oseafoodgrill.com

"They take fish seriously" at this Smithtown seafooder known for its "exciting" preparations, from the "millennium lobster" to "unique" sushi, served by a "helpful" staff in "modern", white wood-paneled surroundings ("can you have an elegant beachy atmosphere? this does!"); while the tab might have you "fishing for your credit card", many recommend the Wednesday night wine dinners for "value."

Hudson & McCoy *Seafood* | 17 | 17 | 17 | $44 |

Freeport | 340 Woodcleft Ave. (bet. Atlantic & Guy Lombardo Aves.) | 516-868-3411 | www.hudsonmccoy.com

"Mostly a summer hangout on the Nautical Mile", this Freeport sea-fooder draws a "younger crowd" to the "hopping" outdoor bar with "loud rock bands" on warm weekends; the fish tends to "fall a little short", though, and service is "lacking", so many deem it "pricey for the quality" overall.

Hudson's Mill *American* | 22 | 21 | 22 | $42 |

Massapequa | 5599 Merrick Rd. (Carman Mill Rd.) | 516-799-5394 | www.hudsonsmill.com

"It's the whole package for a delightful evening" enthuse diners about this Massapequa "gem" providing "gourmet" New American fare matched with "fantastic wines by the glass" for "much less than you'd pay at a high-end restaurant"; lots of brick and a mahogany bar lend it a "dark cozy" feel, while the "accommodating", informative staff adds to the "charming atmosphere."

Hunan Taste *Chinese*

23 | 16 | 18 | $35

Greenvale | 3 Northern Blvd. (Wellington Rd.) | 516-621-6616
"Out-of-the-ordinary" Chinese food entices at this Greenvale Hunan haven with a "long history" of serving "high-quality meals" that are "far from the typical takeout (and a little more "expensive"); while the staff can generally "handle a crowd", vets advise "skip the popular time frames" as it's "mobbed" and "loud" on the weekends.

Il Capuccino Ristorante *Italian*

19 | 15 | 19 | $40

Sag Harbor | 30 Madison St. (bet. Main & Sage Sts.) | 631-725-2747 | www.ilcapuccino.com
"Still unbeatable for consistency, charm" and the "most insanely delicious garlic knots on the planet", this "family-run" "throwback" in Sag Harbor "caters more to local diners than to glitterati" with its "hearty" Italian food at "reasonable prices"; decorated with hanging Chianti bottles and red-checkered tablecloths, it's "relaxed, homey" and "perfect for a crisp fall night."

Il Classico Ⓜ *Italian*

24 | 21 | 23 | $48

Massapequa Park | 4857 Merrick Rd. (bet. Cartwright & Park Blvds.) | 516-798-8496 | www.ilclassico.com
"Attention to detail" shown in the "heavenly", traditional Northern Italian food, "romantic" room and "top-shelf" service by a staff that "makes you feel like a VIP" keeps this Massapequa Park mainstay "fabulous all around"; "you do pay for the quality", but most feel "happy" to do so; N.B. live music Thursdays makes it extra "enjoyable."

🅩 Il Mulino New York *Italian*

26 | 22 | 24 | $78

Roslyn Estates | 1042 Northern Blvd. (bet. Cedar Path & Searingtown Rd.) | 516-621-1870 | www.ilmulinonewyork.com
"Quintessential" Northern Italian dining awaits at this Roslyn Estates chain link spun off from the "superb" NYC original and featuring the same "excellent" cooking and "great service"; granted, the mood can be "stuffy" and the pricing "exorbitantly high", but ultimately they'll "feed you so much" – the meal comes with "lots of extras" "before you even order" – that a "good walk afterward" is recommended; N.B. the kitchen has recently launched a prix fixe Sunday supper.

Indian Cove *American*

18 | 19 | 17 | $46

Hampton Bays | 258 E. Montauk Hwy. (off Canoe Place Rd.) | 631-728-5366 | www.indiancoverestaurantmarina.com
"Picturesque" with waterside seating overlooking Shinnecock Bay, this "casual" Hampton Bays hang is "enjoyable" for view seekers who like to "sit on the deck at sundown"; as the setting is the "highlight", some critics contend the American seafood menu and service "need revamping", though others are "pleasantly surprised" by the meal; N.B. no lunch on the weekends in the off-season.

	FOOD	DECOR	SERVICE	COST

NEW Indian Wells Tavern M *American* | 15 | 14 | 17 | $36 |

Amagansett | 177 Main St. (bet. Cozzins & Windmill Lns.) |
631-267-0400

"After strolling Amagansett", peckish patrons head to this "publike" newcomer in the former Estia Cantina space by the "well-known" owners of Bostwick's on the Harbor; the "simple", "fairly priced" American dishes are rated as "nothing special" but good for "grazing", and while some call it too "dark" and "generic" in style, it's "friendly" and "lively" enough to get "packed on the weekends in the summer."

Inlet Seafood *Seafood* | 21 | 19 | 16 | $48 |

Montauk | 541 E. Lake Dr. (opp. Montauk Airport) | 631-668-4272 |
www.inletseafood.com

"Truly the last restaurant on Long Island" since it's about as far out as you can get, this "quirky" Montauk "upstart" in an unassuming A-frame is "owned by a cooperative of fishermen" and serves "terrific" cooked seafood as well as "great sushi"; though some report "surly" service and "long waits" (no reservations are taken), that's a minor catch in light of the "salt-air" setting and "breathtaking" sunsets; N.B. closed January to mid-March.

Inn Spot on the Bay *Eclectic* | 19 | 21 | 19 | $58 |

Hampton Bays | 32 Lighthouse Rd. (Foster Ave.) | 631-728-1200 |
www.theinnspot.com

"On a moonlit night, you could fall in love" at this "big secret" in the "little town" of Hampton Bays, "set in a beautiful country home on the water"; some say the Eclectic menu with a seafood focus "should be better" considering the "expense", but others are so lulled by the "ambiance, sunsets" and "pleasant" service, they sigh it's "like visiting a friend."

⊠ In Season American Bistro M *American* | 26 | 19 | 23 | $46 |

Islip | 301 Main St. (bet. Ocean & Pardee Aves.) | 631-581-1029 |
www.inseasonbistro.com

"Talented" chef-owner Christopher Hunter uses "changing" seasonal ingredients to prepare "creative", "first-rate" New American fare "you won't find anywhere else" at this foodie "hit" in Islip and amiably chats up patrons, explaining "some delicious but obscure vegetable you couldn't identify"; it's "small" with "close-together" tables, but both the size and the staff create a "personable atmosphere."

Intermezzo *Italian* | 20 | 15 | 17 | $34 |

Fort Salonga | Village Plaza | 10-12 Fort Salonga Rd./Rte. 25A (Bread & Cheese Hollow Rd.) | 631-261-4840 | www.intermezzorestaurantny.com
Customers "count on" this Fort Salonga Italian that's a "step up from the typical pizza place" with its wood-fired pies and "tasty" pastas; while it's now under "new ownership", it remains "jammed" by visitors who vouch for the "food quality and local flavor", as well as the "good value."

International Delight Cafe ⊭ *Diner* | 18 | 8 | 16 | $19 |

Bellmore | 322 Bedford Ave. (Wilson Ave.) | 516-409-5772

(continued)

International Delight Cafe

Rockville Centre | 241 Sunrise Hwy. (bet. Park & Village Aves.) | 516-766-7557 ◐
www.internationaldelightcafe.com

"Better than a diner", these Bellmore and Rockville Centre "staples" serve up "solid", "generous" American plates for low prices, but "best of all are the waffles and gelato" (in a "gazillion flavors"), so some advise "forget dinner and just order dessert"; even if they don't offer much in the way of ambiance, they work for a "late-night" bite on the weekends (just "bring cash").

Irish Coffee Pub *Continental/Irish*   22 | 21 | 23 | $40

East Islip | 131 Carleton Ave. (bet. Stewart & Wall St.) | 631-277-0007 | www.irishcoffeepub.com

An "emerald gem", this East Islip "mainstay" for Continental and Irish "home cooking" ("potato soup is a must") is essentially a "warm pub on a large scale" where the "decor differs from room to room"; though popular as a "catering facility, it doesn't forget about its lunch and dinner clientele", and satisfied guests say "you get your money's worth."

NEW Island BBQ & Grill Ⓢ Ⓜ *BBQ*   - | - | - | I

Islip | 591 Main St. (bet. Locust & Nassau Aves.) | 631-650-5635

Plenty of different BBQ plates (along with entree-sized salads and sandwiches) make this Islip newcomer on Main Street a hungry-man's hog heaven; the simple interior features a brick-walled separate take-out area (there are cost-effective family combo packs), as well as two small, minimally decorated, wood-floored dining rooms; N.B. only wine and beer are served.

Island Mermaid *American*   20 | 20 | 20 | $46

Fire Island | 780 Bay Walk (Evergreen Walk) | 631-583-8088 | www.islandmermaid.com

"There's nothing like having a cocktail then dinner while the sun is setting" say habitués of this Ocean Beach New American known for the "ultimate view" and "straightforward fun" in the summertime; some say it's just "ok for beach food" and "not cheap by Fire Island standards", but it doesn't disappoint with a "late-night bar crowd and dancing"; N.B. closed October to mid-April.

Ivy Cottage *American*   24 | 19 | 21 | $44

Williston Park | 38 Hillside Ave. (Nassau Blvd.) | 516-877-2343 | www.ivycottagerestaurant.com

This "adorable little" Williston Park American woos guests with "excellent", "inventive" (and slightly "expensive") cuisine served in a "homey" cottage setting; the service is largely "warm" too, but bear in mind it's "difficult to get weekend reservations, so book early."

NEW Izumi *Asian Fusion*   - | - | - | M

Bethpage | Bethpage Mktpl. | 440 N. Wantagh Ave. (Rte. 107) | 516-933-7225 | www.izumifood.com

"Wonderful food presentations" with "unique designs" distinguish this attractive Asian fusion newcomer in the former space of Zen

	FOOD	DECOR	SERVICE	COST

18C in Bethpage; Thai, Chinese and Japanese cooking are on the menu, along with a "delicious" sushi selection, including specialties like the naruto roll, wrapped in cucumber instead of rice.

Jaiya *Thai*   21 | 14 | 17 | $32

Hicksville | 46 W. Old Country Rd. (B'way) | 516-681-3400 | www.jaiya.com

"The spice is not diluted for Americans" at this Hicksville Thai serving "truly authentic" dishes that "singe the lips" and "clear the sinuses"; though it "could use an interior decorator" and the service doesn't impress, fiery food fiends say that finding "the real thing" "more than makes up for it."

Jamesport Country Kitchen *American*   23 | 16 | 21 | $37

Jamesport | 1601 Main Rd. (Manor Ln.) | 631-722-3537 | www.northfork.com/catering

"Local fare from land, sea, farm and vineyard" shines at this Jamesport "gem" where chef-owner Matthew Kar matches "fresh, wholesome" New American cooking with an "excellent Long Island wine list"; as the "plain-Jane" space looks like a "mom-and-pop" shop, it's "nothing fancy", but offers a "memorable meal with wonderful service" for a price that's "right on the mark."

Z Jamesport Manor Inn *American*   24 | 27 | 23 | $54

Jamesport | 370 Manor Ln. (bet. Main Rd. & Sound Ave.) | 631-722-0500 | www.jamesportmanorinn.com

"Recently restored to its original beauty" by owner Matthew Kar (Jamesport Country Kitchen), this "stylish" revival of a Jamesport landmark house sets the stage for "inventive", "well-executed" New American dishes with "local East End flair"; as the service is "warm and gracious", most say it's worth the "beaucoup" bucks (and a "bargain" for Sunday brunch and prix fixe dinners); N.B. closed Tuesday.

Z Jedediah's *American*   26 | 28 | 26 | $64

Jamesport | Jedediah Hawkins Inn | 400 S. Jamesport Ave. (bet. Main Rd. & Peconic Bay Blvd.) | 631-722-2900 | www.jedediahhawkinsinn.com

Voted No. 1 for Decor on Long Island, a "magnificent" 19th-century "sea captain's house" that's been "lovingly restored" and landscaped provides the backdrop for this Jamesport destination and its "brilliant" seasonal New American cuisine – now prepared with a more casual take by chef Matt Murphy (Antares Cafe), who replaced Tom Schaudel post-Survey; the "fabulous" staff maintains "professional pacing" as well, making the meal a "memorable experience."

NEW Jeff's Seafood & Galley *Seafood*   – | – | – | I

East Northport | Elwood Plaza | 1965 Jericho Tpke. (Elwood Rd.) | 631-858-2393 | jeffsseafoodandgalley.food.officelive.com

Savvy seafarers head to this East Northport hole-in-the-wall to shop at the seafood market and chow down on cooked fin fare including battered Boston cod and Billy Bob's crab cakes; decorated with fish netting and murals, the space is bare-bones but a few tables and chairs allow for dining inside.

	FOOD	DECOR	SERVICE	COST

Jewel of India *Indian*

| 20 | 15 | 18 | $31 |

Syosset | 347 Jericho Tpke. (Florence Ave.) | 516-677-9898 |
www.jewelofindiarestaurant.com

For an abundance of "excellent" tandoori dishes and other "nicely spicy" eats, guests go for this Syosset Indian where the lunch buffet "can't be beat for quality and price"; sure, "the decor is rather worn", but "in a crowded field" its cuisine "stands out."

Jimmy Hays *Steak*

| 25 | 21 | 23 | $60 |

Island Park | 4310 Austin Blvd. (Kingston Blvd.) | 516-432-5155 |
www.jimmyhayssteakhouse.com

"This is the place to go" for "incredible" steaks, "delicious" sides and "sublime" seafood say fans of this Island Park "treasure" tended by a "knowledgeable" staff; the "dark clubby setting" with a mahogany bar completes the picture, so while it's too "busy" for some, most feel the "waits" and the tab are "well worth it."

NEW Jin East *Japanese*

| ▽ 25 | 23 | 20 | $43 |

Garden City | 988 Franklin Ave. (bet. 9th & 10th Sts.) | 516-877-0888 |
www.jineast.com

"Fresh seafood" in "appealing" presentations is enhanced by "beautiful", "peaceful" surroundings at this "friendly" new Garden City Japanese; despite high-end prices, early samplers say it's quickly becoming a "favorite."

JLX Bistro *French*

| 13 | 17 | 13 | $51 |

Sag Harbor | 16 Main St. (bet. Nassau & Water Sts.) | 631-725-9100 |
www.jlxbistro.com

Jean-Luc's "breezy" bistro on a busy Sag Harbor corner has some "attractive" faux-French touches, but monsieurs and madames caution "stick to the sure things" when ordering, since "anything with higher aspirations can be chancy"; "spotty, slow service" is another sore point, leading observers to opine "this overpriced star is beginning to fade."

John Harvard's Brew House ● *Pub Food*

| 16 | 15 | 16 | $27 |

Lake Grove | Smith Haven Plaza | 2093 Smithhaven Plaza
(bet. St. Nicholas Ave. & Tower St.) | 631-979-2739 |
www.johnharvards.com

It's all about the "constantly changing menu of craft brews" at this "no-frills" brewpub franchise in Lake Grove where the "typical" American menu is outperformed by the "nice suds selection" (after a few pints "you can convince yourself you made it into Harvard"); complaints about "nonexistent service" are blunted by "good-value" pricing.

Jolly Fisherman & Steak House Ⓜ *Seafood/Steak*

| 20 | 15 | 19 | $48 |

Roslyn | 25 Main St. (bet. E. B'way & Old Northern Blvd.) | 516-621-0055 |
www.jollyfishermanrestaurant.com

"Reminiscent of the old seafood houses in Boston", this "been-there-forever" surf 'n' turfer overlooking Roslyn Pond offers a "wide selection" of "simply prepared" dishes, often catering to "family outings"; critics knock that "nothing has changed since the average customer was young" (the "room is older than McCain"), but it remains "well respected" among its clientele.

Jonathan's *American* | 19 | 19 | 19 | $38 |

Garden City Park | 3000 Jericho Tpke. (Herricks Rd.) | 516-742-7300 | www.jonathans-rest.com

Often "crowded with family groups", this "homey" Garden City Park "staple" has multiple rooms to "accommodate large parties" dining on New American fare that's "well prepared" if "not exciting"; since prices are "moderate" and service is "efficient", most find it a "reliable" choice, especially for Sunday brunch.

Jonathan's Ristorante *Italian* | 23 | 22 | 22 | $52 |

Huntington | 15 Wall St. (bet. Gerard & Main Sts.) | 631-549-0055 | www.jonathansristorante.com

"Sophisticated but not stuffy", this "nifty Huntington haunt" delivers "first-class" Italian fare with a few "snazzy" specials, presented by an "excellent" staff; "spacious surroundings" with French doors add to the upscale ambiance, making it sought out for "special occasions."

JT's Corner Cafe *American* | 23 | 12 | 19 | $24 |

Nesconset | 204 Smithtown Blvd. (Joseph Pl.) | 631-265-5267 | www.jtscornercafe.com

"You'd never expect to dine so well at a place that looks like this" assert samplers of this Nesconset "storefront" where the "chef takes chances" and produces "gourmet twists" on New American standards from morning to night; considering the "excellent value" and "friendly" service, few mind the "small-town" "country kitchen setting", deeming it a "diamond in the rough"; N.B. beer and wine are now served.

JT's Place *Pub Food* | 18 | 14 | 19 | $35 |

Hampton Bays | 26 W. Montauk Hwy. (bet. Ponquogue Ave. & Springville Rd.) | 631-723-2626

Hampton Bays beach bums "hang out and enjoy a meal with family and friends" at this "casual" pub specializing in "burgers and steaks" along with other "satisfying" American eats; most feel it's "fairly priced", but bargain-hunters head for the prix fixe dinner Sunday–Monday.

Kabul Afghani Cuisine *Afghan* | 22 | 16 | 21 | $31 |

Huntington | 1153 E. Jericho Tpke. (bet. Dix Hills Rd. & Park Ave.) | 631-549-5506 | www.kabulny.com

A rare "cultural exchange" inspires diners at this "authentic", "family-run" Huntington Afghan that excels with "delicious kebabs and vegetarian dishes" among other "superb" options; "welcoming" service, an "intimate" dining room and "fun" Friday night belly dancing make it even more of a "bargain."

Kawasaki Japanese Steakhouse *Japanese*   ▽ | 19 | 14 | 19 | $32 |

Long Beach | 22 E. Park Ave. (bet. Edwards & Riverside Blvds.) | 516-889-6699

"Go for the show, but enjoy the food" hint hibachi fans of this Long Beach Japanese where the steak and sushi are "surprisingly delicious";

bear in mind there are "lots of kids" (along with "21-year-olds" downing "super-sized beverages"), which makes for a "noisy" meal.

King Umberto *Italian*

23	15	22	$35

Elmont | 1343 Hempstead Tpke. (Meacham Ave.) | 516-352-3232 | www.kingumberto.com

"They make you feel like you just stepped into *nonna's* kitchen" at this "old established" Elmont Italian where the "sumptuous" dishes, "crunchy-crust pizza" and "nice wine selections" from an "extensive" list are served by an "outstanding" staff whose "advice comes with experience"; "festive" and "crowded" (reservations are recommended), it's a choice place to bring a group and "order lots."

NEW Kiraku *Japanese*

-	-	-	M

Glen Head | 127 Glen Head Rd. (bet. Benjamin & Wall Sts.) | 516-676-3632

This attractive new Japanese restaurant in Glen Head is more atmospheric than most, with a blue light glowing under the sushi bar, and offers the option of tatami booths for group dining; specialties like the multilayered Godzilla roll and miso black cod are standouts, while lunch specials help lure bargain-hunters.

Kiran Palace *Indian*

23	11	20	$24

Hicksville | Delco Plaza | 67-75 E. Old Country Rd. (S. B'way) | 516-932-5191

NEW Commack | Commack Corners | 6092 Jericho Tpke. (Commack Rd.) | 631-462-0003

Selden | Parkhill Plaza | 1230 Middle Country Rd. (bet. Highview & Parkhill Drs.) | 631-716-2400

"Rock solid" Indian cooking that's intensely "hot and spicy" (and features "unique" regional specialties like chicken chettinad) draws a fire-loving following to this "inexpensive" subcontinental trio; though the interiors "don't look like much", a staff that's "eager to be helpful and explain the menu" makes customers feel "like a king and queen."

Kirin Hibachi *Japanese*

▽ 20	16	21	$28

St. James | Shoppes at Green Hills | 556-22 N. Country Rd. (Acorn Rd.) | 631-584-9000

"Popular for parties" and "lots of fun" for kids, this "noisy" St. James Japanese offers "good" if "one-dimensional" hibachi dishes "cooked in front of you", as well as a "nice sushi menu"; it's a bit of a "hole-in-the-wall", but tends to "exceed expectations" for the price.

Kiss'o *Japanese*

22	17	21	$36

New Hyde Park | Lake Success Shopping Ctr. | 1532 Union Tpke. (bet. Lakeville & New Hyde Park Rds.) | 516-355-0587 | www.kisso-sushi.com

Sushi savants say the "melt-in-your-mouth" raw fish at this Japanese "jewel" in New Hyde Park is "so fresh it wiggles"; while the rolls are a bit "standard" for some, and the decor is fairly plain, "low tables" in separate tatami rooms offer a change of pace, and the "courteous" service keeps it a "favorite."

	FOOD	DECOR	SERVICE	COST

⊠ Kitchen A Bistro ⊅ *French* — 28 | - | 23 | $44

St. James | 404 N. Country Rd. (Edgewood Ave.) | 631-862-0151 |
www.kitchenabistro.com

"Phenomenal" fare "continues to astound" at this St. James French
bistro, voted No. 1 for Food on Long Island, where "genius" chef-
owner Eric Lomando "pays attention to detail in every dish",
achieves "poetry" in seafood and changes the menu "at his whim";
it relocated post-Survey to the former Mirabelle space, but is still
quite "intimate", and the no-corkage BYO policy means "you can't
beat the price"; N.B. "make your reservations waaay in advance"
and "bring cash."

NEW Kitchen A Trattoria ⊠ M ⊅ *Italian* — - | - | - | M

St. James | 532 N. Country Rd. (Lake Ave.) | 631-584-3518 |
www.kitchenatrattoria.com

In a bright, open space that seems larger than when its big sister,
Kitchen A Bistro, resided here (it's now located about a mile down
the road), this Italian newcomer in St. James is the latest venture
by renowned chef-owner Eric Lomando, who garnered top food
honors this year for A Bistro; spruced up with new lighting, it remains simple and casual, offering pasta dishes and *secondi* including sea scallops and stuffed roast quail, and the budget-friendly
BYO policy is still in effect; N.B. reservations are taken for Friday-
Saturday nights only.

Koenig's *Continental/German* — 18 | 14 | 19 | $36

Floral Park | 86 S. Tyson Ave. (Mayflower Pl.) | 516-354-2300 |
www.koenigsrestaurant.com

"Rib-sticking goodness" is the specialty of this German-Continental
stalwart in Floral Park, where "favorites like the roast beef sandwich
are what brings people back"; sure, critics call the "old-school" cuisine not for the "diet-conscious", and "in the last 30 years, the only
things that have changed are the tablecloths and the prices", but
most agree "they don't make them like this anymore."

Kohaku *Japanese* — 23 | 12 | 19 | $32

Huntington Station | 2089 New York Ave. (bet. E. 22nd & 23rd Sts.) |
631-351-9888

"Scrumptious sushi" and "authentic" cooked dishes make for a "nice
slice of Japan on the island" at this moderately priced Huntington
Station "standby" with its "own style" when it comes to cuisine;
though the room is "not much to look at" and the service "slow",
fans affirm the "food carries the day."

⊠ Kotobuki M *Japanese* — 27 | 18 | 20 | $40

Roslyn | Harborview Shoppes | 1530 Old Northern Blvd. (Bryant Ave.) |
516-621-5312

Babylon | 86 Deer Park Ave. (Main St.) | 631-321-8387

Hauppauge | 377 Nesconset Hwy. (Hauppauge Rd.) | 631-360-3969

"All hail" the "exceptional", "über-fresh" sushi and other "succulent" dishes offering "amazing value" at this "top" Japanese trio with
a "huge following"; it's generally "impossible to get a table without

a minimum 30-minute wait" (no reservations are taken), the interior is "tight" and service "needs improving", so savvy souls recommend "sit at the sushi bar if you want some peace and quiet."

Kumo Sushi *Japanese*

| 24 | 18 | 20 | $38 |

Plainview | Manetto Hill Mall | 18 Manetto Hill Rd. (Washington Ave.) | 516-681-8881 | www.kumosushi.net

"The crowds tell the story" at this "bustling", "reasonably priced" Japanese "hiding in a little shopping center in Plainview", where the "outstanding" sushi puts it "right up there" with LI's (and "Manhattan's") more established places; while the room, decorated with dark wood and granite accents, can get "noisier than Giants Stadium" and service is sometimes "rushed", fans say it's still "enjoyable to sit at the bar and watch the chefs do their thing."

Kurabarn Ⓜ *Japanese*

| 22 | 18 | 21 | $37 |

Huntington | 479 New York Ave. (bet. High & Hillcrest Sts.) | 631-673-0060 | www.kurabarn.com

"Unpretentious in both food and decor", this "terrific", "affordable" Japanese offers "wonderful" sushi and "well-prepared" "country" cooking in a Huntington house with "low-key", "rustic charm"; as the staff "makes you feel special", reviewers call it a "nice choice to return to" and "feel like family."

Kurofune Ⓢ *Japanese*

| 25 | 15 | 23 | $37 |

Commack | 77 Commack Rd. (1 block south of Jericho Tpke.) | 631-499-1075

This "original Commack sushi restaurant is still going strong", serving "top-grade", "authentic" Japanese specialties in "knowledgeable", "welcoming" style; it's a bit "dated" and "lacks the upscale feel" of some competitors, but the "bang for the buck" keeps it a "weekly favorite."

La Bella Vita Café *Italian*

| ∇ 21 | 16 | 19 | $34 |

East Meadow | 2485 N. Jerusalem Rd. (bet. Sterling & Taft Sts.) | 516-785-8898

"You can see true love coming from the kitchen" purr pleased patrons who appreciate the "solid Italian" menu and "imaginative specials" delivered for a "fair price" at this "half pizza place, half restaurant" in East Meadow; though the digs are "small and noisy", the patio makes it a little more spacious in the summer.

La Bottega *Italian*

| 24 | 14 | 18 | $23 |

Carle Place | 465 Westbury Ave. (Cherry Ln.) | 516-408-3190 Ⓢ
Garden City | 147 Nassau Blvd. (bet. Newmarket Rd. & Stratford Ave.) | 516-486-0935
NEW **Massapequa Park** | 4883 Merrick Rd. (bet. Cartwright & Park Blvds.) | 516-799-4444
Merrick | 2012 Merrick Rd. (Wynsum Ave.) | 516-223-0800
Oceanside | 3216 Long Beach Rd. (Montgomery Ave.) | 516-543-4540

(continued)

(continued)

La Bottega .

Rockville Centre | 234C Merrick Rd. (Village Ave.) | 516-593-4930
www.labottegagourmet.com

Caffe Barocco *Italian*

Garden City | 143 Nassau Blvd. S. (7th St.) | 516-292-0144 |
www.caffebarocco.com

"The ingredients are a step up from the average joint" at this Italian
mini-chain specializing in "must-try" panini ("every kind you can
imagine") and "amazing salads" that "sell like hotcakes"; "laid-
back", "cozy" and a little "crammed", it might "transport you back to
the old country", but plan to "wait" or else "get takeout."

La Bussola *Italian*   23 | 19 | 22 | $51

Glen Cove | 40 School St. (bet. Glen St. & Highland Rd.) | 516-671-2100 |
www.labussolaristorante.com

"A great place to rip off a slice of bread and go dunking", this Glen
Cove Italian (that spun off Piccola Bussola) has been "drawing a
bevy of loyal regulars for years" with its "perfect" pastas and a
"customer-oriented" staff that's "not locked into the menu"; while
the specials can make it "expensive", and the room is "dark" but "not
exactly romantic", most diners deem it a "dependable mainstay."

La Capannina Ⓜ *Italian*   23 | 21 | 20 | $51

Northport | 688 Fort Salonga Rd./Rte. 25A (Ray Pl.) | 631-912-0922 |
www.capanninarestaurant.com

Enthusiasts affirm the "elegant" setting in a "cozy house in Northport"
and a Northern Italian menu that's "traditional without being dull"
set this "sophisticated" "gem" apart; the longtime owner "loves to
visit and chat with patrons", pleasing those who appreciate his "flair
and knowledge", even if a few find the whole package a bit "old hat."

La Coquille *French*   24 | 21 | 23 | $63

Manhasset | 1669 Northern Blvd. (Manhasset Woods Rd.) |
516-365-8422 | www.la-coquille-manhasset.com

Manhasset *amis* give "high marks all around" to this "classic French"
"special-occasion place" that's been "expanded and beautified"
with a "chic ambiance" under new ownership, while maintaining the
same caliber of "distinct", "savory" cuisine with a "presentation on
par with the best in the city", along with "top-notch" service to
"make your evening a real joy"; it's on the "pricey" side, but the
Sunday–Thursday prix fixe makes it a touch more accessible.

La Cuvée Wine Bar & Bistro *French*   ∇ 20 | 18 | 20 | $52

Greenport | Greenporter Hotel | 326 Front St. (4th Ave.) | 631-477-0066 |
www.thegreenporter.com

"A nice surprise" in the retro Greenporter Hotel, this petite, pared-
down French bistro offers "limited" but largely "excellent" bites to
match its "eclectic wine list" highlighting local vintages; though
some cite "uneven" service, the "relaxed atmosphere" appeals –
whether on the deck in summer or by the fire in winter; N.B. weekend
hours vary in the off-season.

La Famiglia ⓜ *Italian*

20 | 15 | 19 | $33

Plainview | 641 Old Country Rd. (bet. Seaford-Oyster Bay Pkwy. & S. Oyster Bay Rd.) | 516-938-2050
Smithtown | 250 W. Main St. (Brooksite Dr.) | 631-382-9454
www.lafamiglia-ny.com

"Doggy bags are guaranteed" at this Smithtown and Plainview duo that's "always a safe bet" for family-style "red-sauce" Italian plates provided by an "accommodating" if sometimes "overwhelmed" staff; "don't take a date" for quiet conversation, but those seeking a meal for "large gatherings" where "sharing is the order of business" (and "kids can run all over") will find a felicitous, "affordable" fit.

La Ginestra *Italian*

24 | 18 | 23 | $54

Glen Cove | 50 Forest Ave. (bet. Elliott Pl. & Walnut Rd.) | 516-674-2244 | www.laginestrarestaurant.com

This upscale "Sicilian mainstay" in a converted Glen Cove house has been "delivering great Southern Italian cuisine for two decades", and the food's a "delight to the eye" as well as "the palate"; further-more, patrons praise the owners as "hands-on", "cordial and wel-coming", and note that though there's "nothing much to see in terms of decor", it's "homey", "civilized" and "perfect for a cold night."

La Gioconda ⓜ *Continental/Italian*

21 | 18 | 23 | $39

Great Neck | 21 N. Station Plaza (bet. Bond & Park Sts.) | 516-466-2004 | www.lagiocondarestaurant.com

"If you want comfort and red sauce", head to this "lovingly run" res-taurant "across the street from the railroad station" in Great Neck for "delicious" Continental–Southern Italian cuisine served up by a "superb" staff and overseen by "owners who really care about their customers"; "small and intimate", it's appreciated by many as an "authentic eatery in an area where the tabs tend to be pricey."

Laguna Grille *Nuevo Latino*

18 | 16 | 18 | $31

Westbury | 1610 Old Country Rd. (bet. Fulton St. & Merrick Ave.) | 516-745-1400
Woodbury | Woodbury Village Shopping Ctr. | 7927 Jericho Tpke. (Southwoods Rd.) | 516-682-8000
www.lagunagrille.com

"Funky fusion" with an "island flair" attracts fans to these modestly priced Westbury and Woodbury Nuevo Latinos that are "known" for their "super salads", "tasty" margaritas and "casual, fun" vibe; "col-orful" and "shopping-mall kitschy", they're "very kid-friendly", so expect the "booster-chair set" to join you for lunch.

ⓩ Lake House ⓜ *American*

27 | 24 | 25 | $61

Bay Shore | 240 W. Main St. (bet. Garner Ln. & Lawrence Ave.) | 631-666-0995 | www.thelakehouserest.com

"Delectable" New American creations by "truly talented" chef/co-owner Matthew Connors are "nothing short of superlative" at this "extraordinary" "find" that "would shine in NYC" but boasts a "tranquil lake setting" in Bay Shore; enthused epicures say a "cock-tail by the fire pit" is a fine way to start, and "first-rate" service keeps

them "delighted" all the way to the "expensive but worth-it" check;
N.B. open for lunch Tuesday–Friday.

La Marmite *French/Italian*   25 | 21 | 24 | $55

Williston Park | 234 Hillside Ave. (bet. Campbell Ave. & Mineola Blvd.) |
516-746-1243 | www.lamarmiterestaurant.com

"Attention to detail" informs both the "excellent" French–Northern
Italian fare and "pampering" service at this "special-occasion" place
in Williston Park that's "withstood the test of time"; the chandelier-
adorned room conveys "quiet elegance", but reviewers recommend it
"could use a little sprucing up" to regain "some of its sheen."

NEW **La Nonna Bella Ristorante** ⑤ *Italian*   – | – | – | M

Garden City | 660 Franklin Ave. (7th St.) | 516-248-0366

In the Garden City space most recently occupied by Taste, this
Italian newcomer offers both a casual bar area and a more formal
dining room with red velvet chairs and banquettes, each with their
own entrances; named for owner and co-chef Anna Maola's grand-
mother, the restaurant gives a nod to its inspiration with dishes like
Nonna's Famous Meatballs, made from a 100-year-old recipe.

La Novella Ristorante Ⓜ *Italian*   ∇ 19 | 12 | 20 | $44

East Meadow | 364 E. Meadow Ave. (Prospect Ave.) | 516-794-6248 |
www.lanovella.com

A small but devoted following "loves this local place" in East Meadow
where "nicely presented", somewhat pricey Northern Italian dishes
are provided by a "staff that goes out of its way" for you; still, some
critics contend it's best for the "faithful whose faces they recognize."

La Pace with Chef Michael Ⓜ *Italian*   24 | 21 | 24 | $61

Glen Cove | 51 Cedar Swamp Rd. (3rd St.) | 516-671-2970 |
www.lapaceglencove.com

"Everything is top-shelf" according to advocates of this Glen Cove
stalwart where chef-owner Michael Mossallam prepares "outstanding Tuscan cuisine" with an "inventive" touch; given the "exceptional" service and "romantic" (if a bit "staid") atmosphere, most
find it a "wonderful dining experience" that justifies the "expense."

La Panchita *Mexican/Spanish*   21 | 16 | 21 | $27

Smithtown | 67 W. Main St. (bet. Karl & Maple Aves.) | 631-360-0627

The "Spanish and Mexican dishes are equally delish" at this "dependable" Smithtown stop for fajitas, paella and "great sangria"
with "no nuevo nonsense"; since the staff is "terrific" and tabs are
"reasonable", few mind the "outdated" decor.

La Parma *Italian*   23 | 15 | 21 | $41

Oceanside | 410 Merrick Rd. (Saratoga St.) | 516-763-1815
Williston Park | 707 Willis Ave. (Henry St.) | 516-294-6610 Ⓜ
Huntington | 452 Jericho Tpke. (bet. Chicory & Sheppard Lns.) |
631-367-6360 Ⓜ
www.laparma.com

"Red sauce is king" and "garlic abounds" at this Italian trio that hits
a "home run every time" with its "humongous", "piled-high" plates

served family-style to "big groups" ("go with at least six people"); sure, it's "crowded and noisy", and the decor comparatively "boring", but the "charismatic" staff ensures everyone can "enjoy" and "*mangia* to their heart's content."

La Parmigiana M *Italian* | 20 | 10 | 17 | $36 |

Southampton | 48 Hampton Rd. (bet. Main & Pine Sts.) | 631-283-8030 | www.laparm.com

"You feel as if nana is still frying the meatballs for Sunday dinner" at this "family-run" Southampton Italian plating up "huge" portions for "sharing" in "very casual" digs; some critics carp that "quantity wins out over quality" and the place "desperately needs at least a coat of paint", but diners still "show up in droves" to tuck into the "affordable" meal; N.B. closed for two weeks in February.

La Piazza *Pizza* | 21 | 14 | 17 | $26 |

Merrick | 2191 Merrick Rd. (bet. Frankel & Lincoln Blvds.) | 516-546-2500
Plainview | Crossroads Shopping Ctr. | 1137 Old Country Rd. (Manetto Hill Rd.) | 516-938-0800
www.lapiazzaonline.com

"Easy on the budget", these Merrick and Plainview Italian joints are "always jumping" with families chowing down on "crunchy"-crust brick-oven pies and a "wide variety of pastas"; even if "jockeying for position" on "long lines" "gets crazy" and the surroundings "lack character", hooked customers "keep coming back for more."

☑ La Piccola Liguria M *Italian* | 26 | 19 | 25 | $60 |

Port Washington | 47 Shore Rd. (bet. Mill Pond & Old Shore Rds.) | 516-767-6490

"Phenomenal" waiters recite an "unending specials list" and "make everything sound wonderful" at this "top culinary stop" in Port Washington offering "expensive" seasonal Northern Italian cuisine "beyond compare"; "charming" and "romantic" if a bit "quaint", it has such a strong following that "reservations are a must" for the "memorable dining experience."

La Pizzetta M *Italian* | 20 | 13 | 19 | $34 |

East Norwich | 1008 Oyster Bay Rd. (bet. Hawthorne Rd. & Northern Blvd.) | 516-624-7800 | www.lapizzetta.net

"Delicious personal pizzas", homemade pasta, "daily specials" and other "solid Italian fare" make this "always packed", "no-reservations" East Norwich eatery a "staple" "for locals"; the "warm", "quick" staff and "reasonable" prices make up for the "plain" decor and "chaotic" atmosphere when "lots of kids" are in-house, plus you can always "take the food to go."

☑ La Plage *Eclectic* | 26 | 18 | 23 | $59 |

Wading River | 131 Creek Rd. (Sound Rd.) | 631-744-9200 | www.laplagerestaurant.net

Guests feel like they've "stumbled onto a secret" at this "laid-back", "rustic" "gem" on the north shore of Wading River, where the "fabulous", "artfully presented" Eclectic fare via chef Wayne Wadington continues to impress; though a handful takes issue with the "cramped" setting and a "beach view that's across a parking lot", most focus on the "inspired" dishes served by an "efficient" staff.

La Primavera *Italian* 23 | 19 | 23 | $52

Hicksville | 294 N. Broadway (16th St.) | 516-938-0220 |
www.laprimaverali.com

"Old-school", "welcoming" service, "comforting" fare (such as "to-die-for" signature duck) and a weekend piano player "keep them coming back" to this unassuming Hicksville Northern Italian; though a few critics call the menu "unexciting" and "pricey" given the modest location, regulars retort the "prix fixe is a steal."

NEW La P'tite Framboise *French* - | - | - | M

Port Washington | 294 Main St. (bet. Bank & Jackson Sts.) | 516-767-7164 |
www.reststarinc.com

The latest venture from the restaurant group behind Bistros Cassis and Citron, this inviting newcomer in Port Washington (replacing Pomodoro by the same team) follows its siblings' format with vintage Parisian photos and a moderate menu studded with French comfort dishes such as coq au vin and bouillabaisse; offering a set special every night, it's reminiscent of a casual, convivial Left Bank bistro.

Lareira *Portuguese* 20 | 14 | 19 | $41

Mineola | 66 E. Jericho Tpke. (Columbus Pkwy.) | 516-248-2004

Loyalists "love" the "authentic", "attractively served" and "reasonably priced" Portuguese fare – including "outstanding bread" to "dip in wonderful sauces" – at this "pleasant" Mineola "keeper" with a "friendly" staff; even if the "dark", "dated" room "needs a face-lift", it's still a "wonderful place to spend the evening"; N.B. checks are 20% off from 5–6 PM weekdays.

La Rotonda *Pizza* 18 | 14 | 17 | $29

Great Neck | 8 Bond St. (bet. Grace Ave. & N. Station Plaza) | 516-466-9596

"Solid" "homestyle Italian", including "delicious brick-oven pizza" and "excellent" entrees, draw Great Neck families to this reasonably priced "neighborhood" eatery; though there's "better-than-average preparation", the fairly "indifferent" service and modest decor are downsides.

La Spada *Italian* ∇ 23 | 18 | 23 | $51

Huntington Station | 315 Walt Whitman Rd. (bet. Old Walt Whitman & Schwab Rd.) | 631-549-3033 | www.laspadarestaurant.com

With "consistently well-executed" cuisine that's "better than you'd expect given its office building location" on Route 110, this Huntington Station Italian specializing in upscale Roman and Sicilian dishes is an "old standby"; "knowledgeable" servers and an "owner who always greets guests" lend it a "warm" feeling, while the burgundy-toned space is "pretty" enough for most diners.

La Strada *Italian* - | - | - | M

Merrick | 2100 Merrick Ave. (bet. Miller Pl. & Smith St.) | 516-867-5488 |
www.lastradaofmerrick.com

In a setting reminiscent of an Italian courtyard, this brick-floored Merrick trattoria is decorated with wrought-iron chairs, gold-sponged

| | FOOD | DECOR | SERVICE | COST |

walls and a village mural near the bar; wood-fired pizzas, pastas and pricier meat and seafood entrees round out the menu, which includes a few options for children too.

NEW La Tavola *Italian* ▽ 24 | 21 | 20 | $43

Sayville | 183 W. Main St. (bet. Greeley & Greene Aves.) | 631-750-6900 | www.latavolasayville.com

The early buzz on this "welcome new addition" to Sayville from the four brothers who run Ruvo includes praise for the "family recipes" that feature "lots of choices for sharing" (creative crostini, cheese and salumi plates, wood-fired pizzas); the rustic country interior boasts hand-hewn wooden tables and mismatched chairs, while daily happy hours tempt with "house specialty cocktails."

La Terrazza Ⓜ *Italian* ▽ 22 | 17 | 21 | $46

Cedarhurst | 142 Spruce St. (bet. Chestnut St. & Willow Ave.) | 516-374-4949

Five Towners feast "often" and with "delight" at this "intimate" Cedarhurst Italian where the "unusually creative" blackboard specials offer plenty to pique curiosity; given the "helpful", "congenial" service, most feel it's "worth" the cost.

Laundry, The *American* 21 | 19 | 19 | $59

East Hampton | 341 Pantigo Rd. (Spring Close Hwy.) | 631-324-3199 | www.thelaundry.com

"Interesting additions to the menu" keep many customers "coming back" to sample chef Andrew Engle's "inventive" New American "comfort fare" at this East Hampton institution; though some diehards miss the "charming" prior location on Race Lane and say it's "losing its touch" with "uneven" service and "premium"-priced cuisine, others warm up to the new setting, noting an "inviting fireplace" in winter and the "airy" garden room come summer.

La Viola *Italian* 21 | 15 | 20 | $41

Cedarhurst | 499 Chestnut St. (bet. Cedarhurst Ave. & Spruce St.) | 516-569-6020 | www.laviolarestaurant.com

Large groups with big appetites appreciate the "family-style" portions of "lovingly prepared" Italian fare served atop "large tables" by the "personable" staff at this "longtime" Cedarhurst "staple"; even if the "tired" "decor needs work", you don't have to "break the bank" for your rigatoni, and there's "always enough left to take home"; P.S. the "special" monthly opera/Broadway night hits a "high note."

La Volpe Ristorante Ⓜ *Italian* ▽ 21 | 22 | 23 | $38

Center Moriches | 611 Montauk Hwy. (Brookfield Ave.) | 631-874-3819 | www.lavolperestaurant.net

An "attentive owner" and a "service-oriented" staff "make you feel like family" at this "highly recommended" Center Moriches Italian with a rustic Tuscan "farmhouse atmosphere" and an "excellent" menu of classics including personal brick-oven pies; monthly wine-tasting dinners and a new attached pizzeria (opened post-Survey) are further reasons many "can't wait to return."

	FOOD	DECOR	SERVICE	COST

Le Chef *Continental/French* | 21 | 16 | 20 | $45 |

Southampton | 75 Jobs Ln. (bet. Main St. & Windmill Ln.) | 631-283-8581 | www.lechefbistro.com

"It's nice to have a place to fall back on" say the "ladies who lunch" at this "charming bistro" in Southampton where you "can always count on" "consistent" French-Continental fare and "welcoming" service; those who feel "cramped" by "tight tables" during the "good-value" nightly prix fixe go "in winter when le crowds are gone"; N.B. a few sidewalk tables are available in warmer weather.

☑ Legal Sea Foods *Seafood* | 20 | 18 | 19 | $42 |

Garden City | Roosevelt Field Mall | 630 Old Country Rd. (bet. Clinton Rd. & Meadowbrook Pkwy.) | 516-248-4600
Huntington Station | Walt Whitman Mall | 160 Walt Whitman Rd. (Weston St.) | 631-271-9777
www.legalseafoods.com

"Always fresh" fish that would "make Neptune proud" is the bait at these "family-friendly" seafood chain links in Garden City and Huntington Station, and though the "straightforward" menus are "not very adventurous", the food's "skillfully prepared"; "midtier" pricing, "can-do" service and that "famous New England clam chowder" make up for "sterile" settings and "off-putting" crowds with "too many kids"; N.B. the menu of "gluten-free choices" is a "godsend" for many.

Legends *Eclectic* | 21 | 18 | 21 | $42 |

New Suffolk | 835 First St. (bet. King & Main Sts.) | 631-734-5123 | www.legends-restaurant.com

Half "lively" pub and half "quiet", "homey little restaurant", this dual destination in the "small seaside village" of New Suffolk has a "loyal following" for the "tons" of "innovative" options on its Eclectic menu, ranging from pad Thai to pulled pork with Moroccan BBQ sauce; there's an "extensive beer menu" too, but watch out for "crowds on weekends and summer nights" when service can turn from "attentive" to "casual."

Lemonleaf Grill *Thai* | 20 | 12 | 18 | $24 |

Carle Place | 227 Old Country Rd. (bet. Glen Cove Rd. & Meadowbrook Pkwy.) | 516-739-3666
Hicksville | Compare Food Shopping Ctr. | 536 S. Broadway (bet. Farm Ln. & Lewis St.) | 516-939-2288 Ⓜ

"Portions are huge" at this Carle Place and Hicksville duo that "promptly" delivers "tasty" fare at "bargain" prices, albeit in "shabby" shopping-center settings; though novices "rarely go wrong at either location" with a menu that's "not too pretentious or too spicy", Thai-fficionados wish they'd "jazz up" the "oddly plain" dishes "for more adventurous" appetites.

☑ Le Soir Ⓜ *French* | 27 | 20 | 24 | $52 |

Bayport | 825 Montauk Hwy. (Bayport Ave.) | 631-472-9090

Devotees are still drawn to this "landmark" Bayport bistro for chef/co-owner Michael Kaziewicz's "impeccable" French dinners, from "homemade soups" to "magnificent desserts, one better than the next"; though some feel the "dimly lit" room "could use a makeover", both the staff and the Sunday–Thursday prix fixe specials are more than "welcoming."

Library Cafe ⏺ *American* | 17 | 20 | 18 | $30 |
Farmingdale | 274 Main St. (Conklin St.) | 516-752-7678 |
www.thelibrarycafe.com
You "won't get shushed" at this "loud" former library turned pub in Farmingdale (sibling of Babylon's Post Office Cafe), complete with "polished hardwood everywhere" and a "wall of booze with a ladder" for accessing it; there's "nothing flashy" about the "standard" American "barroom food", but a crowd still gathers for "ginormous" happy-hour drinks and "watching sports" on multiple TVs.

🆕 Limani *Mediterranean/Seafood* | – | – | – | VE |
Roslyn | 1043 Northern Blvd. (bet. Middle Neck Rd. & Port Washington Blvd.) | 516-869-8989 | www.limaniny.com
Theatrical and grand, this Mediterranean newcomer in Roslyn (from the team behind Manhattan's Estiatorio Milos) follows the Greek concept of selling fish by the pound and allowing guests to make their selection from a huge iced display; tall ceilings, teak floors, mosaic tile and touches of marble all contribute to the high-end atmosphere, while a glass-enclosed floor-to-ceiling wine display separates private parties from the main dining room.

Livorno Ⓜ *Italian* | ▽ 19 | 14 | 18 | $40 |
Port Washington | 95-97 Manorhaven Blvd. (Edgewood Rd.) | 516-944-2730
Still a secret to those who haven't journeyed "off the beaten path" to the Manorhaven section of Port Washington, this "cool local place" turns out "delicious" Sicilian and Northern Italian dishes (try the signature stuffed pork chop) in a bright room with fresh flowers, French doors and chandeliers; "friendly, relaxed" service and an outdoor brick courtyard for alfresco dining are further draws.

LL Dent Ⓜ *Southern* | 21 | 14 | 22 | $29 |
Carle Place | 221 Old Country Rd. (bet. Glen Cove Rd. & Meadowbrook Pkwy.) | 516-742-0940 | www.lldent.com
"Stick-to-your ribs" "Southern food and plenty of it" "hits the spot" at this "down-home" family-owned Carle Place strip-mall joint that racks up points for the "genuine" fried chicken and catfish, "exceptional corn muffins" and "scrumptious" desserts; the "welcoming" staff – including a chef who "hangs out cracking jokes with guests" – puts its "heart into everything", except the "drab" decor.

Lobster Inn *Seafood* | 18 | 13 | 17 | $43 |
Southampton | 162 Inlet Rd. (Sunrise Hwy.) | 631-283-1525
"Bring your bib and cholesterol pills" to Southampton's "no-fuss, no-flair" fried-fish standby where "reasonably priced" "lobster, lobster, lobster" delivered by an "energetic" staff trumps the "dated" "'70s"-style, barn-sized space overlooking Cold Spring Pond; even if claw-

crackers cry it could be "so much more", seasiders sitting on the "lovely" outdoor deck" sigh "what could be better?"

Lobster Roll *Seafood* | 20 | 13 | 17 | $33 |

Amagansett | 1980 Montauk Hwy. (on Napeague Stretch) | 631-267-3740
Baiting Hollow | 3225 Sound Ave. (Roanoke Ave.) | 631-369-3039
www.lobsterroll.com

Popularly known as 'Lunch' for its "iconic" sign, this Amagansett "legend" in an "old house converted with love" (there's also a newer sibling in Baiting Hollow) offers "glorious" namesake rolls, "pleasing puffers" and chowders boasting the "briny taste of the sea"; citing "off-the-wall" prices for "shrinking portions" and so-so service, however, protesters proclaim it's "living on its history"; N.B. the Amagansett branch is closed November–May, while Baiting Hollow stays open Friday–Sunday in the off-season.

Lodge Bar & Grill, The *Steak* | 19 | 18 | 20 | $50 |

East Hampton | 31 Race Ln. (bet. Gingerbread Ln. & Railroad Ave.) | 631-324-5022

Carnivores claim the bone-in rib-eyes and filet mignon "sometimes reach greatness" at this "friendly" East Hampton steakhouse in a Norman Jaffe–designed space from the folks behind nearby Bamboo; while the "beautiful" ski lodge-style interior with a "cozy fireplace" and long brass bar – as well as the Sunday buffet brunch and prix fixe specials – earn praise, ranchhands rankled by the "overbearing bar scene" and "inconsistent" fare find "room for improvement."

NEW Lola's Kitchen & Wine Bar *American* | – | – | – | M |

Long Beach | 180 W. Park Ave. (Magnolia Blvd.) | 516-431-0044
Vintage neighborhood photos lend a homey feel to this Long Beach newcomer, while natural wicker armchairs and leather sofas in the lounge area encourage guests to relax and stay awhile; highlights on the New American menu include pork osso buco and coconut-crusted St. Peter's fish, not to mention the nightly prix fixe for $20.09.

Lombardi's on the Sound *Italian* | 22 | 24 | 20 | $49 |

Port Jefferson | Port Jefferson Country Club | 44 Fairway Dr. (Village Beach Rd.) | 631-473-1440 |
www.lombardisonthesound.com

With "a view of Long Island Sound like no other" and "delectable" Italian dishes with "plenty of flavor", "there's no place" like this "pricey" Port Jefferson waterfronter run by the same family behind the attached country club and Mamma Lombardi's in Holbrook; expect "generous portions", "warm" service, an "excellent bar crowd" and "stunning sunsets", especially from the outdoor deck, but remember to turn on the GPS because "it's kind of hard to find"; P.S. there's an "extensive" Sunday brunch buffet.

Long River *Pan-Asian* | ∇ 18 | 15 | 17 | $22 |

Kings Park | 4 Main St. (Indian Head Rd.) | 631-544-4666
"Flavorful" Chinese "comfort food", along with Indonesian dishes, have made this Kings Park Pan-Asian a "consistent" option for 10

years; flanked by gold lions at the entrance, the surroundings could use some "sprucing up" and so could the "spotty" service, but the location near the LIRR station means it's an easy "take-out" option.

Los Compadres *Mexican* ▽ 22 | 6 | 17 | $17

Huntington Station | 243 Old Walt Whitman Rd. (bet. Chichester Rd. & Livingston St.) | 631-351-8384

They have "Mexican down pat" admit amigos of this "cheap and tasty" family-run "joint" in Huntington Station where the "guacamole is fresh", the "chimichangas among the best" and the "cordial staff" is "welcoming"; if the downscale surroundings "distract from the meal", you can always take it "to go" and have enough "cash left over for another meal."

Lotus East *Chinese* 20 | 14 | 19 | $28

Mount Sinai | 331 Rte. 25A (Rte. 347) | Mt. Sinai | 631-331-6688
St. James | 416 N. Country Rd. (bet. Clinton & Edgewood Aves.) | 631-862-6030

It's a bit like "riding a time machine" when you visit these "affordable" Mt. Sinai and St. James twins where "nothing changes, but nothing has to" say fans of the "consistent" Chinese fare "circa 1970"; still, others assert the "stale decor" hasn't stood the test of time.

Louie's Oyster Bar & Grill *Seafood* 16 | 19 | 17 | $45

Port Washington | 395 Main St. (Prospect St.) | 516-883-4242 | www.louiesoysterbarandgrille.com

Afishionados flip over the "views" of Manhasset Bay, "especially at sunset", from this Port Washington seafooder with a "nautical" interior, a "fantastic" waterside deck and a "happening" bar scene; but a critical crowd, finding "unexciting" food at "lofty prices" along with "rushed" service, says "skip the meal" and "go for drinks" only; N.B. an early-bird menu is offered weekdays from 4–6 PM.

Love Lane Kitchen *American* 22 | 14 | 18 | $33

Mattituck | 240 Love Ln. (bet. Main Rd./Rte. 25 & Pike St.) | 631-298-8989 | www.lovelanekitchen.com

An "amazing" New American menu that changes weekly depending on available "local ingredients" is matched by an "intriguing selection of wines and beers" and "impressive" house-roasted coffee at this "tucked-away" Mattituck "find" for breakfast, lunch or dinner; a "simple" setting with tables hewn from old barn wood, "low-key" (though sometimes "hit-or-miss") service and "bargain prices" complete the package.

Lucé *Italian* ▽ 24 | 25 | 22 | $62

East Norwich | 1053 Oyster Bay Rd. (bet. Johnson Ct. & Northern Blvd.) | 516-624-8330

Formerly Café Girasole, this East Norwich Italian reopened in 2008 under chef-owner Dino Vlacich (who also ran Roslyn's Mio, currently closed due to a fire) with more elegant decor and an "updated menu"; say *arrivederci* to the open kitchen and sunflower motif, and *buon giorno* to subtle earth tones and dishes such as potato-wrapped halibut and grilled veal paillard with mushroom risotto – just be prepared for a *molto* "pricey" check.

Lucy's Café & Bistro Ⓜ *American*
23 | 16 | 20 | $33

Babylon | 135 Deer Park Ave. (James St.) | 631-669-1640 | www.lucysbistro.com

"Don't spread the good news" about this "hidden treasure" in Babylon Village plead possessive patrons who want the "innovative" New American menu, including "wonderful small plates" (check out the Wednesday night tapas-and-wine special), all to themselves; even though there's "average" service and a "cramped" space, they're outweighed by the "interesting" dishes; N.B. open for dinner and late-night drinks Wednesday–Saturday, and for brunch on the weekends.

Ludlow Bistro Ⓜ *American*
23 | 20 | 23 | $45

Deer Park | 1945 Deer Park Ave. (Schwartz Pl.) | 631-667-9595 | www.ludlowbistro.com

"You can tell the chef cares" at this "trendy" Deer Park New American where the "fabulous", "inventive" dishes, "seasoned to perfection" and served by a staff "determined to exceed expectations", have quickly made it a "favorite"; even if it seems "lost in the middle of nowhere" and the fiercely orange decor can be "disconcerting", you'll "get past it" given the personable owner who "walks around as if he were one of the bus boys."

Luigi Q Ⓢ *Italian*
22 | 18 | 21 | $57

Hicksville | 400B S. Oyster Bay Rd. (Woodbury Rd.) | 516-932-7450

"Obvious pride" goes into the "authentic" dishes – from the "succulent chicken scapariello" to the "imaginatively prepared fish" – on chef-owner Luigi Quarta's menu at this "cozy" Hickville Italian; the "gracious service" "makes everything run smoothly", but dollar-watchers deem it "too expensive for the area."

🆕 Luso *Portuguese*
- | - | - | E

Smithtown | 101 E. Main St. (bet. Bellemeade & Landing Aves.) | 631-406-6820 | www.lusorestaurant.com

Portuguese wood-char barbecue takes the stage at this new Smithtown meatery featuring an all-you-can-eat rodizio menu as well as less expensive à la carte choices including seafood, sides and soups; the space is bright and welcoming, enlivened by gold walls and red accents.

Mac's Steakhouse *Steak*
22 | 23 | 21 | $65

Huntington | 12 Gerard St. (bet. New York & Stewart Aves.) | 631-549-5300 | www.macssteakhouse.com

"From the T-bone to the filet mignon", "they don't miss a beat" at this Huntington steakhouse that beef eaters say has "improved dramatically since new owners took over" last year; the "classy", mahogany-accented surroundings – including 10-ft., century-old carved wooden entrance doors and a 1,200-bottle, glass-walled wine cellar – remain, complemented by a "knowledgeable" staff, a "wonderful" expanded menu and "great" live music most nights; N.B. wine-tasting dinners and two-for-one ladies' nights are held frequently.

Madame Tong's at the JL Beach Club Ⓜ *Chinese/Japanese*

▽ 12 | 19 | 10 | $58

Southampton | 256 Elm St. (bet. Powell Ave. & Pulaski St.) | 631-204-0300 | www.madametongs.com

"Drinks under the stars" on the "rockin'" patio are the main attraction of this "hyped" Southampton hang (and JLX Bistro sib), but "subpar", "overpriced" Chinese and Japanese eats set down by "snobby" servers get reviewers riled up; still, with some of the "best eye candy in the Hamptons", sugar freaks ask "who cares about the food?"

Maguire's *American*

18 | 19 | 18 | $44

Fire Island | 1 Bay Walk (Ocean Rd.) | 631-583-8800 | www.maguiresbayfrontrestaurant.com

The "spectacular" waterfront location of this septuagenarian seasonal New American in Ocean Beach sets it apart from its Fire Island peers; maybe it's the "magnificent sunsets", the "cheery" crowd and the "always flowing drinks" that make the "so-so food" "taste better", but some things "shouldn't change" and most agree this is one of them; N.B. the $42-per-person 'Taste of Fire Island', including parking, roundtrip ferry from Bayshore and three-course dinner, is a summertime treat.

Maikhana Lounge Ⓜ *Indian* (fka Dhaba Indian Cuisine)

- | - | - | M

Jericho | 4400 Jericho Tpke. (Old Jericho Tpke.) | 516-938-3300 | www.cotillioncaterers.com

Curry connoisseurs enthuse that this Jericho Indian (formerly Dhaba) offers "authentic", "tasty" eats that are "among the least expensive" in the area; the "kind of odd" decorations may not be for everyone, but the "friendly" staff ("very nice to kids") and more than "tolerable" noise level keep it comfortable.

Majors Steak House *Steak*

17 | 14 | 18 | $39

East Meadow | 284 E. Meadow Ave. (Fairhaven Rd.) | 516-794-6600

Woodbury | 8289 Jericho Tpke. (bet. Juneau Blvd. & Woodbury Rd.) | 516-367-7300

"Stick with the burger, fries" and a microbrew and "you'll leave happy" from these "low-cost" East Meadow and Woodbury steakhouses that some joke should be called "Minors" given the "tough" cuts that are "closer to Outback than Luger's"; ok for "families" seeking "a quick bite" in a "noisy", "crowded" setting "without a lot of decor", they're "not worth the pennies saved" for true carne-seurs.

Mama's *Italian*

22 | 16 | 20 | $28

Centereach | Centereach Mall | 605 Middle Country Rd. (Holbrook Rd.) | 631-585-1498

Holbrook | 1057 Main St. (bet. Furrows Rd. & Railroad Ave.) | 631-981-6262

(continued)

(continued)

Mama's

Oakdale | LaSalle Commons | 587 Montauk Hwy. (Dale Dr.) |
631-589-9640
www.theoriginalmamas.com

Hungry "crowds of friends" "wait on lines" "out the doors" of this "affordable", "friendly" Italian trio, saying "you gotta love the portions" of *molto bene* fare (including pizza, pasta and heros) that are "generous" enough to feed the "whole family"; a few find the simple, red-brick decor "not the best" (there's "always take-out"), but the Centereach and Oakdale branches host a $13.95 prix fixe every Wednesday.

Mamma Lombardi's *Italian*

23 | 18 | 20 | $40

Holbrook | 400 Furrows Rd. (Patchogue-Holbrook Rd.) | 631-737-0774 |
www.mammalombardis.com

It's "Sicily all the way" at this Holbrook "hometown favorite" where "overwhelming portions" – "no one leaves without a doggy bag" – of "delicious" Southern Italian" served family-style by "attentive servers" "make mamma proud"; a few faultfinders fume about "arrogant" staffers, "dated decor" and "lines that could drive you away" (they don't take reservations), but it's "still a Long Island staple"; N.B. the same family also runs the nearby gourmet food market as well as Port Jefferson's Lombardi's on the Sound.

Mangia Mangia Ⓜ *Italian*

19 | 18 | 18 | $39

Patchogue | 69 E. Main St. (bet. Maple & N. Ocean Aves.) |
631-475-4774 | www.mangiamangianow.com

With "easy access to the theater", this "eclectic" family-run Italian "provides a much-needed upscale restaurant" on Patchogue's Main Street say regulars who relax in the "calming" ambiance complemented by "smart" servers who "don't rush you"; even if there are "no eye-raising flavors here", many leave "deeply satisfied"; N.B. the owners have operated the nearby Delfiore pork store for almost 40 years.

Mangiamo *Italian*

▽ 21 | 18 | 20 | $37

Huntington | 15 New St. (bet. Carver & Main Sts.) | 631-421-4600 |
www.mangiamo-ny.com

The "huge" plates of "excellent" crowd-pleasers – gnocchi bolognese, rigatoni carbonara, veal saltimbocca – are "better than mom used to make" at this "laid-back" Huntington family-style Italian where "every guest feels like a regular"; the "spacious" room features photographs of golden-age film stars and TVs "playing old black-and-white movies", but couples say the prices and portions mean it's "only worthwhile if you're feeding a throng of hungry eighth-graders."

Manucci's *Italian/Pizza*

▽ 19 | - | 20 | $37

Montauk | Kenny's Tipperary Inn | 432 W. Lake Dr. (Flamingo Ave.) |
631-668-4455 | www.manuccis.com

Reopening post-Survey at Kenny's Tipperary Inn, this Montauk red-saucer is adding brick-oven pizza to its "dependable" if fairly "run-of-the-mill" Italian menu, and is now decked out with a fireplace too; expect the same "fast, courteous" staff and "best-buy" Monday night pasta specials – a "favorite" year-round.

Marcia's Kitchen ⓜ *Brazilian* ▽ 21 | 11 | 18 | $26

Huntington | 10 New St. (bet. Carver & Main Sts.) | 631-351-1010

"What a deal" hail hungry Huntington hordes who head to this "delightful", "eager-to-please" Brazilian "carnivore's delight", where the $29.95 "all-you-can-eat" option includes a "never-ending parade" of "delicious" "grilled and rotisseried beef, pork and chicken" and the "pay-by-weight" traditional buffet offers "so many choices"; just "be prepared to wait" for a table in the "tight", "informal" space.

𝗡𝗘𝗪 Mare Luna *Eclectic* ▽ 24 | 21 | 24 | $47

Huntington | 24 Clinton Ave. (bet. Gerard & Main Sts.) | 631-812-0083

With "consistently superior", "elegantly presented" entrees, including a "fabulous" signature tilapia, this new "cute" and "cozy" Huntington Eclectic is "already a favorite" judging by the "jam-packed" dining room; "personal" service, buttressed by a "warm" host who "visits every table", further elevates the experience.

Mario *Italian* 25 | 21 | 24 | $48

Hauppauge | 644 Vanderbilt Motor Pkwy. (bet. Marcus Blvd. & Washington Ave.) | 631-273-9407 | www.restaurantmario.com

"Please don't ever change" plead patrons of this "classic" Hauppauge Northern Italian that "never misses a beat, even after all these years"; "superb" dishes "presented with class", a "wonderful" staff ("willing to alter the recipe to your taste") and "fair prices" make it a "favorite haunt", so even if the decor is "a little stodgy", overall it's "a step above most."

🄳 Maroni Cuisine 🆇🅼⊉ *Eclectic/Italian* 28 | 16 | 25 | $97

Northport | 18 Woodbine Ave. (bet. Main St. & Scudder Ave.) | 631-757-4500 | www.maronicuisine.com

"Prepared to exquisite standards" by "one-of-a-kind" chef-owner Michael Maroni, the "incredible" Eclectic-Italian tasting menu "has to be eaten to be believed" at this Northport destination requiring "reservations exactly a month in advance" for an "absolutely glorious experience"; despite an "oddly casual" interior with "close quarters" and "classic rock music" playing, it feels "close to the best cocktail party ever" – "you'll leave stuffed and satisfied and not care about what you spent", so "sit back and enjoy the ride"; P.S. also "bring lots of cash" and remember to "take home some meatballs in a pot."

Massa's ⓜ *Pizza* 25 | 10 | 19 | $23

Huntington Station | 146 W. Jericho Tpke. (bet. Collins Pl. & Pine Tree Rd.) | 631-935-0200

It's lucky that such "out-of-this-world", "Brooklyn-style" thin-crust pies emerge from the coal ovens of this Huntington Station pizza joint, since the "shabby" interior with "only a few tables" and the sometimes "harried" staff aren't exactly winning awards; just focus on the budget-friendly offerings and you'll be happily "surprised"; N.B. a recent chef-owner change may not be reflected in the Food score.

Matsulin *Pan-Asian*

22 | 15 | 19 | $41

Hampton Bays | 131 W. Montauk Hwy. (Springville Rd.) | 631-728-8838

A "unique" Pan-Asian menu featuring "excellent" sushi and an "interesting variety" of Chinese, Malaysian and Thai dishes sets this Hampton Bays "sleeper" apart; service by a "personable" crew eases the "austere" feel of the dining room inside a former bank building.

Matsuya *Pan-Asian*

▽ 22 | 19 | 22 | $34

Great Neck | Gardens Mall | 6 Great Neck Rd. (bet. Brompton & Middle Neck Rds.) | 516-773-4411 | www.matsuyasushi.com

Surveyors savor the "imaginative" fusion fare, from Thai spring rolls to chicken katsu to "excellent sushi prepared with style", at this Great Neck Pan-Asian; the "accommodating" staff, huge tropical fish tank that "keeps kids occupied" and prices running "below most North Shore" eateries ensure a healthy family turnout.

❷ Matteo's *Italian*

23 | 16 | 20 | $45

Bellmore | 416 Bedford Ave. (Wilson Ave.) | 516-409-1779
Long Beach | 777 W. Beech St. (New York Ave.) | 516-432-8101
Roslyn Heights | 88 Mineola Ave. (bet. Elm & Willow Sts.) | 516-484-0555
Huntington Station | 300 W. Jericho Tpke. (West Hills Rd.) | 631-421-6001 Ⓜ

"Don't bother if you don't like garlic" warn regulars of this "always busy", "old reliable" quartet serving "family-style" portions of "hearty" "Italian soul food"; while you'll often find "amazing", "reasonably priced" dishes and waiters you can "trust to guide you", some picky *paesani* are put off by "long waits" amid "noisy", "zoolike" environs.

Matthew's *Seafood*

▽ 17 | 16 | 18 | $44

Fire Island | 935 Bay Walk (bet. Evergreen & Surfview Walks) | 631-583-8016 | www.matthewsseafood.com

"Serving reliable if not always inventive" fin fare, this Ocean Beach seasonal seafooder is the "go-to" place for Fire Islanders seeking a "breathtaking view of the bay" along with their catch of the day; though dining alfresco gives you that "vacation feeling", the interior needs "updating" and the staff should make "a little more effort"; P.S. the attached market has "fabulous fresh fish."

Matto *Italian*

17 | 16 | 15 | $47

East Hampton | 104 N. Main St. (Cedar St.) | 631-329-0200 | www.mattorestaurant.com

The "casual" setting of this seasonal East Hampton Italian – complete with a zinc-topped bar, pinewood floors and a "pleasant patio" for "people-watching" – is part of the appeal for those who also find "very good homemade pastas" and pizza here; but a sizable portion of patrons is peeved by "indifferent" service and "unimaginative" fare that often "falls short"; N.B. the Food score does not reflect a post-Survey chef change.

Maureen & Daughters' Kitchen ⊄ American | 25 | 19 | 22 | $20

Smithtown | 108 Terry Rd. (Larsen Ave.) | 631-360-9227

The daytime herds who graze on "fabulous varieties" of pancakes, "superb" French toast and oatmeal that's like a "fresh-baked cookie" in a bowl say "no one does a better breakfast" than the folks behind this Smithtown "landmark" set in a Victorian house with a wrap-around porch; the "whimsical" cow motif is "moo-velous" and the service "excellent" "no matter how busy" it gets, but try to go on "off hours" to avoid the "daunting waits"; P.S. lunch features "creative sandwiches served with a pile of homemade potato salad."

Maxxels American/Eclectic | 24 | 21 | 22 | $49

Mineola | Gensel Shopping Ctr. | 526 Jericho Tpke. (bet. Herricks & Wardwell Rds.) | 516-294-3604 | www.maxxels.com

"Outstanding", "imaginative" dishes on a "menu that departs from the ordinary" earns an ardent following for this New American–Eclectic that provides "a little bit of Manhattan in Mineola"; the "intimate atmosphere" (backlit bar, banquettes and whimsical food-related photos) and "gracious" service make it "superior" all around, even if you have to venture into a "strip mall" to get there.

Mediterranean Grill-Kebab Mediterranean | ▽ 19 | 10 | 18 | $27

Hewlett | 10-12 Franklin Ave. (bet. B'way & E. B'way) | 516-374-4203

The "satisfying" Mediterranean food – "authentic" kebabs, Greek salads and the "best whole fish" – at prices "you can't beat" makes this "casual" Hewlett nook a "decent" option for a "quick lunch"; but given the drab setting and a staff that's more "well-intentioned" than "efficient", most advise "don't eat in unless you have to."

Mediterranean Snack Bar ⊄ Greek/Mediterranean | 23 | 9 | 18 | $26

Huntington | 360 New York Ave. (bet. E. Carver & Elm Sts.) | 631-423-8982 | www.medsnackbar.com

If you "get past the lack of ambiance", this "tiny", "reliable" 34-year-old Huntington mainstay comes through with "dependable", "always delish" Med fare, from the "best gyros" and Greek salads to owner Steve Soulellis' "fresh" "catch of the day"; "fair prices", "quick service" and "large portions" ensure there's "always a line" (takeout is an option).

Meeting House, The American | 18 | 18 | 17 | $43

Amagansett | Amagansett Sq. | 4 Amagansett Square Dr. (Montauk Hwy.) | 631-267-2764

"Check your attitude at the door" of this "family-friendly" Amagansett Square American that's filled with a "noisy, upbeat crowd" enjoying "hearty" pub-style "comfort fare" like mac 'n' cheese and meatloaf; it's "nothing fancy" and the "waits are long", but the "personable service" and "lively" bar are pluses.

Melting Pot *Fondue*

18 | 21 | 20 | $49

Farmingdale | 2377 Broadhollow Rd./Rte. 110 (Smith St.) | 631-752-4242 | www.meltingpot.com

"Change-of-pace" mavens and "do-it-yourself" types are fond of this "novel" fondue franchise in Farmingdale for its "interactive" approach, i.e. the chance to "cook your own dinner"; the differently sized "romantic" rooms and "long, slow meals" make it appropriate for "first dates" or "large crowds", and while the morsels are "tasty" ("stick to the cheese and chocolate" say some), you'll "end up spending a lot of money" for them.

NEW Mercato

\- | - | - | M

Kitchen & Cocktails *Italian*

Massapequa Park | Southgate Shopping Ctr. | 4958 Merrick Rd. (Whitewood Dr.) | 516-308-3582 | www.mercatokitchen.com

Affordable and affable, this new casual American-Italian in the Southgate Shopping Center in Massapequa Park eschews typical red-sauce fare (there's no parm on the menu) in favor of specialties like chicken bruschetta, filet Madeira and a Gorgonzola wedge salad; the festive space is adorned with a red tooled leather wall behind the polished cement bar, where bartenders whip up Italian- and Latin-accented cocktails.

Meritage *American/Pan-Asian*

23 | 21 | 20 | $53

Bellport | 14 Station Rd. (S. Country Rd.) | 631-286-3300

The "creative" menu at this Bellport crowd-pleaser is nothing if not diverse, offering "excellent" New American and Pan-Asian options, "surprising specials" and a new sushi bar; the "romantic" setting in a 1930s-era post office with pressed-tin ceilings and outdoor seating, along with "attentive" service, puts it "at the top of the list" for pre- or post-theater dining.

Meson Iberia *Continental/Spanish*

21 | 15 | 23 | $34

Island Park | 4335 Austin Blvd. (bet. Kingston Blvd. & Sagamore Rd.) | 516-897-4911

"Exemplary service" from a staff that "tends to your every need" makes the "traditional" fare at this family-run Spanish-Continental in Island Park that much more "delicious" say fans of the "must-have" paella and "awesome" sangria; even if faultfinders feel some dishes are "better than others" and the surroundings "need updating", most have a "pleasant" experience.

Michael Anthony's Food Bar *Eclectic*

▽ 23 | 14 | 23 | $52

Wading River | 2925 N. Wading River Rd. (bet. Hulse Ave. & Hulse Landing Rd.) | 631-929-8800 | www.michaelanthonysrestaurant.com

The "exuberant" namesake chef "greets diners with the night's specials" at this "creative" Eclectic Wading River transplant from Shelter Island that converts call "one of Long Island's best-kept secrets"; given the "fabulous", "well-presented and -served" dishes, and "no corkage fee when you BYO Long Island wines", most overlook the "amateurish" Tuscan-style decor; N.B. closed Tuesdays.

RESTAURANTS

	FOOD	DECOR	SERVICE	COST

Michaels' at Maidstone Beach *American*   18 | 15 | 20 | $45

East Hampton | 28 Maidstone Park Rd. (off Three Mile Harbor Rd.) |
631-324-0725

Take a long, winding drive down Three Mile Harbor Road to this
"low-key" East Hampton "locals' spot" for "reasonably priced",
"hearty" American offerings, such as roasted LI duck and grilled
rack of lamb; though the "dark", antiques-accented space strikes
some as "dreary" and others say the "new management hasn't improved" things, the "relaxed", "unpretentious" service is a refreshing change of pace; N.B. closed Monday–Tuesday in the winter.

Midori *Japanese*   23 | 20 | 19 | $38

Hewlett | 1483 Broadway (Yale Ave.) | 516-295-5494
Oyster Bay | Pine Hollow Shopping Ctr. | 269 Pine Hollow Rd.
(bet. Peerless & Pine Drs.) | 516-922-8070 Ⓜ
www.midorisushi.com

Fin-atics find a fix at these "underappreciated" sushi sibs in Oyster
Bay and Hewlett where the "beautifully prepared" combinations are
"always fresh"; but a few frown upon "slightly overpriced" fare,
"spotty" service and decor that "lacks ambiance" (at the Pine Hollow
location), recommending the "prettier" Broadway locale.

Milk & Sugar Café *American*   20 | 22 | 18 | $32

Bay Shore | 49 W. Main St. (Park Ave) | 631-969-3655 |
www.milkandsugarcafe.com

Perfect for "lunch with the girls" (or a "bridal shower" brunch) given
the "pretty" "living room atmosphere" and "beautiful couches", this
"adorable" Bay Shore American "awash in a sea of estrogen" ("manly
men beware!") serves breakfast, "casual" dinners and "delicious"
desserts; a "gracious", if sometimes "slow", staff, live weekend jazz
and Monday psychic readings are further pluses, but the "no-
reservations policy" translates to "long waits" at times.

NEW Mill Creek Tavern Ⓜ *Seafood/Steak*   ▽ 23 | 20 | 23 | $44

Bayville | 275 Bayville Ave. (Pine Park Ave.) | 516-628-2000 |
www.millcreekny.com

From the folks behind Mim's, this new "local hot spot" in Bayville is
"getting better by the minute"; with an extensive menu of seafood,
steaks and American fare (the two-pound mussel pots are "worth
waiting for"), a "homey" setting and an owner who "makes you feel
welcome", it's not surprisingly "always packed" – and "loud."

Milleridge Inn *American*   15 | 21 | 19 | $40

Jericho | 585 N. Broadway (bet. Jericho Tpke. & Market St.) |
516-931-2201 | www.milleridge.com

Set in a "charming" 17th-century house with 14 fireplaces and an
adjacent village of Colonial-style shops, this "friendly" Jericho "landmark" is particularly "festive" "during the holidays" when period-
attired carolers stroll the "crowded" dining rooms; although many
find the "mundane", "mass-produced" Traditional American prix
fixe-only menu as "old-fashioned" as the setting ("plating and presentation is not a priority"), there's "no place else like it" to "bring

the grandparents" or mark a "family occasion"; N.B. there's a separate on-site cottage and carriage house for private parties.

Z Mill Pond House *Seafood/Steak*   25 | 24 | 23 | $57

Centerport | 437 E. Main St. (bet. Centershore & Little Neck Rds.) | 631-261-7663

"The Piccolo people do it again" at this Centerport "winner" where the "superb" steak and seafood (including "wonderful" sushi) is complemented by an "attractive" interior and "glorious" terrace seating overlooking Mill Pond; with "fine service" to boot, fans advise "don't wait for a special occasion – it is a special occasion"; P.S. the "bargain" prix fixe lunch may be "one of the best-kept secrets on LI."

Z Mill River Inn *American/Eclectic*   27 | 22 | 26 | $74

Oyster Bay | 160 Mill River Rd. (bet. Glen Cove Oyster Bay Rd. & Lexington Ave.) | 516-922-7768 | www.millriverinn.com

"Now that chef Nick Molfetta is back, order has been restored to the world" cheer champions of his "superb", "seasonally changing" New American–Eclectic menu at this pricey Oyster Bay "jewel box" with a "meticulous" staff; even if it "doesn't look like much from the outside", an interior "fireplace adds to the intimacy" of the "romantic" space, so most save it for "serious celebrations"; P.S. the nightly early-bird special is the "best deal."

Mim's *American*   18 | 16 | 18 | $37

Roslyn Heights | 235 Roslyn Rd. (bet. Jane & Thelma Sts.) | 516-625-7305

Syosset | 33 Berry Hill Rd. (bet. Church St. & Muttontown Eastwoods Rd.) | 516-364-2144

www.mimsny.com

"There's something for everyone" at these Roslyn Heights and Syosset siblings where "solid", "generous portions" of New American eats, lively happy hours and "friendly" servers create "crowd-pleasing" experiences; though some discover "nothing special" to these "high-end diners", dubbing them "jacks of all trades, masters of none", the "reasonable prices" (especially for early birds) are a perk.

Minado *Japanese*   20 | 13 | 14 | $33

Carle Place | 219 Glen Cove Rd. (bet. Old Country Rd. & Westbury Ave.) | 516-294-9541 | www.minado.com

The "extraordinary" "variety" of sushi, plus other seafood, salads and teppanyaki, at this all-you-can-eat Carle Place Japanese buffet is "staggering" say regulars who "go hungry" but "don't leave that way"; though it's "not fancy by any means", the "attentive" staff "constantly refreshes" the selections and families find quite a "kid-friendly" "value" (children are charged based on height).

Minami *Japanese*   ▽ 24 | 19 | 22 | $34

Massapequa | 12 Central Ave. (bet. Grand Ave. & Veterans Blvd.) | 516-799-4799 | www.minamijapaneserestaurant.com

Fin-atics find the "flavors wow the palate" at this "always reliable" Massapequa Japanese serving "otherworldly" sushi and sashimi in a "pleasant", if simple, space featuring mahogany floors and a granite bar; a "friendly staff" that "remembers your preferences" is an added plus for patrons who "never leave disappointed."

NEW Mirabelle Tavern *American*   - | - | - | M

Stony Brook | Three Village Inn | 150 Main St. (Shore Rd.) | 631-751-0555 | www.threevillageinn.com

Transforming the restaurant at the historic Three Village Inn in Stony Brook, the Lessing family has enticed Guy Reuge, chef-owner of Mirabelle in St. James for 25 years, to become chef de cuisine, offering an affordable New American menu featuring small plates, Kobe sliders and classics like fish 'n' chips; while the space's beamed ceilings and romantic fireplaces are reminders of the past, new banquettes lend it a chic touch, while the $26 lunch deal (including a glass of wine) is particularly of-the-moment; N.B. the relocated Mirabelle Restaurant is set to open on the same property in spring 2009.

Z Mirko's M *Eclectic*   26 | 23 | 24 | $71

Water Mill | Water Mill Sq. | 670 Montauk Hwy. (bet. Cobb & Old Mill Rds.) | 631-726-4444

"Masterfully prepared" Eclectic fare with "Eastern European flair" is the hallmark of this "highly recommended" Water Mill eatery where the "warm" "husband-and-wife team doesn't miss a trick"; its "inviting" country interior with a fireplace is always packed (there's also seasonal outdoor seating), but "if you can secure a table", it's worth the "expense"; N.B. closed January to mid-February.

Mitchell's *American*   16 | 12 | 17 | $23

Oceanside | 2756 Long Beach Rd. (Harrison Ave.) | 516-255-9544

Valley Stream | 191 Rockaway Ave. (Jamaica Ave.) | 516-825-9708

www.mitchells-restaurant.com

"Not your average diners", these Valley Stream and Oceanside institutions – under separate ownership with common supervision of menus – go a step beyond, offering "homemade" ice-cream topped with "real hot fudge and whipped cream", fresh-squeezed orangeade and "staple" American items in traditional settings outfitted with stainless steel and chrome; even if impatient diners dis "painfully slow" service and "common" fare, more enjoy them for an "informal" meal.

NEW Mitsui *Japanese*   ∇ 23 | 19 | 19 | $37

Bay Shore | 1 W. Main St. (4th Ave.) | 631-630-9890

"Excellent" and "creative" "city-quality sushi" with a "good choice of rolls" at "reasonable prices" makes this Bay Shore Japanese newcomer a "welcome addition to Main Street"; with dark wood–lined "trendy digs" and "gracious" service", fin fans find it's "more sophisticated" than some of its peers.

Mixing Bowl Eatery M *American*   20 | 19 | 21 | $37

Bellmore | 2601 Merrick Rd. (Centre Ave.) | 516-826-7971

"A big improvement" courtesy of reality TV chef Gordon Ramsay has helped "turn around" this Bellmore New American that now boasts a "pretty" living room–like space with candles, pillows and plush chairs that patrons "love"; the menu's "delicious", "health-conscious choices" and a chef-owner who "personally welcomes guests" help make up for "higher prices."

MoCa Asian Bistro *Pan-Asian*

▽ | 23 | 25 | 21 | $41

Hewlett | 1300 Peninsula Blvd. (bet. Gibson Blvd. & Mill Rd.) | 516-295-8888 | www.mocausagroup.com

With a name that stands for 'Modern Culinary Art', this new Hewlett Pan-Asian boasts a predictably "cool", "high-tech" setting (multicolored neon facade, blue-lighted ceilings, backlit bar) that complements the "tasty", "interesting" fusion fare; a "rare find on Long Island", it's often "jammed on weekends" with "sceney" crowds sipping "expensive" cocktails.

Modern Snack Bar Ⓜ *American*

18 | 10 | 20 | $28

Aquebogue | 628 Main Rd. (bet. Church Ln. & Edgar Ave.) | 631-722-3655 | www.modernsnackbar.com

"Step back in time to a James Dean movie" at this "authentic" Aquebogue "throwback" that's been serving "large portions" of "classic comfort food" in a "homey" East End diner setting for nearly 60 years; the "old-fashioned" ("what are you havin', hon?") service, along with "mouthwatering" "mile-high" pies, "famous mashed turnips" and other "wholesome", affordable American eats, leads to "long lines on weekends."

Montebello *Italian*

22 | 17 | 23 | $38

Port Washington | 14 Haven Ave. (bet. Franklin Ave. & Main St.) | 516-767-7828 | www.montebellorestaurant.com

"After a long day in Manhattan", this Northern Italian near the Port Washington train station is just the place to "kick back, relax" and have a "tasty" meal; "family-size portions" that are easily "shared", "prompt" service and pleasing prices outweigh "unsophisticated" decor that "needs attention."

Ⓩ Morton's The Steakhouse *Steak*

24 | 22 | 23 | $68

Great Neck | 777 Northern Blvd. (Susquehanna Ave.) | 516-498-2950 | www.mortons.com

"Consistency abounds" at this Great Neck branch of the "classic" steakhouse chain pairing "well-prepared" chops that "hang off the plate" with "seriously powerful martinis"; "arm-and-a-leg" pricing comes with the territory, along with a "Saran-wrapped presentation" of raw meats (accompanied by an instructional "recitation" by the waiter) – a "shtick" that many find "tired."

Ⓩ Mosaic ⓈⓂ *American*

26 | 21 | 25 | $56

St. James | 418 N. Country Rd. (Edgewood Ave.) | 631-584-2058 | www.eatmosaic.com

The skilled chefs can "put food together (or take it apart) in ways one would not typically imagine", then "beautifully plate it" and couple it with "inspired wine pairings" at this "wonderful" New American whose nightly tasting menu (with an à la carte option) gives locals "something to get excited about" in "sleepy St. James";

"impeccable" service in an "intimate", pale-green space adorned with black-and-white photos completes the "experience."

Mother Kelly's Restaurant *American/Italian* | 21 | 11 | 19 | $31 |

Cedarhurst | 490 Chestnut St. (bet. Cedarhurst Ave. & Spruce St.) | 516-295-5421 | www.motherkellysli.com

An "old favorite" that's "always bustling", this "family-friendly" Cedarhurst Italian-American makes you feel like you've "gone home for Sunday" dinner; "huge" portions of "hearty" red-sauce fare, "fabulous" salads and "can't-be-beat pizza" are served by a "speedy" staff that honors "special requests", so "what it lacks in ambiance" with its "cafeterialike atmosphere", it makes up for with all the rest; N.B. there's a monthly comedy night every third Friday.

Mt. Fuji *Japanese* | ▽ 19 | 16 | 19 | $36 |

Southampton | 1678 North Hwy. (bet. Greenfield & Shrubland Rds.) | 631-287-1700

Best for a "stop-off" on your way out east, this "simple" Southampton Japanese offers "consistent" affordable sushi and cooked dishes in a "welcoming" setting; sure, it's "not an amazing meal" say visitors who get "frustrated that it's not better", but there's a traditional tatami room and a "lovely staff."

NEW Mumon *Japanese* | - | - | - | E |

Garden City | 1300 Franklin Ave. (bet. 13th & 14th Sts.) | 516-747-3388 | www.mumonrestaurant.com

Its name means 'dream' in Japanese, but you certainly wouldn't want to catch any shut-eye at this striking new Garden City arrival, located off the parking lot behind the Winthrop Wellness Pavilion; the lounge has comfy sofas and a glass-topped bar with red leaves shining underneath, and the dining room, accented with gold and terracotta, is illuminated with cylindrical hanging lanterns; sushi is the focus, but Japanese cooking and cocktails are additional draws.

Musashino *Japanese* | ▽ 17 | 9 | 18 | $32 |

Huntington | 301 Main St. (bet. Green & New Sts.) | 631-425-0777

"Decent" Japanese cuisine, including "one-of-a-kind" rolls, for "significantly less cost" than some competitors keep a "crowd" coming to this modest Huntington longtimer; still, some rate it as "run of the mill", lamenting it's "not the sushi mecca it used to be."

Muse Restaurant & Aquatic Lounge *American* | ▽ 21 | 24 | 22 | $58 |

Water Mill | Water Mill Shoppes | 760 Montauk Hwy. (Station Rd.) | 631-726-2606

Chef Matthew Guiffrida's "tuna creations" stand out among the "delicious", "innovative" New American dishes served at this Water Mill "sleeper"; a "unique" saltwater reef "aquarium bar" where the "fish swim under your drinks" is the highlight of the "intimate" (though "too cute" for some) interior, while "terrific service" further marks it as a way "to beat the stuffy Hamptons crowds"; N.B. closed Monday–Wednesday during the off-season.

	FOOD	DECOR	SERVICE	COST

⊘ Nagahama *Japanese* | 26 | 15 | 21 | $35 |

Long Beach | 169 E. Park Ave. (bet. Long Beach & Riverside Blvds.) | 516-432-6446 | www.nagahamasushi.com

Devotees insist "nothing else compares locally" to chef/co-owner Hide Yamamoto's Long Beach Japanese where "fabulous sushi" is crafted from the "freshest" fish; even "cramped quarters" and "ridiculous waits" don't detract from the allure, as "smiling waitresses" deliver "prompt" service.

Nagashima ⊠ *Japanese* | 22 | 13 | 18 | $39 |

Jericho | Jericho Office & Shopping Plaza | 12A-1 Jericho Tpke. (Brush Hollow Rd.) | 516-338-0022

Offering "a little taste of Tokyo in a shopping center", this Jericho Japanese lures fans of sushi and "well-prepared" hot dishes with its combination of "creative presentations" and "very authentic" fare; while some surveyors find the service "indifferent", the majority maintains that it's a "local place" you "can always count on."

Nanking *Chinese/Thai* | ▽ 19 | 23 | 17 | $35 |

New Hyde Park | 2056 Hillside Ave. (bet. Aster Dr. & Marcus Ave.) | 516-352-0009 | www.nankingrestaurantgroup.com

"Pretty" surroundings featuring red-and-gold silk-covered walls and copper-topped tables set the stage for "flavorful", reasonably priced "Chinese-Thai fusion" fare at this New Hyde Parker (with Manhattan and New Jersey branches) that offers a wide "variety of dishes"; naysayers gripe about sometimes "disappointing service", but most appreciate the "interesting concept."

Nautilus Cafe *Seafood/Steak* | 24 | 16 | 23 | $45 |

Freeport | 46 Woodcleft Ave. (bet. Adams & Front Sts.) | 516-379-2566 | www.nautiluscafe.com

"Superb" steaks and "fresh, properly prepared" fish reel Freeporters into this "Nautical Mile" standout across from a canal; even if the ship-themed room "looks like a diner" to some and is "so small" "reservations are required", the "efficient" staff has all hands on deck, so "get a waterside table and go enjoy"; P.S. "the early-bird is a bargain."

Nello Summertimes ❶ *Italian* | ▽ 18 | 21 | 16 | $109 |

Southampton | Nello Summertimes | 136 Main St. (bet. Hampton Rd. & Post Crossing) | 631-287-5500

Sought out for "stargazing" (LeRoy Neiman portraits sometimes match the faces at the tables), this glitzy seasonal Southamptoner situated in a renovated 17th-century inn offers a "beautiful setting" for outdoor summer dining; still, the "outrageously exorbitant" prices for "hit-or-miss" Northern Italian fare are "downright offensive" to the less-impressed, as is the service.

🆕 New Chilli & Curry Restaurant Ⓜ *Indian* | - | - | - | M |

Hicksville | 106 Woodbury Rd. (bet. Charles & Max Aves.) | 516-932-9180

This newcomer to Hicksville's international dining scene offers a combination of Northern Indian and Indian-style Chinese and Thai dishes, such as crispy whole red snapper in a choice of ginger-garlic or chili sauce; a coppery pressed-tin ceiling and a wall-sized Indian tapestry embroidered with gold threads enhance the tiny space, and a thrifty $7.95 lunch buffet is an additional draw.

New Hyde Park Inn *Continental/German* | 20 | 22 | 22 | $42 |

New Hyde Park | 214 Jericho Tpke. (bet. 2nd & 3rd Sts.) | 516-354-7797 | www.innatnhp.com

"What a turnaround" exclaim Hyde Parkers who liken the "upscale remodeling" of this Continental-German "landmark" to a "Cinderella" transformation; the "vastly improved" fare and "welcoming, professional" staff add further appeal, as does a working fireplace in the dining room.

New Paradise Cafe *American/Eclectic* | 21 | 17 | 20 | $58 |

Sag Harbor | 126 Main St. (bet. Nassau & Spring Sts.) | 631-725-6080

The "inventive" New American–Eclectic menu is "varied enough for the most choosy table" or diner at the copper-top bar of this "delightful" Main Street "mainstay" in Sag Harbor; though a few grouse that it's "overpriced" and "noisy", blissed-out brethren note a "warm", "attentive" staff and a "small deck out back that's a wonderful retreat."

Nicholas James Bistro Ⓜ *American* | 21 | 16 | 21 | $37 |

Merrick | 2057 Merrick Rd. (bet. Hewlett & Merrick Aves.) | 516-546-4805 | www.njbistro.com

This "moderately priced" Merrick New American that serves "well-prepared cosmopolitan" fare is an "always reliable" choice say fans who dub it a "little jewel of a local hangout"; a "friendly staff" and "relaxed atmosphere" help make it "popular for lunch" too.

Nichol's *American* | 18 | 13 | 18 | $37 |

East Hampton | 100 Montauk Hwy. (Cove Hollow Rd.) | 631-324-3939

"Big portions" of American eats – e.g. burgers, pot pie, eggs Benedict – please "locals" and "in-the-know" weekenders at this "relaxed" East Hamptoner where the service "makes you feel at home" whether in the "rustic" publike interior or on the patio; either way, the "price is just right."

NEW Nick & Charley Steak House *Steak* | - | - | - | E |

Williston Park | Herricks Shopping Center | 432 Hillside Ave. (Herricks Rd.) | 516-747-1744

Set in a little Williston Park strip mall, this pricey new Italian steakhouse nevertheless has a notable pedigree in owner Niko Milovcevich and chef Michael Haber (veterans of Peter Luger) and chef Giuseppe Capobianco (ex-chef-owner of Cafe Picasso); large photos of old New York, including shots of the Yankees, adorn the upscale casual setting.

∄ Nick & Toni's *Italian/Mediterranean* | 23 | 21 | 22 | $68 |

East Hampton | 136 N. Main St. (bet. Cedar St. & Miller Terrace) | 631-324-3550 | www.nickandtonis.com

"Inspired" yet "not overly fussy" rustic Italian-Med dishes and wood-fired specialties live up to the "hype and hustle" at this star-studded

East Hampton "staple"; "knowledgeable" servers and surprisingly intimate rooms round out what fans call "one of the best dining experiences in the Hamptons", which explains why the "price almost doesn't matter" and it's so packed that the big question is "how do you get a reservation?"

Nick Diangelo   *Italian/Steak* | 21 | 20 | 20 | $43 |

Long Beach | 152 W. Park Ave. (bet. Magnolia & National Blvds.) | 516-889-3366 | www.georgemartingroup.com

"American steak crossed with hearty Italian" scores a winning combo at this Long Beach link in the George Martin chain where "heaping plates of" pasta, chicken, beef and other dishes make for family-friendly dining; it can be "noisy" and "crowded", especially on weekends, but the "dark-wood" interior and "attentive" staff ease the squeeze.

Nick's   *Pizza* | 23 | 17 | 20 | $28 |

Rockville Centre | 272 Sunrise Hwy. (bet. Morris & Park Aves.) | 516-763-3278 | www.nicksrvc.com

Pie partisans praise the "state-of-the-art thin-crust pizza" that's dished out whole ("no slices offered") at this Rockville Centre Italian (related to the Forest Hills and Manhattan branches) – but "don't ignore" the rest of the menu, or risk missing "mouthwatering pasta", calzones and "incredible" "large-enough-for-two" salads; with a "tin ceiling, old photos on the wall and Sinatra playing", plus "no pretensions", it's all a "casual place" "should be."

Nico at the Mansion ⓜ *Italian* | ▽ 21 | 26 | 22 | $51 |

Islip | 712 Main St. (bet. Rte. 111 & S. Bay Ave.) | 631-581-1900 | www.nicoatthegatsby.com

Some may be "surprised" at the recent transition to an Italian menu at the "beautiful" 130-year-old restored Victorian Gatsby Mansion in Islip (site of the former Gatsby's), but most are happy to find a "magnificent presentation" and "charming" staff; three "well-appointed" dining rooms are "classy all around", making it a contender for "special occasions" as easily as "a drink at the bar and dinner."

Nisen ⓜ *Japanese* | 25 | 18 | 21 | $39 |

Commack | 5032 Jericho Tpke. (Larkfield Rd.) | 631-462-1000 | www.nisensushi.com

"Once you've eaten here, you'll be disappointed in sushi anywhere else" claim roll relishers of the "fabulous fresh and creative" fare at this "intimate" Commack Japanese; even with tables in two private tatami rooms, it's "always jam-packed", but the "considerate" service and "reasonable prices" make the "wait" "worth it."

Ⓩ Nisen Sushi   *Japanese* | 26 | 27 | 22 | $59 |

Woodbury | Woodbury Village Shopping Ctr. | 7967 Jericho Tpke. (Southwoods Rd.) | 516-496-7000 | www.nisensushi.com

"Exquisite" raw and cooked Japanese cuisine sates discriminating diners who "aren't sure which is more mouthwatering, the innovative sushi or the trendy crowd" at this "hip" Woodbury "scene"; yes, it will cost you an "arm and a leg", but the atmosphere delivers "a bit of

	FOOD	DECOR	SERVICE	COST

Manhattan" "chic" – just "make sure you have reservations"; N.B. DJs and live music stir up extra excitement Thursday–Saturday nights.

Noma Ⓜ American

▽ 20 | 20 | 21 | $47

Huntington | 70 Gerard St. (bet. Clinton Ave. & W. Neck Rd.) | 631-923-1570 | www.nomarestaurant.com

"Sophisticated decor" and a "tasty, varied" menu make this Huntington New American a "pleasant surprise" for locals; the "owner always greets you with a warm welcome", but nigglers insist the "little things just aren't right" and "prices are steep", though most concede that the "valet parking is very handy."

Nonnina Ⓜ Italian

24 | 25 | 22 | $54

West Islip | 999 Montauk Hwy. (bet. Gladstone Ave. & Oak Neck Rd.) | 631-321-8717 | www.nonninarestaurant.com

"Wow!" exclaim surveyors who aver you can't miss with this "superb" "modern" Italian in West Islip where "just about everything is first-rate"; while some suggest the staff should "check the attitude", most report "excellent service" in an "elegant" setting with a "relaxing fireplace for a drink before dining" that all completes an "expensive", "wonderful experience."

☒ North Fork Table & Inn American

28 | 25 | 27 | $71

Southold | North Fork Inn | 57225 Main Rd./Rte. 25 (bet. Boisseau & Laurel Aves.) | 631-765-0177 | www.northforktableandinn.com

"A true star in the fork" by NYC expats who "know how to do it", this "sublime" Southolder "lives up to the hype" – and the "expense" – with a "marvelous" New American menu by Gerry Hayden (ex Aureole) showcasing "plentiful local" ingredients with "astonishing twists that work", as well as "irresistible desserts" by Claudia Fleming (ex Gramercy Tavern); set in a "glowing dining room with a country house feel" and tended by a "warm, youthful" and "knowledgeable" staff, it earns the No. 1 score for Service on Long Island; N.B. closed Tuesday–Wednesday in the off-season.

Novitá Wine Bar and Trattoria Italian

23 | 23 | 21 | $47

Garden City | 860 Franklin Ave. (bet. 9th St. & Stewart Ave.) | 516-739-7660 | www.novita-ny.com

It's "heaven for oenophiles" at this "lively" Garden City Italian where an "amazing wine list" and "extensive" selections by the glass (100 choices are preserved in a custom-built unit) pair with "unique" dishes including "zeppoles for dessert"; the "cool contemporary decor" and a "knowledgeable" staff add to the allure, so though it's "a bit pricey", it's a dapper "date spot and a nice place to meet" friends.

NU Restaurant & Lounge Continental

– | – | – | E

Hauppauge | Hyatt Regency Long Island | 1717 Motor Pkwy. (bet. Blydenburgh Rd. & Hoffman Ln.) | 631-784-1234 | www.longisland.hyatt.com

In a sleek setting that features polished brown granite tables and accents of ivory and gold, this lobby dining room in Hauppauge's

	FOOD	DECOR	SERVICE	COST

Hyatt Regency hotel offers Continental fare ranging from steak and fish to barbecue babyback ribs; an affordable wine list and an upscale dessert selection add to the appeal.

Oak Chalet ⓜ *Continental/German* | 20 | 19 | 21 | $37 |

Bellmore | 1940 Bellmore Ave. (bet. Beltagh Ave. & Natta Blvd.) | 516-826-1700 | www.oakchalet.net

"Solid", "reasonably priced" Continental-German "staples" channel "dining the way it was years ago" at this Bellmore "classic" that also boasts "fantastic" "beers on tap"; a staff that "makes sure you are taken care of in the most loving way" and a "cozy, warm, chalet"-like setting with a "roaring fireplace" contribute to the *gemütlichkeit*.

Oakland's *Seafood* | 17 | 21 | 17 | $46 |

Hampton Bays | Dune Rd. (Rd. H, at Shinnecock Inlet) | 631-728-6900 | www.oaklandsrestaurant.com

Those who "like eating at the water's edge" say this Hampton Bays seasonal seafooder with "views of Shinnecock Inlet" and "spectacular sunsets" provides a "consistently" "fabulous" setting that "almost justifies" the "pricey", "uneven" American fare; throw in summertime "college-student servers who try hard, but are sloppy", and some conclude that a "drink at the outdoor bar" or "lunch is the way to go."

Oak Room at Carlyle on the Green *American* | 23 | 25 | 24 | $50 |

Farmingdale | Bethpage State Park | 99 Quaker Meeting House Rd. (Round Swamp Rd.) | 516-501-9700 | www.carlyleonthegreen.net

"Excellent" American fare tees off at this "fine-dining" Farmingdale spot situated beside the Bethpage Black golf course, where the staff makes diners "always feel special" and "beautiful decor" featuring dark-wood paneling, chandeliers and a candle-filled fireplace complements the outdoor scenery; it's all so "lovely", guests ask if you've "got green to dine by the green", "what else do you need?"; N.B. live music Saturday evenings.

Oar Steak & Seafood Grill *Seafood/Steak* | 20 | 18 | 18 | $38 |

Patchogue | Sun Dek Marina | 264 West Ave. (Mulford St.) | 631-654-8266 | www.theoar.com

Whether arriving by land or sea, diners are lured to the "relaxing" waterside dining at this "reasonably priced" Patchogue place serving "good" seafood and steaks in the Sun Dek Marina near the Fire Island ferries; an oar-bedecked room lends a "nautical feel", and live music on the outdoor deck on summer weekends helps make it an even more "friendly" hangout.

Oasis Waterfront Restaurant & Bar ⓜ *American* | 23 | 22 | 21 | $63 |

Sag Harbor | Mill Creek Marina | 3253 Noyac Rd. (Ruggs Path) | 631-725-7110 | www.oasishamptons.com

"Fish dishes reign supreme" at this "unsung" New American "waterside" "gem" outside Sag Harbor at the Mill Creek Marina that has "excellent views" and a "clean, simple" interior; the "accommodating", "conscientious" staff with "no Hamptons attitude" is an "especially welcome gift in August" according to regulars who call it "expensive but worth it."

Oaxaca Mexican Food Treasure *Mexican* | 23 | 11 | 22 | $24 |

Huntington | 385 New York Ave. (bet. Main & W. Carver Sts.) | 631-547-1232

Amigos attest this Huntington "find" dishes out "terrific" Mexican food that's the "real deal", including "unbeatable mole"; so forget the "hole-in-the-wall" "luncheonette atmosphere", because a "cheery staff" that "goes out of its way to satisfy" plus "bang for the buck" make it "a must"; N.B. serves wine and beer only.

NEW Oevo *Italian* | - | - | - | E |

Great Neck | 421 Northern Blvd. (bet. Lakeview & Merrivale Rds.) | 516-504-9690

Wood-fired pizzas and entrees such as a 16-oz. veal chop lure Great Neck diners to this high-end Italian newcomer, an offshoot of Manhattan's Da Ciro; set in the former Brunello space, the redecorated dining room has a contemporary look with an understated beige-and-brown palette.

Olde Speonk Inn *American* | 17 | 14 | 19 | $48 |

Speonk | 190 Montauk Hwy. (bet. Mill & N. Phillips Aves.) | 631-325-8400 | www.theoldespeonkinn.com

"Reliable" American fare spotlighting seafood is served at this historic Speonk roadhouse decorated in country-inn style; "the bar is a great place to have a bite and listen to live music on the weekends", there's a pub room with big screens for sports fans, and while some say overall it's "not exciting, at least it's not the Hamptons scene"; N.B. closed Tuesdays.

Old Mill Inn *American* | 17 | 17 | 17 | $46 |

Mattituck | 5775 W. Mill Rd. (Naugles Rd.) | 631-298-8080 | www.theoldmillinn.net

"If you can find" this New American "hidden" away in an "old-time authentic mill" overlooking Mattituck Inlet, expect an "interesting take on local fare", especially in the seafood specials; service is "hit-or-miss", but the "romantic" decor (with a fireplace by the bar) recalls the interior of an old yacht, plus the deck is "a treat" where summer diners can "watch the boats" cruise by.

Old Stove Pub *Greek* | 18 | 10 | 14 | $61 |

Sagaponack | 3516 Montauk Hwy. (bet. Sagg & Town Line Rds.) | 631-537-3300

"Welcome back" say Hamptonites heralding the revival of this classic steakhouse take on Greek in Sagaponack where chef Colin Ambrose (Estia's Little Kitchen) is at the helm and harking back to the menu of the '70s (at the restaurant's peak); some call the "charming place" "delightfully tacky", though there are grumbles that the staff "needs training" and prices are "high", since offerings apart from the "excellent steaks" are "a little shaky"; N.B. closed Mondays–Wednesdays in the off-season.

	FOOD	DECOR	SERVICE	COST

Olive Oils *Italian*

	-	-	-	I

Point Lookout | 28 Lido Blvd. (Bellmore Ave.) | 516-432-0000
Located in little Point Lookout on the tip of the Long Beach peninsula, this Italian offers a menu including pizzas, panini and pastas in a simple setting of bare wooden tables – plus one that's embedded with colorful shells that was crafted by the owner; summer sidewalk seating is shielded from pedestrians by a border of flower-filled planters.

Oliver Bon Dinant Ⓜ *French*

	25	13	23	$45

Williston Park | 82 Hillside Ave. (bet. Broad St. & Willis Ave.) | 516-747-6337 | www.oliverbondinantrestaurant.com
It's like "stepping into a cafe on the outskirts of Paris" for Francophiles enraptured by the "fantastic", "imaginative" dishes with "big flavors" that are created at this "small" Williston Park "bistro with flair"; the "price is right" and the "delightful owner and his wife" add to the bonhomie, so the "storefront location should not discourage anyone."

O'Mally's ◑ *Pub Food*

	16	13	18	$32

Southold | 44780 North Rd./Rte. 48 (bet. Hortons Ln. & Youngs Ave.) | 631-765-2111
Southold diners dig into "reliable" pub grub at this "family"-friendly joint known for its "wide variety" of midpriced American fare – especially burgers "any way you want" them; the decor is "cozy and relaxing" and the staff is "friendly", but best of all, "late-night hours make it a welcome stop for weekend warriors."

Once Upon a Moose Ⓜ *Sandwiches*

	▽ 19	18	18	$26

Sea Cliff | 304 Sea Cliff Ave. (Central Ave.) | 516-676-9304 | www.onceuponamoose.net
"Delicious homemade sandwiches and desserts" are "prepared with love" at this "adorable", "kitschy brunch and lunch place that's popular with locals" in the "quirky seaside town" of Sea Cliff; in the "quaint" setup, you "eat in the midst of stuff to buy" while being "served by a friendly staff"; N.B. under new owners, a liquor license, extended hours and live entertainment are in the works.

105 Harbor *American*

	20	22	20	$52

Cold Spring Harbor | 105 Harbor Rd. (bet. Flora St. & Terrace Pl.) | 631-367-3166 | www.105harbor.com
"Dazzling" water views from the "delightful" upstairs dining room and a "crackling fire" downstairs in the winter keep customers returning to this "cozy" New American in Cold Spring Harbor, where the "tasty" meals, including a "scrumptious Sunday brunch", are delivered by a "pleasant" staff; though a few feel the "food and prices aren't in sync", they admit that if you "keep looking out the window, you won't notice."

𝗡𝗘𝗪 101 Bar & Grill *American/Seafood*
(fka Jackson Landing)

	20	19	19	$43

Bellmore | 2565 Bellmore Ave. (Public Hwy.) | 516-785-5353 | www.101bargrill.com
"Nestled in a residential area" in Bellmore, this "cute", "lively" eatery – which changed its name from Jackson Landing and introduced some

less expensive menu items post-Survey – provides "well-prepared" New American fare with a seafood focus; some find the quality "amateurish", however, with "sweet" but "hit-or-miss" service.

On 3 *American*

| 24 | 19 | 22 | $56 |

Glen Head | 32 Railroad Ave. (bet. Prospect & School Sts.) | 516-656-3266 | www.on3newyork.com

"Trendy city hot spot meets friendly neighborhood comfort" zone at this adult-centric New American "gem" near the Glen Head train station, where the "excellent", "inventive" fare is "beautifully presented" and the "friendly" chef-owner and staff "aim to please"; nitpickers call it "quite expensive" and nix the "tight seating", but make tracks to the "secluded" "outdoor garden" for summer dining.

Onzon Thai House *Thai*

| 24 | 10 | 17 | $27 |

Bellmore | 2618 Merrick Rd. (Bellmore Rd.) | 516-409-6113

"Amazing", "different-from-the-usual" Thai with "just-right" spicing lures fans to Bellmore for "one of the best"; true, it's a "hole-in-the-wall" and "service can be slow", but the "nice" staff and affordable grub add up to a "local favorite"; P.S. "BYO is an added bonus."

Orchid *Chinese*

| 24 | 19 | 22 | $34 |

Garden City | 730 Franklin Ave. (bet. 7th St. & Stewart Ave.) | 516-742-1116

"Cantonese lives" in Garden City at this "top-notch" midpriced Chinese presenting plates that are "pretty to look at and even better to eat"; the subterranean setting has "mirrors to make it pleasant" and an "over-the-top" bronze ceiling for what admirers call a "sophisticated atmosphere" that's abetted by "attentive and professional" waiters, all ensuring a "classy" dining experience.

⚡ Orient, The *Chinese*

| 26 | 10 | 19 | $26 |

Bethpage | 623 Hicksville Rd. (bet. Courtney & Fiddler Lns.) | 516-822-1010

For "wonderfully prepared, fresh" Cantonese, Hunan and Sichuan fare, "gracious host Tommy" Tan's Bethpage Chinese is the "undisputed" choice say aficionados who "get over the lack of decor" and "let the waiter recommend a special dish or two" from the "extensive menu"; though it's "always crowded" and "rushed" ("especially on weekends"), the "price is great", so there's "no need to trudge into Chinatown" – even for "terrific dim sum."

Osaka ⓩ *Japanese*

| ▽ 23 | 15 | 18 | $37 |

Huntington | 328 W. Main St. (bet. Green & Prospect Sts.) | 631-673-7271

"Top-notch Japanese" lures fish fanciers to this "wee" midpriced "hidden treasure" where they're "rewarded" with sushi that's "sweet to the taste in its freshness"; with a "plain" exterior, "unprepossessing" decor and "pleasant" service, many feel it's as "close to Japan" as you can get in Huntington.

Oscar's of St. James *American*

| 22 | 21 | 21 | $51 |

St. James | 552 N. Country Rd. (bet. Acron Rd. & Lake Ave.) | 631-584-4600 | www.oscarsofstjames.com

Devotees declare that the "pretty", "flavorful and unique dishes" on this New American's "seasonal menu" are "obviously created by a culinary artist" – chef Philippe Corbet (ex Bouley); the former beach house setting in St. James with "New England–style decor" boasts two fireplaces, and the "staff makes you feel at home" despite the "noise"; "fair" tabs and live music (Thursdays and Sundays) help make it "a favorite" "for a date, special occasion or dinner with friends."

NEW Oso *Seafood/Steak*
`-` | `-` | `-` | `E`

Southampton | Southampton Inn | 91 Hill St. (1st Neck Ln.) | 631-283-1166 | www.southamptoninn.com

The verdict's still out on this fledgling surf 'n' turfer in the Southampton Inn where the "outer court is like dining alfresco in Italy", but some balk at the "basement"-like dining room and "uneven service"; still others deem it a "great breakfast spot", a "good value for the Hamptons (especially the prix fixe)" and a "well-kept secret."

Osteria da Nino *Italian*
`23` | `19` | `22` | `$46`

Huntington | 292 Main St. (bet. Green & New Sts.) | 631-425-0820 | www.ninosrusticitalian.com

"Rustic Italian fare that brings Rome and Florence right to your table" pleases *paesani* at this somewhat high-end Huntington "find" where "you can't go wrong with any dish"; the "hospitable" staff makes you "feel right at home", and the "intimate" atmosphere is usually so "pleasurably quiet" "you can actually hear yourself talk", to which locals say "nicely done."

NEW Osteria Toscana *Italian*
`-` | `-` | `-` | `E`

Huntington | 69 Wall St. (Central St.) | 631-549-7074 | www.osteriatoscana.com

The Reststar Group (Bistro Cassis) teamed with chef-owner Joseph Maulo for this Huntington Italian with a Tuscan touch that serves fresh pastas made in-house, plus entrees such as split lobster sautéed with garlic; the warm decor features hardwood floors and huge, colorful posters on brick walls, as well as a private upstairs dining room with a fireplace.

Ozumo Japanese Restaurant *Japanese*
∇ `21` | `13` | `20` | `$32`

Bethpage | 164 Hicksville Rd. (Hempstead Tpke.) | 516-731-8989

Ozumo Sushi House Ⓜ *Japanese*

Oceanside | 144 Mott St. (Oceanside Rd.) | 516-872-8686

"They know their customers" at these "neighborhood Japanese joints" in Oceanside and Bethpage where the midpriced menu includes "fresh fish" for the sushi set as well as appealing bento boxes; the Hicksville Road sib has pictures of sumo wrestlers on the wall (Ozumo is the Super Bowl of sumo) plus tatami options, so diners can "sit on the floor or at a table" while being tended to by a "staff that really cares."

Pace's Steak House *Steak*
`23` | `20` | `21` | `$61`

Hauppauge | 325 Nesconset Hwy. (bet. Brooksite Dr. & Hauppauge Rd.) | 631-979-7676

Port Jefferson | 318 Wynn Ln. (Main St.) | 631-331-9200 | www.pacessteakhouse.com

"Bring your appetite and your wallet" to this "real-deal" chophouse and seafooder with branches in Hauppauge and Port Jeff that offers

	FOOD	DECOR	SERVICE	COST

"steaks so big" carnivores think they "went to heaven"; though some beef that it's "crowded and noisy", the "dark, masculine decor" and service that's "on point when you have a question" seals the meaty deal for most.

Paddy McGees *Seafood* | 16 | 18 | 16 | $38 |

Island Park | 6 Waterview Rd. (Pettit Pl.) | 516-431-8700

"Basic seafood" comes "second" at this Island Parker on Reynolds Channel where boaters "pull up" and "get a table outside" "for the view", while "on summer weekends" the "youth" revel in a "raucous" "party atmosphere"; those who "don't care how noisy it gets" or balk at "disappointing" service hit the "best Sunday brunch around for the price"; N.B. open for private parties only in winter.

Page One Ⓜ *American/Eclectic* | 22 | 17 | 24 | $41 |

Glen Cove | 90 School St. (bet. Highland Rd. & North Ln.) | 516-676-2800 | www.pageonerestaurant.com

"Wonderful" chef/co-owner Jeanine Dimenna is the "ultimate pro", preparing "outstanding, innovative dishes" at this American-Eclectic "class act" in Glen Cove with an "attentive, professional" staff (earning a boost in the Service score this year); though a few quibble that the interior could use a little "redecorating", locals laud the "live jazz Sunday nights" and "reasonable prices", saying it's "under the radar but shouldn't be."

Painters' *Eclectic* | 18 | 19 | 18 | $38 |

Brookhaven Hamlet | 416 S. Country Rd. (Montauk Hwy.) | 631-286-6264 | www.paintersrestaurant.com

It's the "place to go if you think you've been everywhere" assert adventurous fans of the "imaginative menu that changes with the seasons" at this "one-of-a-kind", "funky, arty" Eclectic in Brookhaven Hamlet; the decor of "undiscovered artists' works" for sale, plus the "younger crowd", Thursday DJ and "wonderful bands" (Friday-Saturday) keep things lively.

🆕 Palio Ristorante *Italian* | - | - | - | VE |

Jericho | 399 Jericho Tpke. (Merry Ln.) | 516-433-9100

In a subtle setting highlighted by vivid barside paintings of the Palio (a horse race in Sienna), this new Jericho Italian offers a high-end menu from chef Massimo Fedozzi, whose background includes European restaurants and Manhattan's I Tre Merli; a dedication to natural and organic ingredients and earth-friendly practices shows in touches such as menus printed on recycled paper and converting the cooking oil to biodiesel fuel.

Palm, The *Seafood/Steak* | 25 | 19 | 23 | $69 |

East Hampton | Huntting Inn | 94 Main St. (Huntting Ln.) | 631-324-0411 | www.thepalm.com

"Old-school dining" is alive and well at this "distinguished" chain carnivorium in The Huntting Inn, drawing plenty of "movers and shakers" with its "enormous" steaks and lobsters plated in a "beautiful" setting adorned with celebrity "caricatures"; sure, the tabs are reminiscent of "mortgage payments" and service can career from "top-notch" to "surly", but ultimately it's "consistently good."

Z Palm Court
at the Carltun M *American/Continental*

| 24 | 27 | 24 | $60 |

East Meadow | The Carltun | Eisenhower Park (Merrick Ave.) | 516-542-0700 | www.thecarltun.com

A "relaxed, elegant" mansion setting – with "sensational" touches such as painted flying monkeys decorating the ceiling – prompts dazzled diners to "get dressed up and splurge" on "exquisite", "innovative" dishes at this Continental–New American in East Meadow; "impeccable service" and a "killer wine list" add to a "classy" "experience" in the "grand style" that's "worth it" for "special occasions"; P.S. "go for lunch and you won't break the bank."

Z Panama Hatties *American*

| 26 | 22 | 25 | $70 |

Huntington Station | Post Plaza | 872 E. Jericho Tpke. (bet. Cooper Ave. & Emerald Ln.) | 631-351-1727 | www.panamahatties.com

"Don't be fooled by the outside, it's definitely worth" seeking out this "oasis" in a Huntington Station strip mall enthuse epicures enthralled with chef-owner Matthew Hisiger's "out-of-this-world", "perfectly prepared" New American cuisine; "very professional, friendly service" augments the "culinary experience", as does an "elegant" interior with pressed-tin ceilings – and not surprisingly, "it will really cost you."

Pancho's Border Grill *Tex-Mex*

| 19 | 16 | 19 | $28 |

Bethpage | 4119 Hempstead Tpke. (Stewart Ave.) | 516-579-5500
Great Neck | 10 Grace Ave. (bet. Bond St. & Middle Neck Rd.) | 516-829-5305
Pancho's Cantina *Tex-Mex*
Island Park | 4245 Austin Blvd. (Audubon Blvd.) | 516-897-8300
www.panchostexmex.com

For "always reliable", "basic" Tex-Mex that's dished out in "substantial portions", hungry hombres head to this trio for its large menu of "traditional" fare that's "served with a smile"; parents applaud the "decent prices" and "relaxed atmosphere", saying it's "a great place to take kids."

Panini Café at Diane's *Sandwiches*

| ▽ 23 | 16 | 15 | $34 |

Roslyn | 23 Bryant Ave. (bet. Roosevelt Ave. & Skillman St.) | 516-621-2522

The location under the Roslyn viaduct camouflages the "excellent" fare offered at this cafe attached to Diane's Bakery, where the panini, salads and such are "delicious" and "creative", and the "baked goods are superb"; though a few cite service that's "not on par" with expectations "at this price point", pluses include a little back terrace and "neat upstairs seating."

Papa Razzi *Italian*

| 18 | 18 | 17 | $32 |

Westbury | 1500 Jericho Tpke. (Glen Cove Rd.) | 516-877-7744 | www.paparazzitrattoria.com

Westbury locals proclaim this "chain Italian" is "not a bad choice" "for the area", with its "consistent" fare, moderate prices and "accom-

	FOOD	DECOR	SERVICE	COST

modating service"; since it seats 300, you "can always get a table" in the "family-friendly" digs decorated with chandeliers and tablecloths.

Paradise Island *Vietnamese*   ▽ 19 | 6 | 13 | $24

Williston Park | 344 Hillside Ave. (Concord Ave.) | 516-248-1140
Though it's fairly low-profile, this Williston Park Vietnamese offers an "extensive" selection of dishes that are "well prepared and nicely presented", if not "elaborately creative"; the surroundings are "beyond minimal" but they're "neat", and fans applaud the "value for the money" – especially since it's BYO only.

Pasta-eria *Italian*   23 | 12 | 18 | $27

Hicksville | Woodbury Shopping Ctr. | 440 S. Oyster Bay Rd. (Woodbury Rd.) | 516-938-1555
"Amazing" pies and pasta "never disappoint" devotees of this Hicksville Italian situated on a "shopping strip", with a "cramped" dining room "in the back of the pizzeria"; service is "what you'd expect" for a "neighborhood" joint, but given such "fair prices", it's "definitely worth the 15–20 minute wait."

Pasta Pasta *Italian*   23 | 20 | 22 | $41

Port Jefferson | 234 E. Main St. (Prospect St.) | 631-331-5335 | www.pastapasta.net
Regulars return for "creative" pasta specials among a "wide variety" of "exceptional" Italian fare that's served at this "cozy" Port Jeff "delight"; some note that normally "attentive", "friendly" service can "suffer a bit" on weekends, when reservations are especially "recommended", and when the otherwise "romantic", "lively" atmosphere can seem "cramped" and "a bit noisy" – but it's always "worth it."

🆕 Pasta Vino Italian Bistro *Italian*   ▽ 23 | 19 | 21 | $39

Mineola | 149 Mineola Blvd. (Harrison Ave.) | 516-294-1715 | www.pastavinobistro.com
Mineolans praise the Italian food "prepared as though it were made by your grandma" at this "casual" new storefront that's "not to be missed"; though a few dub it the "noisiest place on Long Island", most cheer the "value", "cute" bistro-style decor and "attentive" service that makes them "feel welcome."

Pastrami King Ⓜ *Deli*   19 | 11 | 16 | $24

Merrick | 196 Merrick Rd. (bet. Bernard St. & Meadowbrook Pkwy.) | 516-377-4300 | www.pastramiking.com
"Pastrami is truly king" at this "Jewish-style" (but not kosher) Merrick deli and Eclectic eatery with "huge" sandwiches "you'll kvell over"; cravers confess it's choice for "cheating on a diet", and if "the service can vary" and the "informal dining room" offers little "in the way of decor", knowledgeable noshers note "that's not why we eat there."

Patio at 54 Main, The *American*   19 | 19 | 19 | $52

Westhampton Beach | 54 Main St. (Potunk Ln.) | 631-288-0100 | www.thepatiowhb.com
"Steady" steak, seafood and other New American eats make for a "happy crowd" at this "friendly" Westhampton Beach "tradition"

where the glassed-in patio creates a "dreamy" interior; advocates advise going on the weekends, when live music and a "lively bar scene" make for a "pleasant experience" – and one that can be "expensive", unless you catch the prix fixe before 6:30 PM.

Pearl East *Chinese*   23 | 19 | 20 | $36

Manhasset | 1191 Northern Blvd. (bet. Maple St. & Norgate Rd.) | 516-365-9898

"Fine Chinese cuisine" with "unusual" flourishes and "outstanding presentation" pleases patrons of this midpriced Manhasset eatery where the "quality of the ingredients is the finest"; the "updated" "beautiful interior" featuring Asian antiques is "stylish and understated", and though the service is "sometimes slow", the "darling" owner "makes sure everything is to your liking", so it's "always a pleasure."

Pentimento Ⓜ *Italian*   21 | 20 | 21 | $45

Stony Brook | Stony Brook Village Ctr. | 93 Main St. (bet.Christian Ave. & Rte. 25A) | 631-689-7755 | www.pentimentorestaurant.net

"Innovative" Italian cuisine "changes with the seasons" at this "quaint" Stony Brook "mainstay" that's a "respite from the usual" with a "warm, welcoming" atmosphere; it's recommended for "sitting outside" and enjoying a "bargain" lunch, and even those who feel it's "inconsistent" find it "can also score a major hit."

Pepi's Cucina Di Casa *Italian/Seafood*   ▽ 16 | 15 | 18 | $40

Southold | 400 Old Main Rd. (off Main Rd./Rte. 25) | 631-765-6373

Its "unique setting on the water", including a "dock for boaters", makes this "kid-friendly" Italian-seafooder at Southold Bay a summer destination, and its renovated interior with a fireplace increases winter pleasure as well; despite the "generous portions", quibblers dub the fare "inconsistent" and the service "quirky", but "go for the view on a sunny day" and "when everything clicks, it's thoroughly enjoyable."

Peppercorns *Continental*   18 | 17 | 20 | $35

Hicksville | 25 E. Marie St. (B'way) | 516-931-4002 | www.peppercornsny.com

"Not-bad" Continental dishes are served in "generous portions" at this "moderately priced" Hicksville "pub-style" steakhouse where the "pro" waiters make you "feel like a regular"; add in a "down-to-earth" setting featuring historic local photos, and most say it offers "more than you'd expect" from a neighborhood haunt.

PeraBell Food Bar *American/Eclectic*   24 | 19 | 22 | $35

Patchogue | 114 W. Main St. (bet. Clare Rose Blvd. & Railroad Ave.) | 631-447-7766 | www.perabellfoodbar.com

"Flavors abound" with "bargains to be found" on the "scrumptious" "seasonal" menu at this chef-owned American-Eclectic in Patchogue where the "innovative" midpriced fare and "fierce" cocktails are served by an "attentive" staff; in the "small, pub-style" setting, patrons either "catch the game" in the "cute bar area" or head for the "cozy ambiance" of the "candlelit" – if "tight" – dining quarters.

	FOOD	DECOR	SERVICE	COST

Per Un Angelo *Italian*

| 21 | 18 | 21 | $46 |

Wantagh | Jones Beach Hotel | 3275 Byron St. (bet. Atlantic Blvd. & Willow St.) | 516-783-6484

This "upscale" Wantagh "find" "hidden away" in the Jones Beach Hotel serves "old-fashioned" "Northern Italian cuisine", delivered with "European"-style service that fits the bill for "special occasions"; while detractors declare it "amateurish" and "out-of-date", the mostly "older crowd" of devotees finds it "pleasant", especially when the keyboardist entertains with Italian tunes (Wednesday-Thursday and Saturday).

☑ Peter Luger ⊕ *Steak*

| 27 | 17 | 21 | $71 |

Great Neck | 255 Northern Blvd. (bet. Jayson Ave. & Tain Dr.) | 516-487-8800 | www.peterluger.com

Named Long Island's Most Popular restaurant for the 16th year running, this "mecca of beef" in Great Neck (spun off from the Brooklyn original) serves up "superb", "melt-in-your-mouth" steaks and sides in a "masculine" setting – and some even claim the "waiters aren't as grumpy as people say"; indeed, "they pour a healthy drink to make you forget" the hefty tab – just remember to bring a debit card or cash (and "lots of it").

P.F. Chang's China Bistro *Chinese*

| 19 | 20 | 18 | $34 |

Westbury | Mall at the Source | 1504 Old Country Rd. (Merchants Concourse) | 516-222-9200 | www.pfchangs.com

Expect "major hustle-bustle" at this "noisy" Chinese chain link in Westbury where the "sanitized", "mass-produced" menus "aren't really authentic" yet do "appeal to most palates" (when in doubt, the "lettuce wraps rule"); no one minds the "spotty" service and "ersatz" Sino decor since they "have the formula down" – starting with "nothing-fancy" prices and an overall "fun" vibe.

PG Steakhouse *Steak*

| 22 | 15 | 18 | $64 |

Huntington | 1745 E. Jericho Tpke. (Ware Ave.) | 631-499-1005 | www.pgsteakhouse.com

Cow connoisseurs contend that "for the price", this Huntington chophouse is "one of the better steak places around"; most advise "don't be put off by the exterior" or the humble decor "when you get inside", because once there, you'll find a "friendly local" place "that tries to please."

Piccola Bussola *Italian*

| 22 | 16 | 20 | $40 |

Mineola | 159 Jericho Tpke. (bet. Mineola Blvd. & Willis Ave.) | 516-294-4620
Huntington | 970 W. Jericho Tpke. (bet. Round Swamp Rd. & Sheppard Ln.) | 631-692-6300
www.piccolabussolarestaurant.com

This duo of Mineola and Huntington "family-style" Italians dishes up "old-school" cuisine "done right" in portions "fit for a gluttonous king"; the "pleasant" service and "moderate prices" help attract "large groups", keeping it "busy and noisy", and most proclaim that even though it "isn't exactly a looker", you "can't go wrong."

☑ Piccolo *American/Italian* | 26 | 21 | 24 | $57 |

Huntington | Southdown Shopping Ctr. | 215 Wall St. (bet. Mill Ln. & Southdown Rd.) | 631-424-5592 | www.piccolorestaurant.net

Customers crave the "stellar" dishes on the "inventive" New American–Italian menu accompanied by a "surprising wine list" at this "warm, inviting" Huntington "favorite" with a "fantastic" staff that makes "you feel like you're being served by friends"; a piano player (Sunday–Thursday) adds a "nice touch" to the "expensive" meal, which is so "transporting", "reservations are a must."

Piccolo's Ⓜ *Italian* | 23 | 17 | 22 | $40 |

Mineola | 150 E. Jericho Tpke. (Congress Ave.) | 516-248-8110

Pasta partisans praise the "many different kinds" of "homemade ravioli" ("try the duck") at this "accommodating" Mineola mainstay featuring "real" Northern Italian cooking for "reasonable prices"; though the space is "not notable", it more than passes muster for an "unassuming" "neighborhood spot."

Pie, The *Pizza* | 20 | 16 | 19 | $22 |

Port Jefferson | 216 Main St. (Arden Pl.) | 631-331-4646 | www.thepie.tv

Offering thin-crust, "coal-fired-oven pies" with "unique toppings" and "fresh" ingredients plus "terrific" "family-style" salads at a "reasonable price", this Port Jeff pizzeria is a "comfortable" "kid-friendly" place where the staff is "eager to please"; as an added plus, "you can watch the chef twirling the dough over his head" from one of the large booths.

NEW Pier 441 Ⓜ *Seafood* | ▽ 19 | 18 | 18 | $43 |

Centerport | 441 E. Main St./Rte. 25A (bet. Centershore Rd. & Little Neck Rds.) | 631-261-2828 | www.pier441.com

"Enjoyable" fare and a "water view" of Mill Pond "makes you feel as though you're on vacation" at this nautical-themed Centerport seafooder recently reinvented by owners who are "wonderful hosts"; while some say the latest incarnation needs some "fine tuning", the "reasonable" prices make it "worth the visit."

Pier 95 Ⓜ *Mediterranean* | 23 | 20 | 22 | $49 |

Freeport | 95 Hudson Ave. (bet. Norton & Overton Sts.) | 516-867-9632 | www.pier95.com

"Mouthwatering fresh seafood" with a Portuguese influence is served in an "upscale", "romantic" setting at this pricey Freeport Mediterranean that's "attractively located" by the waterfront; with "prompt", "accommodating" service, it adds up to a "triple coup."

Pierre's *French* | 21 | 19 | 18 | $58 |

Bridgehampton | 2468 Main St. (bet. Bridgehampton-Sag Harbor Tpke. & Hull Ln.) | 631-537-5110 | www.pierresbridgehampton.com

"Authentic? *oui!*" declare Francophiles fond of this Bridgehampton "bistro with a buzz" that serves French fare in a "bright, cheery" setting with a "wonderful patisserie" up front and "charming" chef-owner Pierre Weber as the "engaging host"; though servers can dish out "Parisian" "attitude" and some argue the "prices outweigh the experience", most find it a "memorable treat"; P.S. jazz musicians perform on Tuesday and Sunday nights.

☑ Pine Island Grill ⓜ American
17 | 26 | 16 | $49

Bayville | Crescent Beach Club | 333 Bayville Ave. (bet. Ships Ln. & Sound Beach Ave.) | 516-628-3000 | www.thecrescentbeachclub.com

"Right on the beach with an amazing view" of Long Island Sound and the sunset from "almost every seat", this New American in Bayville's Crescent Beach Club has a "magic", "romantic" touch; alas, the "pricey" fare is "merely adequate" and the staff "always seems to be new", but if you "go when the weather is nice and sit outside on the deck", it's a "winner."

Pita House Mediterranean/Turkish
23 | 14 | 19 | $27

NEW East Setauket | Heritage Sq. | 100-27 S. Jersey Ave. (Rte. 25A) | 631-675-9051
Patchogue | 680 Rte. 112 (bet. E. Woodside & Old Medford Aves.) | 631-289-2262
www.pita-house.com

Offering a "touch of the exotic", this Patchogue pita kitchen and its "welcome" new East Setauket branch "can't be beat, dollar for dollar and bite for bite" for Mediterranean-Turkish kebabs, "addictive dips" and such – all with "spice for the adventurous"; service is "friendly" at both (but the spin-off outshines the original's "dismal decor"), so the "only thing missing is the belly dancer."

Pizza Place ⊘ Pizza
▽ 21 | 10 | 18 | $19

Bridgehampton | 2123 Montauk Hwy. (Hildreth Ln.) | 631-537-7865

For pizza toppings way beyond pepperoni, pie-sani need look no further than the "creative" thin-crust slices at this Bridgehampton "joint" offering more than 30 options – such as Hawaiian and bacon-cheeseburger – on a family-geared menu that also includes soup and fried chicken; it's wallet-friendly, but "don't expect anything fancy" say locals who admit the "setting and service leave much to be desired."

Planet Bliss Eclectic/New World
▽ 20 | 17 | 16 | $43

Shelter Island | 23 N. Ferry Rd. (Duval Ave.) | 631-749-0053 | www.planet-bliss.com

This "quirky", seasonal Shelter Islander offers "farm-fresh, locally sourced ingredients" in "inventive" Eclectic–New World dishes that fans attest are "worth the trip on the ferry"; the "funky setting" at the multihued Victorian is like a trip back to "the '60s", best enjoyed while dining at one of the "pleasant porch-side tables" or "hanging out" at the "happening bar."

☑ Plaza Cafe American
26 | 21 | 25 | $71

Southampton | 61 Hill St. (bet. 1st Neck & Windmill Lns.) | 631-283-9323 | www.plazacafe.us

"It's not just a celebrity hangout" exclaim enthusiasts who thrill to the "outstanding", "imaginative" New American menu highlighted by "wonderful seafood" at chef-owner Douglas Gulija's "sophisticated" Southampton "treat"; the staff is "attentive and knowledgeable" and the atmosphere "spacious" and "subdued", so even though it's "quite expensive", nobody is complaining.

Poco Loco *Mexican* | 17 | 14 | 18 | $31 |

Roslyn | 1431 Old Northern Blvd. (bet. E. B'way & Skillman St.) | 516-621-5626

Under new ownership, this Mexican stalwart in Roslyn serves up "lethal margaritas" and "typical" south-of-the-border fare in a "cozy" (some say "divey") space that's supplemented by a patio in the summer; though the service ranges from "attentive" to "slow", the "popular bar" makes it "the place to be on Cinco de Mayo."

Pollo Rico Latin Bistro *Pan-Latin* | - | - | - | M |

Centereach | 2435 Middle Country Rd. (bet. Hammond Ln. & Oak St.) | 631-471-0585

Patchogue | Rent Ctr. | 350-12 E. Main St. (bet. Case & Evergreen Aves.) | 631-475-4200 M

www.polloricolatinbistro.com

Owned by a mother-and-son team, this lively Centereach Pan-Latin bistro (with a take-out counter in Patchogue) features dishes from paella to guava-marinated ribs, served in homey surroundings enlivened with a trompe l'oeil mural of a garden courtyard, as well as small, three-dimensional depictions of houses collected in South America; strolling guitarists and a harpist lend it extra atmosphere on weekend nights.

☑ Polo Restaurant *American* | 25 | 26 | 26 | $68 |

Garden City | Garden City Hotel | 45 Seventh St. (bet. Cathedral & Hilton Aves.) | 516-877-9352 | www.gardencityhotel.com

"Superb in every way", this New American in the Garden City Hotel provides "memorable" food and the "finest" service in an "ornate" setting where all the "small touches" make it a "wonderful place to celebrate"; true, it all comes at "Manhattan prices", but most find it's "well worth it"; P.S. a formal tea on Saturday and the "exquisite" Sunday brunch come "highly recommended."

Pomodorino *Italian* | 17 | 15 | 18 | $33 |

Seaford | 3915 Merrick Rd. (Jackson Ave.) | 516-826-1555

Syosset | 4 Berry Hill Rd. (bet. Berry Hill & Cold Spring Harbor Rds.) | 516-802-5665

Hauppauge | 648 Vanderbilt Motor Pkwy. (bet. Orient & Washington Aves.) | 631-951-0026

Huntington | 326 W. Jericho Tpke. (bet. Jones St. & Oakwood Rd.) | 631-425-1196

www.pomodorino.com

Families find this checked-tablecloth Italian chainlet a "dependable" option for "generous portions" of "decent" pasta and pizza at reasonable prices, enjoying the "novelty" of pay-as-you-drink bottles of house wine on every table; others label them "too boring to comment on", unless it's to say they could use "overhauls."

NEW Porters on the Lane *Seafood/Steak*

FOOD	DECOR	SERVICE	COST
-	-	-	E

Bellport | 19 Bellport Ln. (bet. Bell St. & S. Country Rd.) | 631-803-6067 | www.portersonthelane.com

The couple behind Carla Marla's ice cream parlor across the street has renovated the old Bellport Chowder House and launched this surf 'n' turfer with a raw bar and creative New American fare via chef Sean Blakeslee (alumnus of Manhattan's One if by Land, Two if by Sea); wood floors, pressed tin ceilings, a stone fireplace and subtle nautical decor create a cozy ambiance, plus there's porch seating and live piano on Thursdays.

Porto Bello *Italian*

FOOD	DECOR	SERVICE	COST
18	19	18	$44

Greenport | Stirling Harbor Marina | 1410 Manhanset Ave. (bet. Beach Rd. & Champlain Pl.) | 631-477-1515 | www.portobellonorthfork.com

"Back in its original location" with "views of the boats" in Greenport's Stirling Harbor Marina, this "pleasant" Italian with crisp blue-and-white decor offers "attractively priced", "huge portions" and "enough variety that you won't get bored"; still, reviewers report there's nothing too "adventurous" on the menu, and the "young staff" is either "efficient" or "out to lunch" depending on the day.

Post Office Cafe ❶ *American*

FOOD	DECOR	SERVICE	COST
18	17	18	$29

Babylon | 130 W. Main St. (bet. Carll & Deer Park Aves.) | 631-669-9224 | www.thepostofficecafe.com

Pub-crawlers appreciate the "bar scene" and "quick service" at this American "hangout" (sib to Farmingdale's Library Cafe) set in a former Babylon post office; so just "stick with the basics" – burgers, beers, wings – and give in to the "noisy", quirky atmosphere, complete with carousel horses, a fake chicken hanging from the ceiling and the original teller window intact; N.B. there's live music several nights a week.

Post Stop Cafe *American*

FOOD	DECOR	SERVICE	COST
16	15	18	$37

Westhampton Beach | 144 Main St. (bet. Mill Rd. & Sunset Ave.) | 631-288-9777

"Sit on the porch and watch the action" on Main Street at this "reliable" Westhampton Beach American set in a "small" 1914 post office with oak floors and lace curtains; partyers find it "awesome for that morning-after breakfast" accompanied by "people-watching", but sober sorts snort that the rest of the menu is too "ambitious for the chef's talents" and the service is not up to par.

Z Prime *American*

FOOD	DECOR	SERVICE	COST
22	27	21	$69

Huntington | 117 New York Ave. (bet. Ketewomoke Dr. & Youngs Hill Rd.) | 631-385-1515 | www.restaurantprime.com

An "elegant yet casual" setting with floor-to-ceiling windows and "spectacular" "views of the bay" is the prime attraction at this "romantic" Huntington New American (which shares owners with H2O and Tellers), but the "excellent", "beautifully presented" dishes aren't far behind; though some cite "inconsistency" in the service, most reviewers "can't wait to go back."

	FOOD	DECOR	SERVICE	COST

Pumpernickels *German* — 20 | 16 | 20 | $40

Northport | 640 Main St. (Fort Salonga Rd./Rte. 25A) | 631-757-7959
Belly up to the Bavarian bar at this Northport landmark for "old-fashioned" and reasonably priced "German comfort food", from sauerbraten "you never get tired of" to "big bowls of red cabbage"; a "dark", "tired" interior is outshined by the "bend-over-backwards" staff, including a chef who "cooks off-the-menu items", "attentive", traditionally garbed servers and "personable" bartenders.

Q East ●Ⓜ *American/Mediterranean* — 23 | 24 | 21 | $67

Quogue | Inn at Quogue | 47 Quogue St. (Jessup Ave.) | 631-288-3463 |
www.qrestauranteast.com
"Terrific", "fantastically presented" New American–Mediterranean dishes and a "cool", stylish room that "looks like it's in New York City" make this eatery in the Inn at Quogue a "breath of fresh air in the Hamptons"; even if some patrons "don't love the prices", most are satisfied with "top"-quality service; N.B. closed Monday–Wednesday during the winter.

Quetzalcoatl *Mexican* — 17 | 17 | 19 | $29

Huntington | 296 Main St. (bet. Green & New Sts.) | 631-427-7834
The folks behind the nearby Oaxaca run this "more upscale" bi-level Huntington Mexican providing "traditional dishes" as well as "Tex-Mex for gringos"; an "attractive" interior is decorated with rain-forest murals and Mayan sculptures, the service is "warm" and the margaritas "perfect", though some "disappointed" diners declare it "a bit ordinary."

Rachel's Cafe Ⓜ *Italian* — 23 | 15 | 21 | $38

Syosset | 57 Berry Hill Rd. (bet. Church & East Sts.) | 516-921-0303 |
www.rachelscafe.net
With an "innovative" menu that includes "dynamic specials, astounding old standards" and "awesome desserts", this "tiny" family-run Syosset Italian is a reasonably priced option; even if claustrophobes feel "cramped" in the "crowded" space and others grumble over "slow" service, at least the staff "doesn't rush you" and always accommodates "special requests."

Rachel's Waterside Grill *American/Seafood* — 19 | 15 | 18 | $39

Freeport | 281 Woodcleft Ave. (bet. Manhattan & Suffolk Sts.) |
516-546-0050 | www.rachelswatersidegrill.com
Guests say the seafood is "always good but never spectacular" at this year-round Nautical Mile mainstay "on the canal in Freeport"; while crabs cry over the "unappealing" room, "average" service and "crowds on weekends", the "pretty water view" and "dependable" quality are draws; N.B. closed Monday in the off-season.

Ram's Head Inn *American/Eclectic* — 21 | 23 | 20 | $59

Shelter Island | Ram's Head Inn | 108 Ram Island Dr. (N. Ram Island Dr.) |
631-749-0811 | www.shelterislandinns.com
The "gorgeous setting with a lawn that spreads to the water" means the "view is the meal" at this seasonal American-Eclectic in a 1929

inn overlooking Shelter Island's Coecles Harbor; on balmy days "ask to eat on the terrace" where you'll dine on "consistently" pleasing, if "heftily priced", dishes accompanied by an "extensive wine list" and a "beautiful sunset."

Rangmahal *Indian*
23 | 15 | 22 | $35

Hicksville | 355 S. Broadway (Lawnview Ave.) | 516-942-7256 | www.rangmahalrestaurant.com

"Just follow your nose" to this "awesome" Hicksville Indian where each dish has its own "exotic, distinctive flavor" and the "friendly" staff knows the difference between "hot and sweating hot" spice; despite lacking decor and a cost that's "expensive" for the genre, most reviewers "roll home happy."

Ravagh *Persian*
∇ 22 | 10 | 16 | $34

Roslyn Heights | 210 Mineola Ave. (bet. High St. & Powerhouse Rd.) | 516-484-7100

"It still looks like a diner on the outside" but "they pay attention to the food" on the inside declare disciples of this Persian outpost in Roslyn Heights, where "great kebabs" and other "exotic" dishes for "bargain" prices help make up for the homely setting and iffy service.

red bar brasserie *American/French*
23 | 20 | 22 | $62

Southampton | 210 Hampton Rd. (bet. Lewis St. & Old Town Rd.) | 631-283-0704 | www.redbarbrasserie.com

"Unique flavor combinations that work" distinguish the "terrific" New American–French dishes ("try the amazing duck") at this "sceney" Southampton stunner that's "so loud you can't hear your dinner companion raving about the food"; with a "beautiful", candlelit interior (too "dark" for a few), "professional, caring" service and a "lively bar", it's a "class act" that "doesn't come cheap."

Red Dish Grille & Martini Bar *American*
21 | 18 | 20 | $42

Commack | 6300 Jericho Tpke. (west of Commack Rd.) | 631-462-6042 | www.reddishgrille.com

The titular "delicious" martinis whet the palate for "tasty", "inventive" New American fare at this "upscale" surprise in an "unassuming" Commack strip mall; a "happening bar scene" and frequent live music ratchet up the "noise" in the "small" space, and the high "prices need to be revisited", but the "young crowd is bent on drinking" regardless; P.S. the three-course special (Monday–Friday 4–6 PM and all day Sunday) is a real "deal."

Red Fish Grille *American/Seafood*
23 | 16 | 20 | $43

Plainview | Woodbuy Row Plainview Ctr. | 430 Woodbury Rd. (east of S. Oyster Bay Rd.) | 516-932-8460 | www.redfishgrille.com

"Every course made me look forward to the next" rave regulars of this "fairly priced" Plainview New American where the "fabulous" chef "works wonders" (especially with seafood) and the "helpful staff" keeps the "crowded" room under control; still, the "unappealing" space doesn't cater to conversationalists who resort to "earplugs" and their "BlackBerries" to communicate.

	FOOD	DECOR	SERVICE	COST

Red Restaurant & Bar *American*

24 | 21 | 23 | $53

Huntington | 417 New York Ave. (bet. High & W. Carver Sts.) |
631-673-0304 | www.redrestaurantli.com

"You can taste the passion" of the chef-owner in every "outstanding",
"beautifully presented" dish at this stylish Huntington New American
that offers a "magical experience"; a curved zinc bar, velvet lounge
chairs, plenty of red (on walls, pillows and tables) and a "secret
backyard patio" are matched by "attentive" service that includes an
"expert" sommelier, but traditionalists tsk it "tries too hard to be hip."

Rein Bar & Bistro *American/Eclectic*

▽ 23 | 24 | 23 | $45

Garden City | Garden City Hotel | 45 Seventh St. (bet. Cathedral &
Hilton Aves.) | 516-877-9385 | www.gardencityhotel.com

With a "chic", "city-style" lounge boasting plush fabrics, a fireplace
and big-screen TVs, this American-Eclectic in the Garden City Hotel
is a less formal alternative to the neighboring Polo Restaurant; "excellent" "classics with an extra twist", "martinis in every flavor", a
"terrific" staff and "live entertainment" Thursday–Saturday make it
a "wonderful" ("if pricey") "place to eat and relax."

ⓩ Rialto Ⓜ *Italian*

26 | 20 | 25 | $57

Carle Place | 588 Westbury Ave. (bet. Glen Cove Rd. & Post Ave.) |
516-997-5283 | www.rialtorestaurantli.com

An "absolutely fabulous" meal awaits at this "pricey" Carle Place
Italian where the "whole fish is prepared to perfection" and the
"gnocchi pesto is out of this world"; "gracious" servers treat the
"well-heeled patrons" like "kings", so it's only the "stodgy" setting
that needs help.

Ristorante Forestieri Ⓜ *Italian*

▽ 21 | 19 | 20 | $50

Hauppauge | 760 Townline Rd. (bet. Amber Ct. & Hoffman Ln.) |
631-265-7475

A "fine" taste of "Tuscany" and a "familylike atmosphere" attract
fans to this "cozy" Northern Italian sleeper set in a Victorian-style
Hauppauge house; for many, "attentive" owners Art and Carol Grillo
"are the best part", though a few opine that it's "slightly overpriced";
N.B. the Food score does not reflect a recent chef change.

Ristorante Gemelli Ⓜ *Italian*

22 | 23 | 23 | $48

Babylon | 175 E. Main St. (bet. Cooper St. & Totten Pl.) | 631-321-6392 |
www.gemellirestaurant.com

"Authentic Italian cooking at its finest" is served at this Babylonian
(near the fine-food market of the same name), where the villa-style
room is "so pretty you'll think you're in Tuscany"; there's a "warm"
staff and a chef who "constantly tries new things", so this is "the
place to take your spouse for a special occasion."

Ristorante Italiano Toscanini *Italian*

▽ 22 | 18 | 24 | $40

Port Washington | 179 Main St. (bet. Madison & Monroe Sts.) |
516-944-0755 | www.toscaninipw.com

"The owner's dedication" infuses this Port Washington trattoria
with "charm and superb cooking" cheer ciao hounds who applaud

the "consistently delicious menu" that's supplemented by "many creative specials"; "extraordinary service" and a "comfortable" (if "small") interior sporting murals of the Tuscan countryside make it a "definite keeper."

Ritz Cafe, The *Continental* | 18 | 13 | 19 | $35 |

Northport | 42 Woodbine Ave. (bet. 5th & Scudder Aves.) | 631-754-6348
Little more than "a bar with some tables", this "comfy neighborhood hangout" near the docks in Northport serves Continental "staples" that are better than you'd expect given the "crowded", "divelike" setting; a "friendly" staff keeps things moving, but it's just too "loud" for some folks.

☑ Riverbay Seafood Bar & Grill *Seafood* | 22 | 18 | 20 | $50 |

Williston Park | 700 Willis Ave. (bet. Charles & Henry Sts.) | 516-742-9191 | www.riverbayrestaurant.com
It's "hard to go adrift" with any of the dishes at this nautically themed Williston Park seafooder housed in a former Masonic Hall and run by the same owner as Manhattan's Central Park Boathouse; "top-quality" fish, including sushi, "excellent salads and sides" and a "terrific" Sunday brunch satisfy most, but sullen skippers cite "noisy" environs and rising prices as drawbacks.

Riverview *American/Continental* | 19 | 22 | 19 | $50 |

Oakdale | 3 Consuelo Pl. (off Shore Dr.) | 631-589-2694 | www.riverviewoakdale.com
With a "spectacular view of the Great South Bay", this waterfront Oakdale American-Continental more than earns its moniker; the recently renovated bar is another "visual home run" (summer happy hours "rock") and the Sunday brunch buffet is a "winner", but salty sailors snort over "disorganized" service and "just ok" fare that "doesn't justify the price" or match the vista; N.B. there's an outdoor deck for warmer months.

Riviera Grill *Italian* | ∇ 24 | 18 | 24 | $51 |

Glen Cove | 274 Glen St. (bet. Elm & Hendrick Aves.) | 516-674-9370 | www.rivieragrillrestaurant.com
"Excellent" multiregional Italian and a "congenial", "almost familial" staff are the hallmarks of this Glen Cove eatery that earns extra points for the complimentary bottle of "ice-cold homemade limoncello" and biscotti that end the meal; the simple setting includes arched windows and paintings of the Italian countryside, but the real "masterpieces" are on the plate.

Robata of Tokyo *Japanese* | ∇ 21 | 12 | 18 | $30 |

Plainview | 1163 Old Country Rd. (Manetto Hill Rd.) | 516-433-5333 | www.robatasushi.com
For "exceptional sushi" that "almost swims to your plate", as well as a "variety" of cooked options (tempura, yakitori, soba), Plainview locals head to this "authentic" Japanese "joint" "tucked away in a strip mall"; while the downmarket decor makes it "better for takeout", it still maintains a "faithful following."

	FOOD	DECOR	SERVICE	COST

Robert's *Italian*
24 | 21 | 21 | $68

Water Mill | 755 Montauk Hwy. (bet. Nowedonah Ave. & Station Rd.) | 631-726-7171

The "inventive" seasonal Italian menu featuring "fantastic" dishes and "memorable desserts", coupled with an "elegant", "cozy farmhouse" setting complete with a fireplace, keeps Robert Durkin's Water Mill standby perennially packed; the only downsides for a few doubters are sometimes "sporadic" service and the "pricey" check.

Robinson's Tea Room Ⓜ *Tearoom*
24 | 23 | 23 | $22

Stony Brook | Stony Brook Village Ctr. | 97 E. Main St. (bet. Christian Ave. & Rte. 25A) | 631-751-1232

For the best high tea "this side of England" Anglophiles amble to this "cutesy", "lace-curtained" Stony Brook teahouse where the "mouth-watering" "homemade" scones with fresh clotted cream, salads, omelets and a "huge selection" of "fresh brews" are so popular you "have to make reservations"; the "obliging" staff, a "lovely" location in the "heart of the village" and "charming" touches like "mismatched teacups and saucers" make it "perfect for a ladies' lunch."

NEW Rocco's Italian Kitchen Ⓜ *Italian*
23 | 17 | 21 | M
(fka Mazzi)

Huntington Station | 493 E. Jericho Tpke. (bet. Depot & Melville Rds.) | 631-421-3390

Formerly Mazzi, but still run by the same owner and chef, this "tiny", "terrific" Huntington Station house changed post-Survey from American-Continental to a less expensive Italian menu, and has been renovated with a more Tuscan look (not reflected in the ratings); despite the "tight" space, lovebirds deem it "romantic" "for a date."

Rock 'n Sake *Japanese*
23 | 21 | 18 | $36

Port Washington | 90 Main St. (bet. Evergreen & Haven Aves.) | 516-883-7253 | www.rocknsakeny.com

"Young", "trendy" sushi-lovers head to this "hip", "loungey" Port Washington Japanese (with a Manhattan branch) where the "flavorful" rolls "melt in your mouth"; the "nightclubby" space can get "too loud", "dark" and "crazy" (catch the "Godzilla movies projected onto the bathroom floors") and the service "could be better", but it's a "delicious" "taste of NYC in the 'burbs"; P.S. "go without the kids."

Romantico of Capri Ristorante *Italian*
19 | 19 | 22 | $42

Port Washington | 45A Shore Rd. (bet. Mill Pond & Old Shore Rds.) | 516-767-0077

An "exceptional" staff that "never rushes" you is the highlight of this Port Washington Northern Italian with a "pretty" setting of exposed brick archways and Tuscan frescoes; the menu is "not huge", but it's a "cut above the standard" in this category (try the "extraordinary" braised items such as lamb osso buco), while "reasonably priced wines", senior discounts and an early-bird special make it more affordable.

	FOOD	DECOR	SERVICE	COST

Roots M *American* ▽ 24 | 22 | 21 | $47

Sea Cliff | 242 Sea Cliff Ave. (bet. Central & Roslyn Aves.) | 516-671-7668
"Delicious" "comfort dishes with a creative twist" – from bacon-wrapped meatloaf to a "killer mac 'n' cheese – highlight chef-owner and artist David Santoro's Italian-influenced rustic American menu at this family-run Sea Cliff find "tucked into" a "romantic" Tudor-style building; the "quirky" industrial-meets-earthy decor includes recycled wood furnishings built by the owner, and the "attentive" service brings it all together, but a "loud" space, "uncomfortable seats" and an "unwillingness to alter a dish or allow substitutes" ("leave food allergies at home") disturb some diners.

☒ Rothmann's Steakhouse *Steak* 25 | 22 | 23 | $69

East Norwich | 6319 Northern Blvd. (Oyster Bay Rd./Rte. 106) | 516-922-2500 | www.chasrothmanns.com
"Among the upper echelon of steakhouses", this "expensive" East Norwich veteran combines "outstanding" cuts with an "elegant" atmosphere and a "courteous" staff that brings you "back to the Gold Coast's Golden Age"; though it gets "horrifically noisy" and you may have to "bring your tranquilizer gun to tame the cougars at the happening bar" (where you'll have a "long wait" for your table), many maintain this "top-shelf" meat mecca "still has it after all these years"; P.S. there's a "wonderful" Sunday brunch.

Rowdy Hall *Pub Food* 19 | 14 | 18 | $36

East Hampton | 10 Main St. (bet. Fithian Ln. & The Circle) | 631-324-8555 | www.rowdyhall.com
The "huge burgers" "still take the gold" at this East Hampton pub-grub palace from the crew behind Nick & Toni's, "tucked away" on a mews off Main Street; the staff "tries hard to please" even when it's "mobbed" (after the "next-door movies" let out) and the "typical", "pass-the-heart-pump" fare "won't hurt your pocketbook", but any love for the "casual" setting (there's a fireplace, copper-topped bar and outdoor seating) is often dampened by the "noise."

RS Jones M *Southwestern* 21 | 19 | 23 | $35

Merrick | 153 Merrick Ave. (bet. Miller Pl. & W. Loines Ave.) | 516-378-7177 | www.rsjones.com
For an "unusual" finger lickin' "mix of Southern and Cajun", cow-pokes canter to this "lively" country-style Merrick Southwestern that "never fails to satisfy"; "funny" servers "lead you on what to order" from the expansive menu that includes "highly recommended" daily chalkboard specials, while the "funky", "cozy" space sports swinging saloon-style doors and "live music" several nights a week; N.B. there's a prix fixe every Tuesday, and reservations are accepted only for groups of six or more.

NEW Ruby's Famous BBQ Joint *BBQ* – | - | - | M

East Meadow | 2367 Hempstead Tpke. (bet. Clearmeadow Dr. & Newbridge Rd.) | 516-280-6657 | www.rubysfamousbbqjoint.com
Western-themed decor welcomes hombres to this BBQ tenderfoot in a little East Meadow shopping plaza that dishes out gut-busting

	FOOD	DECOR	SERVICE	COST

fare including ribs (Kansas City or Memphis style), pulled chicken and brisket in ample portions for moderate prices.

Runyon's *American*
17 | **14** | **17** | **$30**

Seaford | 3928 Merrick Rd. (bet. Jackson Ave. & Smith Ln.) | 516-221-2112

Runyon's Roadside Tavern *American*

East Meadow | 2172 Hempstead Tpke. (Carman Ave.) | 516-794-8065
www.runyons.com

At these separately owned "pub"-style places, the "dependable" eats – steaks, burgers, meatloaf – are "nothing spectacular", but the "active" "after-work bar scene", outdoor seating (in East Meadow) and OTB touch-screen wagering (in Seaford) are pluses; the "fair" service and "old-feeling" decor, however, are "a shame."

⊠ Ruth's Chris Steak House *Steak*
24 | **21** | **23** | **$63**

Garden City | 600 Old Country Rd. (Clinton Rd.) | 516-222-0220 | www.ruthschris.com

"Nothing beats a steak sizzling in butter" at this "special-occasion" Garden City chain link where the "melt-in-your-mouth" chops are "cooked to perfection" and presented on "hot plates"; sure, the "old-fashioned" space "could use a refreshing", but service is "attentive" and the "off-the-charts" pricing manageable "so long as your boss doesn't care how much you spend."

Ruvo *Italian*
21 | **20** | **21** | **$44**

Greenlawn | 63 Broadway (Smith St.) | 631-261-7700
Port Jefferson | 105 Wynn Ln. (Main St./Rte. 25A) | 631-476-3800
www.ruvorestaurant.com

You can expect "comforting", reasonably priced Southern Italian with "flair" at this family-owned Greenlawn and Port Jefferson duo whose "warm" rustic settings include woodcut art by the owners' father; though a few complain about "loud" rooms and "smallish" portions, there's a "wonderful" martini selection and "friendly", "competent" service; N.B. the Broadway outpost has an adjoining market.

Sabai Thai Bistro *Thai*
- | **-** | **-** | **M**

Miller Place | 825 Rte. 25A (bet. Harrison & Tyler Aves.) | 631-821-1780 | www.sabaithairestaurant.com

A giant golden statue greets guests at the door of this Miller Place Thai, and the rest of the room is just as dramatic, featuring granite-topped tables, gold walls and a variety of gongs; freshly made sauces brighten a roster of favorites, while the low-priced wine list helps keep tabs modest.

Sagamore Steakhouse *Steak*
23 | **22** | **22** | **$66**

Syosset | 650 Jericho Tpke. (Cedar St.) | 516-496-8000 | www.sagamoresteakhouse.com

Loyalists "love" this "masculine" bi-level beef haven in Syosset for its "excellent" steaks, surf 'n' turf nights, "professional service" and "see-and-be-seen" set that "packs the huge bar at happy hour" for "ginormous drinks"; still, cranky carnivores call it a "pricey" proposition that's "no better, no worse" than other chopshops; N.B. there's live jazz every Wednesday and Friday night.

	FOOD	DECOR	SERVICE	COST

Sage Bistro *French*

25 | 17 | 22 | $40

Bellmore | 2620 Merrick Rd. (bet. Centre & St. Marks Aves.) | 516-679-8928 | www.bistrosage.com

Francophiles flip for the "wonderfully prepared", "moderately priced" bistro fare – "excellent mussels", duck à l'orange, coq au vin – at this Bellmore sibling of Oceanside's Brasserie Persil, insisting there's "better French here than in Paris"; though it gets "crowded" in the "cramped", "nothing-special" space, a "caring" staff "makes you feel welcome" while you "wait."

Salamander's General Store *Eclectic*

∇ 21 | 14 | 15 | $27

Greenport | 414 First St. (bet. Center & South Sts.) | 631-477-3711

"Marvelous fried chicken" is only one of the Eclectic draws at this seasonal gourmet grab-and-go grocery that has only two indoor tables, but expands to a garden for summer supping in Greenport; "just about anything coming out of the kitchen is delicious", especially the "inspired salads" and the freshly made doughnuts on Saturdays, so it's "worth a drive from anywhere" despite sometimes "frantic" service.

NEW Sally's Cocofé *Eclectic/Kosher*

- | - | - | I

Huntington | 273 Main St. (bet. New York Ave. & Wall St.) | 631-546-7541 | www.sallyscocofe.com

With a kosher Eclectic menu of salads, pizzas, panini and interesting entrees – and a serious focus on chocolate (both in dishes like the chocolate teriyaki salmon and in a huge selection of desserts and drinks) – this Huntington newcomer courts the serious cocoa-vore; a stylish setting of ivory suede high-backed booths suitable for a romantic tête-à-tête is a further draw.

Salsa Salsa *Californian/Mexican*

23 | 10 | 18 | $17

NEW Bayport | 893 Montauk Hwy. (bet. Barrett & Sylvan Aves.) | 631-419-6464

Port Jefferson | 142 Main St. (bet. Mill Creek Rd. & Wynn Ln.) | 631-473-9700

Smithtown | Maple Commons Shopping Ctr. | 320 Maple Ave. (Rte. 111) | 631-360-8080

www.salsasalsa.net

"Huge, awesome burritos" and the "best salad wraps on the North Shore" among other appealing Cal-Mex choices are served "with a smile" at "bargain prices" in these "always packed" "go-tos"; but "don't come for the atmosphere", particularly in Smithtown, just for the "tasty", "reasonable" eats.

Salvatore's Ⓜ ⊅ *Pizza*

24 | 15 | 19 | $20

Port Washington | 124 Shore Rd. (bet. Manhasset Ave. & Soundview Dr.) | 516-883-8457

Pie at Salvatore's, The ⊅ *Pizza*

Bay Shore | 120 E. Main St. (bet. 1st & 2nd Aves.) | 631-206-1060

www.salvatorescoalfiredpizza.com

"Classic coal-oven" pie with a "crisp, light crust" and "fresh toppings" "puts Long Island squarely on the map" crow "pizza snobs" who praise the "extremely friendly" owners for having "perfected the tomato-to-cheese ratio" at this Port Washington and Bay Shore duo; those who are "helplessly addicted" say they can afford to "gorge", and enjoy the "casual atmosphere" with the entire family.

Sam's *Pizza*

19 | 11 | 17 | $31

East Hampton | 36 Newtown Ln. (bet. Main St. & Osborne Ln.) | 631-324-5900 | www.samseasthampton.com

"Stick with the thin-crust pizza" and you'll never be disappointed say pie partisans of this "local hangout" in East Hampton peddling "cheap" Italian with "absolutely no pretense" (especially when it comes to the lacking decor or the rest of the "not so hot" fare); sure, "nothing ever changes" here, but regulars "hope it stays the way it is for another 50 years."

Samurai *Japanese*

▽ 20 | 18 | 20 | $37

Huntington | 46A Gerard St. (Wall St.) | 631-271-2588 | www.samuraihibachi.com

Patrons praise the nightly "antics" at this Huntington Japanese steakhouse offshoot of nearby Tomo, where the "solid" hibachi experience features lots of "fire and flipping" by chefs who "put on a great show"; the food, which includes sushi, "isn't bad" and "kids enjoy all the activity", so even if it's best shared with a "preteen birthday crowd", it's still "reliable" "fun."

San Marco ⊠ *Italian*

24 | 19 | 25 | $48

Hauppauge | 658 Motor Pkwy. (bet. Kennedy Dr. & Marcus Blvd.) | 631-273-0088 | www.sanmarcoristorante.com

The "enormous selection" of Northern Italian fare "delights the palate" at this Hauppauge "old-worlder" where there's "no need to break the bank" for "beautiful presentations", "impeccable" black-tie service (the waiters wheel around appetizer and dessert carts) and an "elegant" atmosphere; even if a few dis the "dated" decor, all the "fanfare" makes up for it.

Sant Ambroeus *Italian*

24 | 18 | 20 | $69

Southampton | 30 Main St. (bet. Meetinghouse Ln. & Wall St.) | 631-283-1233 | www.santambroeus.com

"Authentic" Milanese dishes shine at this "fabulous" "gem" on Southampton's Main Street, a "sophisticated" sister to restaurants in Manhattan and Italy that boasts an espresso bar with the "best cappuccino ever", "super-tasty" gelato and "sublime" desserts; regulars relish the "personable" service" and "sidewalk seating" in summer, but with dinner costing close to "the price of an Italian vacation" you might go "into shock at the bill"; N.B. closed February–April.

Sapporo *Japanese*

20 | 15 | 20 | $35

Wantagh | 3266 Merrick Rd. (1 block east of Wantagh Pkwy.) | 516-785-3853

"Unfailingly fresh" sushi, "inventive" rolls, "delicious" teriyaki and other Japanese selections served by a "cordial staff" are "so much better than the decor" at this Wantagh veteran say modernists forced to look past the "outdated", "Shogun-esque" interior; but

	FOOD	DECOR	SERVICE	COST

those who choose floor seating in the "traditional" tatami room have a "Zen-like" experience to go with the "wonderful" fare.

Saracen *Italian* | 17 | 18 | 15 | $61 |

Wainscott | 108 Wainscott Stone Rd. (Montauk Hwy.) | 631-537-6255

"Is this an upscale Italian wannabe or a hot disco?" ask guests of this "over-the-top" Wainscott locale with "lots of attitude"; the "uneven" food and "spotty" service are drawbacks, but some simply "go for the drinks and the scene."

Sarin Thai *Thai* | 22 | 17 | 20 | $33 |

Greenvale | 43 Glen Cove Rd. (Wellington Rd.) | 516-484-5873 | www.sarinthaicuisine.com

The "refined" dishes at this "reliable", affordable Greenvale Thai are "fresh, flavorful and have a real bite of fire" say fans who are "never let down"; once you get past the "tight" parking situation and settle into the "peaceful", "airy" room tended by a "kind" staff, you'll have a "relaxing" evening.

Savanna's *American* | 20 | 19 | 18 | $62 |

Southampton | 268 Elm St. (Powell Ave.) | 631-283-0202 | www.savannassouthampton.com

Trendy types "come for the buzz" at this high-end New American where "young", "beautiful people rejoice" in a "Southampton scene" that's so loud you "can't hear yourself think"; still, others who "expect better" decry the "tiny" tastings, high prices and "haughty" service that outweigh an "interesting" menu; N.B. closed November–May.

Schooner *Seafood/Steak* | 16 | 16 | 16 | $42 |

Freeport | 435 Woodcleft Ave. (Richmond St.) | 516-378-7575 | www.theschooner.com

The "view's the thing" at this waterfront standard-bearer on Freeport's Nautical Mile where "beautiful vistas" from indoor and outdoor tables appeal despite steak and seafood dishes with "little flair", merely "adequate" service and "old" decor; still, "your grandparents would like" the "reliable" "time-warp-to-the-'60s" menu, finding "a reason" why it's "still around" after 40 years.

Scrimshaw Ⓜ *American* | 22 | 21 | 19 | $53 |

Greenport | Preston's Wharf | 102 Main St. (bet. Front St. & Greenport Harbor) | 631-477-8882 | www.scrimshawrestaurant.com

Greenporters gravitate to this small waterfront New American for "superb", "imaginative" fare featuring "local ingredients" often spiked with a "hint of Asian" flair; the "sophisticated dockside setting" and a "cheerful" staff make it a "worthwhile" excursion, even if a handful cite "inconsistencies" and "high tabs"; P.S. "romantics" should sit on the outdoor deck at sunset with "views of Shelter Island."

Sea Basin *Italian* | ∇ 18 | 15 | 20 | $35 |

Rocky Point | 624 Rte. 25A (bet. B'way & Polk St.) | 631-744-1643 | www.seabasin.com

Reviewers have mixed feelings about this "reliable, if standard", Italian seafooder in Rocky Point: proponents praise both the "friendly" owner who's "always there to make sure you're happy" and the "hearty portions" of "reasonably priced" food (try the rack of lamb "to die for" and "locally caught" fish), but detractors deride "diner-like" "dated" decor and "average" offerings.

Seafood Barge   *Seafood*   21 | 19 | 20 | $51

Southold | Port of Egypt Marina | 62980 Main Rd. (bet. Albacore Dr. & Bay Home Rd.) | 631-765-3010 | www.seafoodbarge.com

"Watch an osprey gliding" over the bay as you "sip local wines and enjoy some of the North Fork's freshest seafood" at this waterfront Southold vet where the "inventive" dishes from a "seasonally changing" menu are "prepared with skill" by new chef Noah Schwartz; even if the "nautical" blue-and-white decor is a tad "dated" and hungry wallet-watchers gripe it's "overpriced and underportioned", many feel it's an "underrated classic."

Sea Grille   *American/Italian*   ∇ 18 | 19 | 19 | $51

Montauk | Gurney's Inn | 290 Old Montauk Hwy. (bet. Fir Ln. & Maple St.) | 631-668-2345 | www.gurneys-inn.com

You "couldn't find a prettier beach location if you tried" say admirers of this American-Italian in Montauk's Gurney's Inn, where the "magnificent ocean views" "from every table" upstage the "spotty", "slightly overpriced" food and service; nostalgics, however, appreciate the "throwback" ambiance that includes weekend music and dancing.

Sea Levels   🅂🅼 *American/Seafood*   ∇ 24 | 20 | 23 | $42

Brightwaters | 391 N. Windsor Ave. (Orinoco Dr.) | 631-665-8300 | www.sealevelsrestaurant.com

Chef-owner John Peter Montgomery brings a "pleasant surprise" to Brightwaters with his "innovative", seasonally changing New American dishes originating above and below sea level, from the Urban Cowboy steak to the "to-die-for" fin fare; a staff that "makes you feel right at home", along with a "cozy" interior, a mahogany bar and live music Friday–Saturday make it a "lively" local "hot spot."

Second House Tavern   🅼 *American*   ∇ 18 | 17 | 19 | $47

Montauk | 161 Second House Rd. (bet. Industrial Rd. & S. Dewey Pl.) | 631-668-2877 | www.secondhousetavern.com

This newcomer in a renovated 1920s building that was formerly home to Ruschmeyers offers New and Traditional American fare to mixed reviews; fans "love" the buttermilk fried chicken, "excellent specials" and the "cozy" space overlooking Montauk's "lovely" Fort Pond, while critics cite "mediocre" eats and uneven service, acknowledging it's "still working out the kinks."

Seeda Thai   *Thai*   21 | 14 | 19 | $30

Valley Stream | 28 N. Central Ave. (½ block north of Merrick Rd.) | 516-561-2626 | www.seedathai.com

"Well-seasoned" Thai food "full of delicious subtleties" is dished up at this Valley Stream "contender" where diners simply "can't go wrong for the price", whether it's the coconut soup or the sticky rice with mangoes ("nothing better"); while the "low-lit", "small" space means "bunch-ups at the door", an "efficient" staff eases the strain.

Sempre Vivolo 🗷 *Italian*

FOOD	DECOR	SERVICE	COST
25	22	24	$56

Hauppauge | 696 Vanderbilt Motor Pkwy. (Old Willets Path) | 631-435-1737

Delivering "classic", "old-school" Italian, this "*sempre* dependable" Hauppauge veteran with "fantastic" fare and a "quiet", "formal" atmosphere is the "place to unwind"; the "tuxedoed" staff "can't do enough to please", but a few modernists mumble the "tired" room is "in a time warp"; N.B. jacket required on Saturday night.

Sen *Japanese*

FOOD	DECOR	SERVICE	COST
24	18	19	$54

Sag Harbor | 23 Main St. (bet. Bay & Madison Sts.) | 631-725-1774 | www.seninthehamptons.com

Peckish prospectors strike "sushi gold" at this "trendy" "Sag Harbor phenomenon" serving "superb", "slightly modernized" Japanese dishes that occasionally call for a "king's ransom"; with a "professional" (and sometimes "belly button"–baring) staff and a "SoHo" feel, it packs in "all the beautiful people" in the summer, so "be prepared to line up" and "bring your Zen patience"; N.B. its neighboring spin-off, formerly Sen Spice & Lounge, is reopening in spring 2009 as Phao Thai Kitchen.

1770 House
Restaurant & Inn *Continental*

FOOD	DECOR	SERVICE	COST
25	25	24	$65

East Hampton | 1770 House | 143 Main St. (Dayton Ln.) | 631-324-1770 | www.1770house.com

"Dark and romantic" with "fireplaces warming the rooms", this "beautifully appointed" Continental in a "historic" East Hampton inn provides a "sanctuary" for feasting on "fine cooking" served by a "polished" staff; many "make it a point to visit the old speakeasy bar downstairs", boasting a more "relaxed", "convivial" atmosphere and "delicious" pub menu option, while others savor the "savings" of the early prix fixe dinner in the "garden on a summer evening."

Seventh St. Cafe *Italian*

FOOD	DECOR	SERVICE	COST
19	19	19	$40

Garden City | 126 Seventh St. (bet. Franklin & Hilton Aves.) | 516-747-7575 | www.seventhstreetcafe.com

For a "respite during a day of downtown shopping", head to this "friendly" Victorian-style Garden City Italian turning out "satisfying", decently priced, if predictable, fare from pastas to salads; though spoilsports say the menu is "tired" and the interior is "so noisy" and "bright" "you'll leave with a headache", you can always wait until summer and "sit outside."

75 Main St. *American*

FOOD	DECOR	SERVICE	COST
18	18	17	$47

Southampton | 75 Main St. (bet. Jobs Ln. & Nugent St.) | 631-283-7575

A "fantastic location" with a sidewalk "scene" on Main Street is the lure for a "lively" crowd at the latest "revival" of this Southampton New American; critics sniff that the ownership "constantly changes, but the lackluster service seems to be a staple", and while the cuisine is "decent enough", it's "just not as good as it could – or should – be" for the price.

	FOOD	DECOR	SERVICE	COST

Shagwong *American*
18 | 15 | 15 | $37

Montauk | 774 Main St. (bet. Edgemere & Essex Sts.) | 631-668-3050 | www.shagwong.com

Plenty of old salts stand by this "stalwart" in the "middle of Montauk" – both in geography and spirit, with "so much history" – serving "reliable" seafood and other "darn good chow" on the American "pub-grub" menu; always "full of locals" who love the "tavern atmosphere", it's even "bustling" in the winter when it's "the only show in town."

Shang Hai Pavilion *Chinese*
▽ 23 | 12 | 19 | $25

Port Washington | 46 Main St. (bet. Bayles & Maryland Aves.) | 516-883-3368

Shang Hai Pavilion II *Chinese*
NEW **Bellmore** | 2725 Merrick Rd. (bet. Centre & S. St. Marks Aves.) | 516-221-2332

The "must-have" "juicy" soup dumplings are "yum-mazing" at this budding Bellmore and Port Washington duo whose inexpensive Shanghai specialty "adds some excitement" to a Chinese menu that's often "just ok" otherwise; despite a "mediocre" atmosphere and uneven service, addicted diners deem it "deserving of its popularity."

Sherwood Asian
▽ 17 | 18 | 20 | $34

Cuisine *Chinese/Japanese*

Glen Cove | 187 Glen St. (Pearsall Ave.) | 516-656-8888

An "aesthetically pleasing" room with "lovely ambiance" sets apart this hard-to-find (and "never crowded") Glen Cove place offering a "huge menu" of "reliable", reasonably priced Chinese and Japanese food; though the cooking doesn't make a big impression, the "service is tops", so all in all it's a "most pleasant" dining experience.

Shiki *Japanese*
23 | 14 | 19 | $37

Babylon | 233 E. Main St. (Cooper St.) | 631-669-5404
Smithtown | 97 E. Main St. (bet. Bellemeade & Landing Aves.) | 631-366-3495
www.shiki-longisland.com

Sushi-seekers "love the food enough to overlook" the "drab decor" at these Japanese standbys in Babylon and Smithtown featuring plenty of "fresh, clever combinations"; with "pleasant" service and a "reasonable cost", they're a "must to do and redo", especially when you "refuse to wait in line" elsewhere.

Shiro of Japan *Japanese*
22 | 19 | 21 | $40

Carle Place | 401 Old Country Rd. (Carle Rd.) | 516-997-4770 | www.shiroofjapan.com

Hibachi "done the right way" draws a crowd to this Carle Place "family favorite" where the Japanese chefs keep the show "fresh and fun", and "kids love to watch them cook"; in addition to tableside grilling, the "sushi bar is a find" with "out-of-this-world" rolls, so even if it adds up to an "expensive night out", most call it a "cut above" the rest.

	FOOD	DECOR	SERVICE	COST

Shogi Ⓜ *Japanese*   ▽ 23 | 12 | 24 | $32

Westbury | 584 Old Country Rd. (bet. Longfellow & Tennyson Aves.) | 516-338-8768

"Everyone is made to feel like a friend" at this Japanese place in Westbury where the hostess "knows all of her customers by name" and the chefs "go out of their way to make what you want"; "quaint" and "small", it offers the kind of "value" that makes it a local "favorite."

Show Win *Japanese*   22 | 14 | 19 | $38

Amagansett | 40 Montauk Hwy. (bet. Cross & Indian Wells Plain Hwys.) | 631-267-7600 | www.showwinsushi.com
Northport | 325 Fort Salonga Rd./Rte. 25A (bet. Reservoir & Woodbine Aves.) | 631-261-6622 | www.sushishowwin.com

Reviewers recommend the "unbeatable variety of rolls" – many of them "named after people in town" – at this Japanese duo in Amagansett and Northport; despite the star treatment, the service leads some to nickname it 'Slow Win', so "sitting at the sushi bar" is often best.

Ⓩ Siam Lotus Thai Ⓜ *Thai*   26 | 15 | 24 | $33

Bay Shore | 1664 Union Blvd. (bet. 4th & Park Aves.) | 631-968-8196 | www.siamlotus.info

"Artfully presented", "outstanding" Thai specialties are spiced to "delight any palate" (though "even adventure-seekers need to think twice before asking for native Thai heat") at this "brilliant" Bay Shore "gem" offering lots of daily specials; while there's "not much ambiance", most visitors assure that it's "more than made up for" by the "caring family owners" who make an effort to keep "everyone happy."

Silver's *Eclectic*   22 | 15 | 18 | $42

Southampton | 15 Main St. (bet. Jobs Ln. & Nugent St.) | 631-283-6443 | www.silversrestaurant.com

Salivating Southamptonites wish this "simple" lunch-only Eclectic in the center of town were open for dinner, but chef-owner Garrett Wellins (whose family has run the location through several incarnations since 1923) "makes a singular BLT" and "sublime lobster bisque" and has no plans to expand his hours; the "small" checkered-floor setting lends it an "unpretentious" "charm", though the "hefty" price tag is a deterrent for some.

NEW Simply Fondue *Fondue*   – | – | – | E

Great Neck | The Gardens | 24 Great Neck Rd. (bet. Brompton & Middle Neck Rds.) | 516-466-4900 | www.simplyfonduelongisland.com

This slick new dipping DIYer perched above a grocery store in The Gardens shopping plaza in Great Neck features a series of rooms with booths and table seating, all outfitted with burners for cooking the four-course fondue prix fixe of salad, cheese, entree and a chocolate finale; lots of options are offered in each category, with extensive wine and martini choices to boot.

	FOOD	DECOR	SERVICE	COST

Simply Thai *Thai*

| 20 | 13 | 17 | $26 |

Rockville Centre | 274 Merrick Rd. (Davison Pl. & Park Ave.) | 516-255-9340

"Bold flavors" bring a following to this busy Rockville Centre Thai offering "well-prepared" food for "inexpensive" tabs; some warn the "sparse" decor "isn't very inviting" and "service on a Saturday night can be tough to take" (reservations are recommended on the weekends), but it largely comes through as a "decent neighborhood place."

☑ Smokin' Al's Famous BBQ Joint *BBQ*

| 24 | 16 | 19 | $31 |

NEW **Massapequa Park** | 4847 Merrick Rd. (bet. Harbor Ln. & Park Blvd.) | 516-799-4900

Bay Shore | 19 W. Main St. (bet. 4th & 5th Aves.) | 631-206-3000
www.smokinals.com

"Dig in with both hands" for some of the "best" BBQ "north of the Mason-Dixon line" at this "carnivore's delight" in Bay Shore (with a new Massapequa spin-off) delivering "amazing" pulled pork, "unbeatable" brisket and ribs that "simply melt off the bone"; since it's "always packed", the wait can be "interminable" and the service "harried", but the "authentic" 'cue keeps fans "hickory happy."

Snapper Inn *Seafood*

| 17 | 19 | 18 | $45 |

Oakdale | 500 Shore Dr. (½ mi. west of Vanderbilt Blvd.) | 631-589-0248 | www.thesnapperinn.com

"Waterside dining is the thing" at this Oakdale "icon" situated on a "beautiful rolling lawn" stretching out to the Connetquot River; otherwise the seafood rates as "just ok" and the service "mediocre", so some only go "for the view and the cocktails"; N.B. hours vary by season, so call ahead.

Snaps *American*

| 22 | 13 | 20 | $44 |

Wantagh | 2010 Wantagh Ave. (south of Sunrise Hwy.) | 516-221-0029 | www.snapsrestaurant.com

"Hidden" in a Wantagh strip mall, this little "NYC restaurant on Long Island" offers chef/co-owner Scott Bradley's "sophisticated" New American dishes that add up to a "dining experience, not just eating"; the service is "friendly", but patrons "just wish the decor would step up and match the food" as well as the somewhat "expensive" tabs.

Soigné *Continental/French*

| 25 | 23 | 25 | $54 |

Woodmere | 1066 Broadway (Franklin & Hartwell Pls.) | 516-569-2259

"First-class all the way", this "delightful" Woodmere destination shines with "superb", "beautifully presented" French-Continental cuisine and "lovely service" in a "quiet, refined" setting complete with "lace napkins", making it "perfect for a romantic dinner"; such "elegance" doesn't come cheap, but the early prix fixe is "a steal."

☑ Solé *Italian*

| 26 | 15 | 21 | $39 |

Oceanside | 2752 Oceanside Rd. (Merle Ave.) | 516-764-3218 | www.soleny.com

Diners declare there are "not enough superlatives" for the "swoonworthy" Italian "masterpieces" prepared at this Oceanside Italian that "surprises" "in the middle of suburbia"; the staff is generally "attentive", so while the "tight" yellow-accented space "may be lacking" and there's usually a "long wait" (since reservations are only taken for five or more), most say it's "justifiably crowded" given the impressive "value for the money."

Soundview *American* ▽ 19 | 19 | 20 | $46

Glen Cove | Glen Cove Golf Club | 109 Lattingtown Rd. (E. Beach Rd.) | 516-676-9781 | www.soundviewglencove.com

A "beautiful view" across the fairways to Long Island Sound in the distance is the main draw of this New American option at the Glen Cove Golf Club; backed by a "basic" but "well-prepared" menu, "sweet" service and a huge terrace and outside bar, duffers deem it "a real find."

Southampton Publick House *Pub Food* 16 | 15 | 17 | $36

Southampton | 40 Bowden Sq. (N. Main St. & N. Sea Rd.) | 631-283-2800 | www.publick.com

"If you love handcrafted beer, this is the place to go" say Southampton hops hounds, though most agree the microbrewery's "top-notch" suds outdo the "filling", "traditional" American pub grub; "kid-friendly" during the day, the atmosphere can get "rowdy" at night when the bar scene takes over.

Southside Fish & Clam *Seafood* 18 | 6 | 8 | $26

Lindenhurst | 395 W. Montauk Hwy. (bet. 4th & 5th Sts.) | 631-226-3322 | www.southsidefishandclam.com

"Step right up for your plastic tray of deliciously fresh seafood" dished out on "paper plates" at this Lindenhurst self-serve counter and market that "looks like a mess hall"; though some find the fish "lackluster" and "not as cheap as it used to be", others appreciate the "uncomplicated" eats and say it's still a "bargain for the lobster."

Souvlaki Palace *Greek* ▽ 20 | 10 | 17 | $22

Commack | 57 Commack Rd. (Jericho Tpke.) | 631-858-1482

"Bustling at lunchtime", this compact Commack Greek specializing in "wonderfully prepared" fish and "street-fare" classics also offers "a lot for your money at dinner"; it's a bit of "a dump" and service gets mixed reviews, but "if you don't need atmosphere, this place is for you."

Spare Rib, The *BBQ* 17 | 13 | 16 | $28

Hicksville | 600 W. Old Country Rd. (bet. Charlotte St. & E. Wantagh State Pkwy.) | 516-433-5252
Commack | 2098 Jericho Tpke. (Indian Head Rd.) | 631-543-5050
www.spareribonline.com

"Be prepared to get messy" warn sauce slurpers, as "lots of napkins are required" for the "finger lickin' good" ribs that will "threaten anyone's diet" at this low-cost Commack and Hicksville duo; on the downside, some don't see "much to rave about", and complain about "so-so" service and "looong waits" ("bring a chair and patience if you want to eat here" on the weekend).

	FOOD	DECOR	SERVICE	COST

NEW Speranza Fine Italian Food Studio ◐ Ⓜ *Italian* | - | - | - | VE |

Woodbury | 7940 Jericho Tpke. (Piquets Ln.) | 516-922-2400
This new Woodbury Italian strikes an unconventional pose with a TV screen outside the entry, a rotating display of desserts in the foyer and a long, glowing red bar; a dining room done up in soft greens and purples is the backdrop for upscale dishes with prices to match from chef Michael Meehan (ex Mill River Inn), and there's also a more casual lounge menu of sliders and such.

Spicy's Barbecue *BBQ* | 19 | 4 | 13 | $18 |

Bellport | 501 Station Rd. (Atlantic Ave.) | 631-286-2755
Riverhead | 225 W. Main St. (bet. Griffing & Osborn Aves.) | 631-727-2781
"Make sure to have your cardiologist on speed-dial" because the BBQ ribs and chicken wings at these "standout" joints in Bellport and Riverhead are a "real guilty pleasure"; the locations feel "pretty rough" ("not exactly a place to take the family"), so while "true road-food dive" fans eat in, others recommend ordering to go.

NEW Sri Thai *Thai* | ▽ 21 | 15 | 19 | $28 |

Huntington | 14 New St. (bet. Main & W. Carver Sts.) | 631-424-3422
"The best thing that's happened to Huntington dining in a long time" according to pad Thai partisans, this "buzzed"-about arrival approaches the "quality and taste of cooking in Thailand" with its "properly spiced" specialties; offering "pleasant" environs and "good value" too, it's become the "newfound favorite" of many.

Star Confectionery ⊄ *American* | ▽ 21 | 18 | 20 | $17 |

Riverhead | 4 E. Main St. (Roanoke Ave.) | 631-727-9873
At this "old-fashioned luncheonette with great burgers, sandwiches", big American breakfasts and homemade ice cream in Riverhead, "you won't leave hungry or broke"; owned and run by the same family since the 1920s, the digs are "still fun" with many of their original turn-of-the-century fixtures.

Starr Boggs *American/Seafood* | 25 | 22 | 22 | $68 |

Westhampton Beach | 6 Parlato Dr. (Library Ave.) | 631-288-3500 | www.starrboggs.com
"Who cares about traffic on the LIE when you know dinner awaits?" at this Westhampton Beach "blast" ask Starr-struck fans of the chef's "uniquely satisfying" seafood and New American fare served amid "lovely", "clubby" surroundings; while the check can be sizable, "top-notch" service and perks like the "don't-miss" Monday lobster bake in the summer keep it "jumping"; N.B. closed January to mid-April.

Stella Ristorante Ⓜ *Italian* | 24 | 18 | 22 | $44 |

Floral Park | 152 Jericho Tpke. (bet. Belmont & N. Tyson Aves.) | 516-775-2202 | www.stellaristorante.com
"They feed you like you're family" at this "upscale" Floral Park Italian where the "high-quality" cuisine includes parmagiana dishes that are "second to none"; true, the "menu hasn't changed in decades",

the "old-world" decor is "nothing to write home about" and even if you have a reservation, you may "have to wait", but most affirm it's "been around forever and should continue" to be so.

Steven's Pasta Specialties *Italian*
23 | 17 | 21 | $32

Long Beach | 120 E. Park Ave. (bet. Long Beach & Riverside Blvds.) | 516-897-7012 | www.stevenspasta.com

"Terrific" pastas and other "well-prepared" dishes come out of the open kitchen at this Long Beach Italian that's "informal" yet "calming" with "uncluttered" gray-and-black-toned decor; as chef-owner Steven Guasco is a "most hospitable host", some tout it as the type of "standby" that "should be a staple in every community."

Steve's Piccola Bussola *Italian*
25 | 17 | 22 | $42

Syosset | 41 Jackson Ave. (Underhill Blvd.) | 516-364-8383
Westbury | 649 Old Country Rd. (Tennyson Ave.) | 516-333-1335
www.stevespiccolabussola.com

"Bring a hefty appetite" to these Syosset and Westbury Italians where "out-of-this-world" "family-style platters" of "delectably sauced" dishes are served by a "saucily delightful" staff; while the "weekend waits" "might kill you" and the "loud, cramped" environs aren't for everyone, most maintain it's "worth a trip from anywhere" in order to leave "stuffed and smiling"; N.B. reservations only for parties of six or more.

☑ Stone Creek Inn Ⓜ *French/Mediterranean*
26 | 24 | 24 | $65

East Quogue | 405 Montauk Hwy. (bet. Carter Ln. & Wedgewood Harbor) | 631-653-6770 | www.stonecreekinn.com

"A serious restaurant where you can enjoy yourself", this French-Med in East Quogue "excites the palate" with "expertly prepared" seasonal fare served amid "simple yet elegant" surroundings by a "professional, accommodating" staff; connoisseurs conclude it's the "complete package", though the high cost keeps it a "special-occasion" place for some.

Stonewalls *American/French*
24 | 21 | 23 | $51

Riverhead | Woods at Cherry Creek Golf Club | 967 Reeves Ave. (bet. Doctors Path & Roanoke Ave.) | 631-208-3510 | www.stonewalls-restaurant.com

This "lovely" New American-French eatery, "a real surprise" set in the Woods at Cherry Creek Golf Club in Riverhead, almost always "hits the mark" with its "seasonal", "priced-right" repasts; "warm" service and "pleasant" views of the course round out the "grown-up dining experience."

Stresa *Italian*
24 | 22 | 23 | $59

Manhasset | 1524 Northern Blvd. (¼ mi. east of Shelter Rock Rd.) | 516-365-6956 | www.stresarestaurant.com

"Classy" and "creative", this "fine" Italian in Manhasset offers "first-rate" fare and a "user-friendly" wine list in an upscale, "celebratory" setting that draws an "older" clientele; "European-style" service is a plus, so while some "stress" over "crowds" and preferential treatment for "regulars", the majority insists it's "superior all around."

	FOOD	DECOR	SERVICE	COST

Suki Zuki *Japanese* | 23 | 12 | 15 | $45

Water Mill | 688 Montauk Hwy. (opp. the Windmill) | 631-726-4600
"One of the best" sushi options "on the East End", this Water Mill Japanese offers an "eclectic" menu of "fresh" rolls and "delicious" robata-grilled items that deliver "for the dollar"; handling a room that's "small" and "always busy" (from "hopping" to "mob-scene", including "families with screaming kids"), the service "sometimes lacks finesse", so bring "plenty of patience" in season.

Sullivan's Quay *Pub Food* | 17 | 18 | 19 | $33

Port Washington | 541 Port Washington Blvd. (Revere Rd.) |
516-883-3122 | www.sullivansquay.com
Reviewers rely on this "rustic" Port Washington pub for a "burger and brew" along with slightly "pricey" Irish-American "special dishes" served by a staff that's "happy to see you"; karaoke Thursdays and other occasional entertainment add to the "lively atmosphere."

Sundried Tomato Cafe *Italian/Pizza* | 22 | 10 | 19 | $26

Nesconset | Nesconset Plaza | 127-3 Smithtown Blvd. (bet. Mayfair Ave. & Southern Blvd.) | 631-366-6310 | www.lisundriedtomato.com
Sure, the specialty slices are a "knockout", but "take the time to sit and enjoy the huge dishes" of "satisfying" Italian home cooking at this "friendly" Nesconset pizzeria and restaurant that "can't be beat for the price"; as the room is "fairly basic", some prefer it for takeout.

Sunset Beach *French/Pan-Asian* | 17 | 21 | 13 | $61

Shelter Island Heights | Sunset Beach Hotel | 35 Shore Rd.
(across from Crescent Bch.) | 631-749-2001 | www.sunsetbeachli.com
"Glitz and glamour" abound at this Shelter Island destination where the "view rivals the Riviera" ("sit upstairs and watch the sunset" or "ask for a table in the sand") and the scene, chock-full of "designer bag-toting Europeans and New Yorkers" and "pretentious" servers, is something out of *La Dolce Vita* (or a "David Lynch film"); while the "expensive" "French bistro" and Pan-Asian eats get mixed reviews, most approve of the "exotic" cocktails.

NEW Surf Lodge *American* | ▽ 21 | 26 | 16 | $60

Montauk | 183 Edgemere St. (bet. Elwell St. & Industrial Rd.) |
631-668-2632 | www.thesurflodge.com
"Fabulous", "innovative" New American fare feeds "plenty of beautiful people" at this Montauk hot spot, opened last year with Sam Talbot of "*Top Chef*" fame helming the kitchen; while the "cool scene" has a breezy beach-bum vibe, some weary wayfarers wince at the "hype" or bemoan the fact that come mid-summer they "just couldn't get in"; N.B. closed November–May.

NEW Surf 'N Turf | - | - | - | M
Mediterranean Grill *Greek/Turkish*

Merrick | 2205 Merrick Rd. (bet. Fox & Lincoln Blvds.) | 516-992-0918 |
www.surfnturfgrill.com
It may be tiny, but this little Greek-Turkish nook in Merrick is big on style and flavor, outfitted with an oak bar, polished mahogany floors

and dark wainscoting climbing halfway up the walls; dishes like whole branzino grilled over hot lava rocks, varied kebabs and a shrimp and skirt steak combo mean it lives up to its name.

Surfside Inn *Continental/Seafood* ▽ 19 | 19 | 18 | $44

Montauk | Surfside Inn | 685 Old Montauk Hwy. (bet. School Ln. & Washington Dr.) | 631-668-5958

If you were "any closer to the ocean, you'd be wet" say admirers of the "sweeping" seaside backdrop afforded at this "old-time" Montauker serving a "decent" Continental seafood menu; despite upmarket tabs, most find the "cozy" coastal house a "refreshing" stop that's worth "adding to the list" – just be sure to sit outside or "by the window."

Sushi Ya *Japanese* 22 | 16 | 20 | $35

Garden City | 949 Franklin Ave. (bet. 9th & 10th Sts.) | 516-873-8818
NEW **New Hyde Park** | 2311 Jericho Tpke. (Nassau Blvd.) | 516-741-2288
www.sushiyagc.com

Adults savor the "creative platings" of sushi and "tasty" bento box combinations, while kids get a kick out of "entertainment" at the hibachi tables of this moderately priced Japanese duo in Garden City and New Hyde Park; though "nothing special" to some, fans say the owners "go the extra mile" to keep it a "family favorite."

Sweet Mama's *Diner* 18 | 18 | 18 | $22

Northport | 9 Alsace Pl. (Fort Salonga Rd./Rte. 25A) | 631-261-6262 | www.sweetmamaskitchen.net

"Breakfast a notch or three above the usual diner fare" ("available all day") brings pancake pals to this "bustling" Northport nook that also serves "traditional homey American" fare for lunch and dinner; its "bright and sunny" "'50s-style" looks amp up the appeal, though some feel the "atmosphere trumps the flavor" and it's "not the same since it was sold" last year.

Swingbelly's Beachside BBQ ❷ *BBQ* 21 | 14 | 18 | $27

Long Beach | 909 W. Beech St. (Wisconsin St.) | 516-431-3464 | www.swingbellysbbq.com

"Right in the middle of the Long Beach bar scene", this BBQ joint packs its own buzz with "big" plates of "fall-off-the-bone" ribs and other "impressive" slow-cooked 'cue washed down with a "bucket of beers"; it's "laid-back" with the "games always on", making it a ready choice for "relaxing" "after the beach."

NEW **Table 9** *American/Italian* - | - | - | VE

East Hills | 290 Glen Cove Rd. (Red Ground Rd.) | 516-625-9099 | www.table9restaurant.com

A new sister to Mill Pond House and Piccolo, this refined American-Italian in East Hills (formerly the home of Brivo and L'Endroit) brings together the cuisines of both sibs for a high-end menu that's big on homemade pastas, seafood and steaks; the space has a subtle, slightly formal look, with beige-and-brown tones and chandelier lighting, but the prix fixe specials for lunch and Monday–Thursday dinner add an extra-welcoming touch.

	FOOD	DECOR	SERVICE	COST

Taiko ⓜ *Asian Fusion* — 24 | 16 | 20 | $39

Rockville Centre | 15 S. Village Ave. (bet. Lincoln Ave. & Merrick Rd.) | 516-678-6149 | www.taikorestaurant.com

"Regulars" are "rewarded" with "dazzling" rolls ("big props to the chefs") at this family-run Rockville Centre "classic" composing "work-of-art" sushi as well as appealing Asian fusion dishes; what some call "ragged" decor can be a drawback, but most report the slightly "pricey" food is "well worth any negatives."

Tai-Show *Japanese* — 22 | 16 | 21 | $34

Levittown | 170A Gardiners Ave. (Hempstead Tpke.) | 516-731-1188
Massapequa | 4318 Merrick Rd. (Harrison Ave.) | 516-798-1119
Massapequa | 4320 Merrick Rd. (Harrison Ave.) | 516-798-3958
NEW **East Setauket** | 316 Main St. (bet. Deering St. & Shore Rd.) | 631-751-2848
Oakdale | 1543 Montauk Hwy. (Vanderbilt Ave.) | 631-218-0808
www.taishow.com

"Expertly made" sushi and cooked dishes draw a following to this Japanese quintet with a "huge, diverse" menu; the service is "dependable" and "welcoming", and while there's "not much" to the decor, some locations add extra enticement with hibachi tables and chefs who "put on a show."

Takara ⓩ *Japanese* — ▽ 26 | 19 | 21 | $43

Islandia | Islandia Shopping Plaza | 1708 Veterans Memorial Hwy. (bet. Blydenburg Rd. & Sycamore Ln.) | 631-348-9470 | www.takara-sushi.com

"Outstanding", "exciting" sushi earns high praise from a small sampling of surveyors for this Islandia Japanese where the chefs are "a blast" and the owner accommodates in "quintessential dignified" style; with booth seating and karaoke on Saturday nights, dinner takes on a festive feel.

Tandoor Grill ⓜ *Indian* — 21 | 17 | 21 | $30

Rockville Centre | 222 Sunrise Hwy. (bet. N. Park & N. Village Aves.) | 516-766-4440 | www.tandoorgrill.com

Both "adventurous and not so adventurous" eaters satisfy their appetites at this Rockville Centre Indian offering "plentiful", "tasty" subcontinental specialties – some of the "best" outside of "Little India" (i.e. Hicksville); though a few critics complain of "institutional" looks, its "convenient location" and "value" (especially for the lunch buffet) win out.

Tava *Turkish* — 19 | 20 | 20 | $37

Port Washington | 166 Main St. (Monroe St.) | 516-767-3400 | www.tavarestaurantandbar.com

Folks tip their fezzes to the "wonderful" owners of this Turkish delight in Port Washington for its "flavorful", moderately priced cuisine, "clublike" "candlelit atmosphere" and "attentive, nonintrusive service"; all in all it's an "exciting addition" to the village scene that's a "step above the others", offering perks like wine-pairing dinners and live music Thursday–Saturday.

	FOOD	DECOR	SERVICE	COST

NEW Tel Aviv *Israeli/Kosher*

| - | - | - | M |

Great Neck | 613 Middle Neck Rd. (bet. Beach Pl. & Fairview Ave.) | 516-466-6136 | www.tlvrestaurant.com

Israeli meze, grilled meats, veggie dishes and exotic desserts (like rosewater panna cotta) make up most of the kosher menu at this moderately priced Great Neck newcomer, while specials such as sashimi and Thai curry draw on international flavors; casual and contemporary, it features pared-down design elements like bare butcher block tables, a plane-ticket motif on the menu and soft lighting to warm up the room; N.B. Friday and Saturday hours vary with the season.

Z Tellers American Chophouse *Steak*

| 26 | 26 | 24 | $66 |

Islip | 605 Main St. (bet. Locust & Nassau Aves.) | 631-277-7070 | www.tellerschophouse.com

"Who needs bulls and bears when you have steers like this?" ask sanguine steak lovers smitten by the "first-class" filets and rib-eyes "like butter" (not to mention "amazing" seafood) "served with style" in this "soaring" space, a former Islip bank building that "makes you feel like a VIP"; the "inviting" bar, walk-in "wine cellar vault" and a staff "at your beck and call" add to the "luxurious" meal, so most don't mind shelling out the "big bucks"; N.B. a post-Survey chef change is not reflected in the Food score.

NEW Tequila Jacks *Caribbean*

| - | - | - | E |

Port Jefferson | 201 Main St. (on Arden Pl. bet. E. Main & Main Sts.) | 631-331-0960 | www.tequilajacksportjeff.com

Seafoam green tones evoke the Caribbean at this Port Jefferson catch (where Elk St. Grille had been for many years) featuring such upscale island items as Bahamian spiced beef tenderloin and jumbo prawns with papaya puree; complementing the tropical flavors, tequila flights and margaritas muddled with fresh fruit do justice to the name.

Terry G's Steak & Seafood Grill *Steak*

| ▽ 17 | 12 | 18 | $35 |

Farmingdale | 354 Main St. (bet. Conklin St. & Rte. 109) | 516-845-9300 | www.terrygs.com

It "looks like a bar" up front, but patrons are "pleasantly surprised" by the "good, affordable" steaks coming out of the kitchen at this eatery "tucked away in the village of Farmingdale"; still, as most say the "tired" dining room could use some "brightening up", its new striped paint job adds a little color; N.B. a recent chef change and New American additions on the menu may not be reflected in the Food score.

Tesoro Ristorante M *Italian*

| 22 | 17 | 23 | $49 |

Westbury | 967 Old Country Rd. (bet. New York Ave. & Sylvester St.) | 516-334-0022 | www.tesorosrestaurant.com

Wowing with "white-glove" treatment, the "extraordinary" staff makes fans "feel important" as they feast on "all the classics" at this "consistent", "old-world" Westbury Italian; the decor is a bit "sad looking", though, so many root for a "makeover."

☒ Thai Gourmet Ⓜ⌀ Thai — 26 | 13 | 18 | $26

Port Jefferson Station | Common Plaza | 4747-24 Nesconset Hwy. (bet. Terryville Rd. & Woodhull Ave.) | 631-474-0663

"Food is front and center" at this "tiny" Port Jefferson Station BYO where "fresh", "spicy" dishes (such as "addictive pad Thai") are served "direct from the fire"; true, the "hole-in-the-wall" digs demand "long wait times" (and "cash only"), but it's a real "bargain", so "bring friends and a few bottles of wine" and "enjoy a fabulous evening."

Thai Green Leaf Thai — 22 | 12 | 19 | $24

Massapequa | 27 Carmans Rd. (bet. E. Walnut & Hemlock Sts.) | 516-799-8666 Ⓜ

East Northport | 1969 Jericho Tpke. (Daly Rd.) | 631-462-8666

Loyal fans feel "lucky to know" about this Thai twosome where the "vibrant" cuisine is "full of color and flavor" and the "helpful" crew will "customize the spice to your liking"; both the East Northport and Massapequa locations are "minimally decorated" and "reasonably priced", but the latter locale offers sushi as well.

Thai House Thai — 21 | 15 | 20 | $30

Smithtown | 53 W. Main St. (Maple Ave.) | 631-979-5242

"What a find!" exclaim those who stumble on this "asset to Smithtown" offering a "wide selection" of "delightful" Thai cooking for "moderate prices"; "recently renovated" under new ownership, it strikes most as "just right" and deserving of a "stronger following."

Thai Table Thai — 22 | 17 | 19 | $27

Rockville Centre | 88A N. Village Ave. (Sunrise Hwy.) | 516-678-0886

"Step into serenity" and savor the "Zen-like vibe" say visitors about this Rockville Centre Thai offering "palate-pleasing" dishes for "reasonable prices"; with a "sweet" staff, it's a "friendly local place" that's "always busy and for good reason."

Thai USA Thai — 21 | 10 | 18 | $29

Huntington | 273 New York Ave. (bet. Gerard St. & Union Pl.) | 631-427-8464

Surveyors have a "soft spot" for this "little Thai house" in Huntington where the food is "delicious and well prepared" and service is generally "pleasant and efficient"; so even if some patrons plead "please paint the place", it fits the bill for those who "aren't looking for a scene."

34 New Street Ⓜ Eclectic — 20 | 15 | 18 | $32

Huntington | 34 New St. (bet. Main & W. Carver Sts.) | 631-427-3434 | www.34newstreet.com

"Mouthwatering" margherita pies, "interesting" toppings and "fantastic specials" "surprise" at this Eclectic Huntington "sleeper" with a pizza counter up front and white-tablecloth dining in back; despite its "plain-wrapper appearance", and a menu some critics call "too extensive" and "inconsistent", the "low prices" and "friendly" (if "slow") service make it a "good family place."

Thomas's Ham & Eggery Diner ⌷ *Diner* | 23 | 10 | 18 | $17 |

Carle Place | 325 Old Country Rd. (bet. E. Gate Blvd. & Mitchell Ave.) | 516-333-3060

"A must for any breakfast lover", this "cute" Carle Place coffee shop dating back to 1946 delivers "fresh eggs to order in a hot skillet" along with "winning" pancakes and waffles; the owners and staff "treat you right", though on weekends "the wait can be an hour long", so "if you're sitting there reading this, you're already late to get in line."

Thom Thom *Seafood/Steak* | 21 | 20 | 20 | $44 |

Wantagh | 3340 Park Ave. (bet. Beech St. & Wantagh Ave.) | 516-221-8022 | www.thomthomrestaurant.com

"Asian meets steakhouse" at this "modern" Wantagh option whose "solid" menu also features seafood (like "feisty hot" calamari); still, some critics contend it "keeps getting less interesting", recommending "stick with the apps" and "wonderful" if "expensive" martinis; N.B. a mid-Survey renovation may not be reflected in the Decor score.

Thyme Restaurant & Café Bar *American* | 20 | 19 | 20 | $46 |

Roslyn | 8 Tower Pl. (bet. Main St. & Old Northern Blvd.) | 516-625-2566 | www.thymenewyork.com

"Roslynites love" this "cozy" "little place" "next door to the movie theater" that's graced with a "tranquil view" of the pond; though "uneven" at times, its "intriguing" menu of "tasty" New American dishes is "attentively" served and complemented by "live background music" on the weekends, plus the "prix fixe dinner is a bargain."

Tide Runners *American* | ∇ 17 | 22 | 16 | $41 |

Hampton Bays | 7 North Rd. (bet. Montauk & Sunrise Hwys.) | 631-728-7373 | www.tiderunners.com

"Eat outside if you can" to enjoy the "location by the canal" at this Hampton Bays "hangout" serving a somewhat "expensive", seafood-heavy American menu; even if many find the food less exciting than the actual tides below, and some snipe the "rowboats drift faster than the staff", "lunch on the deck in the summer" and "tidbits at happy hour" remain "a treat"; N.B. closed mid-September to May.

Tierra Mar *American/Seafood* | 22 | 25 | 22 | $68 |

Westhampton Beach | Westhampton Bath & Tennis Hotel | 231 Dune Rd. (Jessup Lane Bridge) | 631-288-2700 | www.ontheatlantic.com

"Who can resist the setting?" ask admirers of this beachfront beacon in the Westhampton Bath & Tennis Hotel, where draping blue-and-white fabric plays off the "spectacular" views of the ocean and the dunes; many also commend the "costly" but "refreshing" seafood-focused New American cuisine and "not stuffy" service, completing the picture for a "moonlit summer evening."

Toast *Eclectic* | 23 | 16 | 19 | $20 |

Port Jefferson | 242 E. Main St. (Thompson St.) | 631-331-6860 | www.toastcoffeehouse.com

"Fantastic gourmet breakfasts" (such as "dreamy" sweet potato pancakes) and "creative" Eclectic lunches are the daytime draw at this "winning", "eccentric" Port Jefferson eatery, which also stays open for tapas, fondue and wine on Friday–Saturday nights; local art on the walls "fits the vibe" and "spruces up an otherwise plain dining room", while "personable" service and a low cost "for the area" add to the appeal.

NEW Toast & Co. *American*   17 | 15 | 14 | $24

Huntington | 62 Stewart Ave. (bet. Main St. & New York Ave.) | 631-812-0056

"Different menu choices for breakfast" and lunch pique patrons' curiosity at this Huntington New American offering "comforting" daytime fare in a "funky little place" that "feels like it should be in Greenwich Village"; though the "cheerful" service can be "a bit unorganized", the seating "tight" and the kitchen "inconsistent", a "mellow vibe" prevails; N.B. a new menu introduced mid-Survey may not be reflected in the Food score.

Z Toku *Asian Fusion*   24 | 27 | 22 | $63

Manhasset | The Americana | 2014C Northern Blvd. (Searingtown Rd.) | 516-627-8658 | www.tokumodernasian.com

"God arrived, and he made Toku" aver hip habitués of this "trendy", "urbane" addition to the Miracle Mile in Manhasset's The Americana, whose "stunning", temple-influenced surroundings create a "sparkling" backdrop for "wonderful" sushi and "decadent", "not-your-usual" Asian fusion plates; a "courteous" staff navigates the "chichi" scene of "beautiful, well-dressed" people, so "bring your Benjamins" to fit right in.

Tokyo M *Japanese/Korean*   ▽ 23 | 12 | 21 | $30

East Northport | Laurelwood Ctr. | 192 Laurel Rd. (bet. Bellerose & Dickinson Aves.) | 631-754-8411

Locals feel "lucky to live around the corner" from this long-standing East Northport eatery serving "fresh sushi", tempura and other Japanese and Korean specialties courtesy of a "delightful, warm" staff; despite Japanese screens and other decorations, the "small" space is called "not so pretty", "but don't worry" since it's "reliable" and a real "value."

Tomo Hibachi Steak House *Japanese*   19 | 18 | 17 | $36

Huntington | 286 Main St. (New St.) | 631-271-6666 | www.tomohibachi.com

"Typical cook-in-front-of-you fun" can be found at this Huntington hibachi house that satisfies those with a "big appetite for red meat", "good sushi" and a "loud", "raucous" atmosphere; all in all, you really "pay for the show", so "open your mouth and you might receive a tasty morsel flipped by a chef!"

Tony's Asian Fusion *Asian Fusion*   21 | 16 | 18 | $33

East Quogue | 337 Montauk Hwy. (Seashore Ave.) | 631-728-8850 | www.tonysasianfusion.com

Tony's Fusion Express *Asian Fusion*

Hampton Bays | 1 W. Main St. (Squiretown Rd.) | 631-728-1799

(continued)

Tony's Fusion West *Asian Fusion*
Westhampton Beach | 23 Sunset Ave. (bet. Hanson Pl. & Main St.) |
631-288-8880 | www.tonysfusionwest.com

Tony's Sushi *Asian*
East Moriches | 466 E. Main St. (Atlantic Ave.) | 631-878-9575 |
www.tonyssushi.net

At "any one of Tony's restaurants", the Chinese-Japanese-Thai menu is nothing if not diverse – from the large "hibachi grill in back" at the East Quogue branch to the full dining rooms of Westhampton Beach and East Moriches to the takeout-only counter-service of Hampton Bays, "they have it all"; samplers say the Thai is "particularly good" among the "bang-for-the-buck" options, so "uneven" service hardly ruffles the "Asian-starved East End."

Top of the Bay *American* | - | - | - | E |
Fire Island | 1 Dock Walk | 631-597-6028

Perched on the second floor of a building at the Cherry Grove ferry dock, this romantic seasonal bistro, with subdued mood lighting and a large bar, has wraparound windows offering spectacular views of the Great South Bay and bobbing boats in the harbor; its New American menu is more high-end than most on Fire Island, but still offers comforting dishes with regional influences by the chef.

Torcellos *Italian* | 18 | 12 | 18 | $30 |
East Northport | Elwood Shopping Ctr. | 1932 Jericho Tpke. (Elwood Rd.) |
631-499-8792 | www.torcellos.com

"Homestyle Italian" dishes and pizzas are plated up in "tremendous" portions ("I think they give each person a pound of pasta!") at this East Northport "go-to" that's an "excellent value"; while the "outdated" room has diners "sitting on top of" each other, it's still a "convenient", "friendly" option.

Touch of Venice, A *Italian* | 19 | 18 | 20 | $42 |
Mattituck | Matt-A-Mar Marina | 2255 Wickham Ave. (bet. Bayer & Farmer Rds.) | 631-298-5851 | www.touchofvenice.com

"Lots of fresh fish and local produce" go into the "rustic" cuisine at this "family-run" Italian with a "lovely secluded setting" in the Matt-A-Mar Marina in Mattituck; "warm" with "excellent" service, it's "cozy by the fireplace in winter" and an "oasis" in the summer, plus there's a dock if you want to arrive by boat; N.B. hours vary in the off-season, so call ahead.

Townline BBQ *BBQ* | 18 | 14 | 15 | $28 |
Sagaponack | 3593 Montauk Hwy. (Townline Rd.) | 631-537-2271 |
www.townlinebbq.com

Sagaponack sunbathers "fill up after a day at the beach" at this take on a Texan roadside BBQ joint from the Nick & Toni's group; it's "relaxed and casual" with "self-serve" trays, sliding barnwood walls and a pool table by the bar, and while some call the 'cue "average" and "a bit pricey", others assert it's a "welcome alternative to the fancy fare of the Hamptons."

	FOOD	DECOR	SERVICE	COST

Trata East ☻ *Greek/Seafood*   22 | 21 | 17 | $71

Water Mill | 1020 Montauk Hwy. (bet. Deerfield & Scuttle Hole Rds.) |
631-726-6200 | www.trata.com

"Delectable fish" and other "fresh, innovative" Greek specialties
stand out at this Water Mill sister to NYC's Trata Estiatorio that's
"chic" with "easy, breezy Mediterranean decor" and often "quite a
scene"; "rushed" service can ruffle reviewers, however, who also
warn about "getting stung" on the check; N.B. closed November
to mid-March.

Trattoria Diane Ⓜ *Italian*   25 | 21 | 23 | $58

Roslyn | 21 Bryant Ave. (bet. Roosevelt Ave. & Skillman St.) |
516-621-2591

"Colorful" Northern Italian dinners with "awesome" desserts "shine"
at this "pretty" Roslyn trattoria with "NYC quality"; "competent",
"cordial" service adds to the "refined" feel, and while it's on the
"pricey" side, wallet-watchers single out the Sunday night prix fixe
as the "bargain of the century."

Trattoria Di Meo *Italian*   21 | 15 | 20 | $45

Roslyn Heights | 183 Roslyn Rd. (Donald St.) | 516-621-4895 |
www.trattoriadimeo.com

It's "like eating at your grandma's" say pleased *paesani* who appreciate the 40 years of "classic", "consistent" Italian cooking at this
family-owned Roslyn Heights vet; with a "homey" setting and "just
the right amount of attention" from the "gracious" owners and staff,
it's an "old favorite" for "easy, tasty" meals.

Tre Bambini *Italian*   21 | 19 | 20 | $44

Lynbrook | 159 Sunrise Hwy. (Huntington Ave.) | 516-599-5858 |
trebambini.kpsearch.com

Homemade pastas enhance the "always fresh" cuisine, while crystal
chandeliers and rich draperies lend an "old-world feeling" to this
Northern Italian in Lynbrook; though somewhat "expensive", locals
prize it as a "lovely place to meet friends" for a "midweek escape."

Tricia's Café Ⓜ *American*   ▽ 21 | 13 | 15 | $22

Babylon | 26 E. Main St. (Fire Island Ave.) | 631-422-7879 |
www.triciascafe.com

Babylon boosters cheer the "cheap", "down-home" eats at this coffee shop serving up all-American fare in a '50s-style space decorated with old-time photos; while service can be "unpredictable",
it's an "affordable" option for the "entire family."

Trio *American*   ▽ 21 | 17 | 20 | $41
(aka Frederick & Co.)

Holbrook | Holbrook Country Club | 700 Patchogue-Holbrook Rd.
(Somerset Dr.) | 631-585-4433 | www.triofinefood.com

"Creative, well-prepared" New American dishes and a "nice view of
the golf course" are the prime attractions of this Patchogue transplant
set in the Holbrook Country Club; with prix fixe lunches and early-bird
specials, it offers savvy customers "a lot of food for a little price."

	FOOD	DECOR	SERVICE	COST

Trumpets on the Bay _American/Continental_ | 22 | 25 | 23 | $54 |

Eastport | 58 S. Bay Ave. (south of Montauk Hwy.) | 631-325-2900 | www.trumpetsonthebay.com

"Get a table overlooking the water and you'll have a terrific evening" assure admirers of this "hard-to-find" Eastport "winner" where "quiet, gracious" surroundings set the stage for "magical" summer sunsets; while the Continental-American menu has some stiff competition in the scenery, it's often "wonderful" and "worth it in every respect."

Tsubo ☒ _Japanese_   ▽ | 22 | 13 | 22 | $32 |

Syosset | 18 Cold Spring Rd. (Jackson Ave.) | 516-921-8154

You "can't beat it for the price" approve patrons of this "neighborhood" Syosset Japanese slicing "large cuts" of "quality" sushi into "amazing specials"; even if the food is low on "imagination" and the decor doesn't entice, "friendly" servers keep it an appealing option.

Tula Kitchen ☒ _Eclectic_ | - | - | - | M |

Bay Shore | 41 E. Main St. (bet. 3rd & 4th Aves.) | 631-539-7183 | www.tulakitchen.com

Decidedly un-crunchy in style, this Bay Shore innovator that's a "cross between fine dining and a countercultural experience" provides "delicious, nourishing" and reasonably priced Eclectic fare with lots of veggie choices (as well as poultry and fish) by chef-owner Jackie Sharlup; the setting has a "New York" vibe, fueled by "lovely deep red" walls, velvety pillow-topped chairs and a dramatic chandelier, and benefits from "engaged" service.

Tulip _Mediterranean/Turkish_ | 20 | 15 | 20 | $38 |

Great Neck | 4 Welwyn Rd. (bet. Gilchrest Rd. & Shoreward Dr.) | 516-487-1070 | www.tulipbarandgrill.com

"Forget about plane tickets to Turkey", the "tasty" Mediterranean "soul food" "satisfies" at this "moderately priced" Great Necker that earns kudos for "authentic" eats; the owner "makes you feel at home", and while it's a little "frenetic" on the weekends, most onlookers "love the belly dancing on Friday nights."

Tupelo Honey _American_ | 22 | 23 | 21 | $48 |

Sea Cliff | 39 Roslyn Ave. (bet. Sea Cliff & 10th Aves.) | 516-671-8300 | www.tupelohoneyrestaurant.com

"A sexy place to surprise your honey", this "colorful" Sea Cliff "escape" stimulates the senses with its "mosaic-tiled tables", curvy bar and "inventive", "refreshing" New American menu with Caribbean accents; rounded out by "excellent" drinks, an "engaging" staff and "wonderful" outdoor seating, it's a "happening" "local place where laughing out loud is fine"; N.B. winter hours vary, so call ahead.

Turquoise _Seafood_ | 23 | 13 | 19 | $42 |

Great Neck | 33 N. Station Plaza (bet. Bond St & Park Pl.) | 516-487-3737

It's "not glamorous", but this Great Neck seafooder attracts crowds for "fresh catches" "prepared to perfection" as well as "tasty" accompaniments like the "best Israeli salad"; despite the "downer" of "tight quarters with little ambiance", it's "just a stone's throw from the train station", service has "improved" and the early-bird is a "real bargain."

Turtle Crossing *BBQ/Southwestern*   21 | 11 | 16 | $37

East Hampton | 221 Pantigo Rd. (bet. Cross Hwy. & Egypt Ln.) | 631-324-7166 | www.turtlecrossing.com

"No muss, no fuss, just darn good BBQ" calls customers to this Southwestern pit stop in East Hampton delivering "smoky" ribs and "killer margs" in a "casual" space livened up by bands Thursday–Friday; "it's no bargain" and some "can't tell if they want to be kid-friendly or happy hour–friendly", but many feel it strikes a balance with "quality for the money" and a "vacation" vibe.

Tuscan House *Italian*   21 | 19 | 21 | $53

Southampton | 10 Windmill Ln. (Jobs Ln.) | 631-287-8703

"Hearty" fare such as the osso buco, 15 pastas and a "thin-crust brick-oven" pizzette (often enjoyed "at the bar") brings a "taste of Italy" to Southampton, with a "fine location" "convenient" to after-noon shopping; a few complain about the "cost", but others are appeased by the "attention to detail" all around.

Tutto Il Giorno *Italian*   ∇ 22 | 19 | 19 | $55

Sag Harbor | 6 Bay St. (Rector St.) | 631-725-7009

"Constant celebrity sightings" lend cachet to this Sag Harbor arrival that also delivers "delicious" Italian dishes and outdoor summer seating that's a "pleasure"; its "second incarnation" under a new team gets props for a "wonderful revamp" of the interior (by Gabby Karan De Felice, Donna's daughter) that provides a bit more space, though it is still "intimate" and reservations are only taken in the off-season, so "get there early to avoid a wait"; N.B. closed Mondays and weekday afternoons in the winter.

Tutto Pazzo *Italian*   21 | 21 | 19 | $42

Huntington | 84 New York Ave. (bet. Ketewomoke Dr. & Youngs Hill Rd.) | 631-271-2253 | www.tuttopazzo.com

"Vibrant" Italian cuisine is served with "pride" at this Huntington haunt where the "enjoyable" atmosphere is enhanced by a back patio that's perfect for "parties", "families" or "just dinner on a summer night"; some patrons suggest it's just "standard", but it remains "popular" with "lots of regulars who love it."

Tweeds Restaurant & Buffalo Bar *American*   20 | 20 | 19 | $46

Riverhead | J.J. Sullivan Hotel | 17 E. Main St. (bet. East & Roanoke Aves.) | 631-208-3151 | www.tweedsrestaurant.com

"Be adventurous" and try the bison steaks or burgers (they "rule!") at this "winter favorite" in Riverhead offering "lots of different foods to try" on the New American menu; partial to its "pub atmosphere" and "19th-century decor (complete with buffalo head)", people also praise the "easygoing entertainment" by a piano player weekend nights; P.S. "if you have too much to drink", you can always stay at the hotel.

	FOOD	DECOR	SERVICE	COST

21 Main *Steak* | 24 | 22 | 23 | $60 |

West Sayville | 21 Montauk Hwy. (Cherry Ave.) | 631-567-0900 | www.21main.com

"Brontosaurus-size bone-in rib-eyes" served with "panache" are "perfect for a big night out" at this West Sayville steakhouse where "even waiting at the bar is pleasant" given the "warm, welcoming" style, "well-versed" bartenders and "piano music on the weekends"; with "sparkling wood floors and upbeat decor", it's "elegant yet not pretentious", adding up to a "good splurge."

Twin Harbors *Seafood*   ▽ | 22 | 10 | 23 | $37 |

Bayville | 341 Bayville Ave. (Greenwich Ave.) | 516-628-1700

It's "like visiting family without the fighting" at this "inviting" Bayville "hideaway" specializing in "excellent" seafood and "prompt, cheerful" service since 1964; some customers complain it's "getting tired", but for others that's part of the "bargain."

Umberto's *Italian/Pizza* | 21 | 15 | 18 | $27 |

Garden City | 361 Nassau Blvd. S. (bet. Cambridge & Princeton Aves.) | 516-481-1279

New Hyde Park | 633 Jericho Tpke. (Lakeville Rd.) | 516-437-7698 | www.originalumbertos.com

Wantagh | Cherrywood Shopping Ctr. | 1180 Wantagh Ave. (Jerusalem Ave.) | 516-221-5696 | www.originalumbertos.com

Huntington | 138 E. Main St. (Loma Pl.) | 631-935-1391 | www.umbertosofeastmain.com

Angoletto Café *Italian/Pizza*

New Hyde Park | 1598 Hillside Ave. (New Hyde Park Rd.) | 516-358-2010

Village Pizzeria ⊟ *Italian/Pizza*

Floral Park | 169 Tulip Ave. (bet. Iris & Plainfield Aves.) | 516-775-0612

"Mamma mia, it's the best pizzeria" – especially for the "grandma and Sicilian" slice – rave parlor partisans about this "midrange" mini-chain, though some say you "must go to the original New Hyde Park location to get the real feel"; while other dishes only get "satisfactory" scores, and "service can be slow", most say it's "worth the wait" for a ticket to pie "heaven"; N.B. the Huntington branch is separately owned.

Uncle Bacala's *Italian/Seafood* | 18 | 16 | 19 | $37 |

Garden City Park | 2370 Jericho Tpke. (bet. Herricks Rd. & Marcus Ave.) | 516-739-0505 | www.unclebacala.com

"They'll keep the dishes coming until you scream 'uncle'" at this "decent neighborhood place" in Garden City Park proffering "affordable" "straightforward" Southern Italian favorites with a seafood focus; even if the "wait is ridiculous on Saturdays", it usually works for a "large crowd or a night out with da boys."

Uncle Dai *Chinese* | 17 | 10 | 17 | $24 |

Glen Cove | 26 School St. (bet. Glen St. & Highland Rd.) | 516-671-1144

Customers "count on" this Glen Cove "staple" for "quick", "well-done" Chinese food that's a "relief to the pocketbook"; there's "nothing too exciting" and the decor is "depressing", so some say "takeout is the only way to go", while others ride it out for the "free wine – a big plus."

Union Station Restaurant & Tavern *American*

19 | 19 | 20 | $40

Smithtown | 155 W. Main St. (Elliott Pl.) | 631-265-3300 | www.unionstationrestaurantsmithtown.com

On-board locals "love the bar" at this latest inhabitant of the former Smithtown Hotel, calling it "the place to eat" with a "lively atmosphere" and a "professional" staff; otherwise, the "old-fashioned" dining room can feel a bit "stuffy", and the "basic" New American steaks and other dishes get "mixed reviews", but most find it's "above average" with "enough choice on the menu to please all."

Varney's ☒ *American/Seafood*

▽ 24 | 7 | 18 | $34

Brookhaven | 2109 Montauk Hwy. (Cemetery Rd.) | 631-286-9569

Eaters who "aren't picky about their surroundings" "go for the food" at this "utilitarian" Brookhaven nook that's home to "outstanding" American cooking (the "simple seafood dishes are most successful"); since the "portions are big", "sharing is a definite possibility."

Venere Ristorante *Italian*

20 | 13 | 21 | $34

Westbury | 841 Carman Ave. (bet. Lake & Land Lns.) | 516-333-2332 | www.ristorantevenere.com

"Now this is an Italian restaurant!" approve patrons of this Westbury "tradition" serving up "classic dishes with consistency"; so even if "all the old parmigiano standards" and columned digs aren't for everyone, it's still "fine for family outings" with "caring, on-the-ball" service and "value" for the dollar.

Vespa Cibobuono *Italian*

22 | 19 | 21 | $49

Great Neck | 96 Northern Blvd. (bet. Buttonwood & Westminster Rds.) | 516-829-0005 | www.vespany.com

"Fresh pastas" and other "inspired" Northern Italian creations have earned a loyal following for this "adorable" Great Neck cafe that's somewhat "pricey" but "does it right"; decorated with Italian movie posters, the "hip", "date"-friendly setting is so atmospheric you "feel like you're in a little Italian village with your own Vespa and girl/boyfriend", about to "ride off into the sunset."

Villa D'Este *Italian*

20 | 16 | 20 | $42

Floral Park | 186 Jericho Tpke. (bet. Flower & Tyson Aves.) | 516-354-1355 | www.villadesterestaurant.com

"Surprise bargains abound" for those who go the prix fixe route at this "homey" Floral Park Italian offering "simple", "old-fashioned" cuisine; with "welcoming" service from a "longtime" staff, it draws lots of "repeat customers."

Village Lanterne Ⓜ *German*

- | - | - | E

Lindenhurst | 143 N. Wellwood Ave. (bet. Auburn & Bristol Sts.) | 631-225-1690 | www.thevillagelanterne.com

Prosit! applaud patrons who are taken with the "excellent" "variety of German specialties" (including "delicious" baked goods) and a *"wunder-bar"* of Bavarian beers at this Lindenhurst arrival from the owner of Black Forest Bakery; adorned with tapestries, steins and lanterns, the interior is "cozy", though several customers contend "they still haven't worked out the kinks" when it comes to service.

Vincent's Clam Bar *Italian*   ▏–▕–▕–▕ M ▏

Carle Place | Carle Place Commons | 179 Old Country Rd. (Glen Cove Rd.) | 516-742-4577 | www.vincentsclambar.com

"If you want a quiet, romantic night, this is not the place, but the energy is contagious" advise advocates of this Carle Place Italian that was originally affiliated with the 1904 Little Italy landmark (although no more) and exudes the same old-school atmosphere; "straightforward saucy" dishes, a clam and oyster bar and "efficient" service keep it hopping, plus you can "buy their sauce" to go.

☑ Vine Street Café *American*   ▏27▕20▕23▕ $63 ▏

Shelter Island | 41 S. Ferry Rd. (1½ mi. north of South Ferry) | 631-749-3210 | www.vinestreetcafe.com

Wayfarers wax ecstatic about the "novel", "exquisite" American dishes at this "expensive""Manhattan-quality" "destination" that "makes Shelter Island a happening place"; while the "Jaguars lined up outside" can be "a little daunting", the "bustling", "bistro-type" space (renovated post-Survey) with a "lovely porch" is "unpretentious" and tended in "relaxed" style, rewarding a "trip on the ferry"; N.B. closed Tuesday–Wednesday in the winter.

Vine Wine + Cafe ◑Ⓜ *American*   ▏22▕22▕19▕ $39 ▏

Greenport | 100 South St. (1st St.) | 631-477-6238 | www.vinewinebar.com

"Brightening an out-of-the-way corner" in "picturesque Greenport", this "casual yet sophisticated" New American offers "upscale inventive small plates" and "fabulous cheeses" to accompany its "terrific" wine selection; as most of the seating is outside on the patio and wraparound porch, smitten sippers say it's the "perfect place to hang on a summer evening" and "people-watch"; N.B. hours are limited in the off-season, so call ahead.

🆕 Vintage Port ☒Ⓜ *French*   ▏–▕–▕–▕ I ▏

Port Washington | 109D Main St. (bet. Central Dr. & Irma Ave.) | 516-883-1033

Part wine bar and part French small-plates venue, this new Port Washington offshoot of Bistro du Village (just down the street) offers savory crêpes, sandwiches and cheese platters, complemented by a variety of ports; a copper tile–topped bar, exposed-brick walls and tables with mosaic work (by co-owner Laraine Le Dily) lend it an artful, yet rustic, touch.

☑ Vintage Prime Steakhouse *Steak*   ▏26▕22▕24▕ $65 ▏

St. James | 433 N. Country Rd. (Clinton Ave.) | 631-862-6440

A "rare find" in St. James, this "meat-eaters' heaven" provides "mouthwatering mains" and sides in an atmosphere suited to an "intimate dinner or a group of eight"; "professional" service enhances

	FOOD	DECOR	SERVICE	COST

the meal, so while "the more Western decor may throw you off a little" and prices are "steep", most affirm it's "well worth it."

Vittorio's Restaurant & Wine Bar *American/Italian*

| 24 | 21 | 24 | $47 |

Amityville | 184 Broadway (Greene Ave.) | 631-264-3333 | www.vittorios.biz

The "spot-on" staff "continues to surpass all expectations" at this "highly recommended" Amityville option offering "delicious", "large" plates of American-Italian cuisine as well as a steakhouse menu on Wednesday that "can't be beat"; sure, "it ain't cheap", but that's taken in stride since it's "cozy" and "welcoming", and "eating at the bar and mingling with the regulars is as much fun as having a full-course meal."

Viva Juan *Mexican*

| 17 | 12 | 16 | $26 |

Farmingdale | 169 Main St. (S. Front St.) | 516-586-5601 ●
Selden | 280 Middle Country Rd. (bet. New Ln. & Patchogue-Mt. Sinai Rd.) | 631-698-8172

"Standard combo-plate food with an emphasis on drinks" can be found at these "party"-friendly Farmingdale and Selden hangouts that critics call your "typical pseudo-Mexican places"; even if the management "needs to put some effort and money into renovating" as well as cooking, gung-ho guests say "go for the pitchers of margaritas" and karaoke in Farmingdale on the weekends – "what a hoot!"

Viva La Vida *Mexican/Spanish*

| ▽ 23 | 17 | 24 | $37 |

Oakdale | 1611 Montauk Hwy. (bet. Idlehour & Vanderbilt Blvds.) | 631-589-2300 | www.viva-la-vida.com

"Authentic" Spanish and Mexican cuisine (featuring appealing options "if you're not into tacos and enchiladas") and "out-of-this-world" drinks make a "wonderful" combo at this moderately priced Oakdale locale; since the servers "trip over themselves to serve you", pampered patrons assure it's an "enjoyable place to be."

Viva Loco *Italian/Mexican*

| 16 | 18 | 17 | $33 |

Bellmore | 2381 Merrick Rd. (bet. Farmers & Ocean Aves.) | 516-679-5900 | www.vivalocorestaurant.com

"The mix of Italian and Mexican means that everyone will be able to find something to eat" at this "hybrid-style" stop in Bellmore, even if detractors dis that it "can't decide what kind of restaurant it is"; even so, patrons belly up to the bar for "lots of variations of margaritas" and are willing to put up with the "nothing-special" food and iffy service for a "hip", "colorful" setting that helps fuel a "big date scene."

Voila! 🅂 *French*

| 23 | 22 | 24 | $47 |

St. James | 244 Lake Ave. (Woodlawn Ave.) | 631-584-5686 | www.voilathebistro.com

Visitors savor a taste of "Provence on Long Island" at this "winning" yet "relatively unknown" St. James bistro that's so "delightful" it "should be packed every night"; the "caring" chef-owner and "outstanding" staff lend a personal touch to the "charming" environs, while the prix fixe deals are a "bargain" and the tasting menu is of the quality "you'd get in Manhattan, but at half the cost."

Walk Street   *American* | 21 | 17 | 21 | $39 |

Garden City | 176 Seventh St. (Franklin Ave.) | 516-746-2592 | www.walkstreetgc.com

Garden City grazers go for the "reliable pub food" at this "modern", "barlike" New American that fits the bill for a "girls' night out" or outdoor meal "in the summertime"; some naysayers note the menu could use some "shaking up" and the lighting is reminiscent of a "dentist's office", but most agree the service "deserves high marks", plus half-price bottles of wine on Mondays add to the value.

Wall's Wharf   *American/Seafood* | 17 | 18 | 17 | $42 |

Bayville | 18 Greenwich Ave. (off Bayville Ave.) | 516-628-9696 | www.wallswharf.com

"Outside on the deck is the way to go" at this beachfront Bayviller that wows with a "wonderful view of Long Island Sound"; many say the New American seafood menu has "improved" of late with "new innovations", but even those who cite "ordinary", "overpriced" fare, an "inexperienced" staff and "interior decor like a bad hotel restaurant" admit it's "fantastic at sunset on a cool summer evening."

Waterview Restaurant   *Continental/Seafood* | 16 | 16 | 18 | $39 |

Port Washington | Brewer Capri Marina E. | 45 Orchard Beach Blvd. (bet. Kaywood & Lindwood Rds. S.) | 516-944-5900 | www.thewaterview.net

"Stunning" views are the star of this Continental seafooder set in the Brewer Capri Marina in Port Washington, where the vista leads some to "overestimate the taste" of the "hit-or-miss" fare; "inconsistent" service and somewhat "depressing" digs are other setbacks, though sedate types recommend it as a "place to relax"; N.B. closed Monday–Wednesday in the winter.

Z Waterzooi Belgian Bistro   *Belgian* | 23 | 18 | 19 | $43 |

Garden City | 850 Franklin Ave. (bet. 9th St. & Stewart Ave.) | 516-877-2177 | www.waterzooi.com

"No one's better at flexing their mussels" than this "young", "upbeat" Belgian bistro in Garden City where the "awesome", shareable pots of moules are prepared in "exciting" ways and matched by "addictive" frites and a "fantastic Belgian beer selection"; though the prices can "sneak up on you", the "decent" service keeps it comfortable for everyone from "local businesspeople to hipsters to shoppers" (just beware of the "unbearable din" at "peak times").

NEW Wave   *American*   ▽ | 20 | 23 | 17 | $52 |
(fka 25 East American Bistro)

Port Jefferson | Danfords on the Sound | 25 E. Broadway (E. Main St.) | 631-928-5200 | www.danfords.com

"Things have been looking up" lately at this New American in the former 25 East space in Danfords on the Sound, having completed a "long overdue" makeover with "pretty" results up front and an "eclectic" touch in the "improved" kitchen; while a few report some "growing pains" and "pricey" tabs, most still appreciate the "view of Port Jeff Harbor" and like to "go for happy hour."

West East Bistro *Asian Fusion* | 24 | 20 | 20 | $37 |

Hicksville | 758 S. Broadway (bet. Hazel St. & Oyster Bay Rd.) | 516-939-6618 | www.westeastbistro.com

A "real find" in a Hicksville strip mall, this "excellent newcomer" stands out with "refreshing", "innovative" and "superbly sauced" Asian fusion dishes, a "classy", "comfortable" dining room and service that's "attentive without being annoying", overseen by a "gracious" owner; commending the "generous portions" and "reasonable" prices too, most customers "can't wait to return."

☒ West End Cafe *American* | 25 | 20 | 21 | $45 |

Carle Place | Clocktower Shopping Ctr. | 187 Glen Cove Rd. (bet. Old Country Rd. & Westbury Ave.) | 516-294-5608 | www.westendli.com

"The cooking continues to amaze" at this "little" Carle Place "jewel" where "sublime" New American dishes are served by a "caring" staff amid "modern" surroundings with a "Manhattan feel"; so "don't let the strip-mall" exterior "dissuade you", just "make a reservation far in advance" and opt for the twilight menu for "unbelievable value."

Westhampton Steakhouse ● *Steak* | 17 | 17 | 20 | $51 |

Westhampton Beach | 142 Mill Rd. (Sunset Ave.) | 631-288-7161 | www.westhamptonsteakhouse.com

Carnivores can't seem to agree on this Westhampton Beach chophouse, with some savoring its "good" steaks and "value" prix fixe deal, while others assert it "runs hot and cold" and "just cannot compare to the big boys on Steak Row"; at least the "friendly" staff "aims to please", and it's set in a "nice building" dating back to the 1890s.

West Lake Clam & Chowder House Ⓜ *Seafood* | 24 | 13 | 18 | $37 |

Montauk | W. Lake Fishing Lodge | 382 W. Lake Dr. (Duryea Ave.) | 631-668-6252

There's "nothing fancy but the food" at this "treasure" off Lake Montauk turning out "beautiful" fish, "freshly made" chowders and "incredible" sushi that's all "shockingly upscale, given the shabby dockside decor"; "earthy" and popular with families (kids can "see the catch coming in"), it's the "kind of off-the-beaten-path find you'd like to keep to yourself", but word has gotten out, so there can be a long "wait."

Wild Fig *Mediterranean/Turkish* | 19 | 13 | 18 | $28 |

Garden City | 829 Franklin Ave. (Stewart Ave.) | 516-739-1002
Glen Cove | 167 Glen St. (bet. Pearsall Ave. & Town Path) | 516-656-5645
www.wildfigonline.com

"Tasty" Med-Turkish dishes, including "full-of-flavor" brick-oven pides (similar to pizzas), are "pleasantly served" at this duo that's a "refreshing change" "from the typical fast-food joint"; both branches are "reasonably priced", but the Garden City location happily "surprises" with a martini list, while Glen Cove (which serves beer and wine) is "a bit more family-friendly."

Wild Ginger *Pan-Asian*   22 | 19 | 19 | $37

Great Neck | The Gdns. | 48 Great Neck Rd. (Middle Neck Rd.) | 516-487-8288 | www.wildgingerrestaurant.net

"Zesty" Pan-Asian fare "wakes up" the taste buds at this "big favorite" in Great Neck set in an "attractive", "jazzed-up" space where "large groups tend to migrate" on the weekends; some wags warn the staff "serves with enthusiasm and clears equally enthusiastically", but those seeking a "quickie dinner" for a "decent price" appreciate the "lightning" speed.

Wild Harvest Ⓜ *Southern*   20 | 20 | 22 | $41

Glen Cove | 64 Forest Ave. (bet. Bryce Ave. & Phillips Rd.) | 516-676-0056 | www.wildharvestrestaurant.com

Chef/co-owner Zane Smith "shows off his Southern roots" with "fantastic" fare ("who knew grits could be so good?") at this new Wild Honey spin-off in Glen Cove that's decorated in "inviting" "ski lodge" style and staffed by a crew that stays "on top of things"; though a few cite "inconsistent" meals, most maintain it's a "comfort-food mecca."

Wild Honey Dining & Wine *American*   24 | 22 | 23 | $47

Oyster Bay | 1 E. Main St. (South St.) | 516-922-4690 | www.wildhoneyrestaurant.com

An "Oyster Bay pearl" "housed in Teddy Roosevelt's summer White House", this "nifty haunt" offers "adventurous" New American cuisine with an "upscale flair" in an atmosphere that's "full of character"; add in "personable" service and a "hopping" scene, and "foodies" feel it's "one of the best meals for your money on the North Shore."

Wildthyme *American*   ▽ 18 | 15 | 16 | $58

Southampton | 129 Noyac Rd. (bet. Bay & Oak Aves.) | 631-204-0007

"Off the beaten path" in the North Sea hamlet of Southampton, this "simple but tastefully decorated" place provides "fresh flavors in new combinations", featuring a Northeastern American menu with Mediterranean and Asian influences and offering the "bargain" of two-for-one entrees on Sunday nights; "inconsistency" is an issue, however, as critics contend the kitchen "underperforms" and service can be "spotty", concluding the meal "should be better for the price."

World Pie ➊ *Pizza*   20 | 13 | 17 | $36

Bridgehampton | 2402 Montauk Hwy. (bet. Bridgehampton-Sag Harbor Tpke. & Corwith Ave.) | 631-537-7999

"Pies you would never have imagined, but are happy they did" "please" pizza lovers at this "solid" Bridgehampton staple that invites "sitting outside in the summer", with a "family-friendly" vibe during the day followed by a "surprisingly seductive" scene in the

	FOOD	DECOR	SERVICE	COST

"late" hours; indeed, it's "one of the more affordable meals" in town, though it may add up to "more than you planned on paying for a pizza and a glass of wine."

Yamaguchi Ⓜ *Japanese* | 24 | 14 | 20 | $39 |

Port Washington | 63 Main St. (Herbert Ave.) | 516-883-3500
Admirers are "enthralled" by the "superior" sushi served in "gorgeous presentations" at this "busy" Port Washington vet that also prepares "traditional Japanese dishes in accordance with the seasons"; despite what some call "top-dollar" tabs, the decor "could use work" ("wish they'd dim the lights after the second sake") and service can be "patchy", but most are charmed by the "thoughtful hosts" who ensure "you'll be well taken care of, if you're a repeat customer."

Yama Q Ⓢ Ⓜ *Japanese* | - | - | - | M |

Bridgehampton | 2393 Montauk Hwy. (bet. Ocean Rd. & School St.) | 631-537-0225
Tucked away in a tiny Bridgehampton building, this Japanese bento box offers a "quirky" selection of moderately priced, "health-oriented" dishes spanning sushi and sashimi, vegetarian combos and steak teriyaki; granite-topped tables and wood walls add to the earthy feel.

Yokohama *Asian Fusion* | 23 | 17 | 21 | $38 |

East Northport | 3082 Jericho Tpke. (Verleye Ave.) | 631-462-2464 | www.liyokohama.com
"Number one in my book" according to boosters, this "enjoyable" East Northport nook earns raves for its "terrific, inventive" sushi and "eclectic", "attractive" Asian fusion dishes served by a "congenial" staff; though the "casual" space could use an "update" and the "wait is long on the weekend", most maintain they're "never disappointed."

Yuki's Palette Ⓢ *Japanese* | 21 | 13 | 20 | $33 |

Westbury | Poet Corner Shopping Ctr. | 611 Old Country Rd. (bet. Longfellow & Tennyson Aves.) | 516-334-5009

Yuki's Palette Too Ⓜ *Japanese*

🆕 **Merrick** | 151 Merrick Ave. (Loines Ave.) | 516-867-8738
South Shore sushi sleuths savor the "fresh, fresh, fresh" creations composed for "amazing taste explosions" at this Westbury Japanese and its new Merrick spin-off that shows "the chef's much-deserved popularity has grown"; a "warm, inviting" staff and value "for your buck" are also pluses, so despite "zero ambiance", the loving clientele stays "loyal."

🆕 Zim Zari *Californian/Mexican* | - | - | - | I |

Massapequa Park | Southgate Shopping Ctr. | 4964 Merrick Rd. (Whitewood Dr.) | 516-809-6960 | www.zimzari.com
Set in the same shopping center as its sister restaurant, Mercato, this Massapequa Park newcomer shows its coastal Southern California leanings with a huge beach mural, surfboards hanging on the walls and a bright blue glow from the bar; the inexpensive menu

focuses on Cal-Mex dishes with healthy options, offering tacos and burritos that can be wrapped in lettuce instead of tortillas, as well as some dishes tossed with organic soba noodles.

Zorba the Greek *Greek* | 19 | 11 | 16 | $22 |

Hicksville | 620 S. Oyster Bay Rd. (Old Country Rd.) |
516-932-9701
Port Jefferson Station | 572 Port Jefferson Plaza (Rte. 112) |
631-473-9220

Greek to Go *Greek*
Stony Brook | Smithpoint Plaza | 2460 Nesconset Hwy. (Stony Brook Rd.) |
631-689-2222

"Hearty", "plentiful" Greek food "fills the craving" for "budget"-conscious customers of these "reliable", separately owned outposts; the decor ranges from minimal to "a bit much" depending on the location (the Port Jeff locale has recently upgraded), but works when you want to "swing by for takeout" or a "quick" lunch.

INDEXES

Cuisines

Includes restaurant names, locations and Food ratings.

AFGHAN

Ariana	**Huntington**	21
Kabul Afghani	**Huntington**	22

AMERICAN (NEW)

Antares Cafe	**Greenport**	24
Argyle Grill	**Babylon**	21
☑ Barney's	**Locust Valley**	26
Bayview Inn	**S Jamesport**	21
Beacon	**Sag Harbor**	24
Bella Vita Grill	**St. James**	21
Bellport	**Bellport**	23
Bistro 44	**Northport**	21
Bistro M	**Glen Head**	25
Bliss	**E Setauket**	22
Blond	**Miller Pl**	22
Blue	**Blue Pt**	19
Blue Room	**E Northport**	24
Bob's Place	**Floral Pk**	21
NEW Brass Rail	**Locust Valley**	–
Breakwater Cafe	**Montauk**	–
Broadway Beanery	**Lynbrook**	22
Butterfields	**Hauppauge**	20
Cafe Joelle	**Sayville**	23
Catfish Max	**Seaford**	23
☑ Chachama Grill	**E Patchogue**	28
Chadwicks	**Rockville Ctr**	–
NEW Charlotte's	**Cold Spring**	20
Cirella's	**Huntington Station**	21
City Cellar	**Westbury**	20
Coach Grill	**Oyster Bay**	22
Coast Grill	**Southampton**	18
Collins & Main	**Sayville**	24
☑ Country House	**Stony Brook**	22
NEW Crew Kitchen	**Huntington**	25
Crossroads Cafe	**E Northport**	20
Delano Mansion	**Woodbury**	–
☑ Della Femina	**E Hampton**	24
Desmond's	**Wading River**	22
NEW Dish	**Water Mill**	–
Downtown	**Mineola**	–
Duke Falcon's	**Long Bch**	23

East by Northeast	**Montauk**	21
☑ E. Hampton Point	**E Hampton**	20
E. B. Elliot's	**Freeport**	18
Emerson's	**Babylon**	23
Fifth Season	**Port Jefferson**	24
Four Food Studio	**Melville**	20
Fresno	**E Hampton**	22
Gabrielle's	**Rockville Ctr**	22
George Martin	**Rockville Ctr**	22
Graffiti	**multi.**	20
Grasso's	**Cold Spring**	25
NEW Grey Horse	**Bayport**	22
Grill Room	**Hauppauge**	22
Harbor Bistro	**E Hampton**	22
Hemingway's	**Wantagh**	18
☑ Honu	**Huntington**	22
Horace/Sylvia's	**Babylon**	17
Hudson's Mill	**Massapequa**	22
☑ In Season Amer.	**Islip**	26
Island Mermaid	**Fire Is**	20
Jamesport Country	**Jamesport**	23
☑ Jamesport Manor	**Jamesport**	24
☑ Jedediah's	**Jamesport**	26
Jonathan's	**Garden City Pk**	19
JT's Corner Cafe	**Nesconset**	23
☑ Lake House	**Bay Shore**	27
Laundry	**E Hampton**	21
Library Cafe	**Farmingdale**	17
NEW Lola's	**Long Bch**	–
Love Lane Kitchen	**Mattituck**	22
Lucy's Café	**Babylon**	23
Ludlow Bistro	**Deer Park**	23
Maguire's	**Fire Is**	18
Maxxels	**Mineola**	24
Meritage	**Bellport**	23
☑ Mill River Inn	**Oyster Bay**	27
Mim's	**multi.**	18
NEW Mirabelle Tavern	**Stony Brook**	–
Mixing Bowl	**Bellmore**	20
☑ Mosaic	**St. James**	26
Muse	**Water Mill**	21

New Paradise	**Sag Harbor**	21
Nicholas James	**Merrick**	21
Noma	**Huntington**	20
☑ North Fork Table	**Southold**	28
Oasis Waterfront	**Sag Harbor**	23
Old Mill Inn	**Mattituck**	17
105 Harbor	**Cold Spring**	20
NEW 101 Bar & Grill	**Bellmore**	20
On 3	**Glen Head**	24
Oscar's	**St. James**	22
☑ Palm Court	**E Meadow**	24
☑ Panama Hatties	**Huntington Station**	26
Patio/54 Main	**Westhampton Bch**	19
☑ Piccolo	**Huntington**	26
☑ Pine Island	**Bayville**	17
☑ Plaza Cafe	**Southampton**	26
☑ Polo	**Garden City**	25
☑ Prime	**Huntington**	22
Q East	**Quogue**	23
Rachel's Waterside	**Freeport**	19
red bar	**Southampton**	23
Red Dish Grille	**Commack**	21
Red Fish	**Plainview**	23
Red Rest.	**Huntington**	24
Robinson's	**Stony Brook**	24
Sagamore Steak	**Syosset**	23
Savanna's	**Southampton**	20
Scrimshaw	**Greenport**	22
Sea Levels	**Brightwaters**	24
Second House	**Montauk**	18
75 Main St.	**Southampton**	18
Snaps	**Wantagh**	22
Soundview	**Glen Cove**	19
Starr Boggs	**Westhampton Bch**	25
Stonewalls	**Riverhead**	24
NEW Surf Lodge	**Montauk**	21
Thyme	**Roslyn**	20
Tierra Mar	**Westhampton Bch**	22
NEW Toast & Co.	**Huntington**	17
Top of the Bay	**Fire Is**	–
Trio	**Holbrook**	21
Tupelo Honey	**Sea Cliff**	22
Tweeds	**Riverhead**	20
Union Station	**Smithtown**	19
Vine Wine/Cafe	**Greenport**	22

Walk St.	**Garden City**	21
Wall's Wharf	**Bayville**	17
NEW Wave	**Port Jefferson**	20
☑ West End	**Carle Pl**	25
Wild Honey	**Oyster Bay**	24

AMERICAN (REGIONAL)

Wildthyme	**Southampton**	18

AMERICAN (TRADITIONAL)

☑ American Hotel	**Sag Harbor**	24
Barrister's	**Southampton**	16
Birchwood	**multi.**	18
B.K. Sweeney's	**multi.**	18
Blue Sky Bistro	**Malverne**	23
Bridgehampton Candy	**Bridgehampton**	15
Brook House	**Stony Brook**	–
Buckram Stables	**Locust Valley**	18
Cafe Max	**E Hampton**	21
Canterbury	**Oyster Bay**	18
Chalet Bar	**Roslyn**	18
☑ Cheesecake Factory	**multi.**	20
Chequit Inn	**Shelter Is Hts**	19
Claudio's	**Greenport**	15
Cooperage Inn	**Baiting Hollow**	20
Declan Quinn's	**Bay Shore**	19
Driver's Seat	**Southampton**	15
Estia's Kitchen	**Sag Harbor**	21
Fairway	**Sagaponack**	18
56th Fighter Group	**Farmingdale**	15
Garden Grill	**Smithtown**	19
George Martin Grill	**multi.**	21
Golden Pear	**multi.**	17
Gonzalo's	**Glen Cove**	20
Hildebrandt's	**Williston Pk**	19
Houston's	**Garden City**	21
H.R. Singleton's	**Bethpage**	17
Indian Cove	**Hampton Bays**	18
NEW Indian Wells Tav.	**Amagansett**	15
International Delight	**multi.**	18
Ivy Cottage	**Williston Pk**	24
John Harvard's	**Lake Grove**	16
JT's Place	**Hampton Bays**	18

Maureen's Kitchen | **Smithtown**	25
Meeting House | **Amagansett**	18
Michaels'/Maidstone | **E Hampton**	18
Milk & Sugar Café | **Bay Shore**	20
Milleridge Inn | **Jericho**	15
Mitchell's | **multi.**	16
Modern Snack | **Aquebogue**	18
Mother Kelly's | **Cedarhurst**	21
Nichol's | **E Hampton**	18
Oakland's | **Hampton Bays**	17
Oak Room | **Farmingdale**	23
Olde Speonk Inn | **Speonk**	17
O'Mally's | **Southold**	16
Page One | **Glen Cove**	22
PeraBell | **Patchogue**	24
Post Office Cafe | **Babylon**	18
Post Stop Cafe | **Westhampton Bch**	16
Ram's Head | **Shelter Is**	21
Rein | **Garden City**	23
Riverview | **Oakdale**	19
Roots | **Sea Cliff**	24
Runyon's | **multi.**	17
Sea Grille | **Montauk**	18
Shagwong | **Montauk**	18
Southampton Publick | **Southampton**	16
Star Confectionery | **Riverhead**	21
Sullivan's Quay | **Port Washington**	17
Sweet Mama's | **Northport**	18
NEW Table 9 | **E Hills**	-
Thyme | **Roslyn**	20
Tide Runners | **Hampton Bays**	17
Tricia's Café | **Babylon**	21
Trumpets | **Eastport**	22
Varney's | **Brookhaven**	24
Z Vine Street | **Shelter Is**	27
Vittorio's | **Amityville**	24

ARGENTINEAN

Café Buenos Aires | **Huntington**	23

ASIAN

NEW Fortune Asian | **Westbury**	-
Thom Thom | **Wantagh**	21
Tony's Fusion | **E Moriches**	21

ASIAN FUSION

Azuma | **Greenlawn**	-
Blue Fin | **Great Neck**	23
Cho-Sen | **multi.**	18
NEW Cove Star | **Glen Cove**	-
Danú | **Huntington**	19
NEW Haiku | **Woodbury**	-
Hinata | **Great Neck**	22
NEW Izumi | **Bethpage**	-
Taiko | **Rockville Ctr**	24
Z Toku | **Manhasset**	24
Tony's Fusion | **multi.**	21
West East | **Hicksville**	24
Yokohama | **E Northport**	23

BAKERIES

BayKery | **Oyster Bay**	19

BARBECUE

BBQ Bill's | **Greenport**	18
Big Daddy's | **Massapequa**	23
BobbiQue | **Patchogue**	19
Famous Dave's | **multi.**	19
Foody's | **Water Mill**	19
Harbor-Q | **Port Washington**	-
NEW Island BBQ | **Islip**	-
NEW Ruby's BBQ | **E Meadow**	-
Z Smokin' Al's BBQ | **multi.**	24
Spare Rib | **multi.**	17
Spicy's BBQ | **multi.**	19
Swingbelly's | **Long Bch**	21
Townline | **Sagaponack**	18
Turtle Crossing | **E Hampton**	21

BELGIAN

Z Waterzooi | **Garden City**	23

BRAZILIAN

Churrasc. Riodizio | **Roslyn Hts**	21
Marcia's Kitchen | **Huntington**	21

BURGERS

American Burger | **multi.**	17
Barrister's | **Southampton**	16
Bay Burger | **Sag Harbor**	19
NEW Bobby's Burger | **Lake Grove**	-
Buckram Stables | **Locust Valley**	18
Chalet Bar | **Roslyn**	18

George Martin Grill | multi. 21
Gonzalo's | **Glen Cove** 20
O'Mally's | **Southold** 16
Post Stop Cafe |
  Westhampton Bch 16
Rowdy Hall | **E Hampton** 19

CAJUN

Bayou | **N Bellmore** 23
Big Daddy's | **Massapequa** 23
Blackbirds' Grille | **Sayville** 18
B.Smith's | **Sag Harbor** 16

CALIFORNIAN

Salsa Salsa | multi. 23
NEW Zim Zari | **Massapequa Pk** -

CARIBBEAN

Antares Cafe | **Greenport** 24
Cooke's In | **Huntington** 23
NEW Gulf Coast Kitchen |
  Montauk -
NEW Tequila Jacks |
  Port Jefferson -

CHINESE

(* dim sum specialist)
Albert's Mandarin | **Huntington** 21
Ancient Ginger | **St. James** 21
Chi | **Westbury** 25
Dynasty/Pt. Wash. |
  Port Washington 18
Fortune Wheel* | **Levittown** 23
Hunan Taste | **Greenvale** 23
Lotus East | multi. 20
Madame Tong's | **Southampton** 12
Nanking | **New Hyde Pk** 19
Orchid | **Garden City** 24
Z Orient* | **Bethpage** 26
Pearl East | **Manhasset** 23
P.F. Chang's | **Westbury** 19
Shang Hai Pavilion | multi. 23
Sherwood | **Glen Cove** 17
Tony's Fusion | **Westhampton Bch** 21
Uncle Dai | **Glen Cove** 17

COFFEEHOUSES

Broadway Beanery | **Lynbrook** 22
Golden Pear | multi. 17
Hampton Coffee | multi. 19

COFFEE SHOPS/ DINERS

Bozena Polish | **Lindenhurst** 22
Bridgehampton Candy |
  Bridgehampton 15
International Delight | multi. 18
Mitchell's | multi. 16
Star Confectionery | **Riverhead** 21
Sweet Mama's | **Northport** 18
Thomas's Ham | **Carle Pl** 23
Tricia's Café | **Babylon** 21

CONTINENTAL

Babylon Carriage | **Babylon** 19
Barolo | **Melville** 25
Bayview Inn | **S Jamesport** 21
Bellport | **Bellport** 23
Cafe Testarossa | **Syosset** 20
Z Camille's | **Carle Pl** 24
Chadwicks | **Rockville Ctr** -
Chez Kama | **Great Neck** -
Cirella's | **Melville** 21
Claudio's | **Greenport** 15
Cooperage Inn | **Baiting Hollow** 20
Crabtree's | **Floral Pk** 20
Z Dave's Grill | **Montauk** 26
Frederick's | **Melville** 22
Irish Coffee | **E Islip** 22
Koenig's | **Floral Pk** 18
La Gioconda | **Great Neck** 21
Le Chef | **Southampton** 21
Meson Iberia | **Island Pk** 21
New Hyde Park | **New Hyde Pk** 20
NU | **Hauppauge** -
Oak Chalet | **Bellmore** 20
Z Palm Court | **E Meadow** 24
Peppercorns | **Hicksville** 18
Ritz Cafe | **Northport** 18
Riverview | **Oakdale** 19
1770 House | **E Hampton** 25
Soigné | **Woodmere** 25
Surfside Inn | **Montauk** 19
Trumpets | **Eastport** 22
Waterview Rest. |
  Port Washington 16

CREOLE

Bayou | **N Bellmore** 23
Cooke's In | **Huntington** 23

CUBAN

NEW Cafe Havana | **Smithtown**	17
Havana Beach Club | **Montauk**	-

DELIS

Ben's Deli | **multi.**	19
Deli King | **New Hyde Pk**	18
Pastrami King | **Merrick**	19

DESSERT

Bridgehampton Candy | **Bridgehampton**	15
Broadway Beanery | **Lynbrook**	22
Z Cheesecake Factory | **multi.**	20
Fresco Crêperie | **Long Bch**	23
Hildebrandt's | **Williston Pk**	19
Once Upon a Moose | **Sea Cliff**	19
NEW Sally's Cocofé | **Huntington**	-

ECLECTIC

Abel Conklin's | **Huntington**	22
Babette's | **E Hampton**	20
NEW Bennett's | **Locust Valley**	-
NEW Brick & Rail | **Wantagh**	-
Cafe Joelle | **Sayville**	23
Cafe Max | **E Hampton**	21
Canterbury | **Oyster Bay**	18
Chalet Bar | **Roslyn**	18
Chequit Inn | **Shelter Is Hts**	19
Chi | **Westbury**	25
Cirella's | **Huntington Station**	21
Collins & Main | **Sayville**	24
Duke Falcon's | **Long Bch**	23
Epicurean Room | **Central Islip**	-
Frisky Oyster | **Greenport**	24
Z Grand Lux | **Garden City**	19
Hideaway | **Fire Is**	20
Inn Spot/Bay | **Hampton Bays**	19
Z La Plage | **Wading River**	26
Legends | **New Suffolk**	21
NEW Mare Luna | **Huntington**	24
Z Maroni Cuisine | **Northport**	28
Maxxels | **Mineola**	24
Michael Anthony's | **Wading River**	23
Z Mill River Inn | **Oyster Bay**	27
Z Mirko's | **Water Mill**	26

Muse | **Water Mill**	21
New Paradise | **Sag Harbor**	21
Page One | **Glen Cove**	22
Painters' | **Brookhaven Hamlet**	18
Pastrami King | **Merrick**	19
PeraBell | **Patchogue**	24
Planet Bliss | **Shelter Is**	20
Ram's Head | **Shelter Is**	21
Rein | **Garden City**	23
Salamander's | **Greenport**	21
NEW Sally's Cocofé | **Huntington**	-
Silver's | **Southampton**	22
34 New St. | **Huntington**	20
Toast | **Port Jefferson**	23
Tula Kitchen | **Bay Shore**	-

FONDUE

Melting Pot | **Farmingdale**	18
NEW Simply Fondue | **Great Neck**	-

FRENCH

Z American Hotel | **Sag Harbor**	24
Z Barney's | **Locust Valley**	26
Chez Noëlle | **Port Washington**	24
Fresco Crêperie | **Long Bch**	23
La Coquille | **Manhasset**	24
La Marmite | **Williston Pk**	25
Le Chef | **Southampton**	21
Z Le Soir | **Bayport**	27
Oliver Bon Dinant | **Williston Pk**	25
Pierre's | **Bridgehampton**	21
red bar | **Southampton**	23
Soigné | **Woodmere**	25
Z Stone Creek | **E Quogue**	26
Stonewalls | **Riverhead**	24
NEW Vintage Port | **Port Washington**	-

FRENCH (BISTRO)

Almond | **Bridgehampton**	21
Z Bistro Cassis | **Huntington**	24
Bistro Citron | **Roslyn**	21
Bistro du Village | **Port Washington**	24
Bistro Toulouse | **Port Washington**	21
Emerson's | **Babylon**	23
JLX Bistro | **Sag Harbor**	13
Z Kitchen A Bistro | **St. James**	28

La Cuvée	**Greenport**	20
NEW La P'tite Framboise	**Port Washington**	–
Sage Bistro	**Bellmore**	25
Sunset Beach	**Shelter Is Hts**	17
Voila!	**St. James**	23

FRENCH (BRASSERIE)

| Brasserie Cassis | **Plainview** | 23 |
| **NEW** Brasserie Persil | **Oceanside** | 25 |

GERMAN

Koenig's	**Floral Pk**	18
New Hyde Park	**New Hyde Pk**	20
Oak Chalet	**Bellmore**	20
Pumpernickels	**Northport**	20
Village Lanterne	**Lindenhurst**	–

GREEK

NEW Alexandros	**Mount Sinai**	–
Chicken Kebab	**Roslyn Hts**	20
Ethos	**Great Neck**	21
Greek Village	**Commack**	19
Hellenic Snack	**E Marion**	20
Med. Snack	**Huntington**	23
Old Stove Pub	**Sagaponack**	18
Souvlaki Palace	**Commack**	20
NEW Surf 'N Turf	**Merrick**	–
Trata East	**Water Mill**	22
Zorba/Greek	**multi.**	19

HEALTH FOOD

(See also Vegetarian)
| Babette's | **E Hampton** | 20 |

INDIAN

Akbar	**Garden City**	21
Curry Club	**multi.**	22
Diwan	**multi.**	–
Diya	**Valley Stream**	–
Hampton Chutney	**Amagansett**	22
House of Dosas	**Hicksville**	23
House of India	**Huntington**	22
Jewel of India	**Syosset**	20
Kiran Palace	**multi.**	23
Maikhana Lounge	**Jericho**	–
NEW New Chilli/Curry	**Hicksville**	–

| Rangmahal | **Hicksville** | 23 |
| Tandoor Grill | **Rockville Ctr** | 21 |

IRISH

| Irish Coffee | **E Islip** | 22 |
| Sullivan's Quay | **Port Washington** | 17 |

ISRAELI

| **NEW** Tel Aviv | **Great Neck** | – |

ITALIAN

(N=Northern; S=Southern)
Absolutely Mario	**Farmingdale**	21
Allison's	**Sea Cliff**	22
Almarco	**Huntington**	18
Almoncello	N	**Wainscott**	20
NEW A Mano	**Mattituck**	22
Amici	**Massapequa**	21
Angelina's	**multi.**	22
Z Annona	**Westhampton Bch**	23
Aqua East	**Montauk**	20
Armand's	**Southampton**	17
Arturo's	**Floral Pk**	23
Baby Moon	S	**Westhampton Bch**	19
Barolo	**Melville**	25
Basil Leaf	**Locust Valley**	19
Bella Vita Grill	**St. James**	21
Benny's	N	**Westbury**	25
Bevanda	N	**Great Neck**	21
Blue Moon	**Rockville Ctr**	21
Boccaccio	N	**Hicksville**	23
Branzino	N	**Lynbrook**	25
Bravo Nader!	S	**Huntington**	26
Butera's	**multi.**	21
Cafe Baci	**Westbury**	22
Café Formaggio	**Carle Pl**	20
Cafe La Strada	**Hauppauge**	24
Cafe Rustica	**Great Neck**	21
Cafe Symposio	**Bellmore**	18
La Bottega	**multi.**	24
Caffe Laguna	**Long Bch**	19
Caracalla	**Syosset**	23
Carnival	S	**Port Jefferson Station**	20
Caruso's	**Rocky Pt**	22
Casa Rustica	**Smithtown**	25
Chefs of NY	**E Northport**	20
Ciao Baby	**multi.**	18

Restaurant	Rating
NEW Ciao Bella	S	Valley Stream	-
Cielo	Hauppauge	18
Cielo Rist.	N	Rockville Ctr	19
Cimino's	S	Southold	18
Cinelli's	multi.	-
Cipollini	Manhasset	20
NEW Circa	Mineola	-
Cirella's	N	Melville	21
cittanuova	N	E Hampton	18
City Café	Garden City	17
Z Dario's	N	Rockville Ctr	27
Z Da Ugo	N	Rockville Ctr	26
Dee Angelo's	Westhampton Bch	17
DiMaggio's	Port Washington	18
Dodici	Rockville Ctr	23
Edgewater	Hampton Bays	-
18 Bay	Bayville	24
El Parral	Syosset	21
Emilio's	Commack	23
Epiphany	Glen Cove	22
Ernesto's East	Glen Head	20
Fanatico	Jericho	20
NEW Fino Rosso	N	Glen Cove	18
Franina	Syosset	23
Fratelli Iavarone	New Hyde Pk	21
Galleria Dominick	N	Westbury	25
Giulio Cesare	N	Westbury	24
NEW Grappa	Sag Harbor	20
Harvest	N	Montauk	25
Il Capuccino	Sag Harbor	19
Il Classico	N	Massapequa Pk	24
Z Il Mulino NY	N	Roslyn Estates	26
Intermezzo	Ft Salonga	20
Jonathan's Rist.	Huntington	23
King Umberto	Elmont	23
NEW Kitchen A Tratt.	St. James	-
La Bella Vita	E Meadow	21
La Bussola	Glen Cove	23
La Capannina	N	Northport	23
La Famiglia	multi.	20
La Ginestra	S	Glen Cove	24
La Gioconda	S	Great Neck	21
La Marmite	N	Williston Pk	25
NEW La Nonna Bella	Garden City	-
La Novella	N	E Meadow	19
La Pace/Chef Michael	N	Glen Cove	24
La Parma	S	multi.	23
La Parmigiana	Southampton	20
La Piazza	multi.	21
Z La Piccola Liguria	N	Port Washington	26
La Pizzetta	E Norwich	20
La Primavera	N	Hicksville	23
La Rotonda	Great Neck	18
La Spada	S	Huntington Station	23
La Strada	Merrick	-
NEW La Tavola	Sayville	24
La Terrazza	Cedarhurst	22
La Viola	Cedarhurst	21
La Volpe	Center Moriches	21
Livorno	Port Washington	19
Lombardi's	Port Jefferson	22
Lucé	E Norwich	24
Luigi Q	Hicksville	22
Mama's	multi.	22
Mamma Lombardi's	S	Holbrook	23
Mangia Mangia	Patchogue	19
Mangiamo	Huntington	21
Manucci's	Montauk	19
Mario	N	Hauppauge	25
Z Maroni Cuisine	Northport	28
Z Matteo's	S	multi.	23
Matto	E Hampton	17
NEW Mercato	Massapequa Pk	-
Montebello	N	Port Washington	22
Mother Kelly's	Cedarhurst	21
Nello Summertimes	N	Southampton	18
NEW Nick & Charley Steak	Williston Pk	-
Z Nick & Toni's	E Hampton	23
Nick Diangelo	Long Bch	21
Nick's	Rockville Ctr	23
Nico at the Mansion	Islip	21
Nonnina	W Islip	24
Novitá	Garden City	23
NEW Oevo	Great Neck	-
Olive Oils	Point Lookout	-
Osteria da Nino	N	Huntington	23

NEW Osteria Toscana | Huntington — ⌐

NEW Palio Ristorante | Jericho — ⌐

Panini Café | Roslyn 23

Papa Razzi | N | Westbury 18

Pasta-eria | Hicksville 23

Pasta Pasta | Port Jefferson 23

NEW Pasta Vino | Mineola 23

Pentimento | Stony Brook 21

Pepi's Cucina | N | Southold 16

Per Un Angelo | N | Wantagh 21

Piccola Bussola | multi. 22

Z Piccolo | Huntington 26

Piccolo's | N | Mineola 23

Pomodorino | multi. 17

Porto Bello | Greenport 18

Rachel's Cafe | Syosset 23

Z Rialto | N | Carle Pl 26

Rist. Forestieri | N | Hauppauge 21

Rist. Gemelli | Babylon 22

Rist. Italiano Toscanini | Port Washington 22

Riviera Grill | Glen Cove 24

Robert's | Water Mill 24

NEW Rocco's | Huntington Station 23

Romantico/Capri | N | Port Washington 19

Ruvo | S | multi. 21

Sam's | E Hampton 19

San Marco | N | Hauppauge 24

Sant Ambroeus | N | Southampton 24

Saracen | S | Wainscott 17

Sea Basin | Rocky Pt 18

Sea Grille | Montauk 18

Sempre Vivolo | Hauppauge 25

Seventh St. Cafe | N | Garden City 19

Z Solé | Oceanside 26

NEW Speranza | Woodbury — ⌐

Stella Ristorante | Floral Pk 24

Steven's Pasta | Long Bch 23

Steve's Piccola | multi. 25

Stresa | Manhasset 24

Sundried Tomato | Nesconset 22

NEW Table 9 | E Hills — ⌐

Tesoro | Westbury 22

Torcellos | E Northport 18

Touch of Venice | N | Mattituck 19

Tratt. Diane | N | Roslyn 25

Tratt. Di Meo | Roslyn Hts 21

Tre Bambini | N | Lynbrook 21

Tuscan House | Southampton 21

Tutto Il Giorno | Sag Harbor 22

Tutto Pazzo | Huntington 21

Umberto's | S | multi. 21

Uncle Bacala's | S | Garden City Pk 18

Venere | Westbury 20

Vespa Cibobuono | N | Great Neck 22

Villa D'Este | N | Floral Pk 20

Vincent's | Carle Pl — ⌐

Vittorio's | Amityville 24

Viva Loco | Bellmore 16

World Pie | Bridgehampton 20

JAPANESE

(* sushi specialist)

Z Aji 53 | Bay Shore 27

Akari* | Merrick 21

Azuma | Greenlawn — ⌐

Bamboo* | E Hampton 20

Benihana | multi. 18

Benkei Japanese* | Northport 20

Benten* | Miller Pl 25

Blue Fin | Great Neck 23

Blue Ocean* | Bethpage 24

Bonbori Tiki* | Huntington 19

Bonsai* | Port Washington 22

Chez Kama | Great Neck — ⌐

NEW Cove Star | Glen Cove — ⌐

Daruma of Tokyo* | Great Neck 21

Gasho of Japan | Hauppauge 19

NEW Haiku | Woodbury — ⌐

Higashi* | Syosset 20

Hinata | Great Neck 22

Hokkaido* | Albertson 21

Homura Sushi* | Williston Pk 24

NEW Hotoke | Smithtown 26

NEW Izumi | Bethpage — ⌐

NEW Jin East* | Garden City 25

Kawasaki Steak | Long Bch 19

NEW Kiraku | Glen Head — ⌐

Kirin Hibachi | St. James 20

Kiss'o* | New Hyde Pk 22

Kohaku* | Huntington Station 23

☑ Kotobuki*	multi.	27
Kumo Sushi*	Plainview	24
Kurabarn*	Huntington	22
Kurofune*	Commack	25
Madame Tong's*	Southampton	12
Matsuya*	Great Neck	22
Midori*	multi.	23
Minado*	Carle Pl	20
Minami*	Massapequa	24
NEW Mitsui*	Bay Shore	23
Mt. Fuji*	Southampton	19
NEW Mumon	Garden City	–
Musashino*	Huntington	17
☑ Nagahama*	Long Bch	26
Nagashima*	Jericho	22
Nisen*	Commack	25
☑ Nisen Sushi*	Woodbury	26
Osaka*	Huntington	23
Ozumo*	multi.	21
Robata*	Plainview	21
Rock 'n Sake*	Port Washington	23
Samurai	Huntington	20
Sapporo*	Wantagh	20
Sen*	Sag Harbor	24
Sherwood	Glen Cove	17
Shiki*	multi.	23
Shiro of Japan*	Carle Pl	22
Shogi*	Westbury	23
Show Win*	multi.	22
Suki Zuki*	Water Mill	23
Sushi Ya*	multi.	22
Tai-Show*	multi.	22
Takara*	Islandia	26
Thai Green Leaf	Massapequa	22
☑ Toku*	Manhasset	24
Tokyo*	E Northport	23
Tomo Hibachi*	Huntington	19
Tony's Fusion	Westhampton Bch	21
Tsubo*	Syosset	22
West Lake Clam*	Montauk	24
Yamaguchi*	Port Washington	24
Yama Q	Bridgehampton	–
Yokohama	E Northport	23
Yuki's Palette*	multi.	21

KOREAN

Tokyo	E Northport	23

KOSHER/ KOSHER-STYLE

Ben's Deli	multi.	19
Cho-Sen	multi.	18
Colbeh	multi.	21
Deli King	New Hyde Pk	18
Green Melody	Jericho	–
NEW Sally's Cocofé	Huntington	–
NEW Tel Aviv	Great Neck	–

MEDITERRANEAN

NEW Alexandros	Mount Sinai	–
Allison's	Sea Cliff	22
Ayhan's Shish Kebab	multi.	18
Azerbaijan Grill	Westbury	21
Backyard	Montauk	–
Cafe Rustica	Great Neck	21
Crabtree's	Floral Pk	20
Harvest	Montauk	25
NEW Limani	Roslyn	–
Med. Grill	Hewlett	19
Med. Snack	Huntington	23
☑ Nick & Toni's	E Hampton	23
Pier 95	Freeport	23
Pita House	multi.	23
Q East	Quogue	23
☑ Stone Creek	E Quogue	26
Tulip	Great Neck	20
Wild Fig	multi.	19

MEXICAN

Baja Grill	multi.	17
☑ Besito	multi.	23
Cozymel's Mex.	Westbury	16
Goldmine Mex.	Greenlawn	18
Green Cactus	multi.	21
La Panchita	Smithtown	21
Los Compadres	Huntington Station	22
Oaxaca Mexican	Huntington	23
Poco Loco	Roslyn	17
Quetzalcoatl	Huntington	17
Salsa Salsa	multi.	23
Viva Juan	multi.	17
Viva La Vida	Oakdale	23
Viva Loco	Bellmore	16
NEW Zim Zari	Massapequa Pk	–

NEW ENGLAND

Bigelow's | **Rockville Ctr** 24

NEW WORLD

Planet Bliss | **Shelter Is** 20

NUEVO LATINO

Laguna Grille | **multi.** 18

PAN-ASIAN

Asian Moon | **Garden City** 23
Bamboo | **E Hampton** 20
Blue Ocean | **Bethpage** 24
East by Northeast | **Montauk** 21
Elaine's | **Great Neck** 23
Green Melody | **Jericho** -
Lemonleaf Grill | **Hicksville** 20
Long River | **Kings Park** 18
Matsulin | **Hampton Bays** 22
Matsuya | **Great Neck** 22
Meritage | **Bellport** 23
MoCa Asian Bistro | **Hewlett** 23
Sunset Beach | **Shelter Is Hts** 17
Wild Ginger | **Great Neck** 22

PAN-LATIN

Pollo Rico | **multi.** -

PERSIAN

Azerbaijan Grill | **Westbury** 21
Colbeh | **multi.** 21
Ravagh | **Roslyn Hts** 22

PIZZA

Baby Moon | **Westhampton Bch** 19
Blue Moon | **Rockville Ctr** 21
Chefs of NY | **E Northport** 20
Cirella's | **multi.** 21
Eddie's Pizza | **New Hyde Pk** 21
Emilio's | **Commack** 23
Foody's | **Water Mill** 19
Grimaldi's | **Garden City** 23
King Umberto | **Elmont** 23
La Bella Vita | **E Meadow** 21
La Piazza | **multi.** 21
La Pizzetta | **E Norwich** 20
La Rotonda | **Great Neck** 18
Manucci's | **Montauk** 19
Massa's | **Huntington Station** 25

Matto | **E Hampton** 17
Nick's | **Rockville Ctr** 23
Pasta-eria | **Hicksville** 23
Pie | **Port Jefferson** 20
Salvatore's | **multi.** 24
Pizza Place | **Bridgehampton** 21
Sam's | **E Hampton** 19
Sundried Tomato | **Nesconset** 22
Torcellos | **E Northport** 18
Umberto's | **multi.** 21
World Pie | **Bridgehampton** 20

POLISH

Birchwood | **multi.** 18
Bozena Polish | **Lindenhurst** 22

PORTUGUESE

A Taberna | **Island Pk** 23
Churrasq. Bairrada | **Mineola** 24
Heart of Portugal | **Mineola** 20
Lareira | **Mineola** 20
NEW Luso | **Smithtown** -

PUB FOOD

Birchwood | **Southampton** 18
John Harvard's | **Lake Grove** 16
JT's Place | **Hampton Bays** 18
O'Mally's | **Southold** 16
Peppercorns | **Hicksville** 18
Post Office Cafe | **Babylon** 18
Rowdy Hall | **E Hampton** 19
Runyon's | **multi.** 17
Southampton Publick | **Southampton** 16
Sullivan's Quay | **Port Washington** 17

SANDWICHES

Greenport Tea | **Greenport** 20
Hampton Coffee | **multi.** 19
Lucy's Café | **Babylon** 23
Once Upon a Moose | **Sea Cliff** 19
Panini Café | **Roslyn** 23
Pastrami King | **Merrick** 19

SEAFOOD

Ayhan's Fish | **Port Washington** 19
Barrister's | **Southampton** 16
Bigelow's | **Rockville Ctr** 24
NEW Black & Blue | **Huntington** 24

CUISINES

Bostwick's/Harbor | **E Hampton**	20
B.Smith's | **Sag Harbor**	16
Buoy One | **Riverhead**	22
Cafe Max | **E Hampton**	21
Canterbury | **Oyster Bay**	18
Catfish Max | **Seaford**	23
Chequit Inn | **Shelter Is Hts**	19
NEW Cherrystones | **E Hampton**	19
Clam Bar | **Amagansett**	19
Claudio's | **Greenport**	15
Coast Grill | **Southampton**	18
Z Coolfish | **Syosset**	24
Cull House | **Sayville**	19
Cyril's Fish House | **Amagansett**	18
Z Dave's Grill | **Montauk**	26
Dockers Waterside | **E Quogue**	19
Dockside B&G | **Sag Harbor**	19
Duryea's Lobster | **Montauk**	21
fatfish | **Bay Shore**	19
Fiddleheads | **Oyster Bay**	23
NEW Fishbar | **Montauk**	16
Fisherman's Catch | **Point Lookout**	19
Fishery | **E Rockaway**	19
Fulton Prime | **Syosset**	22
George Martin's Coastal | **Long Bch**	20
Gosman's Dock | **Montauk**	17
Harbor Crab | **Patchogue**	18
H2O Seafood | **Smithtown**	23
Hudson/McCoy | **Freeport**	17
Indian Cove | **Hampton Bays**	18
Inlet Seafood | **Montauk**	21
Inn Spot/Bay | **Hampton Bays**	19
NEW Jeff's Seafood | **E Northport**	-
Jolly Fisherman | **Roslyn**	20
Z Kitchen A Bistro | **St. James**	28
Z Legal Sea Foods | **multi.**	20
NEW Limani | **Roslyn**	-
Lobster Inn | **Southampton**	18
Lobster Roll | **multi.**	20
Louie's Oyster | **Port Washington**	16
Matthew's | **Fire Is**	17
NEW Mill Creek | **Bayville**	23
Z Mill Pond House | **Centerport**	25
Nautilus Cafe | **Freeport**	24
Oakland's | **Hampton Bays**	17
Oar Steak | **Patchogue**	20

Old Mill Inn | **Mattituck**	17
NEW 101 Bar & Grill | **Bellmore**	20
NEW Oso | **Southampton**	-
Paddy McGees | **Island Pk**	16
Palm | **E Hampton**	25
Pepi's Cucina | **Southold**	16
NEW Pier 441 | **Centerport**	19
Pier 95 | **Freeport**	23
Z Plaza Cafe | **Southampton**	26
NEW Porters | **Bellport**	-
Rachel's Waterside | **Freeport**	19
Red Fish | **Plainview**	23
Z Riverbay | **Williston Pk**	22
Schooner | **Freeport**	16
Sea Basin | **Rocky Pt**	18
Seafood Barge | **Southold**	21
Sea Grille | **Montauk**	18
Sea Levels | **Brightwaters**	24
Shagwong | **Montauk**	18
Snapper Inn | **Oakdale**	17
Southside Fish | **Lindenhurst**	18
Starr Boggs | **Westhampton Bch**	25
Surfside Inn | **Montauk**	19
Thom Thom | **Wantagh**	21
Tierra Mar | **Westhampton Bch**	22
Trata East | **Water Mill**	22
Turquoise | **Great Neck**	23
Twin Harbors | **Bayville**	22
Uncle Bacala's | **Garden City Pk**	18
Varney's | **Brookhaven**	24
Wall's Wharf | **Bayville**	17
Waterview Rest. | **Port Washington**	16
West Lake Clam | **Montauk**	24

SMALL PLATES

NEW Bennett's | Eclectic | **Locust Valley**	-
NEW Brass Rail | Amer. | **Locust Valley**	-
NEW Charlotte's | Amer. | **Cold Spring**	20
Z Honu | Amer. | **Huntington**	22
Toast | Eclectic | **Port Jefferson**	23
Vine Wine/Cafe | Amer. | **Greenport**	22
NEW Vintage Port | French | **Port Washington**	-

SOUTHERN

Blackbirds' Grille | **Sayville**	18
B.Smith's | **Sag Harbor**	16
Cooke's In | **Huntington**	23
NEW Gulf Coast Kitchen | **Montauk**	-
LL Dent | **Carle Pl**	21
Wild Harvest | **Glen Cove**	20

SOUTHWESTERN

RS Jones | **Merrick**	21
Turtle Crossing | **E Hampton**	21

SPANISH

Casa Luis | **Smithtown**	23
El Parral | **Syosset**	21
La Panchita | **Smithtown**	21
Meson Iberia | **Island Pk**	21
Viva La Vida | **Oakdale**	23

STEAKHOUSES

Abel Conklin's | **Huntington**	22
Benihana | **multi.**	18
NEW Black & Blue | **Huntington**	24
Z Blackstone Steak | **Melville**	23
Blackwells | **Wading River**	21
Bobby Van's | **Bridgehampton**	22
NEW Brooks & Porter | **Merrick**	22
Z Bryant & Cooper | **Roslyn**	26
Burton & Doyle | **Great Neck**	24
Cliff's | **multi.**	21
Clubhouse | **Huntington**	22
Dockers Waterside | **E Quogue**	19
Elbow East | **Southold**	21
Frank's Steaks | **multi.**	20
Fulton Prime | **Syosset**	22
Gasho of Japan | **Hauppauge**	19
NEW Hotoke | **Smithtown**	26
Jimmy Hays | **Island Pk**	25
Jolly Fisherman | **Roslyn**	20
JT's Place | **Hampton Bays**	18
Lodge B&G | **E Hampton**	19
Mac's Steak | **Huntington**	22
Majors Steak | **multi.**	17
NEW Mill Creek | **Bayville**	23
Z Mill Pond House | **Centerport**	25
Z Morton's | **Great Neck**	24
Nautilus Cafe | **Freeport**	24

NEW Nick & Charley Steak | **Williston Pk**	-
Nick Diangelo | **Long Bch**	21
Oar Steak | **Patchogue**	20
Old Stove Pub | **Sagaponack**	18
NEW Oso | **Southampton**	-
Pace's Steak | **multi.**	23
Palm | **E Hampton**	25
Peppercorns | **Hicksville**	18
Z Peter Luger | **Great Neck**	27
PG Steak | **Huntington**	22
NEW Porters | **Bellport**	-
Z Rothmann's Steak | **E Norwich**	25
Z Ruth's Chris | **Garden City**	24
Sagamore Steak | **Syosset**	23
Schooner | **Freeport**	16
Z Tellers | **Islip**	26
Terry G's Steak | **Farmingdale**	17
Thom Thom | **Wantagh**	21
Tomo Hibachi | **Huntington**	19
21 Main | **W Sayville**	24
Z Vintage Prime | **St. James**	26
Westhampton Steak | **Westhampton Bch**	17

TEAROOMS

Greenport Tea | **Greenport**	20
Robinson's | **Stony Brook**	24

TEX-MEX

Pancho's | **multi.**	19

THAI

Bonbori Tiki | **Huntington**	19
Chaophaya | **Kings Park**	21
Jaiya | **Hicksville**	21
Lemonleaf Grill | **multi.**	20
Nanking | **New Hyde Pk**	19
Onzon Thai | **Bellmore**	24
Sabai Thai | **Miller Pl**	-
Sarin Thai | **Greenvale**	22
Seeda Thai | **Valley Stream**	21
Z Siam Lotus | **Bay Shore**	26
Simply Thai | **Rockville Ctr**	20
NEW Sri Thai | **Huntington**	21
Z Thai Gourmet | **Port Jefferson Station**	26
Thai Green Leaf | **multi.**	22

Thai House | **Smithtown**	21
Thai Table | **Rockville Ctr**	22
Thai USA | **Huntington**	21
Tony's Fusion | **Westhampton Bch**	21

TURKISH

Ayhan's Fish | **Port Washington**	19
Ayhan's Shish Kebab | **multi.**	18
Azerbaijan Grill | **Westbury**	21
Chicken Kebab | **Roslyn Hts**	20
Pita House | **multi.**	23
NEW Surf 'N Turf | **Merrick**	-

Tava | **Port Washington**	19
Tulip | **Great Neck**	20
Wild Fig | **multi.**	19

VEGETARIAN

Ariana | **Huntington**	21
Green Melody | **Jericho**	-
House of Dosas | **Hicksville**	23
Yama Q | **Bridgehampton**	-

VIETNAMESE

Paradise Island | **Williston Pk**	19

Locations

Includes restaurant names, cuisines and Food ratings.

Nassau

ALBERTSON

Hokkaido | *Japanese* — 21

BALDWIN

Ayhan's Shish Kebab | *Med./Turkish* — 18

Ben's Deli | *Deli* — 19

BAYVILLE

18 Bay | *Italian* — 24

NEW Mill Creek | *Seafood/Steak* — 23

Z Pine Island | *Amer.* — 17

Twin Harbors | *Seafood* — 22

Wall's Wharf | *Amer./Seafood* — 17

BELLMORE

Cafe Symposio | *Italian* — 18

International Delight | *Diner* — 18

Z Matteo's | *Italian* — 23

Mixing Bowl | *Amer.* — 20

Oak Chalet | *Continental/German* — 20

NEW 101 Bar & Grill | *Amer./Seafood* — 20

Onzon Thai | *Thai* — 24

Sage Bistro | *French* — 25

Shang Hai Pavilion | *Chinese* — 23

Viva Loco | *Italian/Mex.* — 16

BETHPAGE

B.K. Sweeney's | *Amer.* — 18

Blue Ocean | *Pan-Asian* — 24

H.R. Singleton's | *Amer.* — 17

NEW Izumi | *Asian Fusion* — -

Z Orient | *Chinese* — 26

Ozumo | *Japanese* — 21

Pancho's | *Tex-Mex* — 19

CARLE PLACE

Ben's Deli | *Deli* — 19

Café Formaggio | *Italian* — 20

Z Camille's | *Continental* — 24

Ciao Baby | *Italian* — 18

La Bottega | *Italian* — 24

Lemonleaf Grill | *Thai* — 20

LL Dent | *Southern* — 21

Minado | *Japanese* — 20

Z Rialto | *Italian* — 26

Shiro of Japan | *Japanese* — 22

Thomas's Ham | *Diner* — 23

Vincent's | *Italian* — -

Z West End | *Amer.* — 25

CEDARHURST

La Terrazza | *Italian* — 22

La Viola | *Italian* — 21

Mother Kelly's | *Amer./Italian* — 21

EAST HILLS

NEW Table 9 | *Amer./Italian* — -

EAST MEADOW

La Bella Vita | *Italian* — 21

La Novella | *Italian* — 19

Majors Steak | *Steak* — 17

Z Palm Court | *Amer./Continental* — 24

NEW Ruby's BBQ | *BBQ* — -

Runyon's | *Amer.* — 17

EAST NORWICH

Angelina's | *Italian* — 22

La Pizzetta | *Italian* — 20

Lucé | *Italian* — 24

Z Rothmann's Steak | *Steak* — 25

EAST ROCKAWAY

Fishery | *Seafood* — 19

ELMONT

King Umberto | *Italian* — 23

FARMINGDALE

Absolutely Mario | *Italian* — 21

56th Fighter Group | *Amer.* — 15

Library Cafe | *Amer.* — 17

Melting Pot | *Fondue* — 18

Oak Room | *Amer.* — 23

Terry G's Steak | *Steak* — 17

Viva Juan | *Mex.* — 17

FLORAL PARK

Arturo's | *Italian* — 23

Bob's Place | *Amer.* — 21

Crabtree's | *Continental/Med.* 20
Koenig's | *Continental/German* 18
Stella Ristorante | *Italian* 24
Umberto's | *Italian/Pizza* 21
Villa D'Este | *Italian* 20

FRANKLIN SQUARE

Cinelli's | *Italian* -

FREEPORT

E. B. Elliot's | *Amer.* 18
Hudson/McCoy | *Seafood* 17
Nautilus Cafe | *Seafood/Steak* 24
Pier 95 | *Med.* 23
Rachel's Waterside | *Amer./Seafood* 19
Schooner | *Seafood/Steak* 16

GARDEN CITY

Akbar | *Indian* 21
Asian Moon | *Pan-Asian* 23
Ben's Deli | *Deli* 19
B.K. Sweeney's | *Amer.* 18
La Bottega | *Italian* 24
City Café | *Italian* 17
Z Grand Lux | *Eclectic* 19
Grimaldi's | *Pizza* 23
Houston's | *Amer.* 21
NEW Jin East | *Japanese* 25
NEW La Nonna Bella | *Italian* -
Z Legal Sea Foods | *Seafood* 20
NEW Mumon | *Japanese* -
Novità | *Italian* 23
Orchid | *Chinese* 24
Z Polo | *Amer.* 25
Rein | *Amer./Eclectic* 23
Z Ruth's Chris | *Steak* 24
Seventh St. Cafe | *Italian* 19
Sushi Ya | *Japanese* 22
Umberto's | *Italian/Pizza* 21
Walk St. | *Amer.* 21
Z Waterzooi | *Belgian* 23
Wild Fig | *Med./Turkish* 19

GARDEN CITY PARK

Green Cactus | *Mex.* 21
Jonathan's | *Amer.* 19
Uncle Bacala's | *Italian/Seafood* 18

GLEN COVE

NEW Cove Star | *Asian Fusion/Japanese* -
Epiphany | *Italian* 22
NEW Fino Rosso | *Italian* 18
Gonzalo's | *Amer.* 20
La Bussola | *Italian* 23
La Ginestra | *Italian* 24
La Pace/Chef Michael | *Italian* 24
Page One | *Amer./Eclectic* 22
Riviera Grill | *Italian* 24
Sherwood | *Chinese/Japanese* 17
Soundview | *Amer.* 19
Uncle Dai | *Chinese* 17
Wild Fig | *Med./Turkish* 19
Wild Harvest | *Southern* 20

GLEN HEAD

Bistro M | *Amer.* 25
Ernesto's East | *Italian* 20
NEW Kiraku | *Japanese* -
On 3 | *Amer.* 24

GREAT NECK

Bevanda | *Italian* 21
Blue Fin | *Asian Fusion/Japanese* 23
Burton & Doyle | *Steak* 24
Cafe Rustica | *Italian/Med.* 21
Chez Kama | *Continental/Japanese* -
Cho-Sen | *Asian Fusion/Kosher* 18
Colbeh | *Persian* 21
Daruma of Tokyo | *Japanese* 21
Elaine's | *Pan-Asian* 23
Ethos | *Greek* 21
Hinata | *Asian Fusion/Japanese* 22
La Gioconda | *Continental/Italian* 21
La Rotonda | *Pizza* 18
Matsuya | *Pan-Asian* 22
Z Morton's | *Steak* 24
NEW Oevo | *Italian* -
Pancho's | *Tex-Mex* 19
Z Peter Luger | *Steak* 27
NEW Simply Fondue | *Fondue* -
NEW Tel Aviv | *Israeli/Kosher* -
Tulip | *Med./Turkish* 20
Turquoise | *Seafood* 23
Vespa Cibobuono | *Italian* 22
Wild Ginger | *Pan-Asian* 22

GREENVALE

Ben's Deli	*Deli*	19
Hunan Taste	*Chinese*	23
Sarin Thai	*Thai*	22

HEWLETT

Graffiti	*Amer.*	20
Med. Grill	*Med.*	19
Midori	*Japanese*	23
MoCa Asian Bistro	*Pan-Asian*	23

HICKSVILLE

Boccaccio	*Italian*	23
Diwan	*Indian*	-
House of Dosas	*Indian*	23
Jaiya	*Thai*	21
Kiran Palace	*Indian*	23
La Primavera	*Italian*	23
Lemonleaf Grill	*Thai*	20
Luigi Q	*Italian*	22
NEW New Chilli/Curry	*Indian*	-
Pasta-eria	*Italian*	23
Peppercorns	*Continental*	18
Rangmahal	*Indian*	23
Spare Rib	*BBQ*	17
West East	*Asian Fusion*	24
Zorba/Greek	*Greek*	19

ISLAND PARK

A Taberna	*Portug.*	23
Jimmy Hays	*Steak*	25
Meson Iberia	*Continental/Spanish*	21
Paddy McGees	*Seafood*	16
Pancho's	*Tex-Mex*	19

JERICHO

Fanatico	*Italian*	20
Frank's Steaks	*Steak*	20
Green Melody	*Kosher/Pan-Asian*	-
Maikhana Lounge	*Indian*	-
Milleridge Inn	*Amer.*	15
Nagashima	*Japanese*	22
NEW Palio Ristorante	*Italian*	-

LAWRENCE

Cho-Sen	*Asian Fusion/Kosher*	18

LEVITTOWN

Fortune Wheel	*Chinese*	23
Tai-Show	*Japanese*	22

LOCUST VALLEY

Z Barney's	*Amer./French*	26
Basil Leaf	*Italian*	19
NEW Bennett's	*Eclectic*	-
NEW Brass Rail	*Amer.*	-
Buckram Stables	*Amer.*	18

LONG BEACH

Caffe Laguna	*Italian*	19
Duke Falcon's	*Amer./Eclectic*	23
Fresco Crêperie	*French*	23
George Martin's Coastal	*Seafood*	20
Green Cactus	*Mex.*	21
Kawasaki Steak	*Japanese*	19
NEW Lola's	*Amer.*	-
Z Matteo's	*Italian*	23
Z Nagahama	*Japanese*	26
Nick Diangelo	*Italian/Steak*	21
Steven's Pasta	*Italian*	23
Swingbelly's	*BBQ*	21

LYNBROOK

Branzino	*Italian*	25
Broadway Beanery	*Amer.*	22
Tre Bambini	*Italian*	21

MALVERNE

Blue Sky Bistro	*Amer.*	23

MANHASSET

Benihana	*Japanese*	18
Cipollini	*Italian*	20
La Coquille	*French*	24
Pearl East	*Chinese*	23
Stresa	*Italian*	24
Z Toku	*Asian Fusion*	24

MASSAPEQUA/ MASSAPEQUA PARK

Amici	*Italian*	21
Big Daddy's	*BBQ/Cajun*	23
Ciao Baby	*Italian*	18
Hudson's Mill	*Amer.*	22
Il Classico	*Italian*	24
La Bottega	*Italian*	24
NEW Mercato	*Italian*	-
Minami	*Japanese*	24
Z Smokin' Al's BBQ	*BBQ*	24

Tai-Show | *Japanese* 22

Thai Green Leaf | *Thai* 22

NEW Zim Zari | *Cal./Mex.* -

MERRICK

Akari | *Japanese* 21

NEW Brooks & Porter | *Steak* 22

George Martin Grill | *Burgers* 21

La Bottega | *Italian* 24

La Piazza | *Pizza* 21

La Strada | *Italian* -

Nicholas James | *Amer.* 21

Pastrami King | *Deli* 19

RS Jones | *SW* 21

NEW Surf 'N Turf | *Greek/Turkish* -

Yuki's Palette | *Japanese* 21

MINEOLA

Churrasq. Bairrada | *Portug.* 24

NEW Circa | *Italian* -

Downtown | *Amer.* -

Heart of Portugal | *Portug.* 20

Lareira | *Portug.* 20

Maxxels | *Amer./Eclectic* 24

NEW Pasta Vino | *Italian* 23

Piccola Bussola | *Italian* 22

Piccolo's | *Italian* 23

NEW HYDE PARK

Deli King | *Deli* 18

Eddie's Pizza | *Pizza* 21

Fratelli Iavarone | *Italian* 21

Kiss'o | *Japanese* 22

Nanking | *Chinese/Thai* 19

New Hyde Park | 20
  Continental/German

Sushi Ya | *Japanese* 22

Umberto's | *Italian/Pizza* 21

NORTH BELLMORE

Bayou | *Cajun/Creole* 23

OCEANSIDE

NEW Brasserie Persil | *French* 25

Cinelli's | *Italian* -

La Bottega | *Italian* 24

La Parma | *Italian* 23

Mitchell's | *Amer.* 16

Ozumo | *Japanese* 21

Z Solé | *Italian* 26

OYSTER BAY

BayKery | *Bakery* 19

Canterbury | *Amer./Eclectic* 18

Coach Grill | *Amer.* 22

Fiddleheads | *Seafood* 23

Midori | *Japanese* 23

Z Mill River Inn | *Amer./Eclectic* 27

Wild Honey | *Amer.* 24

PLAINVIEW

Ayhan's Shish Kebab | 18
  Med./Turkish

Brasserie Cassis | *French* 23

Green Cactus | *Mex.* 21

Kumo Sushi | *Japanese* 24

La Famiglia | *Italian* 20

La Piazza | *Pizza* 21

Red Fish | *Amer./Seafood* 23

Robata | *Japanese* 21

POINT LOOKOUT

Fisherman's Catch | *Seafood* 19

Olive Oils | *Italian* -

PORT WASHINGTON

Ayhan's Fish | *Seafood/Turkish* 19

Ayhan's Shish Kebab | 18
  Med./Turkish

Bistro du Village | *French* 24

Bistro Toulouse | *French* 21

Bonsai | *Japanese* 22

Chez Noëlle | *French* 24

DiMaggio's | *Italian* 18

Diwan | *Indian* -

Dynasty/Pt. Wash. | *Chinese* 18

Harbor-Q | *BBQ* -

Z La Piccola Liguria | *Italian* 26

NEW La P'tite Framboise | *French* -

Livorno | *Italian* 19

Louie's Oyster | *Seafood* 16

Montebello | *Italian* 22

Rist. Italiano Toscanini | *Italian* 22

Rock 'n Sake | *Japanese* 23

Romantico/Capri | *Italian* 19

Salvatore's | *Pizza* 24

Shang Hai Pavilion | *Chinese* 23

Sullivan's Quay | *Pub* 17

Tava | *Turkish* 19

NEW Vintage Port	*French*	-⅃
Waterview Rest.	*Continental/Seafood*	16⅃
Yamaguchi	*Japanese*	24⅃

ROCKVILLE CENTRE

Ayhan's Shish Kebab	*Med./Turkish*	18⅃
Bigelow's	*New Eng.*	24⅃
Blue Moon	*Pizza*	21⅃
Chadwicks	*Amer./Continental*	-⅃
Cielo Rist.	*Italian*	19⅃
Z Dario's	*Italian*	27⅃
Z Da Ugo	*Italian*	26⅃
Dodici	*Italian*	23⅃
Frank's Steaks	*Steak*	20⅃
Gabrielle's	*Amer.*	22⅃
George Martin	*Amer.*	22⅃
George Martin Grill	*Burgers*	21⅃
Green Cactus	*Mex.*	21⅃
International Delight	*Diner*	18⅃
La Bottega	*Italian*	24⅃
Nick's	*Pizza*	23⅃
Simply Thai	*Thai*	20⅃
Taiko	*Asian Fusion*	24⅃
Tandoor Grill	*Indian*	21⅃
Thai Table	*Thai*	22⅃

ROSLYN/ ROSLYN HTS./ ROSLYN ESTATES

Z Besito	*Mex.*	23⅃
Bistro Citron	*French*	21⅃
Z Bryant & Cooper	*Steak*	26⅃
Chalet Bar	*Amer./Eclectic*	18⅃
Chicken Kebab	*Greek/Turkish*	20⅃
Churrasc. Riodizio	*Brazilian*	21⅃
Colbeh	*Persian*	21⅃
Green Cactus	*Mex.*	21⅃
Z Il Mulino NY	*Italian*	26⅃
Jolly Fisherman	*Seafood/Steak*	20⅃
Z Kotobuki	*Japanese*	27⅃
NEW Limani	*Med./Seafood*	-⅃
Z Matteo's	*Italian*	23⅃
Mim's	*Amer.*	18⅃
Panini Café	*Sandwiches*	23⅃
Poco Loco	*Mex.*	17⅃
Ravagh	*Persian*	22⅃

Thyme	*Amer.*	20⅃
Tratt. Diane	*Italian*	25⅃
Tratt. Di Meo	*Italian*	21⅃

SEA CLIFF

Allison's	*Italian/Med.*	22⅃
Once Upon a Moose	*Sandwiches*	19⅃
Roots	*Amer.*	24⅃
Tupelo Honey	*Amer.*	22⅃

SEAFORD

Butera's	*Italian*	21⅃
Catfish Max	*Amer./Seafood*	23⅃
Pomodorino	*Italian*	17⅃
Runyon's	*Amer.*	17⅃

SYOSSET

Angelina's	*Italian*	22⅃
Cafe Testarossa	*Continental*	20⅃
Caracalla	*Italian*	23⅃
Z Coolfish	*Seafood*	24⅃
El Parral	*Italian/Spanish*	21⅃
Franina	*Italian*	23⅃
Fulton Prime	*Seafood/Steak*	22⅃
Higashi	*Japanese*	20⅃
Jewel of India	*Indian*	20⅃
Mim's	*Amer.*	18⅃
Pomodorino	*Italian*	17⅃
Rachel's Cafe	*Italian*	23⅃
Sagamore Steak	*Steak*	23⅃
Steve's Piccola	*Italian*	25⅃
Tsubo	*Japanese*	22⅃

VALLEY STREAM

NEW Ciao Bella	*Italian*	-⅃
Diya	*Indian*	-⅃
Mitchell's	*Amer.*	16⅃
Seeda Thai	*Thai*	21⅃

WANTAGH

NEW Brick & Rail	*Eclectic*	-⅃
Green Cactus	*Mex.*	21⅃
Hemingway's	*Amer.*	18⅃
Per Un Angelo	*Italian*	21⅃
Sapporo	*Japanese*	20⅃
Snaps	*Amer.*	22⅃
Thom Thom	*Seafood/Steak*	21⅃
Umberto's	*Italian/Pizza*	21⅃

WESTBURY

Ayhan's Shish Kebab | *Med./Turkish*	18
Azerbaijan Grill | *Mideast.*	21
Benihana | *Japanese*	18
Benny's | *Italian*	25
Cafe Baci | *Italian*	22
Z Cheesecake Factory | *Amer.*	20
Chi | *Chinese/Eclectic*	25
City Cellar | *Amer.*	20
Cozymel's Mex. | *Mex.*	16
Famous Dave's | *BBQ*	19
NEW Fortune Asian | *Asian*	-
Galleria Dominick | *Italian*	25
Giulio Cesare | *Italian*	24
Laguna Grille | *Nuevo Latino*	18
Papa Razzi | *Italian*	18
P.F. Chang's | *Chinese*	19
Shogi | *Japanese*	23
Steve's Piccola | *Italian*	25
Tesoro | *Italian*	22
Venere | *Italian*	20
Yuki's Palette | *Japanese*	21

WILLISTON PARK

Hildebrandt's | *Amer.*	19
Homura Sushi | *Japanese*	24
Ivy Cottage | *Amer.*	24
La Marmite | *French/Italian*	25
La Parma | *Italian*	23
NEW Nick & Charley Steak | *Steak*	-
Oliver Bon Dinant | *French*	25
Paradise Island | *Viet.*	19
Z Riverbay | *Seafood*	22

WOODBURY

Ben's Deli | *Deli*	19
Butera's | *Italian*	21
Delano Mansion | *Amer.*	-
Graffiti | *Amer.*	20
NEW Haiku | *Asian/Japanese*	-
Laguna Grille | *Nuevo Latino*	18
Majors Steak | *Steak*	17
Z Nisen Sushi | *Japanese*	26
NEW Speranza | *Italian*	-

WOODMERE

Soigné | *Continental/French*	25

Suffolk

AMAGANSETT

Clam Bar | *Seafood*	19
Cyril's Fish House | *Seafood*	18
Hampton Chutney | *Indian*	22
NEW Indian Wells Tav. | *Amer.*	15
Lobster Roll | *Seafood*	20
Meeting House | *Amer.*	18
Show Win | *Japanese*	22

AMITYVILLE

Vittorio's | *Amer./Italian*	24

AQUEBOGUE

Modern Snack | *Amer.*	18

BABYLON/ NORTH BABYLON

Argyle Grill | *Amer.*	21
Babylon Carriage | *Continental*	19
Emerson's | *Amer./French*	23
Green Cactus | *Mex.*	21
Horace/Sylvia's | *Amer.*	17
Z Kotobuki | *Japanese*	27
Lucy's Café | *Amer.*	23
Post Office Cafe | *Amer.*	18
Rist. Gemelli | *Italian*	22
Shiki | *Japanese*	23
Tricia's Café | *Amer.*	21

BAITING HOLLOW

Cooperage Inn | *Amer./Continental*	20
Lobster Roll | *Seafood*	20

BAYPORT

NEW Grey Horse | *Amer.*	22
Z Le Soir | *French*	27
Salsa Salsa | *Cal./Mex.*	23

BAY SHORE

Z Aji 53 | *Japanese*	27
Declan Quinn's | *Amer.*	19
fatfish | *Seafood*	19
Z Lake House | *Amer.*	27
Milk & Sugar Café | *Amer.*	20
NEW Mitsui | *Japanese*	23
Salvatore's | *Pizza*	24
Z Siam Lotus | *Thai*	26

Menus, photos, voting and more – free at ZAGAT.com

Z Smokin' Al's BBQ | *BBQ* — 24

Tula Kitchen | *Eclectic* — ⊥

BELLPORT

Bellport | *Amer./Continental* — 23

Meritage | *Amer./Pan-Asian* — 23

NEW Porters | *Seafood/Steak* — ⊥

Spicy's BBQ | *BBQ* — 19

BLUE POINT

Blue | *Amer.* — 19

BRIDGEHAMPTON

Almond | *French* — 21

Bobby Van's | *Steak* — 22

Bridgehampton Candy | *Diner* — 15

Golden Pear | *Coffee* — 17

Pierre's | *French* — 21

Pizza Place | *Pizza* — 21

World Pie | *Pizza* — 20

Yama Q | *Japanese* — ⊥

BRIGHTWATERS

Sea Levels | *Amer./Seafood* — 24

BROOKHAVEN HAMLET

Painters' | *Eclectic* — 18

BROOKHAVEN/ ROCKY POINT

Caruso's | *Italian* — 22

Sea Basin | *Italian* — 18

Varney's | *Amer./Seafood* — 24

CENTEREACH

Mama's | *Italian* — 22

Pollo Rico | *Pan-Latin* — ⊥

CENTER MORICHES

La Volpe | *Italian* — 21

CENTERPORT

Z Mill Pond House | *Seafood/Steak* — 25

NEW Pier 441 | *Seafood* — 19

COLD SPRING HARBOR

NEW Charlotte's | *Amer.* — 20

Grasso's | *Amer.* — 25

105 Harbor | *Amer.* — 20

COMMACK

Ciao Baby | *Italian* — 18

Emilio's | *Pizza* — 23

Greek Village | *Greek* — 19

Kiran Palace | *Indian* — 23

Kurofune | *Japanese* — 25

Nisen | *Japanese* — 25

Red Dish Grille | *Amer.* — 21

Souvlaki Palace | *Greek* — 20

Spare Rib | *BBQ* — 17

DEER PARK

Ludlow Bistro | *Amer.* — 23

EAST HAMPTON

Babette's | *Eclectic* — 20

Bamboo | *Pan-Asian* — 20

Bostwick's/Harbor | *Seafood* — 20

Cafe Max | *Amer./Eclectic* — 21

NEW Cherrystones | *Seafood* — 19

cittanuova | *Italian* — 18

Z Della Femina | *Amer.* — 24

Z E. Hampton Point | *Amer.* — 20

Fresno | *Amer.* — 22

Golden Pear | *Coffee* — 17

Harbor Bistro | *Amer.* — 22

Laundry | *Amer.* — 21

Lodge B&G | *Steak* — 19

Matto | *Italian* — 17

Michaels'/Maidstone | *Amer.* — 18

Nichol's | *Amer.* — 18

Z Nick & Toni's | *Italian/Med.* — 23

Palm | *Seafood/Steak* — 25

Rowdy Hall | *Pub* — 19

Sam's | *Pizza* — 19

1770 House | *Continental* — 25

Turtle Crossing | *BBQ/SW* — 21

EAST MARION

Hellenic Snack | *Greek* — 20

EAST MORICHES

Tony's Fusion | *Asian* — 21

EAST NORTHPORT

Baja Grill | *Mex.* — 17

Blue Room | *Amer.* — 24

Chefs of NY | *Italian* — 20

Crossroads Cafe | *Amer.* — 20

NEW Jeff's Seafood | *Seafood* — ⊥

Thai Green Leaf	*Thai*	22
Tokyo	*Japanese/Korean*	23
Torcellos	*Italian*	18
Yokohama	*Asian Fusion*	23

EAST PATCHOGUE

🅩 Chachama Grill	*Amer.*	28

EASTPORT

Trumpets	*Amer./Continental*	22

EAST SETAUKET

Bliss	*Amer.*	22
Curry Club	*Indian*	22
Pita House	*Med./Turkish*	23
Tai-Show	*Japanese*	22

FIRE ISLAND

Hideaway	*Eclectic*	20
Island Mermaid	*Amer.*	20
Maguire's	*Amer.*	18
Matthew's	*Seafood*	17
Top of the Bay	*Amer.*	-

FORT SALONGA

Intermezzo	*Italian*	20

GREENLAWN

Azuma	*Asian Fusion/Japanese*	-
Goldmine Mex.	*Mex.*	18
Ruvo	*Italian*	21

GREENPORT

Antares Cafe	*Amer./Carib.*	24
BBQ Bill's	*BBQ*	18
Claudio's	*Amer./Continental*	15
Frisky Oyster	*Eclectic*	24
Greenport Tea	*Tea*	20
La Cuvée	*French*	20
Porto Bello	*Italian*	18
Salamander's	*Eclectic*	21
Scrimshaw	*Amer.*	22
Vine Wine/Cafe	*Amer.*	22

HAMPTON BAYS

Edgewater	*Italian*	-
Indian Cove	*Amer.*	18
Inn Spot/Bay	*Eclectic*	19
JT's Place	*Pub*	18
Matsulin	*Pan-Asian*	22

Oakland's	*Seafood*	17
Tide Runners	*Amer.*	17
Tony's Fušion	*Asian Fusion*	21

HAUPPAUGE

Butterfields	*Amer.*	20
Cafe La Strada	*Italian*	24
Cielo	*Italian*	18
Gasho of Japan	*Japanese*	19
Grill Room	*Amer.*	22
🅩 Kotobuki	*Japanese*	27
Mario	*Italian*	25
NU	*Continental*	-
Pace's Steak	*Steak*	23
Pomodorino	*Italian*	17
Rist. Forestieri	*Italian*	21
San Marco	*Italian*	24
Sempre Vivolo	*Italian*	25

HOLBROOK

Mama's	*Italian*	22
Mamma Lombardi's	*Italian*	23
Trio	*Amer.*	21

HUNTINGTON/ HUNTINGTON STATION

Abel Conklin's	*Eclectic/Steak*	22
Albert's Mandarin	*Chinese*	21
Almarco	*Italian*	18
American Burger	*Burgers*	17
Ariana	*Afghan/Veg.*	21
🅩 Besito	*Mex.*	23
🅩 Bistro Cassis	*French*	24
🆕 Black & Blue	*Seafood/Steak*	24
Bonbori Tiki	*Japanese/Thai*	19
Bravo Nader!	*Italian*	26
Café Buenos Aires	*Argent.*	23
🅩 Cheesecake Factory	*Amer.*	20
Cirella's	*Amer./Eclectic*	21
Clubhouse	*Steak*	22
Cooke's In	*Carib./Southern*	23
🆕 Crew Kitchen	*Amer.*	25
Danú	*Asian Fusion*	19
Green Cactus	*Mex.*	21
🅩 Honu	*Amer.*	22
House of India	*Indian*	22
Jonathan's Rist.	*Italian*	23
Kabul Afghani	*Afghan*	22

Kohaku	*Japanese*	23
Kurabarn	*Japanese*	22
La Parma	*Italian*	23
La Spada	*Italian*	23
Z Legal Sea Foods	*Seafood*	20
Los Compadres	*Mex.*	22
Mac's Steak	*Steak*	22
Mangiamo	*Italian*	21
Marcia's Kitchen	*Brazilian*	21
NEW Mare Luna	*Eclectic*	24
Massa's	*Pizza*	25
Z Matteo's	*Italian*	23
Med. Snack	*Greek/Med.*	23
Musashino	*Japanese*	17
Noma	*Amer.*	20
Oaxaca Mexican	*Mex.*	23
Osaka	*Japanese*	23
Osteria da Nino	*Italian*	23
NEW Osteria Toscana	*Italian*	-
Z Panama Hatties	*Amer.*	26
PG Steak	*Steak*	22
Piccola Bussola	*Italian*	22
Z Piccolo	*Amer./Italian*	26
Pomodorino	*Italian*	17
Z Prime	*Amer.*	22
Quetzalcoatl	*Mex.*	17
Red Rest.	*Amer.*	24
NEW Rocco's	*Italian*	23
NEW Sally's Cocofé	*Eclectic/Kosher*	-
Samurai	*Japanese*	20
NEW Sri Thai	*Thai*	21
Thai USA	*Thai*	21
34 New St.	*Eclectic*	20
NEW Toast & Co.	*Amer.*	17
Tomo Hibachi	*Japanese*	19
Tutto Pazzo	*Italian*	21
Umberto's	*Italian/Pizza*	21

ISLANDIA

Takara	*Japanese*	26

ISLIP

(Including Central, East, West)

Epicurean Room	*Eclectic*	-
Z In Season Amer.	*Amer.*	26
Irish Coffee	*Continental/Irish*	22
NEW Island BBQ	*BBQ*	-

Nico at the Mansion	*Italian*	21
Nonnina	*Italian*	24
Z Tellers	*Steak*	26

JAMESPORT

Cliff's	*Steak*	21
Jamesport Country	*Amer.*	23
Z Jamesport Manor	*Amer.*	24
Z Jedediah's	*Amer.*	26

KINGS PARK

Chaophaya	*Thai*	21
Long River	*Pan-Asian*	18

LAKE GROVE

NEW Bobby's Burger	*Burgers*	-
Z Cheesecake Factory	*Amer.*	20
Curry Club	*Indian*	22
John Harvard's	*Pub*	16

LAUREL

Cliff's	*Steak*	21

LINDENHURST

Bozena Polish	*Polish*	22
Southside Fish	*Seafood*	18
Village Lanterne	*German*	-

MATTITUCK

NEW A Mano	*Italian*	22
Love Lane Kitchen	*Amer.*	22
Old Mill Inn	*Amer.*	17
Touch of Venice	*Italian*	19

MELVILLE

Barolo	*Continental/Italian*	25
Z Blackstone Steak	*Steak*	23
Cirella's	*Continental/Italian*	21
Four Food Studio	*Amer.*	20
Frederick's	*Continental*	22

MILLER PLACE

Benten	*Japanese*	25
Blond	*Amer.*	22
Sabai Thai	*Thai*	-

MONTAUK

Aqua East	*Italian*	20
Backyard	*Med.*	-
Breakwater Cafe	*Amer.*	-
Z Dave's Grill	*Continental/Seafood*	26

LOCATIONS

Duryea's Lobster	*Seafood*	21
East by Northeast	*Amer./Pan-Asian*	21
NEW Fishbar	*Seafood*	16
Gosman's Dock	*Seafood*	17
NEW Gulf Coast Kitchen	*Carib./Southern*	-
Harvest	*Italian/Med.*	25
Havana Beach Club	*Cuban*	-
Inlet Seafood	*Seafood*	21
Manucci's	*Italian/Pizza*	19
Sea Grille	*Amer./Italian*	18
Second House	*Amer.*	18
Shagwong	*Amer.*	18
NEW Surf Lodge	*Amer.*	21
Surfside Inn	*Continental/Seafood*	19
West Lake Clam	*Seafood*	24

MOUNT SINAI

NEW Alexandros	*Med.*	-
Lotus East	*Chinese*	20

NESCONSET

JT's Corner Cafe	*Amer.*	23
Sundried Tomato	*Italian/Pizza*	22

NEW SUFFOLK

Legends	*Eclectic*	21

NORTHPORT

Benkei Japanese	*Japanese*	20
Bistro 44	*Amer.*	21
La Capannina	*Italian*	23
☑ Maroni Cuisine	*Eclectic/Italian*	28
Pumpernickels	*German*	20
Ritz Cafe	*Continental*	18
Show Win	*Japanese*	22
Sweet Mama's	*Diner*	18

OAKDALE

Mama's	*Italian*	22
Riverview	*Amer./Continental*	19
Snapper Inn	*Seafood*	17
Tai-Show	*Japanese*	22
Viva La Vida	*Mex./Spanish*	23

PATCHOGUE

BobbiQue	*BBQ*	19
Harbor Crab	*Seafood*	18

Mangia Mangia	*Italian*	19
Oar Steak	*Seafood Steak*	20
PeraBell	*Amer./Eclectic*	24
Pita House	*Med./Turkish*	23
Pollo Rico	*Pan-Latin*	-

PORT JEFFERSON/ PORT JEFFERSON STATION

Carnival	*Italian*	20
Fifth Season	*Amer.*	24
Lombardi's	*Italian*	22
Pace's Steak	*Steak*	23
Pasta Pasta	*Italian*	23
Pie	*Pizza*	20
Ruvo	*Italian*	21
Salsa Salsa	*Cal./Mex.*	23
NEW Tequila Jacks	*Carib.*	-
☑ Thai Gourmet	*Thai*	26
Toast	*Eclectic*	23
NEW Wave	*Amer.*	20
Zorba/Greek	*Greek*	19

QUOGUE/ EAST QUOGUE

Dockers Waterside	*Seafood/Steak*	19
Q East	*Amer./Med.*	23
☑ Stone Creek	*French/Med.*	26
Tony's Fusion	*Asian Fusion*	21

RIVERHEAD

Birchwood	*Amer./Polish*	18
Buoy One	*Seafood*	22
Cliff's	*Steak*	21
Spicy's BBQ	*BBQ*	19
Star Confectionery	*Amer.*	21
Stonewalls	*Amer./French*	24
Tweeds	*Amer.*	20

SAGAPONACK

Fairway	*Amer.*	18
Old Stove Pub	*Greek*	18
Townline	*BBQ*	18

SAG HARBOR

☑ American Hotel	*Amer./French*	24
Bay Burger	*Burgers*	19
Beacon	*Amer.*	24

B.Smith's | *Cajun/Southern* 16
Dockside B&G | *Seafood* 19
Estia's Kitchen | *Amer.* 21
Golden Pear | *Coffee* 17
NEW Grappa | *Italian* 20
Il Capuccino | *Italian* 19
JLX Bistro | *French* 13
New Paradise | *Amer./Eclectic* 21
Oasis Waterfront | *Amer.* 23
Sen | *Japanese* 24
Tutto Il Giorno | *Italian* 22

SAYVILLE

Blackbirds' Grille | *Cajun/Southern* 18
Cafe Joelle | *Amer./Eclectic* 23
Collins & Main | *Amer./Eclectic* 24
Cull House | *Seafood* 19
NEW La Tavola | *Italian* 24

SELDEN

Kiran Palace | *Indian* 23
Viva Juan | *Mex.* 17

SHELTER ISLAND/ SHELTER ISLAND HEIGHTS

Chequit Inn | *Amer./Eclectic* 19
Planet Bliss | *Eclectic/New World* 20
Ram's Head | *Amer./Eclectic* 21
Sunset Beach | *French/Pan-Asian* 17
Z Vine Street | *Amer.* 27

SMITHTOWN

American Burger | *Burgers* 17
Baja Grill | *Mex.* 17
Butera's | *Italian* 21
NEW Cafe Havana | *Cuban* 17
Casa Luis | *Spanish* 23
Casa Rustica | *Italian* 25
Famous Dave's | *BBQ* 19
Garden Grill | *Amer.* 19
NEW Hotoke | *Japanese* 26
H2O Seafood | *Seafood* 23
La Famiglia | *Italian* 20
La Panchita | *Mex./Spanish* 21
NEW Luso | *Portug.* –
Maureen's Kitchen | *Amer.* 25
Salsa Salsa | *Cal./Mex.* 23
Shiki | *Japanese* 23

Thai House | *Thai* 21
Union Station | *Amer.* 19

SOUTHAMPTON

Armand's | *Italian* 17
Barrister's | *Amer.* 16
Birchwood | *Amer./Polish* 18
Coast Grill | *Amer./Seafood* 18
Driver's Seat | *Amer.* 15
Golden Pear | *Coffee* 17
La Parmigiana | *Italian* 20
Le Chef | *Continental/French* 21
Lobster Inn | *Seafood* 18
Madame Tong's | *Chinese/Japanese* 12
Mt. Fuji | *Japanese* 19
Nello Summertimes | *Italian* 18
NEW Oso | *Seafood/Steak* –
Z Plaza Cafe | *Amer.* 26
red bar | *Amer./French* 23
Sant Ambroeus | *Italian* 24
Savanna's | *Amer.* 20
75 Main St. | *Amer.* 18
Silver's | *Eclectic* 22
Southampton Publick | *Pub* 16
Tuscan House | *Italian* 21
Wildthyme | *Amer.* 18

SOUTH JAMESPORT

Bayview Inn | *Amer./Continental* 21

SOUTHOLD

Cimino's | *Italian* 18
Elbow East | *Steak* 21
Z North Fork Table | *Amer.* 28
O'Mally's | *Pub* 16
Pepi's Cucina | *Italian/Seafood* 16
Seafood Barge | *Seafood* 21

SPEONK

Olde Speonk Inn | *Amer.* 17

ST. JAMES

Ancient Ginger | *Chinese* 21
Bella Vita Grill | *Amer./Italian* 21
Kirin Hibachi | *Japanese* 20
Z Kitchen A Bistro | *French* 28
NEW Kitchen A Tratt. | *Italian* –
Lotus East | *Chinese* 20

Z Mosaic | *Amer.* 26
Oscar's | *Amer.* 22
Z Vintage Prime | *Steak* 26
Voila! | *French* 23

STONY BROOK

Brook House | *Amer.* -
Z Country House | *Amer.* 22
Golden Pear | *Coffee* 17
Green Cactus | *Mex.* 21
NEW Mirabelle Tavern | *American* -
Pentimento | *Italian* 21
Robinson's | *Tea* 24
Zorba/Greek | *Greek* 19

WADING RIVER

Blackwells | *Steak* 21
Desmond's | *Amer.* 22
Z La Plage | *Eclectic* 26
Michael Anthony's | *Eclectic* 23

WAINSCOTT

Almoncello | *Italian* 20
Saracen | *Italian* 17

WATER MILL

NEW Dish | *Amer.* -
Foody's | *BBQ/Pizza* 19

Hampton Coffee | *Coffee* 19
Z Mirko's | *Eclectic* 26
Muse | *Amer.* 21
Robert's | *Italian* 24
Suki Zuki | *Japanese* 23
Trata East | *Greek/Seafood* 22

WESTHAMPTON/ WESTHAMPTON BEACH

Z Annona | *Italian* 23
Baby Moon | *Italian* 19
Dee Angelo's | *Italian* 17
Hampton Coffee | *Coffee* 19
Patio/54 Main | *Amer.* 19
Post Stop Cafe | *Amer.* 16
Starr Boggs | *Amer./Seafood* 25
Tierra Mar | *Amer./Seafood* 22
Tony's Fusion | *Asian Fusion* 21
Westhampton Steak | *Steak* 17

WEST SAYVILLE

21 Main | *Steak* 24

Special Features

Listings cover the best in each category and include names, locations and Food ratings. Multi-location restaurants' features may vary by branch.

BOAT DOCKING FACILITIES

Antares Cafe	Greenport	24
Beacon	Sag Harbor	24
Bostwick's/Harbor	E Hampton	20
B.Smith's	Sag Harbor	16
Catfish Max	Seaford	23
Claudio's	Greenport	15
Coast Grill	Southampton	18
Dockers Waterside	E Quogue	19
☑ E. Hampton Point	E Hampton	20
fatfish	Bay Shore	19
NEW Fishbar	Montauk	16
Fisherman's Catch	Point Lookout	19
Gosman's Dock	Montauk	17
Harbor Crab	Patchogue	18
Indian Cove	Hampton Bays	18
Lobster Inn	Southampton	18
Louie's Oyster	Port Washington	16
Oakland's	Hampton Bays	17
Oar Steak	Patchogue	20
Oasis Waterfront	Sag Harbor	23
Old Mill Inn	Mattituck	17
Paddy McGees	Island Pk	16
Pepi's Cucina	Southold	16
Pier 95	Freeport	23
☑ Prime	Huntington	22
Rachel's Waterside	Freeport	19
Ram's Head	Shelter Is	21
Riverview	Oakdale	19
Schooner	Freeport	16
Scrimshaw	Greenport	22
Seafood Barge	Southold	21
Snapper Inn	Oakdale	17
Tide Runners	Hampton Bays	17
Touch of Venice	Mattituck	19
Waterview Rest.	Port Washington	16

BREAKFAST

(See also Hotel Dining)

Ayhan's Shish Kebab	Port Washington	18
Babette's	E Hampton	20

BayKery	Oyster Bay	19
Bridgehampton Candy	Bridgehampton	15
Buckram Stables	Locust Valley	18
Estia's Kitchen	Sag Harbor	21
Fairway	Sagaponack	18
Golden Pear	multi.	17
Hampton Coffee	Water Mill	19
Hellenic Snack	E Marion	20
International Delight	multi.	18
JT's Corner Cafe	Nesconset	23
La Cuvée	Greenport	20
Lombardi's	Port Jefferson	22
Maureen's Kitchen	Smithtown	25
Post Stop Cafe	Westhampton Bch	16
Robinson's	Stony Brook	24
Star Confectionery	Riverhead	21
Sweet Mama's	Northport	18
Thomas's Ham	Carle Pl	23
Tierra Mar	Westhampton Bch	22
Toast	Port Jefferson	23

BRUNCH

Antares Cafe	Greenport	24
Ayhan's Shish Kebab	multi.	18
Barrister's	Southampton	16
☑ Bistro Cassis	Huntington	24
Bistro Citron	Roslyn	21
Blackbirds' Grille	Sayville	18
Bobby Van's	Bridgehampton	22
Breakwater Cafe	Montauk	–
NEW Brick & Rail	Wantagh	–
B.Smith's	Sag Harbor	16
Cafe Joelle	Sayville	23
Cafe Max	E Hampton	21
Canterbury	Oyster Bay	18
☑ Cheesecake Factory	Westbury	20
Cooperage Inn	Baiting Hollow	20
Desmond's	Wading River	22
☑ E. Hampton Point	E Hampton	20
Epicurean Room	Central Islip	–

56th Fighter Group | **Farmingdale**	15	Butterfields | **Hauppauge**	20
Garden Grill | **Smithtown**	19	Caracalla | **Syosset**	23
Gonzalo's | **Glen Cove**	20	Clubhouse | **Huntington**	22
Hemingway's | **Wantagh**	18	Delano Mansion | **Woodbury**	-
H.R. Singleton's | **Bethpage**	17	**Z** E. Hampton Point | **E Hampton**	20
Jonathan's | **Garden City Pk**	19	Franina | **Syosset**	23
JT's Place | **Hampton Bays**	18	Frederick's | **Melville**	22
Library Cafe | **Farmingdale**	17	Fulton Prime | **Syosset**	22
NEW Limani | **Roslyn**	-	George Martin's Coastal | **Long Bch**	20
Lombardi's | **Port Jefferson**	22	Giulio Cesare | **Westbury**	24
Louie's Oyster | **Port Washington**	16	**Z** Il Mulino NY | **Roslyn Estates**	26
Milleridge Inn | **Jericho**	15	**Z** Jamesport Manor | **Jamesport**	24
105 Harbor | **Cold Spring**	20	Jolly Fisherman | **Roslyn**	20
Paddy McGees | **Island Pk**	16	Jonathan's Rist. | **Huntington**	23
Painters' | **Brookhaven Hamlet**	18	La Coquille | **Manhasset**	24
Z Palm Court | **E Meadow**	24	La Pace/Chef Michael | **Glen Cove**	24
Pierre's | **Bridgehampton**	21	**Z** La Piccola Liguria | **Port Washington**	26
Z Pine Island | **Bayville**	17	**NEW** Limani | **Roslyn**	-
Planet Bliss | **Shelter Is**	20	Lombardi's | **Port Jefferson**	22
Z Polo | **Garden City**	25	Mac's Steak | **Huntington**	22
Post Stop Cafe | **Westhampton Bch**	16	Manucci's | **Montauk**	19
Z Prime | **Huntington**	22	**Z** Mill River Inn | **Oyster Bay**	27
Rachel's Waterside | **Freeport**	19	**Z** Morton's | **Great Neck**	24
Ram's Head | **Shelter Is**	21	**NEW** Nick & Charley Steak | **Williston Pk**	-
Rein | **Garden City**	23	Nonnina | **W Islip**	24
Ritz Cafe | **Northport**	18	Oak Room | **Farmingdale**	23
Z Riverbay | **Williston Pk**	22	**NEW** Oevo | **Great Neck**	-
Riverview | **Oakdale**	19	On 3 | **Glen Head**	24
Z Rothmann's Steak | **E Norwich**	25	**NEW** Palio Ristorante | **Jericho**	-
Snapper Inn | **Oakdale**	17	Palm | **E Hampton**	25
Southampton Publick | **Southampton**	16	**Z** Panama Hatties | **Huntington Station**	26
Stonewalls | **Riverhead**	24	Patio/54 Main | **Westhampton Bch**	19
Tierra Mar | **Westhampton Bch**	22	**Z** Peter Luger | **Great Neck**	27
Trumpets | **Eastport**	22	**Z** Piccolo | **Huntington**	26
Z Waterzooi | **Garden City**	23	**Z** Plaza Cafe | **Southampton**	26
Wild Ginger | **Great Neck**	22	**Z** Polo | **Garden City**	25
World Pie | **Bridgehampton**	20	**Z** Prime | **Huntington**	22

BUSINESS DINING

Abel Conklin's | **Huntington**	22	**Z** Riverbay | **Williston Pk**	22
Benihana | **Manhasset**	18	Robert's | **Water Mill**	24
Benny's | **Westbury**	25	**NEW** Rocco's | **Huntington Station**	23
Z Blackstone Steak | **Melville**	23	**Z** Rothmann's Steak | **E Norwich**	25
Bobby Van's | **Bridgehampton**	22	**Z** Ruth's Chris | **Garden City**	24
Z Bryant & Cooper | **Roslyn**	26	Sagamore Steak | **Syosset**	23
Burton & Doyle | **Great Neck**	24		

Menus, photos, voting and more - free at ZAGAT.com

Sea Grille | **Montauk** 18

Sempre Vivolo | **Hauppauge** 25

Show Win | **Northport** 22

NEW Speranza | **Woodbury** –

Z Stone Creek | **E Quogue** 26

Stresa | **Manhasset** 24

NEW Table 9 | **E Hills** –

Z Tellers | **Islip** 26

Tierra Mar | **Westhampton Bch** 22

Trio | **Holbrook** 21

Trumpets | **Eastport** 22

Union Station | **Smithtown** 19

Vespa Cibobuono | **Great Neck** 22

BYO

Bistro du Village | 24
  Port Washington

Deli King | **New Hyde Pk** 18

NEW Dish | **Water Mill** –

Duryea's Lobster | **Montauk** 21

Green Cactus | **Garden City Pk** 21

Green Melody | **Jericho** –

NEW Haiku | **Woodbury** –

International Delight | **Bellmore** 18

NEW Jeff's Seafood | **E Northport** –

Z Kitchen A Bistro | **St. James** 28

NEW Kitchen A Tratt. | **St. James** –

La Bottega | **multi.** 24

Massa's | **Huntington Station** 25

NEW New Chilli/Curry | –
  Hicksville

Onzon Thai | **Bellmore** 24

Paradise Island | **Williston Pk** 19

Z Thai Gourmet | 26
  Port Jefferson Station

CATERING

Akbar | **Garden City** 21

Amici | **Massapequa** 21

Barolo | **Melville** 25

Bayou | **N Bellmore** 23

Bella Vita Grill | **St. James** 21

Bellport | **Bellport** 23

Big Daddy's | **Massapequa** 23

Bistro M | **Glen Head** 25

Blond | **Miller Pl** 22

Butterfields | **Hauppauge** 20

Cafe Baci | **Westbury** 22

Cafe Joelle | **Sayville** 23

Cafe La Strada | **Hauppauge** 24

Caffe Laguna | **Long Bch** 19

Z Camille's | **Carle Pl** 24

Casa Rustica | **Smithtown** 25

Ciao Baby | **multi.** 18

Colbeh | **Great Neck** 21

Cooke's In | **Huntington** 23

Z Coolfish | **Syosset** 24

Curry Club | **E Setauket** 22

Z Dario's | **Rockville Ctr** 27

Z Della Femina | **E Hampton** 24

E. B. Elliot's | **Freeport** 18

Epicurean Room | **Central Islip** –

Fiddleheads | **Oyster Bay** 23

Fratelli Iavarone | **New Hyde Pk** 21

Fresno | **E Hampton** 22

Galleria Dominick | **Westbury** 25

George Martin | **Rockville Ctr** 22

Golden Pear | **multi.** 17

Heart of Portugal | **Mineola** 20

Hokkaido | **Albertson** 21

House of Dosas | **Hicksville** 23

H.R. Singleton's | **Bethpage** 17

Il Classico | **Massapequa Pk** 24

Ivy Cottage | **Williston Pk** 24

Jamesport Country | **Jamesport** 23

Kiran Palace | **Hicksville** 23

La Cuvée | **Greenport** 20

La Famiglia | **Smithtown** 20

La Gioconda | **Great Neck** 21

Laguna Grille | **Woodbury** 18

La Panchita | **Smithtown** 21

La Piazza | **multi.** 21

Z La Plage | **Wading River** 26

La Primavera | **Hicksville** 23

La Terrazza | **Cedarhurst** 22

Lemonleaf Grill | **multi.** 20

Lombardi's | **Port Jefferson** 22

Lotus East | **multi.** 20

Lucy's Café | **Babylon** 23

Mamma Lombardi's | **Holbrook** 23

Z Maroni Cuisine | **Northport** 28

Meritage | **Bellport** 23

Mixing Bowl | **Bellmore** 20

Mother Kelly's | **Cedarhurst** 21

Nagashima | **Jericho** 22

Nicholas James | **Merrick**	21
Nick's | **Rockville Ctr**	23
Nisen | **Commack**	25
Orchid | **Garden City**	24
Oscar's | **St. James**	22
Pace's Steak | **multi.**	23
Page One | **Glen Cove**	22
☑ Palm Court | **E Meadow**	24
Pasta-eria | **Hicksville**	23
Pasta Pasta | **Port Jefferson**	23
Pastrami King | **Merrick**	19
Piccola Bussola | **multi.**	22
Pita House | **Patchogue**	23
Planet Bliss | **Shelter Is**	20
☑ Plaza Cafe | **Southampton**	26
Rachel's Waterside | **Freeport**	19
Rangmahal | **Hicksville**	23
Rist. Forestieri | **Hauppauge**	21
Romantico/Capri | **Port Washington**	19
RS Jones | **Merrick**	21
Salamander's | **Greenport**	21
Salsa Salsa | **multi.**	23
San Marco | **Hauppauge**	24
Sapporo | **Wantagh**	20
Shiki | **multi.**	23
☑ Siam Lotus | **Bay Shore**	26
☑ Smokin' Al's BBQ | **Bay Shore**	24
Snaps | **Wantagh**	22
Soigné | **Woodmere**	25
☑ Solé | **Oceanside**	26
Southside Fish | **Lindenhurst**	18
Spare Rib | **multi.**	17
Starr Boggs | **Westhampton Bch**	25
☑ Stone Creek | **E Quogue**	26
Stresa | **Manhasset**	24
Sundried Tomato | **Nesconset**	22
Taiko | **Rockville Ctr**	24
Tai-Show | **multi.**	22
Tandoor Grill | **Rockville Ctr**	21
Terry G's Steak | **Farmingdale**	17
Tesoro | **Westbury**	22
☑ Thai Gourmet | **Port Jefferson Station**	26
Thai Table | **Rockville Ctr**	22
Thyme | **Roslyn**	20
Umberto's | **New Hyde Pk**	21

Uncle Dai | **Glen Cove**	17
Venere | **Westbury**	20
Viva La Vida | **Oakdale**	23
Voila! | **St. James**	23
Walk St. | **Garden City**	21
☑ West End | **Carle Pl**	25
World Pie | **Bridgehampton**	20

CELEBRITY CHEFS

NEW A Mano | *Tom Schaudel* | **Mattituck**	22
Babylon Carriage | *Danny Gagnon* | **Babylon**	19
NEW Bobby's Burger | *Bobby Flay* | **Lake Grove**	-
NEW Brass Rail | *Kent Monkan* | **Locust Valley**	-
Bravo Nader! | *Nader Gebrin* | **Huntington**	26
☑ Coolfish | *Tom Schaudel* | **Syosset**	24
☑ Kitchen A Bistro | *Eric Lomando* | **St. James**	28
NEW Kitchen A Tratt. | *Eric Lomando* | **St. James**	-
NEW Limani | *Peter Spyropoulos* | **Roslyn**	-
☑ Maroni Cuisine | *Michael Maroni* | **Northport**	28
☑ Mill River Inn | *Nick Molfetta* | **Oyster Bay**	27
NEW Mirabelle Tavern | *Guy Reuge* | **Stony Brook**	-
☑ North Fork Table | *Claudia Fleming/Gerry Hayden* | **Southold**	28
Oscar's | *Philippe Corbet* | **St. James**	22
NEW Palio Ristorante | *Massimo Fedozzi* | **Jericho**	-
☑ Panama Hatties | *Matthew Hisiger* | **Huntington Station**	26
☑ Plaza Cafe | *Doug Gulija* | **Southampton**	26
NEW Speranza | *Michael Meehan/Anthony Trobiano* | **Woodbury**	-
Starr Boggs | *Starr Boggs* | **Westhampton Bch**	25
NEW Surf Lodge | *Sam Talbot* | **Montauk**	21

Menus, photos, voting and more – free at ZAGAT.com

CHILD-FRIENDLY

(Alternatives to the usual fast-food places; * children's menu available)

Albert's Mandarin | **Huntington**	21
Amici | **Massapequa**	21
Angelina's | **E Norwich**	22
Argyle Grill* | **Babylon**	21
Ayhan's Fish* | **Port Washington**	19
Ayhan's Shish Kebab* | **multi.**	18
Babylon Carriage* | **Babylon**	19
Baby Moon | **Westhampton Bch**	19
Baja Grill* | **multi.**	17
Bella Vita Grill* | **St. James**	21
Bellport | **Bellport**	23
Benihana* | **multi.**	18
Benten | **Miller Pl**	25
Big Daddy's | **Massapequa**	23
Bigelow's* | **Rockville Ctr**	24
Bliss* | **E Setauket**	22
Boccaccio | **Hicksville**	23
Bonsai | **Port Washington**	22
Bozena Polish* | **Lindenhurst**	22
Bridgehampton Candy | **Bridgehampton**	15
Butera's* | **Woodbury**	21
Butterfields* | **Hauppauge**	20
Cafe Baci* | **Westbury**	22
Cafe La Strada | **Hauppauge**	24
Cafe Rustica | **Great Neck**	21
Caffe Laguna | **Long Bch**	19
Canterbury* | **Oyster Bay**	18
Casa Luis | **Smithtown**	23
☑ Cheesecake Factory | **Westbury**	20
Chefs of NY | **E Northport**	20
NEW Cherrystones | **E Hampton**	19
Churrasq. Bairrada | **Mineola**	24
Cirella's* | **Huntington Station**	21
Cooke's In* | **Huntington**	23
Cooperage Inn* | **Baiting Hollow**	20
☑ Country House | **Stony Brook**	22
Crossroads Cafe* | **E Northport**	20
Curry Club* | **E Setauket**	22
DiMaggio's* | **Port Washington**	18
Dodici* | **Rockville Ctr**	23
Duke Falcon's | **Long Bch**	23
Eddie's Pizza | **New Hyde Pk**	21
Emilio's* | **Commack**	23
Estia's Kitchen | **Sag Harbor**	21
Fairway* | **Sagaponack**	18
Frank's Steaks | **multi.**	20
Frederick's | **Melville**	22
Galleria Dominick* | **Westbury**	25
George Martin Grill* | **Rockville Ctr**	21
Golden Pear* | **multi.**	17
Goldmine Mex. | **Greenlawn**	18
Gonzalo's* | **Glen Cove**	20
Gosman's Dock* | **Montauk**	17
Graffiti* | **multi.**	20
Green Cactus | **multi.**	21
Grimaldi's | **Garden City**	23
Hampton Chutney* | **Amagansett**	22
Hellenic Snack | **E Marion**	20
House of Dosas | **Hicksville**	23
Il Capuccino* | **Sag Harbor**	19
Indian Cove* | **Hampton Bays**	18
Jamesport Country* | **Jamesport**	23
Jolly Fisherman* | **Roslyn**	20
Kiran Palace | **Hicksville**	23
Kiss'o | **New Hyde Pk**	22
Kurofune | **Commack**	25
La Bussola | **Glen Cove**	23
La Famiglia | **Smithtown**	20
Laguna Grille* | **multi.**	18
La Parma | **multi.**	23
La Parmigiana | **Southampton**	20
La Pizzetta | **E Norwich**	20
La Primavera | **Hicksville**	23
☑ Legal Sea Foods* | **multi.**	20
Lobster Roll* | **multi.**	20
Lombardi's* | **Port Jefferson**	22
Los Compadres | **Huntington Station**	22
Louie's Oyster* | **Port Washington**	16
Lucy's Café | **Babylon**	23
Mamma Lombardi's* | **Holbrook**	23
☑ Matteo's | **multi.**	23
Maureen's Kitchen | **Smithtown**	25
Med. Snack | **Huntington**	23
Meritage | **Bellport**	23
Mim's* | **multi.**	18
Minado | **Carle Pl**	20
Modern Snack* | **Aquebogue**	18
☑ Nagahama | **Long Bch**	26
Nagashima | **Jericho**	22

Nautilus Cafe*	**Freeport**	24	Steve's Piccola	**Westbury**	25
Nicholas James*	**Merrick**	21	Sundried Tomato*	**Nesconset**	22
Nick's	**Rockville Ctr**	23	Sushi Ya*	**Garden City**	22
Oaxaca Mexican	**Huntington**	23	Taiko	**Rockville Ctr**	24
Oliver Bon Dinant	**Williston Pk**	25	Tai-Show*	**Massapequa**	22
O'Mally's*	**Southold**	16	Tandoor Grill*	**Rockville Ctr**	21
Once Upon a Moose*	**Sea Cliff**	19	Terry G's Steak*	**Farmingdale**	17
Orchid	**Garden City**	24	Tesoro	**Westbury**	22
Oscar's*	**St. James**	22	⚡ Thai Gourmet		26
Ozumo*	**Bethpage**	21	**Port Jefferson Station**	
Pace's Steak*	**multi.**	23	Thai Table	**Rockville Ctr**	22
Page One*	**Glen Cove**	22	34 New St.*	**Huntington**	20
Painters'*	**Brookhaven Hamlet**	18	Thomas's Ham*	**Carle Pl**	23
Pancho's*	**multi.**	19	Thom Thom*	**Wantagh**	21
Pasta-eria	**Hicksville**	23	Thyme*	**Roslyn**	20
Pentimento	**Stony Brook**	21	Turtle Crossing*	**E Hampton**	21
Pepi's Cucina*	**Southold**	16	Tutto Pazzo*	**Huntington**	21
Per Un Angelo	**Wantagh**	21	Umberto's	**New Hyde Pk**	21
Pier 95	**Freeport**	23	Uncle Dai	**Glen Cove**	17
Pita House	**Patchogue**	23	Venere*	**Westbury**	20
Planet Bliss	**Shelter Is**	20	Villa D'Este	**Floral Pk**	20
Poco Loco*	**Roslyn**	17	Voila!	**St. James**	23
Pomodorino*	**multi.**	17	World Pie	**Bridgehampton**	20
Post Stop Cafe*		16	Yuki's Palette*	**Westbury**	21

Post Stop Cafe* |
Westhampton Bch

Pumpernickels*	**Northport**	20
Rangmahal	**Hicksville**	23
Red Dish Grille	**Commack**	21
Red Fish*	**Plainview**	23
Rein*	**Garden City**	23
Rist. Gemelli*	**Babylon**	22
⚡ Riverbay	**Williston Pk**	22
RS Jones	**Merrick**	21
Salamander's	**Greenport**	21
Salsa Salsa*	**multi.**	23
Sam's*	**E Hampton**	19
Sapporo*	**Wantagh**	20
Seeda Thai	**Valley Stream**	21
Shiki*	**multi.**	23
Shogi	**Westbury**	23
⚡ Siam Lotus	**Bay Shore**	26
⚡ Smokin' Al's BBQ*	**Bay Shore**	24
Snaps*	**Wantagh**	22
⚡ Solé*	**Oceanside**	26
Spare Rib*	**Commack**	17
Spicy's BBQ	**multi.**	19
Star Confectionery	**Riverhead**	21

DANCING

Blue	**Blue Pt**	19
City Café	**Garden City**	17
56th Fighter Group	**Farmingdale**	15
Hudson/McCoy	**Freeport**	17
Island Mermaid	**Fire Is**	20
Oakland's	**Hampton Bays**	17
Oar Steak	**Patchogue**	20
Riverview	**Oakdale**	19
Saracen	**Wainscott**	17
Sea Grille	**Montauk**	18
Snapper Inn	**Oakdale**	17
Tulip	**Great Neck**	20

DELIVERY/TAKEOUT

(D=delivery, T=takeout)

Albert's Mandarin	T	**Huntington**	21
Amici	T	**Massapequa**	21
Angelina's	T	**multi.**	22
Ayhan's Shish Kebab	D, T	**multi.**	18
Baby Moon	T		19
Westhampton Bch	
Baja Grill	T	**multi.**	17

Bella Vita Grill | T | **St. James**	21
Big Daddy's | T | **Massapequa**	23
Bigelow's | T | **Rockville Ctr**	24
Bliss | T | **E Setauket**	22
Blond | T | **Miller Pl**	22
Bonbori Tiki | T | **Huntington**	19
Bonsai | D, T | **Port Washington**	22
Bridgehampton Candy | T | **Bridgehampton**	15
Buckram Stables | T | **Locust Valley**	18
Butera's | T | **Woodbury**	21
Cafe La Strada | T | **Hauppauge**	24
Caffe Laguna | D | **Long Bch**	19
Chicken Kebab | T | **Roslyn Hts**	20
Churrasq. Bairrada | D, T | **Mineola**	24
Cirella's | T | **multi.**	21
Clam Bar | T | **Amagansett**	19
Collins & Main | T | **Sayville**	24
Cooke's In | T | **Huntington**	23
Curry Club | T | **E Setauket**	22
Cyril's Fish House | T | **Amagansett**	18
DiMaggio's | T | **Port Washington**	18
Duryea's Lobster | T | **Montauk**	21
Dynasty/Pt. Wash. | D | **Port Washington**	18
Eddie's Pizza | T | **New Hyde Pk**	21
Emilio's | T | **Commack**	23
Fortune Wheel | T | **Levittown**	23
Fratelli Iavarone | D | **New Hyde Pk**	21
Frederick's | T | **Melville**	22
Fresco Crêperie | T | **Long Bch**	23
Golden Pear | D, T | **multi.**	17
Goldmine Mex. | T | **Greenlawn**	18
Gonzalo's | D, T | **Glen Cove**	20
Green Cactus | T | **multi.**	21
Grimaldi's | T | **Garden City**	23
Hampton Chutney | T | **Amagansett**	22
Hampton Coffee | T | **Water Mill**	19
Hellenic Snack | T | **E Marion**	20
Hinata | D | **Great Neck**	22
Hokkaido | D | **Albertson**	21
Intermezzo | D | **Ft Salonga**	20
Kawasaki Steak | D | **Long Bch**	19
Kiran Palace | D, T | **Hicksville**	23
Kiss'o | T | **New Hyde Pk**	22
Kohaku | T | **Huntington Station**	23
Kurabarn | T | **Huntington**	22
Kurofune | T | **Commack**	25
Laguna Grille | T | **multi.**	18
La Parma | T | **multi.**	23
La Parmigiana | T | **Southampton**	20
La Pizzetta | T | **E Norwich**	20
La Viola | D | **Cedarhurst**	21
Lemonleaf Grill | D | **multi.**	20
Lobster Inn | T | **Southampton**	18
Lobster Roll | T | **multi.**	20
Lombardi's | T | **Port Jefferson**	22
Long River | T | **Kings Park**	18
Los Compadres | T | **Huntington Station**	22
Lucy's Café | T | **Babylon**	23
ⓩ Maroni Cuisine | T | **Northport**	28
Matsuya | D | **Great Neck**	22
ⓩ Matteo's | T | **multi.**	23
Maureen's Kitchen | T | **Smithtown**	25
Med. Snack | T | **Huntington**	23
Midori | D | **Hewlett**	23
Mim's | T | **multi.**	18
Minami | T | **Massapequa**	24
Modern Snack | T | **Aquebogue**	18
Mother Kelly's | D | **Cedarhurst**	21
Mt. Fuji | T | **Southampton**	19
Musashino | D | **Huntington**	17
ⓩ Nagahama | D, T | **Long Bch**	26
Nagashima | T | **Jericho**	22
Nautilus Cafe | T | **Freeport**	24
Nicholas James | T | **Merrick**	21
Nick's | T | **Rockville Ctr**	23
O'Mally's | T | **Southold**	16
Onzon Thai | T | **Bellmore**	24
Orchid | T | **Garden City**	24
Oscar's | T | **St. James**	22
Ozumo | T | **Bethpage**	21
Pace's Steak | T | **multi.**	23
Pancho's | T | **multi.**	19
Pasta-eria | T | **Hicksville**	23
Pasta Pasta | T | **Port Jefferson**	23
Pearl East | D, T | **Manhasset**	23
Pita House | T | **Patchogue**	23
Pomodorino | T | **multi.**	17
Post Stop Cafe | T | **Westhampton Bch**	16

Pumpernickels | T | **Northport**	20
Rangmahal | D, T | **Hicksville**	23
Ravagh | D, T | **Roslyn Hts**	22
Red Fish | T | **Plainview**	23
Romantico/Capri | D | **Port Washington**	19
Rowdy Hall | T | **E Hampton**	19
RS Jones | T | **Merrick**	21
Salamander's | T | **Greenport**	21
Salsa Salsa | T | **multi.**	23
Sam's | T | **E Hampton**	19
San Marco | T | **Hauppauge**	24
Sant Ambroeus | T | **Southampton**	24
Sapporo | T | **Wantagh**	20
Sarin Thai | T | **Greenvale**	22
Seeda Thai | T | **Valley Stream**	21
Shagwong | T | **Montauk**	18
Shogi | T | **Westbury**	23
Show Win | D, T | **Northport**	22
Z Siam Lotus | T | **Bay Shore**	26
Silver's | T | **Southampton**	22
Z Smokin' Al's BBQ | T | **Bay Shore**	24
Snaps | T | **Wantagh**	22
Southampton Publick | T | **Southampton**	16
Southside Fish | T | **Lindenhurst**	18
Spicy's BBQ | D, T | **multi.**	19
Star Confectionery | T | **Riverhead**	21
Steven's Pasta | D | **Long Bch**	23
Suki Zuki | T | **Water Mill**	23
Sushi Ya | T | **Garden City**	22
Taiko | T | **Rockville Ctr**	24
Tai-Show | T | **multi.**	22
Tandoor Grill | D | **Rockville Ctr**	21
Tesoro | T | **Westbury**	22
Z Thai Gourmet | T | **Port Jefferson Station**	26
Thai Green Leaf | D, T | **multi.**	22
Thai Table | T | **Rockville Ctr**	22
Thai USA | T | **Huntington**	21
34 New St. | D, T | **Huntington**	20
Thomas's Ham | T | **Carle Pl**	23
Thom Thom | T | **Wantagh**	21
Thyme | T | **Roslyn**	20
Tokyo | T | **E Northport**	23
Tony's Fusion | D | **E Quogue**	21

Tratt. Di Meo | T | **Roslyn Hts**	21
Turtle Crossing | T | **E Hampton**	21
Tutto Pazzo | T | **Huntington**	21
Umberto's | T | **New Hyde Pk**	21
Uncle Dai | D, T | **Glen Cove**	17
Venere | T | **Westbury**	20
Wild Ginger | D, T | **Great Neck**	22
World Pie | T | **Bridgehampton**	20
Yamaguchi | T | **Port Washington**	24
Yuki's Palette | T | **Westbury**	21
Zorba/Greek | D, T | **Stony Brook**	19

DINING ALONE

(Other than hotels and places with counter service)

Babette's | **E Hampton**	20
Ben's Deli | **multi.**	19
Bliss | **E Setauket**	22
Bridgehampton Candy | **Bridgehampton**	15
Z Coolfish | **Syosset**	24
Estia's Kitchen | **Sag Harbor**	21
Frisky Oyster | **Greenport**	24
Golden Pear | **multi.**	17
Graffiti | **Woodbury**	20
Hampton Chutney | **Amagansett**	22
Lobster Roll | **Baiting Hollow**	20
Once Upon a Moose | **Sea Cliff**	19
Panini Café | **Roslyn**	23
Salamander's | **Greenport**	21
Sen | **Sag Harbor**	24
Show Win | **Northport**	22
Star Confectionery | **Riverhead**	21
Sushi Ya | **Garden City**	22
Tava | **Port Washington**	19
Townline | **Sagaponack**	18

DRAMATIC INTERIORS

Z American Hotel | **Sag Harbor**	24
Antares Cafe | **Greenport**	24
Chi | **Westbury**	25
City Cellar | **Westbury**	20
Claudio's | **Greenport**	15
Z Country House | **Stony Brook**	22
Delano Mansion | **Woodbury**	–
E. B. Elliot's | **Freeport**	18
56th Fighter Group | **Farmingdale**	15
Fisherman's Catch | **Point Lookout**	19

Four Food Studio | **Melville** 20

Gabrielle's | **Rockville Ctr** 22

Garden Grill | **Smithtown** 19

🆉 Honu | **Huntington** 22

🆉 Jamesport Manor | **Jamesport** 24

🆉 Jedediah's | **Jamesport** 26

Library Cafe | **Farmingdale** 17

NEW Limani | **Roslyn** -

Ludlow Bistro | **Deer Park** 23

Maxxels | **Mineola** 24

Milleridge Inn | **Jericho** 15

NEW Mumon | **Garden City** -

Nanking | **New Hyde Pk** 19

🆉 Nisen Sushi | **Woodbury** 26

Nonnina | **W Islip** 24

Novitá | **Garden City** 23

Oak Room | **Farmingdale** 23

🆉 Polo | **Garden City** 25

Ram's Head | **Shelter Is** 21

Red Rest. | **Huntington** 24

Rist. Gemelli | **Babylon** 22

Riverview | **Oakdale** 19

Robert's | **Water Mill** 24

1770 House | **E Hampton** 25

NEW Speranza | **Woodbury** -

🆉 Tellers | **Islip** 26

Thom Thom | **Wantagh** 21

Tierra Mar | **Westhampton Bch** 22

🆉 Toku | **Manhasset** 24

Tula Kitchen | **Bay Shore** -

Tupelo Honey | **Sea Cliff** 22

Tweeds | **Riverhead** 20

NEW Wave | **Port Jefferson** 20

Wild Harvest | **Glen Cove** 20

ENTERTAINMENT

(Call for days and times of performances)

🆉 American Hotel | piano | **Sag Harbor** 24

Babette's | jazz | **E Hampton** 20

Babylon Carriage | jazz | **Babylon** 19

Backyard | DJ | **Montauk** -

Bayou | bands | **N Bellmore** 23

Big Daddy's | bands | **Massapequa** 23

Blackbirds' Grille | varies | **Sayville** 18

Blond | jazz | **Miller Pl** 22

Blue | DJ | **Blue Pt** 19

Cafe Symposio | piano | **Bellmore** 18

Chequit Inn | rock | **Shelter Is Hts** 19

Ciao Baby | vocals | **multi.** 18

City Café | varies | **Garden City** 17

Collins & Main | piano | **Sayville** 24

Cooke's In | piano | **Huntington** 23

🆉 Coolfish | varies | **Syosset** 24

Curry Club | varies | **E Setauket** 22

Danú | salsa | **Huntington** 19

Dockers Waterside | varies | **E Quogue** 19

🆉 E. Hampton Point | reggae | **E Hampton** 20

E. B. Elliot's | karaoke | **Freeport** 18

fatfish | varies | **Bay Shore** 19

Fiddleheads | varies | **Oyster Bay** 23

Fishery | varies | **E Rockaway** 19

Galleria Dominick | piano | **Westbury** 25

Gosman's Dock | jazz | **Montauk** 17

Grasso's | jazz | **Cold Spring** 25

NEW Grey Horse | blue grass/jazz | **Bayport** 22

Grill Room | varies | **Hauppauge** 22

H2O Seafood | varies | **Smithtown** 23

Hudson/McCoy | varies | **Freeport** 17

Indian Cove | varies | **Hampton Bays** 18

Irish Coffee | Irish | **E Islip** 22

Kabul Afghani | belly dancing | **Huntington** 22

La Coquille | harp | **Manhasset** 24

La Primavera | piano | **Hicksville** 23

Library Cafe | varies | **Farmingdale** 17

Lobster Roll | guitar/vocals | **Baiting Hollow** 20

Lombardi's | varies | **Port Jefferson** 22

Milleridge Inn | piano | **Jericho** 15

🆉 Mill Pond House | piano | **Centerport** 25

🆉 Nisen Sushi | DJ | **Woodbury** 26

Oakland's | varies | **Hampton Bays** 17

Oak Room | varies | **Farmingdale** 23

Oar Steak | varies | **Patchogue** 20

105 Harbor | jazz | **Cold Spring** 20

Pace's Steak | varies | **Port Jefferson** 23

Paddy McGees | DJ | **Island Pk** 16

Painters' | bands | **Brookhaven Hamlet**	18
🛛 Palm Court | varies | **E Meadow**	24
Patio/54 Main | varies | **Westhampton Bch**	19
Per Un Angelo | varies | **Wantagh**	21
🛛 Piccolo | piano | **Huntington**	26
Pierre's | jazz | **Bridgehampton**	21
Pollo Rico | guitar/harp | **Centereach**	-
Post Office Cafe | varies | **Babylon**	18
Ram's Head | varies | **Shelter Is**	21
Red Dish Grille | varies | **Commack**	21
Rein | varies | **Garden City**	23
Rist. Forestieri | varies | **Hauppauge**	21
Riverview | bands | **Oakdale**	19
RS Jones | varies | **Merrick**	21
Saracen | varies | **Wainscott**	17
Sea Grille | DJ/karaoke | **Montauk**	18
Snapper Inn | piano | **Oakdale**	17
Southampton Publick | DJ | **Southampton**	16
Swingbelly's | acoustic | **Long Bch**	21
Takara | karaoke | **Islandia**	26
Tava | piano | **Port Washington**	19
Tide Runners | bands | **Hampton Bays**	17
Tulip | varies | **Great Neck**	20
Tupelo Honey | jazz/pop | **Sea Cliff**	22
Turtle Crossing | bands | **E Hampton**	21
Tweeds | piano | **Riverhead**	20
21 Main | piano | **W Sayville**	24
Village Lanterne | folk | **Lindenhurst**	-
Viva Juan | varies | **multi.**	17
Walk St. | bands | **Garden City**	21

FAMILY-STYLE

Albert's Mandarin | **Huntington**	21
Amici | **Massapequa**	21
Ciao Baby | **multi.**	18
Dynasty/Pt. Wash. | **Port Washington**	18
Fanatico | **Jericho**	20
Harvest | **Montauk**	25
La Famiglia | **Smithtown**	20

La Parma | **multi.**	23
La Parmigiana | **Southampton**	20
La Viola | **Cedarhurst**	21
Mamma Lombardi's | **Holbrook**	23
Mangiamo | **Huntington**	21
🛛 Matteo's | **multi.**	23
Montebello | **Port Washington**	22
Nick Diangelo | **Long Bch**	21
Nick's | **Rockville Ctr**	23
P.F. Chang's | **Westbury**	19
Piccola Bussola | **multi.**	22
Steve's Piccola | **multi.**	25

FIREPLACES

Abel Conklin's | **Huntington**	22
Absolutely Mario | **Farmingdale**	21
Almoncello | **Wainscott**	20
🛛 American Hotel | **Sag Harbor**	24
Angelina's | **Syosset**	22
Armand's | **Southampton**	17
Babylon Carriage | **Babylon**	19
Baby Moon | **Westhampton Bch**	19
🛛 Barney's | **Locust Valley**	26
Basil Leaf | **Locust Valley**	19
Bayview Inn | **S Jamesport**	21
Bellport | **Bellport**	23
Birchwood | **Riverhead**	18
Blackbirds' Grille | **Sayville**	18
🛛 Blackstone Steak | **Melville**	23
Blackwells | **Wading River**	21
Blue | **Blue Pt**	19
NEW Brooks & Porter | **Merrick**	22
🛛 Bryant & Cooper | **Roslyn**	26
Burton & Doyle | **Great Neck**	24
NEW Cafe Havana | **Smithtown**	17
Casa Rustica | **Smithtown**	25
Chalet Bar | **Roslyn**	18
Chequit Inn | **Shelter Is Hts**	19
Churrasc. Riodizio | **Roslyn Hts**	21
Cielo Rist. | **Rockville Ctr**	19
NEW Circa | **Mineola**	-
City Café | **Garden City**	17
Collins & Main | **Sayville**	24
Cooperage Inn | **Baiting Hollow**	20
🛛 Country House | **Stony Brook**	22
Cozymel's Mex. | **Westbury**	16
Crossroads Cafe | **E Northport**	20

🅩 Della Femina | **E Hampton**	24
Driver's Seat | **Southampton**	15
E. B. Elliot's | **Freeport**	18
Famous Dave's | **multi.**	19
56th Fighter Group | **Farmingdale**	15
Fisherman's Catch | **Point Lookout**	19
Franina | **Syosset**	23
Galleria Dominick | **Westbury**	25
Garden Grill | **Smithtown**	19
🆕 Grappa | **Sag Harbor**	20
Hemingway's | **Wantagh**	18
🅩 Honu | **Huntington**	22
Horace/Sylvia's | **Babylon**	17
H.R. Singleton's | **Bethpage**	17
Hudson/McCoy | **Freeport**	17
Il Classico | **Massapequa Pk**	24
Inlet Seafood | **Montauk**	21
Irish Coffee | **E Islip**	22
🅩 Jamesport Manor | **Jamesport**	24
🅩 Jedediah's | **Jamesport**	26
Jimmy Hays | **Island Pk**	25
Jolly Fisherman | **Roslyn**	20
La Capannina | **Northport**	23
La Cuvée | **Greenport**	20
🅩 Lake House | **Bay Shore**	27
La Pace/Chef Michael | **Glen Cove**	24
Laundry | **E Hampton**	21
Legends | **New Suffolk**	21
Lobster Roll | **Baiting Hollow**	20
Lodge B&G | **E Hampton**	19
Madame Tong's | **Southampton**	12
Maguire's | **Fire Is**	18
Majors Steak | **multi.**	17
Mamma Lombardi's | **Holbrook**	23
Mario | **Hauppauge**	25
Michael Anthony's | **Wading River**	23
🆕 Mill Creek | **Bayville**	23
Milleridge Inn | **Jericho**	15
🅩 Mill River Inn | **Oyster Bay**	27
🆕 Mirabelle Tavern | **Stony Brook**	-
🅩 Mirko's | **Water Mill**	26
Nello Summertimes | **Southampton**	18
New Hyde Park | **New Hyde Pk**	20
Nichol's | **E Hampton**	18
Nick Diangelo | **Long Bch**	21
Nonnina | **W Islip**	24
🅩 North Fork Table | **Southold**	28
Oak Chalet | **Bellmore**	20
Olde Speonk Inn | **Speonk**	17
Old Mill Inn | **Mattituck**	17
105 Harbor | **Cold Spring**	20
Oscar's | **St. James**	22
🆕 Osteria Toscana | **Huntington**	-
Palm | **E Hampton**	25
🅩 Palm Court | **E Meadow**	24
🅩 Panama Hatties | **Huntington Station**	26
Papa Razzi | **Westbury**	18
Pepi's Cucina | **Southold**	16
Per Un Angelo | **Wantagh**	21
Piccolo's | **Mineola**	23
Pierre's | **Bridgehampton**	21
🅩 Plaza Cafe | **Southampton**	26
Porto Bello | **Greenport**	18
Post Office Cafe | **Babylon**	18
🅩 Prime | **Huntington**	22
Q East | **Quogue**	23
Ram's Head | **Shelter Is**	21
Rein | **Garden City**	23
Rist. Gemelli | **Babylon**	22
Riverview | **Oakdale**	19
Robert's | **Water Mill**	24
🅩 Rothmann's Steak | **E Norwich**	25
Rowdy Hall | **E Hampton**	19
Runyon's | **Seaford**	17
Sagamore Steak | **Syosset**	23
Saracen | **Wainscott**	17
Savanna's | **Southampton**	20
1770 House | **E Hampton**	25
Seventh St. Cafe | **Garden City**	19
Snapper Inn | **Oakdale**	17
Soigné | **Woodmere**	25
Spare Rib | **Hicksville**	17
Starr Boggs | **Westhampton Bch**	25
🅩 Stone Creek | **E Quogue**	26
Sullivan's Quay | **Port Washington**	17
Surfside Inn | **Montauk**	19
Tesoro | **Westbury**	22
Thyme | **Roslyn**	20
Touch of Venice | **Mattituck**	19

Tratt. Di Meo	Roslyn Hts	21
Trumpets	Eastport	22
Tutto Il Giorno	Sag Harbor	22
Tutto Pazzo	Huntington	21
Tweeds	Riverhead	20
21 Main	W Sayville	24
Umberto's	New Hyde Pk	21
Venere	Westbury	20
❷ Vintage Prime	St. James	26
Viva Loco	Bellmore	16
Wall's Wharf	Bayville	17
Westhampton Steak	Westhampton Bch	17
Wild Harvest	Glen Cove	20

HISTORIC PLACES

(Year opened; * building)

1647	Nello Summertimes*	Southampton	18
1663	1770 House*	E Hampton	25
1672	Milleridge Inn*	Jericho	15
1699	Palm*	E Hampton	25
1710	Country House*	Stony Brook	22
1785	Q East*	Quogue	23
1800	Lobster Roll*	Baiting Hollow	20
1820	105 Harbor*	Cold Spring	20
1821	Old Mill Inn*	Mattituck	17
1826	Garden Grill*	Smithtown	19
1841	Abel Conklin's*	Huntington	22
1842	Chalet Bar*	Roslyn	18
1846	American Hotel*	Sag Harbor	24
1857	Inn Spot/Bay*	Hampton Bays	19
1863	Jedediah's*	Jamesport	26
1865	Babylon Carriage*	Babylon	19
1870	Claudio's	Greenport	15
1872	Chequit Inn*	Shelter Is Hts	19
1876	Nico at the Mansion*	Islip	21
1896	Tweeds*	Riverhead	20
1898	Ayhan's Fish*	Port Washington	19
1900	New Hyde Park*	New Hyde Pk	20
1900	Oscar's*	St. James	22
1900	Porters*	Bellport	-
1902	Silver's*	Southampton	22
1902	Wild Honey*	Oyster Bay	24
1903	Spicy's BBQ*	Riverhead	19
1904	La Marmite	Williston Pk	25
1905	Louie's Oyster	Port Washington	16
1906	Mill Pond House*	Centerport	25
1907	Rothmann's Steak*	E Norwich	25
1911	Star Confectionery	Riverhead	21
1914	Post Stop Cafe*	Westhampton Bch	16
1918	Delano Mansion*	Woodbury	-
1918	Olde Speonk Inn*	Speonk	17
1920	Ayhan's Shish Kebab*	Port Washington	18
1920	Second House*	Montauk	18
1926	Bridgehampton Candy	Bridgehampton	15
1926	Tellers*	Islip	26
1927	Hildebrandt's	Williston Pk	19
1927	Shagwong*	Montauk	18
1929	Backyard*	Montauk	-
1929	Birchwood*	Riverhead	18
1929	Jimmy Hays	Island Pk	25
1929	Ram's Head*	Shelter Is	21
1929	Snapper Inn	Oakdale	17
1930	Meritage*	Bellport	23
1934	Southside Fish	Lindenhurst	18
1935	red bar*	Southampton	23
1937	Blue Moon*	Rockville Ctr	21
1938	Declan Quinn's*	Bay Shore	19
1939	Bigelow's	Rockville Ctr	24
1941	Eddie's Pizza	New Hyde Pk	21
1943	Gosman's Dock	Montauk	17
1943	Mitchell's	Valley Stream	16
1944	Koenig's	Floral Pk	18
1945	Fulton Prime	Syosset	22
1945	Wall's Wharf	Bayville	17
1946	Thomas's Ham	Carle Pl	23

1947	Sam's	E Hampton	19
1948	Duryea's Lobster*	Montauk	21
1950	Modern Snack	Aquebogue	18
1950	Pier 95*	Freeport	23
1955	Carnival	Port Jefferson Station	20
1956	Dockers Waterside*	E Quogue	19
1956	Dockside B&G*	Sag Harbor	19
1957	Jolly Fisherman	Roslyn	20
1958	Cliff's	Jamesport	21

HOLIDAY MEALS

(Special prix fixe meals offered at major holidays)

Benihana	Manhasset	18
Z Country House	Stony Brook	22
Z Jedediah's	Jamesport	26
Milleridge Inn	Jericho	15
Ram's Head	Shelter Is	21

HOTEL DINING

American Hotel
| **Z** American Hotel | Sag Harbor | 24 |

Andrew Hotel
| Colbeh | Great Neck | 21 |

Bayview Inn
| Bayview Inn | S Jamesport | 21 |

Chequit Inn
| Chequit Inn | Shelter Is Hts | 19 |

Garden City Hotel
| **Z** Polo | Garden City | 25 |
| Rein | Garden City | 23 |

Gurney's Inn
| Sea Grille | Montauk | 18 |

Housers Hotel
| Hideaway | Fire Is | 20 |

Huntting Inn
| Palm | E Hampton | 25 |

Hyatt Regency Long Island
| NU | Hauppauge | - |

Inn at East Wind
| Desmond's | Wading River | 22 |

Inn at Quogue
| Q East | Quogue | 23 |

Jedediah Hawkins Inn
| **Z** Jedediah's | Jamesport | 26 |

J.J. Sullivan Hotel
| Tweeds | Riverhead | 20 |

Jones Beach Hotel
| Per Un Angelo | Wantagh | 21 |

Kenny's Tipperary Inn
| Manucci's | Montauk | 19 |

Montauk Manor
| Breakwater Cafe | Montauk | - |

Montauk Yacht Club Resort
| **NEW** Gulf Coast Kitchen | Montauk | - |

Nello Summertimes
| Nello Summertimes | Southampton | 18 |

North Fork Inn
| **Z** North Fork Table | Southold | 28 |

Ram's Head Inn
| Ram's Head | Shelter Is | 21 |

1770 House
| 1770 House | E Hampton | 25 |

Solé East
| Backyard | Montauk | - |

Southampton Inn
| **NEW** Oso | Southampton | - |

Stone Lion Inn
| East by Northeast | Montauk | 21 |

Sunset Beach Hotel
| Sunset Beach | Shelter Is Hts | 17 |

Surfside Inn
| Surfside Inn | Montauk | 19 |

Three Village Inn
| **NEW** Mirabelle Tavern | Stony Brook | - |

West Lake Fishing Lodge
| West Lake Clam | Montauk | 24 |

LATE DINING

(Weekday closing hour)

Carnival	12 AM	Port Jefferson Station	20
Chalet Bar	12 AM	Roslyn	18
Eddie's Pizza	varies	New Hyde Pk	21
George Martin	12 AM	Rockville Ctr	22
Library Cafe	1 AM	Farmingdale	17

Nello Summertimes | 12 AM | **Southampton** — 18

O'Mally's | 12 AM | **Southold** — 16

Post Office Cafe | varies | **Babylon** — 18

Q East | 12 AM | **Quogue** — 23

NEW Speranza | 12 AM | **Woodbury** — -

Swingbelly's | 12:30 AM | **Long Bch** — 21

Trata East | 12 AM | **Water Mill** — 22

Vine Wine/Cafe | 12 AM | **Greenport** — 22

Viva Juan | 12 AM | **Farmingdale** — 17

Westhampton Steak | 12 AM | **Westhampton Bch** — 17

World Pie | 12 AM | **Bridgehampton** — 20

LOCAL FAVORITES

Almond | **Bridgehampton** — 21

Amici | **Massapequa** — 21

Angelina's | **multi.** — 22

Armand's | **Southampton** — 17

Arturo's | **Floral Pk** — 23

Azuma | **Greenlawn** — -

Barrister's | **Southampton** — 16

Bellport | **Bellport** — 23

Benny's | **Westbury** — 25

Bigelow's | **Rockville Ctr** — 24

Z Bistro Cassis | **Huntington** — 24

B.K. Sweeney's | **Garden City** — 18

Blackbirds' Grille | **Sayville** — 18

Blue Moon | **Rockville Ctr** — 21

NEW Brass Rail | **Locust Valley** — -

Bravo Nader! | **Huntington** — 26

Bridgehampton Candy | **Bridgehampton** — 15

Broadway Beanery | **Lynbrook** — 22

Brook House | **Stony Brook** — -

Buckram Stables | **Locust Valley** — 18

Canterbury | **Oyster Bay** — 18

Ciao Baby | **Commack** — 18

Cliff's | **multi.** — 21

Coast Grill | **Southampton** — 18

Cooperage Inn | **Baiting Hollow** — 20

Crossroads Cafe | **E Northport** — 20

Curry Club | **E Setauket** — 22

Z Dario's | **Rockville Ctr** — 27

Z Da Ugo | **Rockville Ctr** — 26

Z Dave's Grill | **Montauk** — 26

Duke Falcon's | **Long Bch** — 23

Duryea's Lobster | **Montauk** — 21

East by Northeast | **Montauk** — 21

Eddie's Pizza | **New Hyde Pk** — 21

Emilio's | **Commack** — 23

Graffiti | **Woodbury** — 20

Greenport Tea | **Greenport** — 20

Hellenic Snack | **E Marion** — 20

Hemingway's | **Wantagh** — 18

Hildebrandt's | **Williston Pk** — 19

Hokkaido | **Albertson** — 21

Il Capuccino | **Sag Harbor** — 19

Ivy Cottage | **Williston Pk** — 24

Jamesport Country | **Jamesport** — 23

Jimmy Hays | **Island Pk** — 25

JT's Corner Cafe | **Nesconset** — 23

Z Kotobuki | **multi.** — 27

La Parmigiana | **Southampton** — 20

La Piazza | **multi.** — 21

Laundry | **E Hampton** — 21

Legends | **New Suffolk** — 21

Lobster Roll | **multi.** — 20

Love Lane Kitchen | **Mattituck** — 22

Ludlow Bistro | **Deer Park** — 23

Maureen's Kitchen | **Smithtown** — 25

Maxxels | **Mineola** — 24

Michaels'/Maidstone | **E Hampton** — 18

NEW Mill Creek | **Bayville** — 23

Mim's | **multi.** — 18

Modern Snack | **Aquebogue** — 18

Z Nagahama | **Long Bch** — 26

Nichol's | **E Hampton** — 18

On 3 | **Glen Head** — 24

Orchid | **Garden City** — 24

Page One | **Glen Cove** — 22

Panini Café | **Roslyn** — 23

Pepi's Cucina | **Southold** — 16

Pierre's | **Bridgehampton** — 21

Rachel's Cafe | **Syosset** — 23

red bar | **Southampton** — 23

Rowdy Hall | **E Hampton** — 19

Ruvo | **Port Jefferson** — 21

Sage Bistro | **Bellmore**	25
Salsa Salsa | **Smithtown**	23
Salvatore's | **Port Washington**	24
Sam's | **E Hampton**	19
Sen | **Sag Harbor**	24
Shagwong | **Montauk**	18
☑ Siam Lotus | **Bay Shore**	26
Silver's | **Southampton**	22
☑ Smokin' Al's BBQ | **Bay Shore**	24
Soigné | **Woodmere**	25
Southampton Publick | **Southampton**	16
Star Confectionery | **Riverhead**	21
Surfside Inn | **Montauk**	19
Taiko | **Rockville Ctr**	24
Tesoro | **Westbury**	22
☑ Thai Gourmet | **Port Jefferson Station**	26
Thomas's Ham | **Carle Pl**	23
Twin Harbors | **Bayville**	22
Umberto's | **New Hyde Pk**	21
Varney's | **Brookhaven**	24
Wall's Wharf | **Bayville**	17
☑ West End | **Carle Pl**	25
Wild Honey | **Oyster Bay**	24

MEET FOR A DRINK

Almond | **Bridgehampton**	21
☑ Annona | **Westhampton Bch**	23
Babylon Carriage | **Babylon**	19
Backyard | **Montauk**	-
Bayou | **N Bellmore**	23
Bayview Inn | **S Jamesport**	21
NEW Bennett's | **Locust Valley**	-
☑ Besito | **Huntington**	23
Birchwood | **Riverhead**	18
B.K. Sweeney's | **Garden City**	18
☑ Blackstone Steak | **Melville**	23
Blackwells | **Wading River**	21
Bobby Van's | **Bridgehampton**	22
NEW Brass Rail | **Locust Valley**	-
B.Smith's | **Sag Harbor**	16
Burton & Doyle | **Great Neck**	24
Café Buenos Aires | **Huntington**	23
Canterbury | **Oyster Bay**	18
Chalet Bar | **Roslyn**	18
Chi | **Westbury**	25
NEW Ciao Bella | **Valley Stream**	-

Cipollini | **Manhasset**	20
cittanuova | **E Hampton**	18
City Cellar | **Westbury**	20
Claudio's | **Greenport**	15
Clubhouse | **Huntington**	22
Coach Grill | **Oyster Bay**	22
Coast Grill | **Southampton**	18
☑ Coolfish | **Syosset**	24
Cyril's Fish House | **Amagansett**	18
☑ E. Hampton Point | **E Hampton**	20
E. B. Elliot's | **Freeport**	18
fatfish | **Bay Shore**	19
Fishery | **E Rockaway**	19
Gabrielle's | **Rockville Ctr**	22
George Martin's Coastal | **Long Bch**	20
George Martin Grill | **Rockville Ctr**	21
☑ Grand Lux | **Garden City**	19
NEW Grappa | **Sag Harbor**	20
NEW Grey Horse | **Bayport**	22
Hemingway's | **Wantagh**	18
Hideaway | **Fire Is**	20
☑ Honu | **Huntington**	22
Horace/Sylvia's | **Babylon**	17
Houston's | **Garden City**	21
Hudson/McCoy | **Freeport**	17
Hunan Taste | **Greenvale**	23
NEW Indian Wells Tav. | **Amagansett**	15
☑ In Season Amer. | **Islip**	26
JT's Place | **Hampton Bays**	18
La Cuvée | **Greenport**	20
☑ La Piccola Liguria | **Port Washington**	26
Legends | **New Suffolk**	21
NEW Limani | **Roslyn**	-
Lobster Inn | **Southampton**	18
Mac's Steak | **Huntington**	22
Madame Tong's | **Southampton**	12
Maguire's | **Fire Is**	18
Mangia Mangia | **Patchogue**	19
Matthew's | **Fire Is**	17
NEW Mirabelle Tavern | **Stony Brook**	-
☑ Morton's | **Great Neck**	24
Muse | **Water Mill**	21
Nello Summertimes | **Southampton**	18

SPECIAL FEATURES

Nick & Toni's | **E Hampton** _23_	Cafe Havana | **Smithtown** _17_
Nonnina | **W Islip** _24_	Charlotte's | **Cold Spring** _20_
Novitá | **Garden City** _23_	Cherrystones | **E Hampton** _19_
Oak Room | **Farmingdale** _23_	Ciao Bella | **Valley Stream** _-_
Oasis Waterfront | **Sag Harbor** _23_	Circa | **Mineola** _-_
Old Mill Inn | **Mattituck** _17_	Cove Star | **Glen Cove** _-_
NEW 101 Bar & Grill | **Bellmore** _20_	Crew Kitchen | **Huntington** _25_
On 3 | **Glen Head** _24_	Dish | **Water Mill** _-_
Painters' | **Brookhaven Hamlet** _18_	Fino Rosso | **Glen Cove** _18_
Z Pine Island | **Bayville** _17_	Fishbar | **Montauk** _16_
Post Office Cafe | **Babylon** _18_	Fortune Asian | **Westbury** _-_
Z Prime | **Huntington** _22_	Grappa | **Sag Harbor** _20_
Red Rest. | **Huntington** _24_	Grey Horse | **Bayport** _22_
Rein | **Garden City** _23_	Gulf Coast Kitchen | **Montauk** _-_
Z Rothmann's Steak | **E Norwich** _25_	Haiku | **Woodbury** _-_
Rowdy Hall | **E Hampton** _19_	Hotoke | **Smithtown** _26_
Saracen | **Wainscott** _17_	Indian Wells Tav. | **Amagansett** _15_
Southampton Publick |	Island BBQ | **Islip** _-_
Southampton _16_	Izumi | **Bethpage** _-_
NEW Speranza | **Woodbury** _-_	Jeff's Seafood | **E Northport** _-_
Sunset Beach | **Shelter Is Hts** _17_	Jin East | **Garden City** _25_
NEW Surf Lodge | **Montauk** _21_	Kiraku | **Glen Head** _-_
Surfside Inn | **Montauk** _19_	Kitchen A Tratt. | **St. James** _-_
Tide Runners | **Hampton Bays** _17_	La Nonna Bella | **Garden City** _-_
Tierra Mar | **Westhampton Bch** _22_	La P'tite Framboise |
Z Toku | **Manhasset** _24_	**Port Washington** _-_
Townline | **Sagaponack** _18_	La Tavola | **Sayville** _24_
Trata East | **Water Mill** _22_	Limani | **Roslyn** _-_
Tupelo Honey | **Sea Cliff** _22_	Lola's | **Long Bch** _-_
Union Station | **Smithtown** _19_	Luso | **Smithtown** _-_
NEW Vintage Port | _-_	Mare Luna | **Huntington** _24_
Port Washington	Mercato | **Massapequa Pk** _-_
Wall's Wharf | **Bayville** _17_	Mill Creek | **Bayville** _23_
Waterview Rest. | _16_	Mirabelle Tavern | **Stony Brook** _-_
Port Washington	Mitsui | **Bay Shore** _23_
Z Waterzooi | **Garden City** _23_	Mumon | **Garden City** _-_
	New Chilli/Curry | **Hicksville** _-_
	Nick & Charley Steak |
	Williston Pk _-_

NOTEWORTHY
NEWCOMERS

Alexandros | **Mount Sinai** _-_	Oevo | **Great Neck** _-_
A Mano | **Mattituck** _22_	101 Bar & Grill | **Bellmore** _20_
Bennett's | **Locust Valley** _-_	Oso | **Southampton** _-_
Black & Blue | **Huntington** _24_	Osteria Toscana | **Huntington** _-_
Bobby's Burger | **Lake Grove** _-_	Palio Ristorante | **Jericho** _-_
Brasserie Persil | **Oceanside** _25_	Pasta Vino | **Mineola** _23_
Brass Rail | **Locust Valley** _-_	Pier 441 | **Centerport** _19_
Brick & Rail | **Wantagh** _-_	Porters | **Bellport** _-_
Brooks & Porter | **Merrick** _22_	

| Rocco's | Huntington Station | 23 |

Rocco's | **Huntington Station** 23
Ruby's BBQ | **E Meadow** ⌐
Sally's Cocofé | **Huntington** ⌐
Simply Fondue | **Great Neck** ⌐
Speranza | **Woodbury** ⌐
Sri Thai | **Huntington** 21
Surf Lodge | **Montauk** 21
Surf 'N Turf | **Merrick** ⌐
Table 9 | **E Hills** ⌐
Tel Aviv | **Great Neck** ⌐
Tequila Jacks | **Port Jefferson** ⌐
Toast & Co. | **Huntington** 17
Vintage Port | **Port Washington** ⌐
Wave | **Port Jefferson** 20
Zim Zari | **Massapequa Pk** ⌐

OFFBEAT

Ariana | **Huntington** 21
Baby Moon | **Westhampton Bch** 19
Backyard | **Montauk** ⌐
Benihana | **multi.** 18
Big Daddy's | **Massapequa** 23
Bliss | **E Setauket** 22
Chalet Bar | **Roslyn** 18
Churrasc. Riodizio | **Roslyn Hts** 21
Cooke's In | **Huntington** 23
Cyril's Fish House | **Amagansett** 18
Hampton Chutney | 22
   Amagansett
House of Dosas | **Hicksville** 23
La Cuvée | **Greenport** 20
LL Dent | **Carle Pl** 21
Los Compadres | 22
   Huntington Station
Melting Pot | **Farmingdale** 18
Midori | **Oyster Bay** 23
New Paradise | **Sag Harbor** 21
Nichol's | **E Hampton** 18
Old Stove Pub | **Sagaponack** 18
Once Upon a Moose | **Sea Cliff** 19
Painters' | **Brookhaven Hamlet** 18
Planet Bliss | **Shelter Is** 20
Poco Loco | **Roslyn** 17
Roots | **Sea Cliff** 24
RS Jones | **Merrick** 21
NEW Sally's Cocofé | **Huntington** ⌐
Samurai | **Huntington** 20
Z Smokin' Al's BBQ | **Bay Shore** 24

Spicy's BBQ | **multi.** 19
Sunset Beach | **Shelter Is Hts** 17
Surfside Inn | **Montauk** 19
Swingbelly's | **Long Bch** 21
Toast | **Port Jefferson** 23
Tomo Hibachi | **Huntington** 19
Townline | **Sagaponack** 18
Tula Kitchen | **Bay Shore** ⌐
Tupelo Honey | **Sea Cliff** 22
Tweeds | **Riverhead** 20

OUTDOOR DINING

(G=garden; P=patio; S=sidewalk;
T=terrace)
Z Annona | T | **Westhampton Bch** 23
Antares Cafe | P | **Greenport** 24
Babette's | S | **E Hampton** 20
Backyard | T | **Montauk** ⌐
Bay Burger | P | **Sag Harbor** 19
BBQ Bill's | P | **Greenport** 18
Beacon | T | **Sag Harbor** 24
Bistro Citron | T | **Roslyn** 21
Blue | P | **Blue Pt** 19
Bostwick's/Harbor | T | 20
   E Hampton
B.Smith's | P | **Sag Harbor** 16
Chequit Inn | P | **Shelter Is Hts** 19
Cimino's | P | **Southold** 18
Cipollini | P | **Manhasset** 20
cittanuova | P, S | **E Hampton** 18
NEW Crew Kitchen | T | 25
   Huntington
Cyril's Fish House | P | 18
   Amagansett
Dee Angelo's | P | 17
   Westhampton Bch
Delano Mansion | T | **Woodbury** ⌐
Z Della Femina | T | **E Hampton** 24
Dockers Waterside | T | **E Quogue** 19
Duryea's Lobster | T | **Montauk** 21
Z E. Hampton Point | P, T | 20
   E Hampton
NEW Fishbar | P | **Montauk** 16
Fishery | T | **E Rockaway** 19
Fresno | P | **E Hampton** 22
Gosman's Dock | P | **Montauk** 17
Graffiti | P | **Woodbury** 20
Harvest | G, P | **Montauk** 25
Hellenic Snack | P | **E Marion** 20

SPECIAL FEATURES

Indian Cove | P | **Hampton Bays** 18

Inn Spot/Bay | T | **Hampton Bays** 19

🗹 Jedediah's | P | **Jamesport** 26

JLX Bistro | P | **Sag Harbor** 13

La Bella Vita | P | **E Meadow** 21

Livorno | P | **Port Washington** 19

Lobster Inn | P | **Southampton** 18

Lodge B&G | P | **E Hampton** 19

Lombardi's | T | **Port Jefferson** 22

Louie's Oyster | T | 16
Port Washington

Madame Tong's | P | **Southampton** 12

Matto | P | **E Hampton** 17

🗹 Mill Pond House | T | 25
Centerport

🗹 Mirko's | P | **Water Mill** 26

🆕 Mumon | T | **Garden City** -

Nello Summertimes | P, T | 18
Southampton

New Paradise | T | **Sag Harbor** 21

Nichol's | P | **E Hampton** 18

🗹 Nick & Toni's | G | **E Hampton** 23

Oakland's | T | **Hampton Bays** 17

Oak Room | T | **Farmingdale** 23

Old Mill Inn | T | **Mattituck** 17

Once Upon a Moose | S | 19
Sea Cliff

🆕 101 Bar & Grill | P | 20
Bellmore

On 3 | G, S | **Glen Head** 24

🗹 Palm Court | P | **E Meadow** 24

Pepi's Cucina | T | **Southold** 16

🗹 Pine Island | T | **Bayville** 17

Planet Bliss | T | **Shelter Is** 20

Poco Loco | P | **Roslyn** 17

Post Stop Cafe | T | 16
Westhampton Bch

Ram's Head | T | **Shelter Is** 21

Savanna's | G | **Southampton** 20

Scrimshaw | P | **Greenport** 22

Sea Grille | P | **Montauk** 18

Starr Boggs | P | **Westhampton Bch** 25

Stonewalls | P | **Riverhead** 24

Sunset Beach | T | **Shelter Is Hts** 17

🆕 Surf Lodge | P | **Montauk** 21

Surfside Inn | P | **Montauk** 19

Tide Runners | T | **Hampton Bays** 17

Tierra Mar | T | **Westhampton Bch** 22

Touch of Venice | P | **Mattituck** 19

Trio | P | **Holbrook** 21

Trumpets | P, T | **Eastport** 22

Tupelo Honey | P, S | **Sea Cliff** 22

🗹 Vine Street | T | **Shelter Is** 27

Waterview Rest. | P | 16
Port Washington

🗹 Waterzooi | P | **Garden City** 23

World Pie | G, P | **Bridgehampton** 20

PEOPLE-WATCHING

Abel Conklin's | **Huntington** 22

🗹 American Hotel | **Sag Harbor** 24

Babette's | **E Hampton** 20

Babylon Carriage | **Babylon** 19

Backyard | **Montauk** -

🗹 Barney's | **Locust Valley** 26

Bobby Van's | **Bridgehampton** 22

B.Smith's | **Sag Harbor** 16

Burton & Doyle | **Great Neck** 24

Cipollini | **Manhasset** 20

cittanuova | **E Hampton** 18

Clam Bar | **Amagansett** 19

🗹 Coolfish | **Syosset** 24

🗹 Della Femina | **E Hampton** 24

🗹 E. Hampton Point | **E Hampton** 20

Grill Room | **Hauppauge** 22

Hudson/McCoy | **Freeport** 17

🗹 Il Mulino NY | **Roslyn Estates** 26

Laundry | **E Hampton** 21

🆕 Limani | **Roslyn** -

Lobster Inn | **Southampton** 18

Lobster Roll | **Amagansett** 20

Madame Tong's | **Southampton** 12

🗹 Mill Pond House | **Centerport** 25

🗹 Mill River Inn | **Oyster Bay** 27

🆕 Mirabelle Tavern | -
Stony Brook

🗹 Morton's | **Great Neck** 24

Muse | **Water Mill** 21

Nello Summertimes | 18
Southampton

🗹 Nick & Toni's | **E Hampton** 23

🗹 Nisen Sushi | **Woodbury** 26

Oasis Waterfront | **Sag Harbor** 23

Palm | **E Hampton** 25

🗹 Panama Hatties | 26
Huntington Station

Ⓩ Peter Luger | **Great Neck**	27
red bar | **Southampton**	23
Rein | **Garden City**	23
Robert's | **Water Mill**	24
Sant Ambroeus | **Southampton**	24
Saracen | **Wainscott**	17
Savanna's | **Southampton**	20
Second House | **Montauk**	18
1770 House | **E Hampton**	25
NEW Speranza | **Woodbury**	-
Starr Boggs | **Westhampton Bch**	25
Ⓩ Stone Creek | **E Quogue**	26
Stresa | **Manhasset**	24
Sunset Beach | **Shelter Is Hts**	17
NEW Surf Lodge | **Montauk**	21
NEW Table 9 | **E Hills**	-
Tierra Mar | **Westhampton Bch**	22
Ⓩ Toku | **Manhasset**	24
Trata East | **Water Mill**	22
Tratt. Diane | **Roslyn**	25
Tutto Il Giorno | **Sag Harbor**	22
Ⓩ Waterzooi | **Garden City**	23
World Pie | **Bridgehampton**	20

POWER SCENES

Ⓩ American Hotel | **Sag Harbor**	24
Ⓩ Barney's | **Locust Valley**	26
Barolo | **Melville**	25
Ⓩ Blackstone Steak | **Melville**	23
Bobby Van's | **Bridgehampton**	22
Ⓩ Bryant & Cooper | **Roslyn**	26
Burton & Doyle | **Great Neck**	24
NEW Crew Kitchen | **Huntington**	25
Ⓩ Della Femina | **E Hampton**	24
Ⓩ E. Hampton Point | **E Hampton**	20
Franina | **Syosset**	23
Ⓩ Il Mulino NY | **Roslyn Estates**	26
La Coquille | **Manhasset**	24
NEW Limani | **Roslyn**	-
Mac's Steak | **Huntington**	22
Ⓩ Mill River Inn | **Oyster Bay**	27
Ⓩ Morton's | **Great Neck**	24
Ⓩ Nick & Toni's | **E Hampton**	23
NEW Palio Ristorante | **Jericho**	-
Palm | **E Hampton**	25
Ⓩ Palm Court | **E Meadow**	24

Ⓩ Panama Hatties | **Huntington Station**	26
Ⓩ Peter Luger | **Great Neck**	27
Ⓩ Polo | **Garden City**	25
Ⓩ Prime | **Huntington**	22
Ⓩ Ruth's Chris | **Garden City**	24
NEW Speranza | **Woodbury**	-
Stresa | **Manhasset**	24
NEW Table 9 | **E Hills**	-
Ⓩ Tellers | **Islip**	26
Ⓩ Toku | **Manhasset**	24

PRIVATE ROOMS

(Restaurants charge less at off
times; call for capacity)

Akari | **Merrick**	21
Ⓩ American Hotel | **Sag Harbor**	24
Babylon Carriage | **Babylon**	19
Barolo | **Melville**	25
Basil Leaf | **Locust Valley**	19
Bella Vita Grill | **St. James**	21
Birchwood | **Riverhead**	18
Blackwells | **Wading River**	21
Blue Moon | **Rockville Ctr**	21
Boccaccio | **Hicksville**	23
B.Smith's | **Sag Harbor**	16
Burton & Doyle | **Great Neck**	24
Cafe La Strada | **Hauppauge**	24
Ⓩ Camille's | **Carle Pl**	24
Carnival | **Port Jefferson Station**	20
Casa Rustica | **Smithtown**	25
Chi | **Westbury**	25
Cielo | **Hauppauge**	18
Coast Grill | **Southampton**	18
Collins & Main | **Sayville**	24
Cooperage Inn | **Baiting Hollow**	20
Ⓩ Country House | **Stony Brook**	22
Crabtree's | **Floral Pk**	20
Curry Club | **E Setauket**	22
Dodici | **Rockville Ctr**	23
Dynasty/Pt. Wash. | **Port Washington**	18
Ⓩ E. Hampton Point | **E Hampton**	20
E. B. Elliot's | **Freeport**	18
Emilio's | **Commack**	23
Fisherman's Catch | **Point Lookout**	19
Frank's Steaks | **Rockville Ctr**	20
Fratelli Iavarone | **New Hyde Pk**	21

SPECIAL FEATURES

Frederick's | **Melville**	22
Galleria Dominick | **Westbury**	25
George Martin | **Rockville Ctr**	22
Giulio Cesare | **Westbury**	24
Gosman's Dock | **Montauk**	17
Grasso's | **Cold Spring**	25
Heart of Portugal | **Mineola**	20
H2O Seafood | **Smithtown**	23
Il Capuccino | **Sag Harbor**	19
Il Classico | **Massapequa Pk**	24
Inn Spot/Bay | **Hampton Bays**	19
Irish Coffee | **E Islip**	22
Ivy Cottage | **Williston Pk**	24
Jaiya | **Hicksville**	21
Jimmy Hays | **Island Pk**	25
Jolly Fisherman | **Roslyn**	20
Kiss'o | **New Hyde Pk**	22
La Marmite | **Williston Pk**	25
☑ La Plage | **Wading River**	26
La Primavera | **Hicksville**	23
Lareira | **Mineola**	20
☑ Legal Sea Foods | **Garden City**	20
NEW Limani | **Roslyn**	-
Lobster Inn | **Southampton**	18
Lombardi's | **Port Jefferson**	22
Louie's Oyster | **Port Washington**	16
Lucé | **E Norwich**	24
Mamma Lombardi's | **Holbrook**	23
Mario | **Hauppauge**	25
☑ Mill Pond House | **Centerport**	25
Mim's | **Roslyn Hts**	18
Minado | **Carle Pl**	20
☑ Morton's | **Great Neck**	24
Mother Kelly's | **Cedarhurst**	21
Nagashima | **Jericho**	22
Nicholas James | **Merrick**	21
Nisen | **Commack**	25
Nonnina | **W Islip**	24
Oasis Waterfront | **Sag Harbor**	23
105 Harbor | **Cold Spring**	20
Orchid | **Garden City**	24
☑ Orient | **Bethpage**	26
Oscar's | **St. James**	22
Pace's Steak | **multi.**	23
☑ Panama Hatties | **Huntington Station**	26
Pasta Pasta | **Port Jefferson**	23
Peppercorns | **Hicksville**	18
Per Un Angelo | **Wantagh**	21
Piccola Bussola | **Mineola**	22
☑ Piccolo | **Huntington**	26
Piccolo's | **Mineola**	23
Pierre's | **Bridgehampton**	21
☑ Pine Island | **Bayville**	17
☑ Polo | **Garden City**	25
Ram's Head | **Shelter Is**	21
☑ Rialto | **Carle Pl**	26
☑ Riverbay | **Williston Pk**	22
Robert's | **Water Mill**	24
NEW Rocco's | **Huntington Station**	23
☑ Rothmann's Steak | **E Norwich**	25
☑ Ruth's Chris | **Garden City**	24
Sagamore Steak | **Syosset**	23
San Marco | **Hauppauge**	24
Saracen | **Wainscott**	17
Seafood Barge | **Southold**	21
Sea Grille | **Montauk**	18
1770 House | **E Hampton**	25
Seventh St. Cafe | **Garden City**	19
Shiki | **multi.**	23
☑ Solé | **Oceanside**	26
Southampton Publick | **Southampton**	16
Southside Fish | **Lindenhurst**	18
☑ Stone Creek | **E Quogue**	26
Sundried Tomato | **Nesconset**	22
Sunset Beach | **Shelter Is Hts**	17
NEW Table 9 | **E Hills**	-
☑ Tellers | **Islip**	26
Tesoro | **Westbury**	22
Thom Thom | **Wantagh**	21
Thyme | **Roslyn**	20
Tierra Mar | **Westhampton Bch**	22
Touch of Venice | **Mattituck**	19
Tratt. Diane | **Roslyn**	25
Tre Bambini | **Lynbrook**	21
Trio | **Holbrook**	21
Umberto's | **New Hyde Pk**	21
Vespa Cibobuono | **Great Neck**	22
Villa D'Este | **Floral Pk**	20
☑ Vintage Prime | **St. James**	26
World Pie | **Bridgehampton**	20

PRIX FIXE MENUS

(Call for prices and times)

Abel Conklin's | **Huntington**	22
Albert's Mandarin | **Huntington**	21
Almond | **Bridgehampton**	21
Angelina's | **Syosset**	22
☑ Annona | **Westhampton Bch**	23
Arturo's | **Floral Pk**	23
Azerbaijan Grill | **Westbury**	21
Babylon Carriage | **Babylon**	19
☑ Barney's | **Locust Valley**	26
Bayou | **N Bellmore**	23
Benny's | **Westbury**	25
Bistro Citron | **Roslyn**	21
Bistro 44 | **Northport**	21
Bistro M | **Glen Head**	25
Bobby Van's | **Bridgehampton**	22
Bob's Place | **Floral Pk**	21
NEW Brick & Rail | **Wantagh**	-
Cafe Max | **E Hampton**	21
Cafe Rustica | **Great Neck**	21
Caracalla | **Syosset**	23
Casa Rustica | **Smithtown**	25
☑ Chachama Grill | **E Patchogue**	28
Chez Noëlle | **Port Washington**	24
Collins & Main | **Sayville**	24
☑ Coolfish | **Syosset**	24
☑ Country House | **Stony Brook**	22
Delano Mansion | **Woodbury**	-
☑ Della Femina | **E Hampton**	24
Desmond's | **Wading River**	22
NEW Dish | **Water Mill**	-
Duke Falcon's | **Long Bch**	23
Fisherman's Catch | **Point Lookout**	19
Fortune Wheel | **Levittown**	23
Gabrielle's | **Rockville Ctr**	22
George Martin | **Rockville Ctr**	22
Higashi | **Syosset**	20
☑ Honu | **Huntington**	22
House of Dosas | **Hicksville**	23
H2O Seafood | **Smithtown**	23
☑ Il Mulino NY | **Roslyn Estates**	26
Indian Cove | **Hampton Bays**	18
☑ Jamesport Manor | **Jamesport**	24
☑ Jedediah's | **Jamesport**	26
Jolly Fisherman | **Roslyn**	20
Jonathan's Rist. | **Huntington**	23
La Coquille | **Manhasset**	24
La Primavera | **Hicksville**	23
NEW La Tavola | **Sayville**	24
Laundry | **E Hampton**	21
Le Chef | **Southampton**	21
NEW Limani | **Roslyn**	-
Lodge B&G | **E Hampton**	19
NEW Lola's | **Long Bch**	-
☑ Maroni Cuisine | **Northport**	28
Milleridge Inn | **Jericho**	15
☑ Mill Pond House | **Centerport**	25
☑ Mill River Inn | **Oyster Bay**	27
Nicholas James | **Merrick**	21
☑ Nick & Toni's | **E Hampton**	23
Page One | **Glen Cove**	22
☑ Palm Court | **E Meadow**	24
☑ Panama Hatties | **Huntington Station**	26
Pearl East | **Manhasset**	23
Pierre's | **Bridgehampton**	21
☑ Plaza Cafe | **Southampton**	26
red bar | **Southampton**	23
Red Rest. | **Huntington**	24
Romantico/Capri | **Port Washington**	19
Roots | **Sea Cliff**	24
RS Jones | **Merrick**	21
Saracen | **Wainscott**	17
Sea Levels | **Brightwaters**	24
1770 House | **E Hampton**	25
Snaps | **Wantagh**	22
Soigné | **Woodmere**	25
Southampton Publick | **Southampton**	16
☑ Stone Creek | **E Quogue**	26
Stonewalls | **Riverhead**	24
Stresa | **Manhasset**	24
NEW Table 9 | **E Hills**	-
Tava | **Port Washington**	19
☑ Tellers | **Islip**	26
34 New St. | **Huntington**	20
Thyme | **Roslyn**	20
Tierra Mar | **Westhampton Bch**	22
Tratt. Diane | **Roslyn**	25
Trumpets | **Eastport**	22
Tupelo Honey | **Sea Cliff**	22
Union Station | **Smithtown**	19

Villa D'Este | **Floral Pk** 20

Voila! | **St. James** 23

QUIET
CONVERSATION

Allison's | **Sea Cliff** 22

Antares Cafe | **Greenport** 24

Ariana | **Huntington** 21

Basil Leaf | **Locust Valley** 19

Bayview Inn | **S Jamesport** 21

NEW Bennett's | **Locust Valley** -

Bevanda | **Great Neck** 21

Breakwater Cafe | **Montauk** -

Brook House | **Stony Brook** -

Cafe Max | **E Hampton** 21

Cafe Symposio | **Bellmore** 18

Z Camille's | **Carle Pl** 24

Caracalla | **Syosset** 23

Chez Noëlle | **Port Washington** 24

Collins & Main | **Sayville** 24

NEW Cove Star | **Glen Cove** -

Delano Mansion | **Woodbury** -

E. B. Elliot's | **Freeport** 18

18 Bay | **Bayville** 24

Ernesto's East | **Glen Head** 20

Estia's Kitchen | **Sag Harbor** 21

Franina | **Syosset** 23

Garden Grill | **Smithtown** 19

Greenport Tea | **Greenport** 20

Hampton Chutney | **Amagansett** 22

Inn Spot/Bay | **Hampton Bays** 19

Z Jedediah's | **Jamesport** 26

Jonathan's Rist. | **Huntington** 23

Kurabarn | **Huntington** 22

La Coquille | **Manhasset** 24

La Pace/Chef Michael | **Glen Cove** 24

Z La Plage | **Wading River** 26

La Spada | **Huntington Station** 23

Mac's Steak | **Huntington** 22

Michaels'/Maidstone | **E Hampton** 18

Z Mill Pond House | **Centerport** 25

Z Mirko's | **Water Mill** 26

Z Mosaic | **St. James** 26

Osteria da Nino | **Huntington** 23

Page One | **Glen Cove** 22

Patio/54 Main | 19
Westhampton Bch

Ram's Head | **Shelter Is** 21

Robert's | **Water Mill** 24

Robinson's | **Stony Brook** 24

NEW Rocco's | **Huntington Station** 23

NEW Sally's Cocofé | **Huntington** -

Sant Ambroeus | **Southampton** 24

Sarin Thai | **Greenvale** 22

1770 House | **E Hampton** 25

Stonewalls | **Riverhead** 24

Stresa | **Manhasset** 24

Thai Green Leaf | **E Northport** 22

Tratt. Diane | **Roslyn** 25

Trumpets | **Eastport** 22

Vespa Cibouono | **Great Neck** 22

RAW BARS

Aqua East | **Montauk** 20

Z Blackstone Steak | **Melville** 23

Blue | **Blue Pt** 19

Blue Room | **E Northport** 24

Buoy One | **Riverhead** 22

Caffe Laguna | **Long Bch** 19

Canterbury | **Oyster Bay** 18

Claudio's | **Greenport** 15

Z E. Hampton Point | **E Hampton** 20

Hudson/McCoy | **Freeport** 17

La Marmite | **Williston Pk** 25

Z Legal Sea Foods | **multi.** 20

Louie's Oyster | **Port Washington** 16

Z Mill Pond House | **Centerport** 25

Noma | **Huntington** 20

Oar Steak | **Patchogue** 20

105 Harbor | **Cold Spring** 20

NEW 101 Bar & Grill | **Bellmore** 20

Paddy McGees | **Island Pk** 16

NEW Porters | **Bellport** -

Z Riverbay | **Williston Pk** 22

Riverview | **Oakdale** 19

Sage Bistro | **Bellmore** 25

Second House | **Montauk** 18

Snapper Inn | **Oakdale** 17

Southside Fish | **Lindenhurst** 18

Tai-Show | **Massapequa** 22

Z Tellers | **Islip** 26

Vincent's | **Carle Pl** -

Waterview Rest. | 16
Port Washington

ROMANTIC PLACES

☑ American Hotel | **Sag Harbor**	24
Antares Cafe | **Greenport**	24
☑ Barney's | **Locust Valley**	26
Benny's | **Westbury**	25
Bistro du Village | **Port Washington**	24
Bistro M | **Glen Head**	25
Blackwells | **Wading River**	21
Bliss | **E Setauket**	22
Blue Room | **E Northport**	24
Cafe Joelle | **Sayville**	23
Caffe Laguna | **Long Bch**	19
Caracalla | **Syosset**	23
Casa Rustica | **Smithtown**	25
Chadwicks | **Rockville Ctr**	-
Chez Noëlle | **Port Washington**	24
Cooperage Inn | **Baiting Hollow**	20
☑ Country House | **Stony Brook**	22
Delano Mansion | **Woodbury**	-
E. B. Elliot's | **Freeport**	18
Elaine's | **Great Neck**	23
Grasso's | **Cold Spring**	25
☑ Jamesport Manor | **Jamesport**	24
☑ Jedediah's | **Jamesport**	26
Kurabarn | **Huntington**	22
La Capannina | **Northport**	23
La Coquille | **Manhasset**	24
☑ Lake House | **Bay Shore**	27
La Pace/Chef Michael | **Glen Cove**	24
☑ La Plage | **Wading River**	26
La Spada | **Huntington Station**	23
☑ Le Soir | **Bayport**	27
Lombardi's | **Port Jefferson**	22
Lucé | **E Norwich**	24
Mac's Steak | **Huntington**	22
☑ Mill Pond House | **Centerport**	25
☑ Mill River Inn | **Oyster Bay**	27
☑ Mirko's | **Water Mill**	26
Nico at the Mansion | **Islip**	21
☑ North Fork Table | **Southold**	28
Oak Room | **Farmingdale**	23
Olde Speonk Inn | **Speonk**	17
105 Harbor | **Cold Spring**	20
NEW 101 Bar & Grill | **Bellmore**	20
NEW Osteria Toscana | **Huntington**	-

☑ Palm Court | **E Meadow**	24
Per Un Angelo | **Wantagh**	21
☑ Piccolo | **Huntington**	26
☑ Pine Island | **Bayville**	17
☑ Plaza Cafe | **Southampton**	26
☑ Polo | **Garden City**	25
Ram's Head | **Shelter Is**	21
Rist. Forestieri | **Hauppauge**	21
Rist. Gemelli | **Babylon**	22
Robert's | **Water Mill**	24
Sant Ambroeus | **Southampton**	24
Sempre Vivolo | **Hauppauge**	25
1770 House | **E Hampton**	25
Soigné | **Woodmere**	25
☑ Stone Creek | **E Quogue**	26
Stresa | **Manhasset**	24
Tierra Mar | **Westhampton Bch**	22
Tratt. Diane | **Roslyn**	25
Trio | **Holbrook**	21
Trumpets | **Eastport**	22
21 Main | **W Sayville**	24
Vespa Cibuobuono | **Great Neck**	22

SENIOR APPEAL

Abel Conklin's | **Huntington**	22
Barrister's | **Southampton**	16
Basil Leaf | **Locust Valley**	19
Cafe Max | **E Hampton**	21
Cafe Rustica | **Great Neck**	21
☑ Camille's | **Carle Pl**	24
Greenport Tea | **Greenport**	20
Jolly Fisherman | **Roslyn**	20
JT's Place | **Hampton Bays**	18
La Primavera | **Hicksville**	23
Le Chef | **Southampton**	21
Lombardi's | **Port Jefferson**	22
Med. Snack | **Huntington**	23
Michaels'/Maidstone | **E Hampton**	18
Milleridge Inn | **Jericho**	15
Modern Snack | **Aquebogue**	18
Nicholas James | **Merrick**	21
Page One | **Glen Cove**	22
Pastrami King | **Merrick**	19
Schooner | **Freeport**	16
Sea Grille | **Montauk**	18
Sweet Mama's | **Northport**	18

| Villa D'Este | **Floral Pk** | 20 |
| Zorba/Greek | **Hicksville** | 19 |

SINGLES SCENES

Almoncello	**Wainscott**	20
Z Annona	**Westhampton Bch**	23
Argyle Grill	**Babylon**	21
Babylon Carriage	**Babylon**	19
Backyard	**Montauk**	-
Bamboo	**E Hampton**	20
B.K. Sweeney's	**Garden City**	18
Z Bryant & Cooper	**Roslyn**	26
Burton & Doyle	**Great Neck**	24
Cafe Testarossa	**Syosset**	20
Cipollini	**Manhasset**	20
Cyril's Fish House	**Amagansett**	18
Z E. Hampton Point	**E Hampton**	20
Four Food Studio	**Melville**	20
George Martin Grill	**Rockville Ctr**	21
Hudson/McCoy	**Freeport**	17
Z Legal Sea Foods	**Huntington Station**	20
Legends	**New Suffolk**	21
Library Cafe	**Farmingdale**	17
NEW Limani	**Roslyn**	-
Madame Tong's	**Southampton**	12
Melting Pot	**Farmingdale**	18
Muse	**Water Mill**	21
Z Nisen Sushi	**Woodbury**	26
Oakland's	**Hampton Bays**	17
Oasis Waterfront	**Sag Harbor**	23
Post Office Cafe	**Babylon**	18
Rein	**Garden City**	23
Z Rothmann's Steak	**E Norwich**	25
Saracen	**Wainscott**	17
Southampton Publick	**Southampton**	16
NEW Speranza	**Woodbury**	-
Sunset Beach	**Shelter Is Hts**	17
NEW Surf Lodge	**Montauk**	21
Z Tellers	**Islip**	26
Tide Runners	**Hampton Bays**	17
Z Toku	**Manhasset**	24
Trata East	**Water Mill**	22
Wall's Wharf	**Bayville**	17
Z Waterzooi	**Garden City**	23
Wild Ginger	**Great Neck**	22

SLEEPERS

(Good food, but little known)

Blue Ocean	**Bethpage**	24
Blue Sky Bistro	**Malverne**	23
Bozena Polish	**Lindenhurst**	22
Caruso's	**Rocky Pt**	22
Chi	**Westbury**	25
Desmond's	**Wading River**	22
Homura Sushi	**Williston Pk**	24
NEW Hotoke	**Smithtown**	26
NEW Jin East	**Garden City**	25
La Spada	**Huntington Station**	23
NEW La Tavola	**Sayville**	24
La Terrazza	**Cedarhurst**	22
Los Compadres	**Huntington Station**	22
Lucé	**E Norwich**	24
NEW Mare Luna	**Huntington**	24
Matsuya	**Great Neck**	22
Michael Anthony's	**Wading River**	23
NEW Mill Creek	**Bayville**	23
Minami	**Massapequa**	24
NEW Mitsui	**Bay Shore**	23
MoCa Asian Bistro	**Hewlett**	23
Osaka	**Huntington**	23
Panini Café	**Roslyn**	23
NEW Pasta Vino	**Mineola**	23
Ravagh	**Roslyn Hts**	22
Rein	**Garden City**	23
Rist. Italiano Toscanini	**Port Washington**	22
Riviera Grill	**Glen Cove**	24
Roots	**Sea Cliff**	24
Sea Levels	**Brightwaters**	24
Shang Hai Pavilion	**multi.**	23
Shogi	**Westbury**	23
Takara	**Islandia**	26
Tokyo	**E Northport**	23
Tsubo	**Syosset**	22
Twin Harbors	**Bayville**	22
Varney's	**Brookhaven**	24
Viva La Vida	**Oakdale**	23

TASTING MENUS

Z Barney's	**Locust Valley**	26
Blue Sky Bistro	**Malverne**	23
Chadwicks	**Rockville Ctr**	-
Chi	**Westbury**	25

Z Coolfish | **Syosset** — 24
Crossroads Cafe | **E Northport** — 20
Daruma of Tokyo | **Great Neck** — 21
Z Della Femina | **E Hampton** — 24
Four Food Studio | **Melville** — 20
Z Jedediah's | **Jamesport** — 26
Z Maroni Cuisine | **Northport** — 28
Z Mill River Inn | **Oyster Bay** — 27
Z North Fork Table | **Southold** — 28
Oscar's | **St. James** — 22
Z Panama Hatties | **Huntington Station** — 26
Z Plaza Cafe | **Southampton** — 26
Red Rest. | **Huntington** — 24
1770 House | **E Hampton** — 25
Snaps | **Wantagh** — 22
Soigné | **Woodmere** — 25
Tupelo Honey | **Sea Cliff** — 22
Voila! | **St. James** — 23

TEEN APPEAL

Baby Moon | **Westhampton Bch** — 19
Bigelow's | **Rockville Ctr** — 24
Blackbirds' Grille | **Sayville** — 18
Green Cactus | **multi.** — 21
La Pizzetta | **E Norwich** — 20
Melting Pot | **Farmingdale** — 18
Salsa Salsa | **Port Jefferson** — 23
Z Smokin' Al's BBQ | **Bay Shore** — 24
Southside Fish | **Lindenhurst** — 18
Turtle Crossing | **E Hampton** — 21

TRENDY

Z Aji 53 | **Bay Shore** — 27
Babette's | **E Hampton** — 20
Babylon Carriage | **Babylon** — 19
Backyard | **Montauk** — -
Bamboo | **E Hampton** — 20
Z Barney's | **Locust Valley** — 26
Z Besito | **Huntington** — 23
Bistro M | **Glen Head** — 25
Bobby Van's | **Bridgehampton** — 22
Z Bryant & Cooper | **Roslyn** — 26
B.Smith's | **Sag Harbor** — 16
Burton & Doyle | **Great Neck** — 24
Chi | **Westbury** — 25
Cipollini | **Manhasset** — 20
cittanuova | **E Hampton** — 18

Z Coolfish | **Syosset** — 24
Z Della Femina | **E Hampton** — 24
East by Northeast | **Montauk** — 21
Frisky Oyster | **Greenport** — 24
Z Honu | **Huntington** — 22
Hudson/McCoy | **Freeport** — 17
Z Il Mulino NY | **Roslyn Estates** — 26
Laundry | **E Hampton** — 21
NEW Limani | **Roslyn** — -
Ludlow Bistro | **Deer Park** — 23
Madame Tong's | **Southampton** — 12
Z Mill River Inn | **Oyster Bay** — 27
Minado | **Carle Pl** — 20
Z Morton's | **Great Neck** — 24
Muse | **Water Mill** — 21
Nello Summertimes | **Southampton** — 18
Z Nick & Toni's | **E Hampton** — 23
Z Nisen Sushi | **Woodbury** — 26
Novitá | **Garden City** — 23
On 3 | **Glen Head** — 24
Z Panama Hatties | **Huntington Station** — 26
Z Peter Luger | **Great Neck** — 27
Z Piccolo | **Huntington** — 26
red bar | **Southampton** — 23
Rein | **Garden City** — 23
Savanna's | **Southampton** — 20
Sen | **Sag Harbor** — 24
NEW Speranza | **Woodbury** — -
Starr Boggs | **Westhampton Bch** — 25
Z Stone Creek | **E Quogue** — 26
Stresa | **Manhasset** — 24
Sunset Beach | **Shelter Is Hts** — 17
NEW Surf Lodge | **Montauk** — 21
Z Toku | **Manhasset** — 24
Trata East | **Water Mill** — 22
Tratt. Diane | **Roslyn** — 25
Tupelo Honey | **Sea Cliff** — 22
Z Waterzooi | **Garden City** — 23
Wild Ginger | **Great Neck** — 22

VALET PARKING

Akbar | **Garden City** — 21
Z American Hotel | **Sag Harbor** — 24
Z Annona | **Westhampton Bch** — 23
Arturo's | **Floral Pk** — 23
Bistro M | **Glen Head** — 25

SPECIAL FEATURES

☑ Blackstone Steak	**Melville**	23	
Bob's Place	**Floral Pk**	21	
Branzino	**Lynbrook**	25	
NEW Brooks & Porter	**Merrick**	22	
☑ Bryant & Cooper	**Roslyn**	26	
Burton & Doyle	**Great Neck**	24	
Café Formaggio	**Carle Pl**	20	
Cafe Testarossa	**Syosset**	20	
Casa Rustica	**Smithtown**	25	
Chi	**Westbury**	25	
Cielo Rist.	**Rockville Ctr**	19	
NEW Circa	**Mineola**	-	
Cirella's	**Melville**	21	
City Café	**Garden City**	17	
Clubhouse	**Huntington**	22	
Crabtree's	**Floral Pk**	20	
NEW Crew Kitchen	**Huntington**	25	
Delano Mansion	**Woodbury**	-	
Desmond's	**Wading River**	22	
fatfish	**Bay Shore**	19	
Fisherman's Catch	**Point Lookout**	19	
Four Food Studio	**Melville**	20	
Franina	**Syosset**	23	
Frank's Steaks	**Rockville Ctr**	20	
Frederick's	**Melville**	22	
Hudson/McCoy	**Freeport**	17	
☑ Il Mulino NY	**Roslyn Estates**	26	
Inn Spot/Bay	**Hampton Bays**	19	
Jimmy Hays	**Island Pk**	25	
Jolly Fisherman	**Roslyn**	20	
La Bussola	**Glen Cove**	23	
La Famiglia	**multi.**	20	
La Marmite	**Williston Pk**	25	
La Pace/Chef Michael	**Glen Cove**	24	
La Parma	**multi.**	23	
La Primavera	**Hicksville**	23	
☑ Legal Sea Foods	**Garden City**	20	
NEW Limani	**Roslyn**	-	
Lombardi's	**Port Jefferson**	22	
Luigi Q	**Hicksville**	22	
Mac's Steak	**Huntington**	22	
Madame Tong's	**Southampton**	12	
Mario	**Hauppauge**	25	
☑ Matteo's	**multi.**	23	
☑ Mill Pond House	**Centerport**	25	
Mim's	**multi.**	18	
☑ Morton's	**Great Neck**	24	

Nautilus Cafe	**Freeport**	24	
Nello Summertimes	**Southampton**	18	
New Hyde Park	**New Hyde Pk**	20	
Nico at the Mansion	**Islip**	21	
Noma	**Huntington**	20	
Nonnina	**W Islip**	24	
Oasis Waterfront	**Sag Harbor**	23	
Pace's Steak	**Hauppauge**	23	
Paddy McGees	**Island Pk**	16	
NEW Palio Ristorante	**Jericho**	-	
Palm	**E Hampton**	25	
☑ Palm Court	**E Meadow**	24	
Pearl East	**Manhasset**	23	
Per Un Angelo	**Wantagh**	21	
☑ Peter Luger	**Great Neck**	27	
Piccola Bussola	**multi.**	22	
NEW Pier 441	**Centerport**	19	
☑ Pine Island	**Bayville**	17	
☑ Polo	**Garden City**	25	
Pomodorino	**Syosset**	17	
Porto Bello	**Greenport**	18	
☑ Prime	**Huntington**	22	
Q East	**Quogue**	23	
Rein	**Garden City**	23	
Rist. Gemelli	**Babylon**	22	
☑ Riverbay	**Williston Pk**	22	
Riverview	**Oakdale**	19	
Robert's	**Water Mill**	24	
NEW Rocco's	**Huntington Station**	23	
Romantico/Capri	**Port Washington**	19	
Runyon's	**E Meadow**	17	
☑ Ruth's Chris	**Garden City**	24	
Sagamore Steak	**Syosset**	23	
San Marco	**Hauppauge**	24	
Saracen	**Wainscott**	17	
Savanna's	**Southampton**	20	
Schooner	**Freeport**	16	
Sea Grille	**Montauk**	18	
☑ Solé	**Oceanside**	26	
NEW Speranza	**Woodbury**	-	
Steve's Piccola	**Westbury**	25	
NEW Surf Lodge	**Montauk**	21	
Surfside Inn	**Montauk**	19	
NEW Table 9	**E Hills**	-	
☑ Tellers	**Islip**	26	

Menus, photos, voting and more – free at ZAGAT.com

Thyme | **Roslyn**	20	
Tierra Mar | **Westhampton Bch**	22	
Tratt. Diane | **Roslyn**	25	
Tratt. Di Meo | **Roslyn Hts**	21	
Tre Bambini | **Lynbrook**	21	
Tutto Pazzo | **Huntington**	21	
21 Main | **W Sayville**	24	
Twin Harbors | **Bayville**	22	
Uncle Bacala's | **Garden City Pk**	18	
Vespa Cibobuono | **Great Neck**	22	
Viva Loco | **Bellmore**	16	
Wall's Wharf | **Bayville**	17	

VIEWS

BBQ Bill's | **Greenport**	18
Beacon | **Sag Harbor**	24
Blackwells | **Wading River**	21
Bostwick's/Harbor | **E Hampton**	20
Breakwater Cafe | **Montauk**	-
B.Smith's | **Sag Harbor**	16
Catfish Max | **Seaford**	23
Chequit Inn | **Shelter Is Hts**	19
Coast Grill | **Southampton**	18
☑ Dave's Grill | **Montauk**	26
Dockers Waterside | **E Quogue**	19
Duryea's Lobster | **Montauk**	21
East by Northeast | **Montauk**	21
☑ E. Hampton Point | **E Hampton**	20
E. B. Elliot's | **Freeport**	18
Edgewater | **Hampton Bays**	-
fatfish | **Bay Shore**	19
Fisherman's Catch | **Point Lookout**	19
Gosman's Dock | **Montauk**	17
NEW Gulf Coast Kitchen | **Montauk**	-
Harbor Bistro | **E Hampton**	22
Harvest | **Montauk**	25
Hideaway | **Fire Is**	20
Hudson/McCoy | **Freeport**	17
Indian Cove | **Hampton Bays**	18
Inlet Seafood | **Montauk**	21
Inn Spot/Bay | **Hampton Bays**	19
Island Mermaid | **Fire Is**	20
Jolly Fisherman | **Roslyn**	20
☑ Lake House | **Bay Shore**	27
☑ La Plage | **Wading River**	26
Lobster Inn | **Southampton**	18
Lombardi's | **Port Jefferson**	22

Louie's Oyster | **Port Washington**	16
Maguire's | **Fire Is**	18
Matthew's | **Fire Is**	17
☑ Mill Pond House | **Centerport**	25
Nautilus Cafe | **Freeport**	24
Oakland's | **Hampton Bays**	17
Oasis Waterfront | **Sag Harbor**	23
Old Mill Inn | **Mattituck**	17
105 Harbor | **Cold Spring**	20
NEW 101 Bar & Grill | **Bellmore**	20
Pepi's Cucina | **Southold**	16
☑ Pine Island | **Bayville**	17
☑ Prime | **Huntington**	22
Ram's Head | **Shelter Is**	21
Riverview | **Oakdale**	19
Saracen | **Wainscott**	17
Schooner | **Freeport**	16
Scrimshaw | **Greenport**	22
Seafood Barge | **Southold**	21
Sea Grille | **Montauk**	18
Second House | **Montauk**	18
Snapper Inn | **Oakdale**	17
Soundview | **Glen Cove**	19
Stonewalls | **Riverhead**	24
Sunset Beach | **Shelter Is Hts**	17
NEW Surf Lodge | **Montauk**	21
Surfside Inn | **Montauk**	19
Thyme | **Roslyn**	20
Tide Runners | **Hampton Bays**	17
Tierra Mar | **Westhampton Bch**	22
Top of the Bay | **Fire Is**	-
Touch of Venice | **Mattituck**	19
Trio | **Holbrook**	21
Trumpets | **Eastport**	22
Wall's Wharf | **Bayville**	17
Waterview Rest. | **Port Washington**	16
West Lake Clam | **Montauk**	24

WATERSIDE

Beacon | **Sag Harbor**	24
Bistro Citron | **Roslyn**	21
Bostwick's/Harbor | **E Hampton**	20
B.Smith's | **Sag Harbor**	16
Catfish Max | **Seaford**	23
Claudio's | **Greenport**	15
Coast Grill | **Southampton**	18
Dockers Waterside | **E Quogue**	19

Duryea's Lobster | **Montauk**	21
East by Northeast | **Montauk**	21
Z E. Hampton Point | **E Hampton**	20
E. B. Elliot's | **Freeport**	18
fatfish | **Bay Shore**	19
NEW Fishbar | **Montauk**	16
Fisherman's Catch | **Point Lookout**	19
Fishery | **E Rockaway**	19
Gosman's Dock | **Montauk**	17
Harbor Bistro | **E Hampton**	22
Harbor Crab | **Patchogue**	18
Harvest | **Montauk**	25
Hideaway | **Fire Is**	20
Indian Cove | **Hampton Bays**	18
Inlet Seafood | **Montauk**	21
Inn Spot/Bay | **Hampton Bays**	19
Island Mermaid | **Fire Is**	20
Z Lake House | **Bay Shore**	27
Lobster Inn | **Southampton**	18
Lombardi's | **Port Jefferson**	22
Louie's Oyster | **Port Washington**	16
Maguire's | **Fire Is**	18
Matthew's | **Fire Is**	17
Z Mill Pond House | **Centerport**	25
Nautilus Cafe | **Freeport**	24
Oakland's | **Hampton Bays**	17
Oar Steak | **Patchogue**	20
Old Mill Inn | **Mattituck**	17
NEW 101 Bar & Grill | **Bellmore**	20
Paddy McGees | **Island Pk**	16
Pepi's Cucina | **Southold**	16
Pier 95 | **Freeport**	23
Z Pine Island | **Bayville**	17
Porto Bello | **Greenport**	18
Z Prime | **Huntington**	22
Rachel's Waterside | **Freeport**	19
Riverview | **Oakdale**	19
Schooner | **Freeport**	16
Scrimshaw | **Greenport**	22
Seafood Barge | **Southold**	21
Snapper Inn | **Oakdale**	17
NEW Surf Lodge | **Montauk**	21
Tide Runners | **Hampton Bays**	17
Tierra Mar | **Westhampton Bch**	22
Top of the Bay | **Fire Is**	-
Touch of Venice | **Mattituck**	19
Trumpets | **Eastport**	22

Wall's Wharf | **Bayville**	17
Waterview Rest. | **Port Washington**	16

WINNING WINE LISTS

Allison's | **Sea Cliff**	22
Z American Hotel | **Sag Harbor**	24
Arturo's | **Floral Pk**	23
Z Barney's | **Locust Valley**	26
Barolo | **Melville**	25
Z Blackstone Steak | **Melville**	23
Blackwells | **Wading River**	21
Branzino | **Lynbrook**	25
Z Bryant & Cooper | **Roslyn**	26
Burton & Doyle | **Great Neck**	24
Butterfields | **Hauppauge**	20
Cafe La Strada | **Hauppauge**	24
Cafe Max | **E Hampton**	21
Caracalla | **Syosset**	23
Chez Noëlle | **Port Washington**	24
City Cellar | **Westbury**	20
Z Coolfish | **Syosset**	24
NEW Crew Kitchen | **Huntington**	25
Z Della Femina | **E Hampton**	24
Dodici | **Rockville Ctr**	23
East by Northeast | **Montauk**	21
Z E. Hampton Point | **E Hampton**	20
Epiphany | **Glen Cove**	22
Fiddleheads | **Oyster Bay**	23
Franina | **Syosset**	23
Fresno | **E Hampton**	22
Galleria Dominick | **Westbury**	25
Harvest | **Montauk**	25
Z Il Mulino NY | **Roslyn Estates**	26
Jamesport Country | **Jamesport**	23
Z Jedediah's | **Jamesport**	26
Jonathan's Rist. | **Huntington**	23
La Capannina | **Northport**	23
La Coquille | **Manhasset**	24
La Cuvée | **Greenport**	20
La Marmite | **Williston Pk**	25
La Pace/Chef Michael | **Glen Cove**	24
Z La Piccola Liguria | **Port Washington**	26
Z La Plage | **Wading River**	26
Z Legal Sea Foods | **Huntington Station**	20

Z Le Soir | **Bayport**	27
NEW Limani | **Roslyn**	-
Lucé | **E Norwich**	24
Mac's Steak | **Huntington**	22
Melting Pot | **Farmingdale**	18
Z Mill Pond House | **Centerport**	25
Z Mill River Inn | **Oyster Bay**	27
Z Mirko's | **Water Mill**	26
Z Morton's | **Great Neck**	24
Z Nick & Toni's | **E Hampton**	23
Novitá | **Garden City**	23
105 Harbor | **Cold Spring**	20
On 3 | **Glen Head**	24
Pace's Steak | **multi.**	23
Z Palm Court | **E Meadow**	24
Z Panama Hatties | **Huntington Station**	26
Pentimento | **Stony Brook**	21
Z Piccolo | **Huntington**	26
Z Plaza Cafe | **Southampton**	26
Z Polo | **Garden City**	25
Z Prime | **Huntington**	22
Ram's Head | **Shelter Is**	21
red bar | **Southampton**	23
Red Rest. | **Huntington**	24
Z Riverbay | **Williston Pk**	22
Robert's | **Water Mill**	24
NEW Rocco's | **Huntington Station**	23
Z Rothmann's Steak | **E Norwich**	25
Z Ruth's Chris | **Garden City**	24
Sagamore Steak | **Syosset**	23
San Marco | **Hauppauge**	24
Seafood Barge | **Southold**	21
Sempre Vivolo | **Hauppauge**	25
1770 House | **E Hampton**	25
Soigné | **Woodmere**	25
Starr Boggs | **Westhampton Bch**	25
Z Stone Creek | **E Quogue**	26
Stresa | **Manhasset**	24
Z Tellers | **Islip**	26
Tierra Mar | **Westhampton Bch**	22
Tratt. Diane | **Roslyn**	25
Tupelo Honey | **Sea Cliff**	22
Union Station | **Smithtown**	19
Vine Wine/Cafe | **Greenport**	22
Z Vintage Prime | **St. James**	26

WORTH A TRIP

Babylon	
Z Kotobuki	27
Bayport	
Z Le Soir	27
Bay Shore	
Z Lake House	27
East Hampton	
Z Nick & Toni's	23
1770 House	25
East Patchogue	
Z Chachama Grill	28
East Quogue	
Z Stone Creek	26
Garden City	
NEW Mumon	-
Hauppauge	
Z Kotobuki	27
Huntington Station	
Z Panama Hatties	26
Jamesport	
Z Jedediah's	26
Locust Valley	
Z Barney's	26
Northport	
Z Maroni Cuisine	28
Oyster Bay	
Z Mill River Inn	27
Roslyn	
Z Il Mulino NY	26
NEW Limani	-
Sag Harbor	
Z American Hotel	24
Southold	
Z North Fork Table	28
St. James	
Z Kitchen A Bistro	28
Wading River	
Z La Plage	26
Water Mill	
Z Mirko's	26
West Islip	
Nonnina	24
Woodbury	
NEW Speranza	-

SPECIAL FEATURES

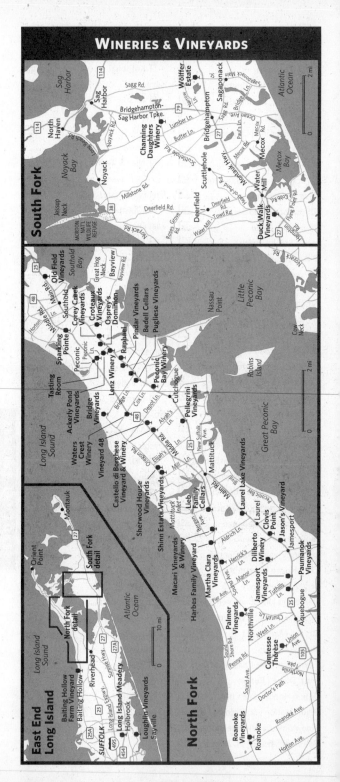

WINERIES & VINEYARDS

Wineries & Vineyards

Ackerly Pond Vineyards
1375 Peconic Ln. | Peconic | 631-765-6861 |
www.ackerlypondvineyards.com

Baiting Hollow Farm Vineyard
2114 Sound Ave. | Baiting Hollow | 631-369-0100 |
www.baitinghollowfarmvineyard.com

Bedell Cellars
36225 Main Rd./Rte. 25 | Cutchogue | 631-734-7537 |
www.bedellcellars.com

Bridge Vineyards
8850 Bridge Ln. | Cutchogue | 917-439-6592 | www.bridgevineyards.com

Castello di Borghese
17150 County Rd. | Cutchogue | 631-734-5111 |
www.castellodiborghese.com

Channing Daughters Winery
1927 Scuttlehole Rd. | Bridgehampton | 631-537-7224 |
www.channingdaughters.com

Clovis Point
1935 Main Rd. | Jamesport | 631-722-4222 |
www.clovispointwines.com

Comtesse Thérèse
Union Ave./Rte. 105 | Aquebogue | 631-871-9194 |
www.comtessetherese.com

Corey Creek Vineyards
45470 Main Rd./Rte. 25 | Southold | 631-765-4168 |
www.bedellcellars.com

Croteaux Vineyards
1450 S. Harbor Rd. | Southold | 631-765-6099 | www.croteaux.com

Diliberto Winery
250 Manor Ln. | Jamesport | 631-722-3416 |
www.dilibertowinery.com

Duck Walk Vineyards
231 Montauk Hwy. | Water Mill | 631-726-7555 | www.duckwalk.com

Grapes of Roth
(Not open to the public, but orders may be placed by phone or online.)
P.O. Box 114 | Sag Harbor | 631-725-7999 |
www.thegrapesofroth.com

Harbes Family Vineyard
715 Sound Ave. | Mattituck | 631-298-0700 |
www.harbesfamilyfarm.com

Jamesport Vineyards
1216 Main Rd./Rte. 25 | Jamesport | 631-722-5256 |
www.jamesport-vineyards.com

Jason's Vineyard
1785 Main Rd./Rte. 25 | Jamesport | 631-926-8486 |
www.jasonsvineyard.com

Laurel Lake Vineyards
3165 Main Rd./Rte. 25 | Laurel | 631-298-1420 | www.llwines.com

Lenz Winery, The
Main Rd./Rte. 25 | Peconic | 631-734-6010 | www.lenzwine.com

Lieb Family Cellars
35 Cox Neck Rd. | Mattituck | 631-298-1942 | www.liebcellars.com

Long Island Meadery
1347 Lincoln Ave. | Holbrook | 631-285-7469 | www.limeadery.com

Loughlin Vineyards
South Main St. | Sayville | 631-589-0027 | www.loughlinvineyard.com

Macari Vineyards & Winery
150 Bergen Ave. | Mattituck | 631-298-0100 |
www.macariwines.com

Martha Clara Vineyards
6025 Sound Ave. | Riverhead | 631-298-0075 |
www.marthaclaravineyards.com

Old Field Vineyards, The
59600 Main Rd./Rte. 25 | Southold | 631-765-0004 |
www.theoldfield.com

Osprey's Dominion
44075 Main Rd./Rte. 25 | Peconic | 631-765-6188 |
www.ospreysdominion.com

Palmer Vineyards
108 Sound Ave./Rte. 48 | Aquebogue | 631-722-9463 |
www.palmervineyards.com

Paumanok Vineyards
1074 Main Rd./Rte. 25 | Aquebogue | 631-722-8800 |
www.paumanok.com

Peconic Bay Winery
31320 Main Rd./Rte. 25 | Cutchogue | 631-734-7361 |
www.peconicbaywinery.com

Pellegrini Vineyards
23005 Main Rd./Rte. 25 | Cutchogue | 631-734-4111 |
www.pellegrinivineyards.com

Pindar Vineyards
37645 Main Rd./Rte. 25 | Peconic | 631-734-6200 | www.pindar.net

Pugliese Vineyards
34515 Main Rd./Rte. 25 | Cutchogue | 631-734-4057 |
www.pugliesevineyards.com

Raphael
39390 Main Rd./Rte. 25 | Peconic | 631-765-1100 |
www.raphaelwine.com

Roanoke Vineyards
3543 Sound Ave. | Riverhead | 631-727-4161 | www.roanokevineyards.com

Sherwood House Vineyards
2600 Oregon Rd. | Mattituck | 631-298-1396 |
www.sherwoodhousevineyards.com

Shinn Estate Vineyards
2000 Oregon Rd. | Mattituck | 631-804-0367 |
www.shinnstatevineyards.com

Sparkling Pointe
(Tasting room opening in summer 2009.)
39750 Rte. 48 | Southold | 631-765-0200 | www.sparklingpointe.com

Tasting Room, The
2885 Peconic Ln. | Peconic | 631-765-6404 | www.tastingroomli.com

Vineyard 48
18910 Rte. 48 | Cutchogue | 631-734-5200 | www.vineyard48.net

Waters Crest Winery
22355 Rte. 48 | Cutchogue | 631-734-5065 | www.waterscrestwinery.com

Wölffer Estate
139 Sagg Rd. | Sagaponack | 631-537-5106 | www.wolffer.com

Wine Vintage Chart

This chart, based on our 0 to 30 scale, is designed to help you select wine. The ratings (by **Howard Stravitz**, a law professor at the University of South Carolina) reflect the vintage quality and the wine's readiness to drink. We exclude the 1991–1993 vintages because they are not that good. A dash indicates the wine is either past its peak or too young to rate. Loire ratings are for dry white wines.

Whites	89	90	94	95	96	97	98	99	00	01	02	03	04	05	06	07
French:																
Alsace	24	25	24	23	23	22	25	23	25	26	22	21	24	25	24	-
Burgundy	23	22	-	27	26	23	21	25	25	24	27	23	26	27	25	23
Loire Valley	-	-	-	-	-	-	-	24	25	26	22	23	27	24	-	-
Champagne	26	29	-	26	27	24	23	24	24	22	26	21	-	-	-	-
Sauternes	25	28	-	21	23	25	23	24	24	29	25	24	21	26	23	27
California:																
Chardonnay	-	-	-	-	-	-	24	23	26	26	25	26	29	25	-	-
Sauvignon Blanc	-	-	-	-	-	-	-	-	-	-	-	26	27	26	27	26
Austrian:																
Grüner Velt./Riesling	-	-	-	25	21	26	26	25	22	23	25	26	26	25	24	-
German:																
German	26	27	24	23	26	25	26	23	21	29	27	24	26	28	24	-

Reds	89	90	94	95	96	97	98	99	00	01	02	03	04	05	06	07
French:																
Bordeaux	25	29	21	26	25	23	25	24	29	26	24	26	24	28	25	23
Burgundy	24	26	-	26	27	25	22	27	22	24	27	25	24	27	25	-
Rhône	28	28	23	26	22	24	27	26	27	26	-	26	24	27	25	-
Beaujolais	-	-	-	-	-	-	-	-	-	-	22	24	21	27	25	23
California:																
Cab./Merlot	-	28	29	27	25	28	23	26	-	27	26	25	24	26	23	-
Pinot Noir	-	-	-	-	-	-	24	23	25	28	26	27	25	24	-	-
Zinfandel	-	-	-	-	-	-	-	-	25	23	27	22	23	23	-	-
Oregon:																
Pinot Noir	-	-	-	-	-	-	-	-	-	-	27	25	26	27	26	-
Italian:																
Tuscany	-	25	23	24	20	29	24	27	24	27	-	25	27	25	24	-
Piedmont	27	27	-	-	26	27	26	25	28	27	-	24	23	26	25	24
Spanish:																
Rioja	-	-	26	26	24	25	-	25	24	27	-	24	25	26	24	-
Ribera del Duero/Priorat	-	-	26	26	27	25	24	25	24	27	20	24	27	26	24	-
Australian:																
Shiraz/Cab.	-	-	24	26	23	26	28	24	24	27	27	25	26	26	24	-
Chilean:																
Chilean	-	-	-	-	-	24	-	25	23	26	24	25	24	26	25	24

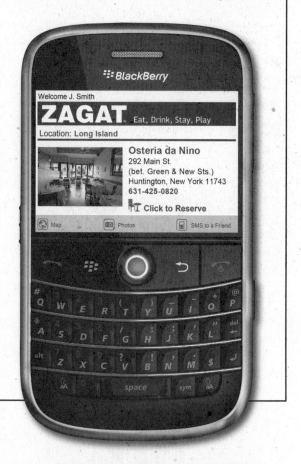